Urban Policy
and the
Exterior City
(Pergamon Policy Studies—41)

Pergamon Policy Studies on Urban Affairs

Perry & Kraemer TECHNOLOGICAL INNOVATION IN AMERICAN LOCAL GOVERMENTS
Clavel, Forester & Goldsmith URBAN AND REGIONAL PLANNING IN AN AGE OF AUSTERITY
Laska & Spain BACK TO THE CITY
Moss PLANNING FOR URBAN WATERFRONTS

Related Titles

Geismar & Geismar FAMILIES IN AN URBAN MOLD
Bernstein & Mellon SELECTED READINGS IN QUANTITATIVE URBAN ANALYSIS
Blowers THE LIMITS OF POWER
Bromley THE URBAN INFORMAL SECTOR: CRITICAL PERSPECTIVES
Chadwick A SYSTEMS VIEW OF PLANNING, 2nd Edition
Davidson & Wibberly PLANNING AND THE RURAL ENVIRONMENT
Faludi ESSAYS ON PLANNING THEORY AND EDUCATION
Fagence CITIZEN PARTICIPATION IN PLANNING
Catalano HEALTH, BEHAVIOR AND THE COMMUNITY
Carter & Hill THE CRIMINAL'S IMAGE OF THE CITY

PERGAMON
POLICY
STUDIES

ON URBAN AFFAIRS

Urban Policy and the Exterior City

Federal, State and Corporate Impacts upon Major Cities

H.V. Savitch

Pergamon Press

NEW YORK • OXFORD • TORONTO • SYDNEY • FRANKFURT • PARIS

Pergamon Press Offices:

U.S.A.   Pergamon Press Inc., Maxwell House, Fairview Park, Elmsford, New York 10523, U.S.A.

U.K.   Pergamon Press Ltd., Headington Hill Hall, Oxford OX3 0BW, England

CANADA   Pergamon of Canada, Ltd., 150 Consumers Road, Willowdale, Ontario M2J, 1P9, Canada

AUSTRALIA   Pergamon Press (Aust) Pty. Ltd., P O Box 544, Potts Point, NSW 2011, Australia

FRANCE   Pergamon Press SARL, 24 rue des Ecoles, 75240 Paris, Cedex 05, France

FEDERAL REPUBLIC OF GERMANY   Pergamon Press GmbH, 6242 Kronberg/Taunus, Pferdstrasse 1, Federal Republic of Germany

Library of Congress Cataloging in Publication Data

Savitch, H   V
  Urban policy and the exterior city.

  Bibliography: p.
  Includes index.
  1. Urban policy—United States.   2. Power (Social sciences)   I. Title.
HN65.S32 1979   301.36'3   79-11552
ISBN 0-08-023390-2

Printed in the United States of America

This book is dedicated to the memory
of my father and to my mother,
folks who made the city a reality.

Contents

Chapter

List of Figures and Tables

Preface

The origins of a book are limitless. They are borne of subjective feelings, objective conditions, an evolution of trial and error, and perhaps most of all conversations with people from many walks of life. This book began with my interest in the city as seen by its politicians and policymakers. The more I spoke with people at city halls, the more I appreciated their actions as reactive gestures to events which were steadily overtaking them. Multinational corporations and official delegates from the state capital and Washington seemed as important to the fate of the city as what its own mayor could do. And with every passing year these external factors seemed more and more important. Believing that too little attention has been given to the city from this perspective, I decided to write this book. A good part of The Exterior City and Urban Policy comes out of this evolution of ideas and other people's experience. For the embryo of that perspective I would like to thank former Mayor of San Francisco Joseph Alioto and the Mayor of Los Angeles, Tom Bradley. My appreciation also goes to mayoral aides John DeLuca in the City of San Francisco and Anton Calleia in Los Angeles. The interviews these officials afforded me enriched my knowledge of the city and provided an intellectual spark for further research.

For those in academe who practice their own brand of policy I would like to acknowledge the talents of Professor Robert Binstock. Professor Binstock has been a perceptive critic and a most quotable commentator. His remarks about policy and public officials are memorable and I have not hesitated to incorporate them into my understanding of politics. Professors Joyce Gelb and Robert Smith also provided criticisms of a first draft which were sufficiently strong to force me into a hot summer's bout with my typewriter. The exemplary scholarship of Professor William Robson has had an intangible, though pervasive, effect on my work. I shall always be indebted to him for the example he sets.

Good friends and colleagues gave me pause for thought and refused to let me get away with vague comments which were not fully documented. For this I thank John Nolan, Executive Director of the Housing Action Council; Jesse Vazquez, Director of Puerto Rican Studies at Queens College; and John Howard, Dean of Social Sciences at SUNY/Purchase. Heidi Most, of the Urban Affairs staff at SUNY/-Purchase, cast a copy editing eye on the manuscript and took on the lonesesome duty at SUNY when I was unavailable. Many thanks also to Ellen Grasso for a typing job well done and deadlines which were promptly met.

My appreciation also goes to Sam Koeppel, both family and friend, who did the illustration for the diagram on page 68. Prior to Mr. Koeppel's intercession, the diagram evoked groans from readers and a very polite nod that this was indeed a "complicated" illustration. The pains associated with that page, I think, have now abated.

At Pergamon Press Dr. Gwen Bell did a yeoman's job in sifting through the manuscript for errors and ambiguities. Her presence made my life easier and her hand made this a better book.

Finally, my deepest appreciation goes to my family who stuck by me through every moment of this writing. My wife Susan painstakingly read through every typed page and made corrections. Without her understanding and encouragement the difficulties would have been inordinate. I appreciate this more than she will ever know or I have ever been able to communicate to her. My sons, Adam and Jonathan, had to endure an absentee father who, even when physically present, could not always put his thoughts to their needs. I hope my family will understand and accept that failing.

It is customary in statements of this kind to absolve those people mentioned from any guilt by association. That I do willingly and without qualification. All errors in fact, emphasis, or judgments are mine alone.

Acknowledgments

Portions of Chapters 1 and 8 are reprinted from "Black Cities; White Suburbs: Domestic Colonialism As An Interpretive Idea" by H. V. Savitch in Volume 439 (September 1978) of THE ANNALS of The American Academy of Political and Social Science. © 1978, by The American Academy of Political and Social Science. All rights reserved.

Fig. 1.1 in the Introduction p. 9 has been adapted from The Congressional Quarterly Almanac, 1969-72. p. 162.

The Poem in Chapter 8, p. 270 is reprinted from "Law Like Love," COLLECTED POEMS OF W. H. AUDEN, edited by Edward Mendelson. All rights reserved, © 1945 by Random House.

Quotations in Chapter 3 are reprinted from MANDATE FOR CHANGE, by Dwight D. Eisenhower. Copyright © 1963 by Dwight D. Eisenhower. Used by permission of Doubleday & Company, Inc.

Support for travel was provided by the Research Foundation of the State University of New York, University Awards Committee.

Introduction

This book begins with the idea that the problems which have riddled cities during the last few decades are not matters of local choice, but are rooted in the larger environment of American society. Social pathology may be nearly synonymous with urban life these days, but its etiology can best be found in forces which are external to the city, not within them.

When I discuss urban decay I refer to the older, traditional cities of the northeast and midwest, not their new, sleed counterparts within the "sunbelt." I mean cities like New York, Philadelphia, Boston, Chicago, or Cleveland; traditional cities of this type have much in common. As a rule they represent the beginning of America's urban endeavor; they have densely concentrated populations; they are rich in ethnic variation; and commerce, recreation, and housing are tightly interwoven through their neighborhoods and downtowns. In sight and in feel traditional cities impart a special quality to urban life. They cannot be mistaken for suburbs nor for oversized shopping centers. Business bustle by day or by evening, and crowds fill city streets with a vibrancy which cannot be duplicated in other surroundings. That vibrancy is often contagious, and the influence of traditional cities spills into the larger regions around them. When a person travels to a different part of the nation he identifies with the big city, not his village. Ask someone from Norwood, Massachusetts or Rocky River, Ohio about their origin and they are as apt to discuss Boston or Cleveland as they are their "home towns."

I have used the term "exterior city" in order to bring attention to cities of this type. The phrase "exterior city" also conveys political relationships which engulf these cities and points up how spheres of power which are outside municipal boundaries shape city conditions.

1

Most accounts of urban society concentrate on the inner dimensions of
the city - what I call the "interior city." In sociology, "groups" and
"community" are studied as the major components of the city. In
economics, municipal taxation and local business choices are analyzed
as the driving forces of the city. In political science, indigenous
"power elites" are uncovered as the chief operators of the city.

The exterior city relies on a different perspective. The urban
past and its future are seen from the vantage of how the larger society
uses policy to create busts and booms, apathy and protest, failure and
success. Urban development is seen as the product of technological
changes of global scope, financial decisions by heads of multinational
corporations, and political outcomes resulting from decisions made in
Washington or the state capitals. The fate of the exterior city hinges
on a technological and demographic upheaval which is beyond its control, but which, nonetheless, uses older cities as repositories for
obsolete industries and unwanted populations. Since the onset of the
1950s, cities have become the sinkholes for an industrial transformation which has yielded inordinate waste, and a demographic impulsion
which has left racial segregation in its wake.

Through all of these events, public policy has been a major
transmitter of change. Governmental policy has spurred a corporate
migration toward the nation's open spaces, it has facilitated the migration of middle class America into the suburbs; and, in attempting
to lessen urban deterioration, it has accelerated it. Thus, when the
cities go into trauma, the currents of shock are often generated from
outside their boundaries. When analysts of the interior city write
about "the collapse of community" or "excessive municipal expenditures" they appreciate only a part of the urban situation, and not the
larger train of circumstances which destroyed those communities or
made those expenditures necessary. I have treated these external
circumstances as taking place within particular spheres of power -
national authority (White House, Congress, the bureaucracy), middle
governments (states, counties, suburbs), and private power (corporate, financial, and other forms of capitalist enterprise). The mix
that takes place within these spheres and between them, as they affect
the exterior city, is treated throughout the book and particularly in
Chapter 2.

Explaining urban decay thus becomes a matter of examining the
city from a different perspective, and revealing it in its national and
interpolitical context. What corporations and the shakers of the
economy do determines what Washington and middle governments will
do, and there are strong reciprocating relationships among all of
these spheres.

Traditionally, there has been an all too artificial separation between the exercise of public and private power. Private power intrudes upon every urban policy, weaving into the fabric of White House decisions, congressional politics, and the actions of middle government. Corporate and financial power are not a visible part of government, but they do have a continual effect upon the social structure. Indeed, placement or withdrawal of assets by manufacturers and bankers can affect whole populations more profoundly than all the reams of antipoverty legislation combined. In this age of national and multinational enterprises, policy analysts cannot ignore the influence of private power, particularly since there is an open question of whose government we actually serve. General Motors employs 681,000 workers; Ford Motor Company, 416,000; General Electric 375,000; and International Business Machines, 288,000 - taken individually each controls more people than most American cities (1). Hopefully, we will shed some light on the power exercised by these giants and the political chemistry created when they interact with public realms of power.

PRIVATISM AND REINFORCING AND MELIORIST POLICY STYLES

Privatism is not just a shortened synonym for common notions of private enterprise or capitalism; it conveys something mightier than an atomized conglomeration of small entrepreneurs. More than this, the term connotes the larger corporate structure in American capitalism and the ability of its individual weight (investments, plant size, generation of commerce, working capital) to make a difference in the size and composition of cities. Privatism encompasses nongovernmental organizations of individuals in the upper reaches of society and the process whereby these organizations expend energy and resources in quest of profits.

Privatism, further, is an attitude rooted in the tradition of America and has shaped its cities. It constitutes the building blocks of the national landscape, and as Sam Bass Warner has made us aware:

... The tradition of privatism has always meant that the cities of the United States depended for their wages, employment, and general prosperity upon the aggregate successes and failures of thousands of individual enterprises, not upon community action.

It has also meant that the physical form of American cities, their
lots, houses, factories, and streets have been the outcome of a
real estate market of profit seeking builders, land speculators
and large investors. Finally, the tradition of privatism has
meant that the local politics of American cities have depended
for their actions, and for a good deal of their subject matter, on
the changing focus of men's private economic activities. (2)

Warner was talking about a single city and privatism's formative
role on the internal development of that city. Embellishing upon his
theme, privatism continues to shape American cities through its external impacts taken in conjunction with national and middle governments. Today, the exterior city is the product of the mega corporation, transcending city limits and national bounds. The common
political dichotomies that flare around discussions of American public
policy - right wing/left wing, conservative/liberal, Republican/Demo-
crat - are adjustments to privatism, and these adjustments set the
parameters for national and urban policies. All else flows from this
proposition and I have dispensed with traditional reliance on the concepts of conservative-Republican and liberal-Democrat, replacing
them respectively with reinforcing and meliorist orientations. This
is done in order to point up the link between policy choices and the
needs of privatism.

The conservative or right wing bent is to reinforce the "push of
privatism" (defined as the intrinsic need for profit and expansion) by
using public policy to further the direction privatism is already pursuing. Hence, if the "push" of private enterprise is toward the suburbs or the "sunbelt" via the increased use of automotive transportation, expenditures made on behalf of highways would enhance this trend
and stimulate "growth" in the economy. Such a policy would also increase the value of land around new highway arteries, generate additional income within the private sector, and stimulate additional business ventures in untried areas of the country. Policies with the
widest appeal among reinforcers are those which resemble "low tax"
strategies and bolster privatism directly by affording it unforeseen
funds to work its own will.

The liberal or left wing disposition is to meliorate the adverse
conditions of society by diverting privatism from its inherent "push."
Meliorists tend to use public policy as an intervener in order to improve the condition of the city, and they have used a variety of circumspect policies to entice corporate investment. Urban renewal, full
employment programs, and even mass transit funding are ways in
which meliorists use policy to compensate those sectors of the nation
that have fallen from privatism's grace.

Reinforcing and meliorist policies both work on the edges of privatism and never affront or compete with it. Reinforcers play to privatism's natural movement or its push, while meliorists coax it with public funds. In no instance is the core of privatism significantly disturbed, and the striking feature of almost all government policy is that it never transcends the limitations placed upon it.

Because neither meliorist nor reinforcing policies can transcend the limitations of the "system" they have failed to meet the intrinsic difficulties of the "urban crisis." Some friendly scholars have suggested that I dispense with this meliorist/reinforcing distinction and instead substitute the conventional references of liberal/-conservative policies. After all, they argue, why add to an already overjargonized social science and muddy the waters with still more vocabulary. As I see it, the mistaken notion that we do pursue liberal or conservative policies clouds our purposes and contributes to our failure.

There is a real and substantial difference between the concept of the reinforcer and that of American conservatism, as there is a sharp distinction between meliorism and American liberalism. American conservatism has traditionally stressed a reduced or minimal role for government in managing economic relations. This book contends that so-called "conservatives" have not reduced that role, but shifted public resources to "reinforce" the growth of prosperous segments of society outside central cities. In short, conservative policies have not been neutral, but highly biased and frequently interventionist. At times a laissez-faire philosophy may be used by conservatives to restrain government, but this is a selective restraint counterbalanced by energetic actions that apply public money to stimulate private profits. One example alluded to throughout this volume deals with inordinate spending for national highways, while fiscal conservatism is applied to mass transit. Another example relates to huge sums allocated for defense spending, with much of the investment spent in non-urban states, while cuts are advocated for community development in central cities.

On a different shade of the ideological spectrum, American liberalism advocates a measured governmental intervention where it is needed to help disadvantaged populations. So-called "liberals" use the rhetoric of this philosophy, but their policies funnel most of the largess to an upper stratum of society. Governmental intercession either provides the barest melioration to the needy, or contradicts itself by diverting assistance away from central cities altogether. Thus, for every urban renewal program made possible by meliorists, far more money has been made available to the suburbs through FHA

mortgage guarantees. Even federal dollars for public works jobs
have intentionally been given to the unemployed on a short-term
transitory basis. These policies may meliorate the festering wounds
of the city and the difficulties of chronic unemployment, but they do
nothing basic to solve these problems. In a word, they fail to realize the liberal rhetoric of governmental assistance for redressing
the stubborn imbalances of our society.

Moreover, the concepts of meliorism and reinforcement offer
greater clarity because they refer exclusively to urban policy choices.
Other issues that more easily lend themselves to liberal/conservative
interpretations are extraneous to this volume and it would not be wise
to bind those orientations to urban policy. Some policymakers may be
liberal when it comes to civil liberties, but quite conservative when
they deal with domestic policy. Two governors of New York State
illustrate the confusions of applying liberal or conservative labels to
all of their actions. Nelson Rockefeller, for example, was the foremost figure in his state's Republican Party and his political orientation varied with the issues. On matters of civil liberties, such as
the death penalty, he was a hardliner and an advocate of strict judicial enforcement. But on statewide urban policies, Rockefeller was
every bit the meliorist and celebrated the marriage between state
government and privatism. By contrast, Hugh Carey was a Democrat
and presumably a liberal, but behaved more like a conservative
governor in manipulating statewide tax and corporate policies. Carey
sought to reinforce the push of privatism through the state, as vigorously as any Republican from the southwest, yet he opposed the death
penalty and was regarded by many members of his party as a liberal.

In truth, Rockefeller's and Carey's political orientations were a
complex bundle of approaches which changed with each issue. Meliorism and reinforcement clarify those approaches by segregating out
policies common to urban issues. Making such distinctions does not
quibble with words, but applies them accurately to describe what
national and middle government policies do to our cities.

"Words are weapons," said Santayana, "and it is dangerous in
politics to borrow them from the arsenal of the enemy." (3) Rather
than borrow from that arsenal, I chose to run the risk of adding to an
already overburdened vocabularly. I also chose to avoid the greater
danger of accepting the commonly held belief that Washington has already done what it could for cities, and is not to blame for their failure. This book attempts to make clear what all those past efforts
were about.

URBAN ANALYSIS AND THE
SELECTION OF PUBLIC POLICIES

In the chapters that follow, public policy will be used as a tool to show how external forces impinge upon the city. Much as the chemist may dip litmus paper into a solution to test for alkalies or acids, so, too, can an urbanist run policies through the complexities of government to test its properties. In this case, I am interested in how power works under federalism and privatism as they interact with the city. Different policies reveal different aspects about urban relationships. Some policies provide breadth over a period of time, others record the intricacies of federal/state/corporate interaction, while still others trace convoluted shifts in political priorities.

To order the selection of policies, I have assessed them according to their spatial relevance to exterior cities and their direct impact upon them. Spatial relevance concerns the territory toward which a given policy is directed, and whether that territory is predominantly urban, rural, or suburban. (4) Direct impact deals with the degree to which urban populations are affected by policies, regardless of whether they are territorially included or singled out as the object of policy. An illustration of how spatial and impact considerations might lead to the selection of different policies is the National Neighborhood Policy Act of 1977 which, from the perspective of spatial relevance, is aimed directly toward traditional cities. The act specifies congested and declining urban communities as the target of legislative intent, and would appear to be a good candidate for examination. Yet from the perspective of impact, the act leaves much to be desired, since its only purpose is to create a twenty-member commission to study a much overworked subject and it contains no real mechanism to bring about any contemplated changes. On the other hand, a proposed policy on the health professions that would make financial aid to medical students contingent upon their willingness to serve in depressed areas, be they urban or rural, would have a direct impact upon the city, though it is not spatially unique to it. The mere availability of better health care within ghettos would not only assist their populations, but provide them with hospitals, clinics, and offshoot benefits. Hence, in the former instance there is urban relevance without significant impact, while in the latter there is impact but not enough relevance to determine how exterior cities fare as the objects of policy.

The aim, then, is to choose policies with both substantial relevance and impact for the city. Such policies rarely present themselves

in neat packages, and we have placed them along a continuum between
the highs and lows of relevance and impact.   Figure I.1 illustrates
the range along which a number of policies might fall.

The policies located to the right of the vertical axis are either
too trivial or idiosyncratic (quadrant II) to reflect anything about the
uses of power, or are too remotely related to cities (quadrant IV) to
reveal anything about the strategy of urban policy.   Those policies to
the left of the vertical axis are all salient, though with potentially
different kinds of yields.   Housing and community development, transportation and poverty policies (quadrant I) are rich in material because
a good deal of these measures are uniquely geared toward traditional
cities.   They also have substantial value as impact because of the
monetary commitments behind them as well as the conflicts they have
engendered in their passage and implementation.   In the simplest
sense, too, these are considered to be major urban policies, negotiated by urban advisers to presidents and shepherded through congressional committees which specialize in the problems of the cities.
Also in quadrant I, the underlined policies are carried out mainly
through middle governments.   The Bay Area Rapid Transit system,
housing finance agencies, and the Urban Development Corporation
were all undertaken by individual states and have had a high spatial
relevance and direct impact upon particular cities.

Revenue sharing, employment and the like (quadrant III) are
policies which are more national in scope and of considerable import.
Irrespective of whether they are intended for urban populations, such
measures are bound to affect them.   In addition, these policies have
ingredients similar to the more spatially related measures.   Each has
a substantial authorization behind it, is marked by a good many political scars, and has the advantage of serving a broad enough clientele
so that its impact on cities brings non-urban contestants into the
struggle.   This is particularly true with revenue sharing, which not
only concerns cities as a distinct category but also puts them at log-
gerheads with suburban townships and counties.   The manner in which
revenue sharing was conceived in the White House, negotiated through
Congress, and ultimately used, may provide us with a valuable test
for assessing the objectives of policymakers.   Turning to middle
government policies in quadrant III, economic incentives for industry
are usually undertaken by the states, while zoning is largely a matter
for townships and counties.   Though these policies are low in spatial
relevance, they have had a significant impact upon the exterior city.
Zoning, for example, is primarily concerned with population density
and land use.   But such prerogatives exercised within suburban jurisdictions have locked the poor into urban ghettoes while absorbing the
best of the exterior city's industry.

spatial relevance (high)

direct impact (high) | direct impact (low)

I	II
housing and community development (urban renewal, model cities and landmark housing, and community development acts)	Neighborhood Policy Act
transportation (mass transit and the highway trust fund)	private bills (special residency bills allowing indidivual alients to immigrate to the U.S. and usually to an urban constituency).
poverty (War On Poverty, Community Action Programs)	
employment (public works provisions for depressed inner cities)	
Bay Area Rapid Transit	
housing finance agencies	
The Urban Development Corporation	
III	**IV**
revenue sharing (general revenue sharing, "special" revenue sharing proposals)	nuclear policy and disarmament
employment (manpower programs, CETA)	agriculture (price supports)
health (training for health professions, medicare, medicaid)	strip mining bans
education (aid to elementary and secondary schools)	national park preserves
law enforcement (Safe Streets Act, aid to police forces)	foreign economic assistance
zoning	foreign policy (treaties, War Powers Act)
economic incentives for industry	

spatial relevance (low)

Note: Underlined policies are mainly those of middle government.

Fig. I.1. The relevance and impact of urban policies.

All told, these policies constitute a list of items which will be
run through the nexus of public and private power. Still, these policy
areas need to be pruned down to specific measures. For the federal
government, the major policy areas include three from quadrant I -
housing and community development, transportation, and poverty.
Within the area of housing and community development, particular
attention will be given to urban renewal, model cities, and the Housing and Community Development Acts of 1968 and 1974. Within the
area of poverty, the examination will turn to Lyndon Johnson's "War
on Poverty" and Richard Nixon's attempt to undo that effort. In transportation policy, special note will be given to the so-called "tap-ins"
on the Highway Trust Fund, which was an effort to divert funds away
from freeways toward urban mass transit. The policy areas for
middle government are specific enough as they stand, and deal with
rapid transit in California and urban development in New York and
Massachusetts.

Specifying measures in quadrant III is easier because direct impact is the sole consideration and some measures have a fuller history
behind them than others. The legislation for "general revenue sharing"
is one measure to follow, both for the reasons stated earlier and because it represents a policy commodity in its rawest form - the
American dollar. Nixon's attempt to replace "categorical" aid to
cities with "special revenue sharing" is also an item that tells us
something about the political conflicts between urban and nonurban
constituencies. The other federal policies in this quadrant will be
dealt with as aspects of categorical aid given to cities and as budget
priorities which changed from one occupant of the White House to
another. Finally, middle government policies of economic incentives
for industry and zoning will be examined most closely in the states of
California, Massachusetts, and New York. These three states are
among the most urbanized states in the Union, and each contains an
exterior city which is followed through this volume.

Before going on to examine these policies, the genesis and dynamic of the exterior city will be explained. Chapter 1 deals with the
transition from interior to exterior city. Chapter 2 describes the
theoretical core of the city's relationship with national, middle government, and private power. The remaining chapters analyze how that
relationship works through each of these spheres.

Urban Policy
and the
Exterior City
(Pergamon Policy Studies—41)

Photograph by Adam Savitch

I

The Dynamic of
the Exterior City

1 The Emergence of the Exterior City

...For in great cities we find an ignorant multitude, largely composed of recent immigrants untrained in self government; we find a great proportion of the voters paying no direct taxes, and therefore feeling no interest in moderate taxation and economical administration; we find able citizens absorbed in their private businesses, cultivated citizens unusually sensitive to the vulgarities of practical politics, and both sets therefore specially unwilling to sacrifice their time and tastes and comfort in the struggle with sordid wire pullers and demagogues. In great cities the forces that attack and pervert democratic government are exceptionally numerous, the defensive forces that protect it exceptionally ill-placed for resistance. Satan has turned his heaviest batteries on the weakest parts of the ramparts.

James Bryce, offering his view
of American cities in 1893.

THE GENESIS OF THE INTERIOR CITY

The interior city is distinguished by an inward orientation fed by the primacy of its urban core and revealed in a cultural and psychological centrism. The concerns of the interior city were taken up with how surrounding environs might contribute to the growth of the city and the enrichment of its political power. The struggles of the interior city were to maximize its own autonomy so that it might be freer to deal with issues which it considered uniquely urban. The pull of the interior

15

city was centripetal, drawing all kinds of activities into its center or
setting conditions so that smaller ventures might flourish around it.

This urban preeminence was limited to perhaps a dozen major
cities across the country which were dominated by the giants - New
York, Chicago, and Philadelphia. Interior cities were the ingatherers
for all manner of commerce, industry, and invention, with waterways
and rail transportation as their nexus. Through this, they were able
to multiply a huge number of economic activities and produce a vast
market for the generation of additional business. Chicago, for example, became the nation's foremost hub for rail transport, at the
spokes of which slaughterhouses conducted their operations, factories
built machinery, and exchanges of all kinds arose to conduct trading.
These industries generated still further activity in the way of banks,
brokers, and a legal-financial apparatus which was serviced by burgeoning department stores and cultural and scientific establishments.
To further the cycle, as the rail lines expanded and aged, their maintenance demanded adjunct employment - tending the yards, repairing
locomotives, building components from Fisherman plates to Pullman
cars - which all fed into the larger urban market place. (1) So powerful was the pull of the giant cities that urban appendages sprang out
from their activities; Gary became Chicago's backyard for steel production, and Newark and Jersey City became way stations between New
York and Philadelphia.

This was a time, too, when the "imperial city," as Kotler describes it, took hold of its rural neighbors and flourished. Centripetal pulls from the growing industrial base necessitated that more
land be put to urban use, so annexation of adjoining villages became
commonplace. Roxbury, Charlestown, and Dorchester Neck (South
Boston) were added to Boston; Pittsburgh annexed Allegheny with a
territory of over 24,000 acres and a population of 140,000; and in
1854 twenty-eight smaller governments were incorporated into the
city of Philadelphia. The capstone of this urban conquest was New
York City's great consolidation of 1897, which, after a history of en-
croachment into surrounding villages and smaller cities, incorporated
them all into five great burroughs with a land mass of 315 square
miles. (2)

The purpose of this incorporation was to speed the transformation of the downtown area into a heartland for commerce and industry,
while the newly added sectors housed its workers. Heretofore, the
city's downtown districts were hardly different from lesser towns and
villages. Places of work and homesites were often joined, building
was of a modest scale, and there was an easy comingling of merchants and ministers with stablekeepers, carters, and laborers. The

industrial city swept this away, with whole streets either converted or
levelled to the ground and rebuilt for the new and massive infusions of
capital. Warner describes Philadelphia as it embarked upon this
transformation and segregated itself into numerous enclaves:

> A quarter of all the city's manufacturing workers, 30,000 and
> more men, women, and children, worked in the principal down-
> town ward of Philadelphia. The great industry in all its branches,
> boot and shoe makers, bookbinders, printers, and paper box
> fabricators, glass manufacturers, machinists, coopers, sugar
> refineries, brewers and cigar makers especially concentrated
> here... Thousands of workers walked to the downtown every day,
> while omnibuses, and just before the Civil War, horse drawn
> streetcars brought shopkeepers and customers. No tall office
> buildings yet outlined the downtown, no manufacturing lofts filled
> entire blocks, but the basic manufacturing-wholesale-retail-
> financial elements had already been assembled by 1860 for the
> future metropolis.
>
> Beyond the downtown convenient transportation had encouraged
> additional manufacturing clusters. They took the common
> American patterns of radiating out from the original urban core
> like a crude spiderweb spun through the blocks of little houses...
> To the north stood the leather and wool districts and machinery
> and textile mills. On the southside garment sweatshops scattered
> through the first slums. To the west, Market Street... had be-
> come a manufacturing axis, especially for furniture woorworking,
> and packing houses. On the northwest the new railroad yards
> there made that section the home of locomotive building and
> metal working. (3)

Patterns of settlement and activity were so markedly oriented
around the urban core that sociologists found it useful to study the
city of Chicago as a series of concentric zones and mini zones emanating out from its business district, the "loop." Each of the larger
zones served a general function: manufacture in one zone, industrial
workers in another, and the owning classes reserving the best locations. That city's polyglot population was further segregated into
numerous divisions with each providing for its denizens a role in the
life of the central city. Their descriptions were vivid and conveyed
a hierarchy of circuses with the performers struggling to make it to
the main event. Thus, we find "hobohemia" portrayed as a deteriorated section of rooming houses for the "homeless migratory man"; the

"Latin Quarter" and the "Black Belt" are stereotyped as places where "free" and "disorderly" spirits could be unleashed; while the immigrants of the teeming "ghetto" look out longingly to fancier neighborhoods with their tall apartment buildings decorated with parquet floors. (4)

It is tempting to compare these cities with their medieval counterparts, where conventional thought has it that when cities lost the power of their walls, they ceased to be. Max Weber, for instance, pointed out that for cities to constitute a "full urban community" they must display several features, including: 1) a fortification, 2) a market, 3) a court of its own and a partially autonomous law in association with a larger polity, and 4) a degree of self-governance or partial autonomy. Weber's thesis was that only in the West, where cities stood apart from rural medievalism and could provide their inhabitants with a political and social alternative ("statlust makt fre") did they reach their fullest potential. (5) Yet a close scrutiny shows that America's interior city could very well be considered the industrial analogue to Weber's urban community. Its walls were defined by municipal boundaries and a peculiar cast of life - hurried, opportunistic, secular - which divided it from the countryside. Its market was the "loop" or downtown, which multiplied the trading of the medieval urban market a thousand fold and absorbed new forms of capital. As political entities, interior cities possessed their own formal institutions encompassing special municipal laws, "strong mayor" systems, a political culture based on payoffs from ward heelers, and the clash of ethnic rivalries.

What distinguished interior cities from the rest of America were not only these qualitative differences, but the way in which they were exercised as the city came to interact with other sectors. The division between urban and nonurban was sharp, and dwellers were acculturated into either one realm or the other, with firmly established identities as to place and class. Interior cities operated as latter day solipsists, conceiving the rest of the world only insofar as it had meaning for the urban realm and with disdain for those who lived outside of it. This is how the derogations "hayseed" and "country bumpkin" came into use, as connotations of unsophisticated and clownish behavior. In the proper company, one could even tolerate jokes about "the farmer's daughter," and the media (which was urban based) came to portray rural folk as ignorant and suspicious of interlopers who came to them from the city. Moreover, relationships with the hinterland were treated as struggles between "we" and "they," or "upstaters" versus "downstaters," and historians of the era could invoke the term "center" opposing the "periphery." One noted philosopher-historian of the time went so far as to see the city embodying the force of history and to discern a "soul of the city" which regarded the country-side as "something different and subordinate." (6)

Such feelings were reciprocated by country townsmen, making the walls between urban and rural worlds still less penetrable. Consider, for example, the following description of attitudes on Long Island just fifty years ago:

> They were fiercely determined to keep their world for them-selves. The bay bottoms, the hell fire preachers in their weather beaten little churches constantly reminded them, were "sacred"... their "priceless natural heritage," and when it came time each year for the townships that bordered on the Great South Bay - Hempstead, Oyster Bay, Babylon, Islip and Brook-haven - to sell leases to mine the bay's underwater crops of shellfish, the baymen crowded into town halls to listen while the leases were awarded - and no outsider was ever given a lease...

> Distrusting anyone "from far away" the baymen especially distrusted anyone from New York. Hating the city - many boasted that they had never been there - they feared that its "foreigners," hordes of long haired Slavs, hook-nosed Jews and unwashed Irishmen, would descend on and befoul their beautiful beaches at the first slackening of their vigilance. (7)

The ecological difference between "urban" and "rural" was accented by their different cultures and the qualities which sprang from the southern and eastern European stock which inhabited the city. This could be seen in how country and city each conducted its political affairs and its contrasting concerns. In the countryside, politics was still managed through town meetings and a personalized relationship between farmer and politician. Rural issues arose intermittently and were resolved by a consensus of outlook. Those issues which were long standing involved taxation, or spilled over onto national questions of tariffs and the price of crops. Despite the land distances which separated farmers, their political activity was direct (meetings, letter writing, petitions) and energized by attendance at the local church or by town newspapers. More so than anyone else, the minister and the editor substituted as professional politicians because they were at the center of communication.

For the city dweller, politics was more structured, organized, and transpired through political parties. Issues floated on public jobs for workers, municipal contracts for business, and political favors

for partisans. The whole fabric of urban politics consisted of a debate over the privileges to be dispensed, and corruption was a thread
that ran through every seam of local power. Professional politicians
were political brokers and the tavern keeper or neighborhood lawyer
was the major trader.

The Trivialization of Urban Policy and
the Politics of Corruption

Machines and Reformers in the
Interior City

Though interior cities incorporated their varied populations within a
common realm, they were not free of political conflict. With only a
few notable exceptions, this conflict was rooted in internal problems
and involved a struggle between forces indigenous to the city. These
forces could be found within the city's numerous ethnic and working
class enclaves (Irish, Italian, Jewish, and Slavic wards), middle
class neighborhoods, downtown merchant organizations, as well as
the city's own patricians who comprised an elite of bankers and business men. Alliances between groups often crisscrossed with many
factions pushing for their own advantage; and it came to the "machines"
and "reformers" to represent, if not organize, political coalitions.
The story of interior city politics can be told as a contest for power
between machine and reform organizations.
        Machine-type politicians have been portrayed as part of a tra-
ditional organizational structure, wedded to patronage and hierarchial
rule. Its hallmarks consisted of an immigrant constituency at its
base, a bland (though not unskilled) mayor or party boss at the top,
and a decision making style which emphasized brokerage amongst
competing interests. (8) In contrast to machine types, reformers
built their support out of a middle class revulsion to boss rule. It
was avowedly moralistic and stressed an open style of organization
rather than underlying interests. (9) Thus, one cutting edge between
machine and reform types was over the conflict between government
by patronage versus impartial government, with the issue of corruption at the center of the controversy.
        In point of fact, the attention given to corruption and patronage
as political issues was as much a reflection of the interior city itself
as the "real issues." Political debates over matters of efficiency,
honesty, and which party could do the best job were simply ways of
carrying out an internal conflict within a realm which itself had a

limited scope. Besides, with a burgeoning urban core and politics in
the grip of two conservative parties, contests for jobs and power were
the quickest paths to gathering public support and recognition.

At the outset, then, we should understand that both machine and
reform politics were stabilizing movements designed to play on different sides of the urban fence so that each could narrowly manage
the city in its own way. Neither propelled itself as a party of social
justice, contemplating a redistribution of income or privilege; and
neither had need to do this, given the nature of the interior city. The
sociological fiction which portrays inner city machines and ward politicians as friends of the poor against the wealthy, ignores the context
and purpose of the political struggle. (10) Immigrant and working
classes were courted by machines only because they were good political currency for bosses to trade for influence, and even such benefits as the poor did receive were ephemeral. Thus, while turkeys
could be given to them at Christmas time (frequently in exchange for
their vote the previous November), or "fixes" made with a local judge
for some minor transgression, machine politicians did not hesitate to
break the back of labor when it fought for permanent demands. In two
major labor strikes (one involving the garment workers in New York
City in 1911, the other centering around Pittsburgh's steel workers in
1919), machine politicians kept faith with business leaders by having
the police arrest and brutalize the striking pickets (in New York,
Tammany-controlled judges sent them off to jail). Not atypical was
the reaction of Boss Ed Crump, from Memphis, who denounced CIO
organizers as "un-American" when they attempted to unionize workers
in that city's Ford and Fisher plants and had them bloodied by the
police. Similar scenes with different characters were played against
labor by Democratic machines in Chicago and Jersey City. (11)

In somewhat that same way, reform politics has its myth makers,
particularly turn-of-the-century writers and modern newspaper edi-
torialists. (12) Much as reformers attempted to "clean up" city hall,
it was a cleaning for limited purposes and sprung from the imperatives of the interior city. This was to ensure the vitality of its central business district, even if it came at the expense of those living in
the adjoining zones of the immigrant poor. In fact, the standard objective tests which reformers substituted for political patronage often
contained a bias against those who were barely literate in English or
those who could not afford the time for schooling. The class and co-
alitional basis of reform was evident in New York City where, after
more than fifty years of power shifts between machine and reform administrations, the most enduring achievement was to award a larger
number of high level posts to upper middle class activists. (13) A

more cynical interpretation holds that the major distinctions between
machines and reformers lay in which groups were to be given the
opportunity to loot the city.

The Issues Fought Out Between
Machine and Reform Politicians

It is a reflection on the relative autonomy of the interior city that its
politics revolved around the habits of individuals rather than impersonal policy choices adopted by government. The power that individual politicians could wield through formal organizations (like the
machines) or ad hoc coalitions (reform groups) was considerable. At
issue in the interior city were the abuses by its most powerful personalities and the capacity of urban populations to tolerate those
abuses. Lincoln Steffens railed against corrupt people, and often
against "merchants and big financiers" who "set out to strip Chicago"
of its wealth. (14) Rarely did Steffens talk about urban policy except
where it involved a bill which granted a franchise to a corrupt railway,
or measures within a city charter designed to combat dishonesty.
Even James Bryce, who came to America with an impressive academic
background, tended to personalize his observations when they were
directed toward big cities. Bryce could inveigh with impunity against
"recent immigrants, untrained in self government" (15) - but not
against public unwillingness to do anything about their impoverish-
ment or the slums in which they lived.
    The interior city had much to prattle over when it came to poli-
tics, but little to undertake when it came to social policy. Welfare
was relegated to soup kitchens largely run by private charities.
Housing was generally entrusted to slum lords who operated under
minimal regulations, and community development had not even been
comprehended. Federal aid to cities was barely in existence and
awarded infrequently for uncommon projects. Only municipal transportation and public sewers drew the attention of urban politicians,
mostly because they provided opportunities for graft.
    What then did machine and reform politicians do in the interior
city? They practiced politics in the purest sense. The quintessential
function of both machines and reformers was to act as broker between
conflicting classes or groups, always keeping in mind that a stable
monetary exchange was the most important asset of the city. Social
change was something to be avoided because it threatened the politician's role as primus intermediary between classes. Only when city
hall began to reel under the weight of corruption and sloppy administration did reformers contemplate change, and, then, to preserve the
system of exchange.

Despite the use of the term "machine," they were not usually streamlined organizations with neat hierarchies and command centers. On the contrary, most big city machines were amorphous groups of political workers, with ill-defined lines of authority. The particular uses of the machine stemmed from the composition of the interior city which, as a heterogeneous and segmented society, required a political clearing house to carry out business. The city's fragmentation into ethnic enclaves, class zones, and commercial interests necessitated an organization which was conventional enough to respect these divisions and could sustain them through an elaborate system of tradeoffs.

This is not to say that machines were unenterprising. On the contrary, bosses had the quality of being able to work closely with as varied a clientele as day laborers and railway presidents, and they often did in building their urban empires. Boss Tweed of New York reorganized municipal enterprises several times, including street cleaning operations, for which he paid an estimated $600,000 in graft to get the job done. Tweed also kept newspaper reporters on his payroll in order to secure favorable stories. He was known to have funneled over $1 million in public funds to Catholic schools in order to ensure a positive disposition toward his projects - an act which might be judged to be a prescient gesture toward aiding parochial schools. (16)

Graft served as a lubricant for these political machines, whether it entailed handing out jobs as sewer inspectors to party followers, or receiving money clandestinely from businessmen anxious for public contracts. The most lucrative of these contracts were in public works (paving streets, building and maintaining drainage canals) or in franchises to operate streetcars. Bonding and insurance houses were also favored since every municipality needs financial coverage in case of loss.

Public improvements of this kind gave something to all urbanites, albeit with great discrepancies in reward. To the immigrants, it gave occasional jobs; to corporations and banks, it provided hefty profits; and to the politicians, it allowed an abundance of "boodle." ("Boodle" is the term used to describe the graft available for distribution during a given regime of boss rule. Apparently there was quite a bit to be enjoyed. Of 18 political bosses counted by one author, 10 amassed fortunes of at least $1 million, which was an astounding sum by early twentieth century standards. One political baron left an estate of over $11 million while another left over $4 million. The well known Boss Crocker of New York was estimated to be worth over $3 million. Boss Tweed, however, was imprisoned and died virtually penniless.

Some bosses also succeeded to careers, heading such concerns as
Erie Railroad, Fairfield Insurance, Marcus Loew Amusement Company and, truth be told, the Brooklyn Bridge!) (17) Because the boss
acted at the interstices of these relationships, the machine was more
concerned about protecting existing power than raising challenges.

Those politicians interested in challenge were the reformers,
whose movement was defined by the protests they could arouse against
the existing political order. In cities like Philadelphia, Chicago, New
York, and San Francisco, the reform movement was shaped by the
deficiencies of the machine. The greater the corruption of the bosses,
the more dramatic became the appeals of reformers. The most effective vehicle for reformers to launch their drive was through a candidate who could imbue the issue with meaning and appeal to aspiration
and ideal. Hence, reformists tended to recruit candidates with an attractive (i.e. clean, courageous, honorable) or dramatic flair about
them. Invariably, these reformists were men of business and the
professions who saw an advantage in reordering political power within
the city, under the banner of honesty and good government. Politicians and young Turks interested in quick political mobility became
reformism's greatest advocates. Here is where the motivations of
principle and self interest were joined, and it provided a reservoir of
energy which was difficult to match.

At the same time, various segments of the business classes
could easily shuttle between machine and reform organizations, depending on their ability to meet commercial demands. Business occupied this comfortable position because of the resources it could
garner for politicians, and also because the interior city was dependent upon it for the continued growth of the urban core. Large banks,
retail outlets, and new industry not only created jobs but enlarged the
tax base and stimulated the local economy, and, so long as machine
mayors maintained a favorable environment, commercial elites did
not resist it. Once, however, the handwriting was on the wall and the
city fell onto bad times, business took to reform politics. The commercial sector perceived that what was bad for the city could also
mean disaster for themselves; civic mindedness prompted the establishment of blue ribbon panels to investigate fraud, and budget committees to curb waste. This, in fact, occurred in New York City
when the Citizen's Union supported the two candidates of that city's
first reform mayor, Seth Low; (18) and some years later in Chicago
when the Municipal Voters' League was formed and took over the City
Council. (19)

Generally, movements of this kind failed to strike a popular
chord amongst the working classes and were in the hands of banking

and industrial interests. One study shows that the early reform
movement in Pittsburgh was almost entirely composed of a financial
oligarchy of the presidents of 14 large banks, officials of Westing-
house, Pittsburgh Plate and Glass, U. S. Steel, the Pennsylvania
Railroad, and other corporate leaders. (20) Likewise, the Chicago
reform.movement of the 1890s was led by the Chicago Civic Federa-
tion, which was well financed and made up of that city's business elite.

The reformist's faith in centralization and charter revision was
based on a perception of the interior city as a controllable entity. Reformers were convinced that these techniques would bring about a
healthy centralization and clear lines of accountability, so that the
city could shape its future direction. In New York, the city charter
was amended to give two of its reform mayors (Fiorello La Guardia
and Robert Wagner) greater managerial and budgetary powers. Administration was also professionalized and placed in new hands, adept
in the science of public management. Similar measures were taken in
Philadelphia under its reform mayors (Richardson Dilworth and Joseph
Clark) to strengthen the organization of city hall.

For the interior city, the historical significance of reform lay in
its credo that all that was needed could be accomplished by better
managing the existing system. Reform put its energy behind the inception of a municipal technology and the good intentions of its administrators. Not until later generations, when a new wave of reformers
took office, would they pay attention to policies for public jobs or help
for the poor. By that time, the city had begun a transformation that
went far beyond a mere shift in its office holders, and though the no-
menclature was bannered at elections, the movement was not the
same.

For all of its political drama, the reform movement bestowed a
legacy which was gradual and developmental. Though reform could do
little to stem the flight of the middle class, it did furnish a rhetoric
of hope and served as a psychological buoy. Some downtown neighborhoods went through a real estate revival and became fashionable
retreats for a new middle class. Though reform did not wipe away
corruption, it did push it into less conspicuous corners and dealt with
the most visible abuses. (21) Finally, though reform did not succeed
in doing away with political organization, it did manage to eliminate
the old fashioned machine - or at least transform it. Reformists
either beat machine candidates at the polls, or the old bosses changed
in order to survive. It is by now a truism to say that success at the
polls also broke the impetus of reform as a movement of challenge.
Each victory over the machine, or each conversion by a boss to reformist methods showed that its cause was growing obsolete.

The Transformation of the
Machine/Reform Dichotomy

The eventual triumph of reform rubbed old dichotomies thin. In some
cases, the old-time bosses faded away and were superseded by reformers who, with the passage of time, became conventional urban
politicians. Charges of "boss rule" and "back room politics" became
handy slogans at election time, but when the heat of the vote subsided,
reformers realized that they, too, needed to head an organization
which arranged quiet concessions. Thus, one man's boss rule became another man's democratic leadership, and one man's back room
politics became another's pragmatic compromise.

In other instances, the reformist melded with the machine politician to create a hybrid which made use of both styles. The best
known leader to merge these styles was Mayor Richard Lee of New
Haven. Lee used his city's old ward heelers to get out the vote, but
kept them at a distance in his administration of city hall. In running
the city, Lee infused his staff with a coterie of technocrats from
Washington and young management types from prestigious business
schools.

Other mayors emerged during the 1960s and 1970s who defy any
categorization. Mayor Philip Rizzo of Philadelphia possessed the
stereotypical traits of the boss (a gruff, dictatorial manner, an ethnic
neighborhood following) but was in a constant and bitter battle with the
machine. Precisely the opposite features described the former Mayor
of Jersey City, Paul Jordon. Jordon cultivated the clean look of the
reformer (an educated professional who dramatized good government)
but worked closely with local bosses in Hudson County and took up his
own brand of patronage.

The most spectacular transformation of the machine/reformist
dichotomy took place under the former Mayor of Chicago, Richard
Daley. Daley was a boss who preempted local reformists with bricks
and mortar, and, to the satisfaction of Chicago's business classes,
rebuilt large sectors of Chicago's downtown Loop. (22) At election
time he also won the enthusiastic endorsement of that city's good
government groups, while using the seediest practices of the machine
to work Chicago's ethnic wards. This seemed like a contradiction to
some observers and a remarkable political feat to others who had always assumed that the purposes of machines and reformers were
mutually exclusive.

Through all of this, it was apparent that the interior city was
changing and the battle between machines and reformers was fast

losing interested spectators, if not the warriors themselves. One
reason why this old dichotomy had begun to fade was that the city now
was caught up in a new set of political relationships and in different
issues. More decisions were taking place outside the city's boundaries which were affecting its future. Urban politics became less in-
ternalized and corruption or good government were no longer the
central issues. More crucial matters were at stake for the city involving federal aid, changes in the welfare system, opportunities for
the poor, funding formulas for community development, and the like.
Urban politics gradually became over-shadowed by urban policy. (23)
To see why this occurred we shall first look at how the exterior city
emerged.

THE GENESIS OF THE EXTERIOR CITY

Census officials and Presidents of the United States tell us that we are
an urban nation. Statistics are cited on behalf of this claim, pointing
out that between 1950 and 1970 the share of the nation's metropolitan
population rose from 62 to 68 percent and by the late 1970s it hovered
at 73 percent. (24) Yet few of our officials tell us what kind of an
urban nation we are, and most Americans would not only refuse to
classify themselves as urbanites but show an outright hostility toward
the city. (25)
      Indeed, some experts reject the notion that we are a nation of
cities, and point out that of the more than 6,000 legally constituted
cities in this nation only five have a population of more than one million and just 51 have more than 250,000 residents. (26) They further
point out that urban densities in America are low compared with those
of Europe, and that at best only 37 percent of the population live in
densities of 1,000 people per square mile, which is a minimum for
urban living. Many states do not even possess a single urban county,
and, if we look toward the year 2000, most urbanized areas will remain at steady densities of about 500 people per square mile. (27)
With this in mind, we might dismiss official claims to "urbanness" as
exaggerated, and see ourselves as a nation of small towns or suburbs
rather than a place where images of Singapore's or Manhattan's
streets await us as the turn of the century approaches.
      One way to appreciate ourselves as a nation of cities is to go
beyond the calculation of size or density to an examination of how all
sectors of the nation have changed as a result of the transformation
from interior to exterior city. Cities are no longer inward oriented,

and they are fast losing their centripetal powers, but so, too, has the
countryside taken on city-like qualities, and it would hardly be accu-
rate to describe ourselves as a nation of modest hamlets.

What the emergence of the exterior city means is that the older,
formerly interior cities are now being shaped from the outside through
myriad pulls in other sectors of the nation. The preeminence of the
urban core is being replaced by new or relocated capital, which is
vested in the surrounding fringes of the cities and open spaces of the
nation. Centripetal pulls are fading and giving way to centrifugal
pulls from a massive urbanization which is occurring outside of traditional contexts and having profound implications for older cities. In
effect, the exterior city is not in control of itself. Unlike the interior
city where growth was taken as an assumption and the major question
to be debated was the division of the spoils, the exterior city must
debate its future in the semantics of survival. The slogans have become all too familiar - "maintain the tax base," "stop white flight,"
"keep private business," and "preserve the neighborhood."

Ecologically, the city has changed in relationship to the former
countryside. Demographically, urban populations have moved into
that countryside but continue to have an impact on the city. These
external changes are as important to the urban future as what the city
does by itself, and we should understand their magnitude before pro-
ceeding further.

Urbanization and the Exterior City

While it is true that only five cities in America contain a population of
one million or more, an equally significant fact is that these cities,
and most smaller ones, are ringed with suburban populations which in
ways render their boundaries invisible. Urban statisticians are inclined these days to talk less of cities or municipalities and more of
great metropolitan areas and megalopoli. The "great metropolitan
area" is defined as a cluster of cities of sprawling suburbs with more
than one million people. In 1960, the United States contained 23 of
these areas which accounted for 38 percent of the total population; a
decade later there were 29 such areas containing 44 percent of the
population; and conservative projections are that by the end of the
century the number of great metropolitan areas will climb to 50 and
compose more than 60 percent of Americans. (28) In other words, if
we pull up those village signposts emblazoned with local Rotary or
Lions Club inscriptions, most Americans do live in massive urban
agglomerations, whether they care to admit it or not.

A broader pattern can be seen if we link up these metropolitan areas with one another and think of them as vast urbanized regions of the country. "Megalopolis" is the popularized and loosely applied description for a vast chain of urban concentrations which are highly interdependent. Originally applied to the Atlantic seaboard with its main links being Boston, New York, Philadelphia, Baltimore, and Washington - or the Bos-Wash complex - it can be seen in other regions of the country as well. We can identify a similar pattern along the lower tier of the Great Lakes which includes Pittsburgh, Cleveland, Akron, Gary, and Chicago to form a Chi-Pitts complex. Another chain of urban links runs up and down the California coast, connecting San Francisco, Los Angeles, Long Beach and San Diego, creating a San-San complex of cities. (29)

This spread of megalopoli has been a major factor in the obliteration of both attitudinal and tangible contrasts between urban and rural life which were so much a part of interior cities. The extension of the city, particularly newer cities which possess their own industry based on low slung buildings fronted by large parking lots, has encouraged mobility and brought an urban culture to the countryside. The great bulk of Americans today are within easy commuting distance of a metropolis or its fringe cities, so that during the present decade over two-thirds of rural nonfarming families are found within urban range.

No longer is there a sharp demarcation between urban and rural qua the interior city. The relationship between the three major geographic sectors of American society (urban, rural, and suburban) is characterized not by relative separation, but by an intricate admixture of dependence, control, and penetration. Moreover, the mode of transportation which blends the nation's population has forever eliminated the central and stable interior city. In its stead is an unhinged exterior city which may be used alternatively with other urban centers.

One way of appreciating the ramifications of this new relationship is to start with the pattern of transportation between exterior cities and outlying areas. Over the last two decades total passenger traffic has more than doubled, going from 508 billion miles to over 1,000 billion miles. Of this increase in travel, automobiles have enjoyed the largest absolute growth, going from 438 billion miles in 1950 to over 1,000 billion 20 years later and absorbing 86 percent of the total miles traveled in the United States. By contrast, railroads have suffered absolute declines and have had their passenger miles cut severely, from 32 billion miles in the 1950s to 11 billion by the early 1970s.

Examining this in relative terms, automobiles by far outpaced all
other modes of transportation during the 1970s with planes, buses,
trains, and waterways following in distant second, third, fourth, and
fifth places. Figure 1.1 provides us with a broad view of these relative patterns since 1929.

Keeping in mind both the absolute and relative dominance of the
automobile, what is significant is the lead held by all modes of fluid
transportation (i.e. automobiles, planes, and buses) over their more
fixed counterparts (i.e. railroads and waterways). Automobiles and
the miasma of highways, cloverleafs, roads, and freeways which
spring up throughout the country are the key to transportation in
America. This fluidity in transportation is one signal of the trend to
provide liaisons with a larger number of lower density and multicentered areas which are outside of the urban core; rather than the
classic "urban hub" idea which existed in Chicago circa 1920.

It can be said that the rapid growth of megalopoli and great metropolitan areas means more than a simple expansion of city living -
more also than a continued urbanization involving more people.
Rather, large numbers of the American people are rapidly changing
by commuting between different geographical areas, residing in different areas from where they were born, and quite literally exchang-
ing roles. It is as if the national psyche has gone through a change of
personality, and this has changed the uses to which populations have
been put in exterior city, suburb, and countryside.

The New Uses of City, Suburb and
Countryside

Fifty years ago, being an urbanite meant that one participated in a
great variety of relationships, confronted others in often impersonal
or specialized roles, and became part of a mechanistic, variegated
society. By contrast, the rural culture was homogeneous, organic,
and based on traditional and personal ties. (30) So unmixed was rural
society that it begot similar opinions, and what one man believed was
the same as what most men accepted as a fact. The urban world was
believed to be a hostile and alien place. Today, it is no longer easy
to compartmentalize these worlds. The person who resides outside of
the city may be more cosmopolitan than one who lives inside of it. If
anything, during the last two decades there has been something of a
population exchange between the two societies. Today, it is not uncommon for affluent corporate executives to commute 50 or 60 miles
each day from urban downtowns to their country homes. The buying

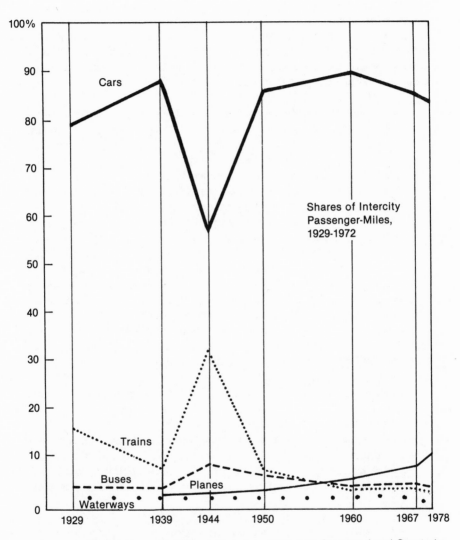

Sources: Adapted from Statistical Abstracts, 1978, and Congressional Quarterly Almanac, 1969-72.

Fig. 1.1. Decline of fixed forms of transportation.

Sources: Adapted from Statistical Abstracts, 1978 and Congresional Quarterly Almanac, 1969-72.

up of vacated farms by an urban middle class and the invasion by commuters of a land beyond the suburban fringe, known as "exurbia," is
another bit of weight on the scale of transformation.

By the same token, farming, which has been the mainstay of traditional family life in the hinterland, is now an agribusiness with all
the trappings of the big urban corporation. Consider the following
case of a potato farmer from Maine:

> Mr. Wilson has a ticker tape in his air-conditioned office at the
> end of one of several storage houses. Every weekday morning at
> 10 o'clock he flicks on a switch and a coil of yellow serpentine
> spins out the prices of Maine potatoes as reported by the New
> York Mercantile Exchange. Perhaps it is the middle of May and
> Mr. Wilson has not yet planted anything, but the Mercantile is
> already quoting what buyers will pay for futures from next No-
> vember through the following April. Mr. Wilson knows pretty
> well what it will cost him to grow 300 acres of potatoes. He has
> checked all the current costs: fertilizer, pesticides, machines,
> and hired labor. The buyers at the Mercantile have done the
> same. Fertilizer sales have been checked, government reports
> on growers' intentions and co-op loans have been probed, and
> some remarks by bankers have not gone unheeded. Mr. Wilson
> senses that there is going to be overproduction again this year.
>
> The buyers on the Mercantile think so too; they are bidding very
> close to costs of production. Their bids do not satisfy Mr. Wil-
> son but he must stay in business. Before he plants a single acre
> he wires his broker to sell two-thirds of his future crop at what
> amounts to a farm price of $2.80 a barrel. This is approxi-
> mately the break-even point for a majority of small producers.
> At this price Mr. Wilson thinks he can net 60 cents, but only be-
> cause he operates on a big scale. While the price is low it will
> cover a lot of cash expenses and a big risk is already eliminated.
> (31)

Corporate agriculture has had its consequences for other rural
folk. Millions of black and white sharecroppers, mostly from the
South and who have been displaced from their land, now settle in the
inner cities. A Chicano and Puerto Rican peasantry has also migrated
to inner cities in search of jobs; and close to half of all Native Americans have left federal reservations for the cities. Harlem, the Okie
sections in uptown Chicago, east Los Angeles, and parts of Minneapo-
lis are grim evidence of this rural trek to the cities.

Urbanization around the exterior city has had contradictory effects which at first appear puzzling. It has broken down urban/ rural distinctions based on place and attitude, while at the same time parochializing society by sorting out members according to class and ethnicity; it has extended and enriched urban life in some aspects, while impoverishing and constricting it in others. Unlike the segregation of the interior city, which for all its faults kept wealth and poverty within the same municipal bounds and left the city with its resources intact, this division has transferred poverty into the city while extracting its resources. In a real sense, exterior cities have become exploited colonies within their own nation, where the weakest and most despised classes are unloaded, and to which the privileged groups commute freely and exploit urban resources. Outer cities and suburbs are able to prosper while the central city decays - values produced or derived from central cities feed the more prosperous sectors outside of it, while unwanted problems are shuttled into it (for a full discussion of this, see Chapter 8, which deals with suburbs and the "colonial syndrome").

Another side of the colonial analogy describes the suburban role as a privileged sector of society. Every morning one can see inner city residents, usually black or Hispanic, at suburban train stations going to work as domestics or gardeners in the most affluent suburbs. The reverse commute has also begun to take hold among blue collar workers in places of manufacture because they cannot afford to move close enough to relocated suburban plants.

Though we are loathe to recognize it, our society has come to resemble that of colonial Africa or present day South Africa. Certain parts of it exact egregious privilege and deplete other parts. Segregation of the poor and color lines sort out the participants while they pass one another each working day in the commuter rush and the reverse commute.

It may be that this has always existed in the class dimensions of American society, but it was never so harshly reinforced by race, ethnicity, and locational disparities. By contrast, the older political and psychological walls of the interior city brought its groups together within the same urban realm and softened the impact of these differences by requiring a measure of internal participation. Moreover, these walls made partial autonomy possible, allowed for simplified political relationships, and enabled a certain portion of the city's resources to be distributed internally. The simultaneous move away from the interior cities to a new urbanization and the penetration of these walls have changed this.

The Idea of the Exterior City

A picture of the exterior city has begun to emerge. The exterior city is large and heterogeneous, with relatively dense concentrations of population and variegated industrial, commercial, and cultural enterprises. Historically, it was the city preeminent - centripetal in its effect on other communities, while at the same time sharply demarcated from the cultures that lay outside of it, and solipsist in outlook.

Depending upon how one wishes to interpret this definition, there are roughly a dozen cities in America which possess these qualities. Elsewhere they may be described as central cities, traditional cities, older cities or any other phrase which comotes urban magnitude and age. The term "exterior" is used throughout this book to convey how these cities have changed and have become enmeshed with larger forces. Ten such cities have been chosen as major points of reference, though the applications of urban policy are broader. Together these ten cities comprise nearly 18 million people or about eight percent of the nation's population. In total their revenues are approximately 20 billion dollars, which is more than the annual expenditures of most nations of the world. The figures for each city, and their cumulative magnitude, can be seen in Table 1.1.

Other cities, like Atlanta or Pittsburgh, might also be classified as "exterior cities," but are not specifically included. Still other urban areas in decline, like Jersey City or Camden, are relevant objects for the urban policies discussed here, but are not "exterior cities." First, members of this latter group contain neither the size nor the economic weight of an exterior city; secondly, these cities never attained the national or regional preeminence of a Chicago or a San Francisco.

A feature of the exterior city is that it is a cosmopolitan center; its commercial variation and mixed populations give it a modicum of international recognition. Six of the cities listed above (New York, Chicago, Philadelphia, San Francisco, Boston, and New Orleans) are distinctly cosmopolitan. The remaining four (Detroit, Baltimore, Cleveland, and St. Louis) are less so, but widely recognized as sources of international trade and travel.

One thing made clear is that the exterior city is not the small municipality located at the outskirts of the metropolitan area. There are many thousands of small cities in America, which are legally incorporated as municipalities. Some are even statistically incorporated into the Census Bureau's definition of the "urban core." More than a few of these are not well off and have been the objects of urban policy, while others are problem free. For our purposes, small cities have been treated as outside of the exterior city or as "suburbs.

Table 1.1.   The Magnitude of Ten Selected
Exterior Cities: Population & Budget

Exterior City	Population: 1975 (in numbers)	Revenue: 1978 (in thousands)
New York	7,481,613	13,827,064
Chicago	3,099,000	1,028,668
Philadelphia	1,815,808	1,010,430
Detroit	1,335,085	760,764
Baltimore	815,698	1,037,067
San Francisco	664,520	759,411
Cleveland	638,793	247,301
Boston	636,725	712,532
New Orleans	550,770	256,036
St. Louis	526,964	266,670

Sources: Department of Commerce, Bureau of the Census, and
The Municipal Year Book: 1978

Another major feature of exterior cities is that a certain amount
of decay is tolerated within them, yet at the same time they are
thought to have enough redeeming value and to be worth millions in
capital investments. This is what also distinguishes New York from
Jersey City, and Camden from Philadelphia. The exterior city still
retains a vast amount of infrastructure and a valuable core which will
not entirely be abandoned. Huge sections of the exterior city may be
left for nought, but its golden nuggets remain. Wall Street is one of
New York's golden nuggets; "Center City" is one of Philadelphia's.
Detroit is on its way to getting the single biggest golden nugget of

them all - a colossal, futuristic complex of hotel and office space
called the "Renaissance Center." "Renaissance Center" will cost an
estimated 337 million dollars of private capital raised by Henry Ford
and the heads of 51 major corporations. To be sure, there are exterior cities which enjoy a surfeit of invested treasure (San Francisco)
while others are dangerously lacking (Cleveland). Without exception,
however, all exterior cities possess some quality which makes them
worth a fight, and it is this struggle that illuminates how public money
is used to bolster private capital in them.

The other side of the coin is that all ten of the referent cities
also possess varying amounts of misery, which can be translated into
official indices of "hardship," "decline," and "distress." One influential study which attempted to measure urban hardship took 55 of the
largest metropolitan areas and listed them according to a composite
index which included unemployment, dependency, education, income,
crowded housing, and poverty. According to this study, the "hardship indices" ranged from a high of 422 to a low of 43. The higher the
index, the greater the hardship. A "hardship index" above 100 meant
that the central city was disadvantaged in relation to the suburbs
around it. All ten of our "exterior cities" were above 100, and in the
top half of the most disadvantaged cities in the nation. The comparative indices of these cities are listed in table 1.2, alongside the ten
most advantaged cities.

Note that the most advantaged cities are all located in the "sunbelt" or in the Far West. These cities are much newer than their
exterior counterparts or have experienced greater development in
recent years. Most advantaged cities also tend to be low density,
spread cities with their business districts sharply set off from their
residential areas. Their flow of human traffic is heavily geared
toward the automobile, and one could argue that in many ways they
more closely resemble large suburbs than they do cities. Urban development and the uses to which land can be put have a great deal to
do with urban prosperity, and we will examine this relationship in the
next chapter.

Of the exterior cities in Table 1.2, Cleveland appears to be in
the most dire condition, followed by Baltimore, Chicago, and St.
Louis. San Francisco comes closest to being well off with the lowest
comprehensive index. This trend is hardly surprising, though some
of these cities exchange places depending upon the criteria used.

Another way to understand the condition of exterior cities is to
look at their rates of job loss and their increase in crime. Job loss
is revealing because it reflects a sense of impending destitution on the
part of the population. Increases in crime reflect desperation and

Table 1. 2. Urban Hardship: Exterior and
Most Advantaged Cities Compared

Exterior City Disadvantaged	Index of Hardship	Ten Most Advantaged Cities	Index of Hardship
Cleveland	331	Omaha	98
Baltimore	256	Dallas	97
Chicago	245	Houston	93
St. Louis	231	Phoenix	85
New York	211	Norfolk	82
Detroit	210	Salt Lake City	80
Philadelphia	205	San Diego	77
Boston	198	Seattle	67
New Orleans	168	Ft. Lauderdale	64
San Francisco	105	Greensboro, N. C.	43

Source: Adapted from Richard P. Nathan and Charles Adams
"Understanding Central City Hardship", Political Science Quarterly
21 (Spring 1976): 51-2.

fear of predators. Both are issues which cut across liberal and conservative persuasions and both issues are intuitively understood as
eating away at the foundations of urban society. Table 1.3 shows just
how exterior cities have fared on these two critical factors.

Once again, the statistics of past years show a trend toward
more crises and more decay. Jobs go down while crime goes up, and
this relationship can only quicken the cycle of poverty and crime that
causes such panic among the middle class. Since 1974, the prospects
for employment in many of these cities have become dimmer. One

Urban Policy and the Exterior City

Table 1.3. Job Loss and Crime in Ten
Exterior Cities: 1970-74

Exterior City	% Job Loss	% Crime Increase
New York	- 6.4%	+ 0.4%
Chicago	-12.1	+90.0
Philadelphia	-12.1	+78.7
Detroit	-18.5	+ 9.1
Baltimore	-12.7	+22.7
San Francisco	- 2.4	- 2.1
Cleveland	n.a.*	+16.7
Boston	n.a.	+71.6
New Orleans	n.a.	+ 9.9
St. Louis	-18.3	+44.6

---

*   n.a. = not available

Sources: U.S. Department of Labor; Federal Bureau of Investigation.

---

can be sure that regardless of additional patrol cars put on city
streets, the problem of urban crime will not abate until there is opportunity for constructive employment.

Taking a larger view of the exterior city, then, it is a seemingly
incompatible combination of surging investment and gnawing decay.
It still has great attraction, yet business and the middle class continue to flee. It is a city which everyone talks of as "dying" because it
is being abandoned, or as "smothering" under the burden of its problems. Yet the attempt to abandon it and the very problems it has

incurred have shown that the exterior city is pretty much inescapable. Movement of former residents out of the exterior city has only increased commutation into it for business, entertainment, or to see familiar faces. Factories which have departed from the urban core often retain intercourse with it through their corporate headquarters which still locate there. Despite the exodus of manufacturing outlets, some exterior cities continue to enjoy a boom in downtown office construction. Moreover, as populations spread and interchange so, too, does the urban crisis. Suburbs and smaller municipalities experience traffic congestion, housing problems, and urban decay in their older areas. For these outlying areas, the urban crisis is acutely felt in the incidence of crime. While much has been made of the crime rate in big cities, suburban crime is also on the rise and proportionately greater than that of the inner city. (32) In a real sense, the sheer magnitude of the exterior city and the crisis it has generated have been nationalized.

The multiple components of the exterior city's crisis has been telescoped by the media into a holistic perception of a national event. The riots of the 1960s, though they occurred in separate places often a distance from one another, were flashed in serial and violent order across television screens, giving one the sense of being afflicted with a national contagion. Events of this kind continue to be flashed through the media in the same way. Crime, pollution caused by industrial abuse, and rising welfare roles are not the exclusive purview of cities, though they are depicted by television cameras on urban streets.

Like a piece of huge timber rolling down a mountainside - vital in some spots and rotting in others - the exterior city quakes the ground around it as it comes down. As the city begins to topple, it implicates one outside government after another in its search for survival. Inevitably, urban politics was bound to change from the emphasis on internal issues to one of policy and the mayors of exterior cities would have to assume new roles.

Politics As Policy In The Exterior City

The Impacted Politics of the Exterior City

It came to the cities, through their mayors, to become the spokesmen for a nation-wide malady called the "urban crisis." The impacted politics of the exterior city had multiple causes and would have multiple effects. Across the country, mayors not only had to contend with

physical decline, but with assuaging demands from competing groups
within their populations, and with having to reach out to other arenas
of power in order to cope with these demands. City halls could no
longer satisfy their constituents by bosses rendering favors or by reformers claiming to improve municipal government. Now urban populations were demanding that their representatives do something about
fundamental living conditions such as full employment, better housing,
and protection against rising crime. Not only was basic legislation
demanded to resolve each crisis, but cities (together with other
governments) were charged with implementing the putative remedies.
For every fuller employment policy there were local public works
projects; for every better housing policy, there were elaborate inspection and loan procedures; for every policy to prevent crime there
were scores of drug rehabilitation centers or halfway houses. These
were efforts which were justified as getting to the root of the "urban
crisis" and they promised results - phrased in either the bombastic
rhetoric of politicians or the jargon of professional grantsmen. Add
to these demands that urban government provide decent and integrated
schools, consumer protection, and recreation centers for the collective well being, and the discrepancy between expectation and ability
to perform seems staggering.

In an effort to meet these pressures, exterior city mayors have
had to promote the urgency of the urban crisis in Washington D. C.,
state capitals, and to a national corporate elite. Charisma, or, more
precisely, the ability to project and utilize personal influence with
audiences outside of municipal boundaries became a sine qua non for
conducting successful politics. New York City's John Lindsay popularized this kind of mayoral style during the 1960s and even attempted
to use the urban issue to catapult himself from city hall to the White
House. The names of mayors competed with those of other public
personalities as political heroes or anti-heroes. Kevin White of
Boston became identified as a popular Kennedyesque figure and was
later victimized by his city's racial strife over busing. Phillip Rizzo
of Philadelphia earned a reputation among his supporters as a "tough
cop-mayor" and among his critics as a "bumptious racist." Moon
Landrieu of New Orleans gained center stage before Congress as de-
fender of New York's economic plight as well as the woes of other
sister cities. Big city mayoralties have always been labeled dead end
streets for politicians, (33) so it was rare for so many mayors to
gain national attention, and the trend continues unabated.

Behind the glimmer of the newspaper headlines and broadcasts,
mayors pushed themselves into substantive policies. At the federal
level, they lobbied for additional mass transit aid, housing construction,

and welfare reform. For every federal program there were extensive commitments from all sides, giving rise to innumerable strands of categorical governments. A skein of mini ambassadors from the cities followed every project implementation and overlaid an already formidable national bureaucracy with local apparati. This became so important a part in governing a city that mayors became their city's chief lobbyist. San Francisco's former mayor Joseph Alioto is purported to have remarked that "No mayor can really do his job unless he spends at least one day per month in Washington." (34)

After that day in Washington each mayor would travel back to his home city where problems were just beginning. For each piece of legislation which was successfully brought to passage, there were the difficulties encountered in making the new programs work, struggling for their political control, and being held responsible for their sound implementation. President Johnson's "War On Poverty" which spawned Community Action Programs (CAP's) was the subject of incessant political struggles between big city mayors and their potential rivals in the communities. Chicago's Richard Daley maintained a tight fisted control over his city's CAP's but other mayors were not as wily, and locally-run CAP's were used against them. In still other instances CAP programs fell into scandal, and city halls were blamed for the misuse of federal funds.

Even the "special revenue sharing" programs of the Nixon-Ford era were subject to internecine warfare between urban politicians. Federal aid given by the Law Enforcement Assistance Administration (LEAA) was often used to bolster a mayor's power of patronage or press favors for constituents within his city. Joseph Alioto not only applied LEAA monies with consummate skill but also used them to control fragments of San Francisco's scattered political structure.

At the corporate level, mayors have gone national as beseechers and salesmen. To encourage business reinvestment, mayors have taken the lead in subsidizing commercial districts, providing tax abatements for new enterprise, and defraying the costs for industrial parks. They have courted the heads of multinational corporations, with spotty success, in order to rebuild cities. Witness, for example, the role auto manufacturers have been induced to play in Detroit, or the rosters of the National Urban Coalition, the Urban League, and similar associations which have been enlisted in efforts to quell the urban crisis. (35)

The notion of the family-dominated, single company town is fast becoming extinct and is being replaced by an absentee-owned and multicentered corporate structure. Such a corporation usually has a capacity for easy relocation and can wield tremendous power through such a decision. It is apparent that cities are beholden to giant corporations, whose board rooms could cause boom or economic chaos, and mayors are anxious to win them over. Through public forums and advertising, mayors and their surrogates are attempting to overcome negative images of their cities by aggressive promotion to corporate heads. Undesirable images of crime ridden and deteriorated slums are countered by sleek pamphlets portraying high rises and new skylines, and newspaper stories on the middle class migration back to the cities and the brownstone revival. Much as the nineteenth century robber barons were replaced by their Harvard educated sons, new mayors have also cultivated respectability. Also, like their corporate counterparts, many urban politicians have developed the sophisticated attributes of national statesman - an impressive demeanor, a broad scope of knowledge, and a personality which exudes confidence to a clientele with international ties.

This is not to say that exterior city politicians can disregard internal concerns. On the contrary, the exterior city compounds internal with external relationships, and its politics refract these difficulties. Thus, the rise of "community control" and the interest in urban decentralization within exterior cities were largely a counterresponse to extended ties with other governments and to overbureaucratization. Some of these efforts at neighborhood control were undertaken at the inspiration of the federal government, which had created the inordinate red tape in the first instance, and afterward laid neighborhood participation in the laps of the cities. The Model Cities Program, passed in 1966, was one such effort at bringing citizen participation to bear on community development problems which had been spawned by planners in Washington.

Other efforts were started by or within cities themselves, as "bottom up" strategies to deal with bureaucratic insensitivity. Thus, school systems were so enmeshed in state regulations and credentialism that community control was introduced to make education responsive to minority group needs. City halls became so extended by a suffusion of federally sponsored programs, that they were unable to deliver services after they were formally committed. As a result, versions of neighborhood decentralization were resorted to where traditional municipal government had failed. Though introduced with great fanfare, these were truncated forms of citizen participation which whet some appetites for control, but did little to effect real change.

The outward thrust of exterior city politics, then, had the reciprocal effect of intensifying internal politics based on the neighborhood and the community. Many actions once taken by outside powers had deleterious impacts on smaller communities within the city. Excavations for highways and land clearances for new business swept away entire neighborhoods or threatened their extinction and aroused the ire of a newly activated citizenry who took to the streets with protest. The community reaction in South Boston to federal court-ordered busing was no less a measure of response to external pressure than were earlier protests over the destruction of neighborhoods by urban renewal.

Whether these neighborhood movements were a response to crises in the school system, urban renewal, or highway excavations, they seem to have endured and taken on a life of their own. What is more ironic is that they have gotten Federal attention and support. In most cities (Chicago, Baltimore, Philadelphia), community activists have sustained the movement through neighborhood corporations. The rise of the "unmeltable ethnic" gained legitimacy overnight as working class people sought to regain control of their neighborhoods. Presidents and presidential candidates were quick to capitalize on the upsurge of neighborhood identity, and even imparted it with national scope. Richard Nixon made much of the neighborhood issue in 1972, campaigning on busing and crime in the wards of Chicago and Cleveland. Neither did the Democratic candidate in 1976 shy away from the neighborhood issue - recall Jimmy Carter's statement about the virtues of "ethnic purity" and the values of the urban community. The nationalization of these issues was also ensconced in Carter's proposed urban policy in 1978, with federal assistance being given directly to community self help organizations. Today there is a bureau within the Department of Housing and Urban Development (HUD) which tends to the neighborhood movement, and a national organization for neighborhoods which lobbies regularly in Washington. The smallest urban communities of a few thousand residents have sought protection and sustenance from larger governments.

This juxtaposition of neighborhood and outside pressures places the exterior city mayor in a difficult and confusing role. To external forces, particularly national corporations, symbolic reassurances are made through slogans ("Cleveland: The New Generation") and propaganda (building models, brochures, newspaper advertisements). For the neighborhoods, different symbols emphasize a battle against heavy odds or against an elusive enemy (anti-urban legislators, vested interests) so that failures can be explained.

While this can be written off as rhetoric, the difficulties it reflects are real, and so, too, is its impact upon an increasingly cynical citizenry. Mayors struggling for survival are prone to push for highly visible short-run achievements, such as giant highway projects

and displays of bricks and mortar to absorb a stagnant labor force.
The phenomenon has been described elsewhere as the "politics of
conspicuous gesture," (36) or as actions which are cosmetic and may
temporarily impress, but which fail to attack fundamental problems.
Secondly, there is a cumulative cost for such gestures, and successor
mayors are bound to pay for them. Every experiment which fails to
produce results and every "white elephant" paid for by citizens has its
upshot in a public which is demoralized and unwilling to venture forth
again.

Multisided Politics and
Proliferating Policies

Politics and policy are the social reflexes of industrial change, and
when the new urbanization jerked its knee the exterior city went into
spasm. The influx of a poor peasantry into the urban core, the exodus of an urban middle class, the startling competition from the suburbs and the sunbelt and the breakup of old neighborhoods all brought
about a different modus operandi for city halls. Much as the exterior
city became geographically extended, so, too, did its politics. Increasingly, urban politics would begin to depend on extensive lobbying
with other governments, a jockeying for prominence between mayors,
and the mastery of technical aid formulas. Success at "politics" was
indicated by success at "policy," the inauguration of new legislation,
and the increased fiscal aid which mayors could present to constituents.

Movement between Washington, D. C. and the exterior city was
decidedly intensified beginning in the mid-1950s when two organizations - the U. S. Conference of Mayors (USCM) and the National
League of Cities (NLC) - emerged as official delegations for the
cities. Each of these organizations grew in proportion to Washington's
response. Thus, in the 15 year interval between 1955 and 1970, the
USCM added close to 200 additional cities to its membership, bringing it to a total of 473, while the NLC saw an eight-fold increase in its
membership, which totaled 410 cities. Both organizations have also
come a long way in the scope of their activity and staff, which went
from fewer than 15 employees and a $200,000 budget in 1954 to nearly
200 employees and a $7 million budget between them, in that same
time period. (37)

Gradually the nation's mayors and city officials evolved a syndicate of local governments in Washington with an army of specialists
working on urban problems. The mere size of this lobbying effort
masks the enormous amount of work which went into its creation.

Through the Eisenhower years when cities began to falter, few people
in Washington paid much attention to them. When John F. Kennedy
came to power, cities could at least be heard, and the swell of legislation during the Johnson years brought a new level of formalized
political activity. Recognition came with the elevation to cabinet
status of a Department of Housing and Urban Development and wan-
dering ambassadors from the cities believed they had found a home.
Legislation which poured out of President Johnson's Great Society
furnished more reasons for building bridges to Congress and the bureaucracy. Policy specialists within USCM/NLC worked with officials
in the White House, in congressional committees, and in the bureaucracy (HUD, Department of Transportation, Commerce, and Health,
Education and Welfare, HEW) on the minutiae of programs. Much of
this required the technical formulation of how community development
monies were to be distributed, what authorizations could be gotten for
capital construction on mass transit, or which was the best method
for stimulating housing construction. Tasks of this kind required
such a steady stream of communication between USCM/NLC and the
federal apparati that a kind of "permanent government" of professional policy makers took root. Between these professionals there
was a tremendous institutional capacity to carry through on urban
policy regardless of what political appointments might be at the top.

What is more, policy action brought opportunities for federal
dollars through grants-in-aid. In 1958, federal aid to states and localities amounted to $7 billion and by 1978 the figure had zoomed to
over $80 billion. (38) Similarly, by the early 1970s there were over
500 separate grant-in-aid programs, four-fifths of which were enacted after 1960. During its first two years, the Nixon administration turned out 143 such programs and could not break the wave of
dollars. (39) Thus, out of the $20 billion in exterior city expendi-
tures cited earlier, more than a third has been met through external
aid.

New policy channels were also needed to guide the flow of federal
dollars, and one governmental mechanism was piled upon another to
manage relations between Washington and the cities. These included
the passage of the Intergovernmental Cooperation Act of 1968, which
paved the way for local Councils of Government (COG's) to consult
with one another on metropolitan-wide problems; the establishment of
A95 reviews to assess the regional impact of federal grants; and the
creation of 10 federal councils to monitor the bureaucracies.

Federal aid has not been without its costs to the city. Usually,
new programs require localities to put up "matching funds" or undertake a "maintenance of effort" to keep up existing programs. In many

cases, federal expenditures also mean increased local expenditures
and, on the average, cities put up 43 cents for each dollar received.
(40) In the longer term, the politics of urban aid turned out to be a
mixed blessing for cities. While their needy populations received
increased amounts for health care and community services, cities
were required to contribute their own share. Since exterior cities
already contained a disproportionate number of citizens in need, their
own budgets were disproportionately higher than other localities.
Table 1.4 shows just how much higher urban expenditures have been
relative to the more affluent, suburban sectors of the nation.

On a per capita basis, total city expenditures are higher than
those of the suburbs in all ten instances. The only category where
suburbs have spent more than cities is in education (almost uniformly)
which is a consequence of suburban growth and the need to school the
children of newly arrived families. Interpolating further from the
first column, the average of the ratios for city/suburban spending is
on the order of 1.38 to 1.00. Continuing to the third column (noneducational expenditures), the average of the ratio jumps to 2.18 to
1.00. For every dollar spent by these suburbs on their entire operating budget, exterior cities have spent $1.38; for every suburban dol-
lar spent on noneducational items, exterior cities have spent $2.18.
While suburbs have been putting a disproportionate amount of their
money into school systems, exterior cities have placed their funds
into police, fire, sanitation, and assorted social services.

Exterior cities may have been successful in boosting the dollars
given to them in the last 20 years, but expectations for more services
and more relief have created a vicious political dynamic. Citizen
demands went beyond the capacity of mayors to handle them, and
there were pressures on expense budgets to match the federal promise.
Homeowners lobbied for better sewer systems, working mothers
asked for day care centers, frightened citizens wanted more police
protection, and the litany of requests became longer as each preceding request was met. Moreover, it is the natural disposition of
politicians to add to their city's offerings. Every mayor delights in
the political pleasure of adding new programs or officiating at the
opening of a new housing complex. During the best of these aid years,
three exterior cities (New York, Philadelphia, and Cleveland) incurred expenditures which exceeded their revenues by more than five
percent. (41) New York continued to succumb to these pressures and
fell headlong into fiscal collapse; Cleveland followed later with its
own "fiscal crisis."

At the level of middle governments, the proliferation of urban
policies has not been as great as the involvement with Washington.

Table 1.4.   Per Capita Expenditures in Ten
Exterior Cities and Their Suburbs, 1970

	Total Expenditures		Educational Expenditures		Non Educational Expenditures	
	City	Suburb	City	Suburb	City	Suburb
New York	894	644	215	332	679	312
Chicago	478	346	158	199	320	147
Philadelphia	495	325	174	203	321	122
Detroit	471	462	177	261	294	201
Baltimore	638	349	222	215	416	134
San Francisco	768	596	209	264	559	332
Cleveland	512	368	210	195	302	173
Boston	531	365	139	177	392	188
New Orleans	334	325	126	123	208	202
St. Louis	463	292	176	187	287	105
Average of the ratios	1.39 : 1.00		1.01 : 1.20		2.08 : 1.00	

Source: Adapted from U.S. Advisory Commission on Intergovernmental Relations, City Financial Emergencies, Table B 25.

Nonetheless, relationships between the exterior city, the states, and
the suburban regions around the urban core are far more complex
today than they were a mere 20 years ago. Much of this has been due
to the lobbying momentum generated in Washington, D.C., and

mayors have plied some of the same tactics at their state capitals.
New York Mayor John Lindsay led a delegation of "big six" cities in
obtaining state aid for urban localities. Milwaukee's Henry Maier
also put together an urban coalition to do battle with the state house in
obtaining a more equitable tax structure for Wisconsin's cities.
Maier dubbed his organization the "Have-nots," and by the early
1970s came through with some achievements for the urban cause.
Through the support of business groups, Chicago's political machine
also won benefits in the Illinois statehouse. An important part of that
machine's success was its command over Democratic votes in the
Illinois legislature as well as former Mayor Daley's ability to spread
his influence beyond Chicago's confines.

The most intense areas of interaction between cities and middle
governments have been in policies toward housing, zoning, and mass
transportation. New York, California, Michigan, and more than 25
other states have established various kinds of housing "finance"
agencies or "development" corporations. Large-scale housing construction perforce entails a certain amount of planning, and these
states have become enmeshed in disputes over the urban future.

Middle governments have also been drawn into zoning disputes
through their state courts. As suburbs were built up around the exterior city, the politics of land played an important part in determining how the urban core was to be used. Though few cities have been
drawn directly into these disputes, they have been represented by
proxy groups of the urban poor who have pressed a legal fight over
their right to reside in the suburbs. Furthermore, how land is used
in the suburbs has a great deal to do with the fiscal plight of the exterior city.

As patterns of communication between cities and the areas outside of them have become more entangled, so, too, has the state's
involvement with transportation. Many states now operate regional
transportation agencies or have cooperated in their establishment.
How these lines get built, where they are built, and who they serve
are key questions for urban policymakers. They are an additional
facet of the extension of exterior city politics to another arena of
government.

In sum, the transition from interior to exterior city has been
gradual but no less decisive. Every change in national development
was like the waves from a giant tide leaving a sediment upon the exterior city. Each spurt of growth in or around the city ensnared it
still deeper in a complex of relationships which had no single beginning nor definitive ending, and which, above all, left city hall with
less means of control than it had earlier. Before moving on to how

federal, middle government, and private power enveloped the exterior city, we will examine the suppositions of policymaking in America. This will enable us to sketch a theory of how urban policy is formed and test it against the actions of policymakers.

2 Political Economy and Policy: How Cities Are Doomed

... Above Ducie Bridge there are some tall tannery buildings, and further up there are dye-works, bone mills and gasworks. All the filth, both liquid and solid, discharged by these works finds its way into the River Irk, which also receives the contents of the adjacent sewers and privies. The nature of the filth deposited by this river may well be imagined. If one looks at the heaps of garbage below Ducie Bridge one can gauge the extent to which accumulated dirt, filth and decay permeates the courts on the steep left bank of the river. The houses are packed very closely together and since the bank of the river is very steep it is possible to see a part of every house. All of them have been blackened by soot, all of them are crumbling with age and all have broken window panes and window frames. In the background there are old factory buildings which look like barracks. On the opposite, low-lying, bank of the river, one sees a long row of houses and factories. The second house is a roofless ruin, filled with refuse, and the third is built in such a low situation that the ground floor is uninhabitable and has neither doors nor windows. In the background one sees the pauper's cemetery, and the stations of the railways to Liverpool and Leeds. Behind these buildings is situated the workhouse. . .

.... It is only industry which has crammed them full of the hordes of workers who now live there. It is only the modern industrial age which has built over every scrap of ground between these old

houses.... and yet this same industry could not flourish except
by degrading and exploiting the workers....

Friedrich Engels, describing
Manchester, England in 1844

PRIVATISM AND THE LIBERAL STATE

The Fiction of the Liberal State

The line between public and private power is ambiguous, and some
would argue that it is meaningless. Yet much of our political thinking
starts from the premise of the state, or public power, operating in a
world apart from the society which houses our private lives. The
usual approaches of social science are to take this separation for
granted and describe public power acting only at critical junctures of
society to resolve problems which have welled up through its groups.
The state often arrives as an intervener, and policy is viewed as
something to be won or lost by diverse classes or groups of individuals. Centrist and right wing interpretations of this process are prone
to see the state functioning as a barometer which registers group demands, or as a mediator which strikes compromises through intricate legislative hairsplitting. Critical writers portray public power
as an arbiter which frequently sides with the most powerful of private
groups in society. (1)

The fabric on which the distinction between the state and private
power is drawn is the fiction of the liberal state, which supposes that
government is capable of acting independently upon classes of individuals in society. This notion, taken from seventeenth and eighteenth
century theorists, suggests that public power is a collective device
which can be used with selective restraint to curb or expand the freedom of its private parts. Early liberalism prescribed the minimal
exercise of this power and saw freedom as a void allowed by the absence of state intrusion so that private energy could be released; or
as John Locke put it, the "liberty to follow my own will in all things
where the rule prescribes not." (2) The successor to this liberalism
was the "positive state," whose policies could be enlisted to expand
newly appreciated economic freedoms, like full employment or old
age pensions. Here the state could act felicitously to assist its private parts, through more, rather than less, intervention.

Whatever the form of liberalism, the implication was that the state would behave in a disinterested manner, as if the clash of its competing parts could ultimately be resolved in some approximation of a public interest. The fiction of the liberal state is its assertion of neutrality and its contention that it can act as an honest broker between groups or classes in society. Dispensing with this fiction means that we approach the state as a mechanism used to adjust the social environment to the needs of industrial movement, and study public power as the product of that movement. This makes the twists of direction from John Locke's minimalist state to "positive liberalism" explicable as an effort to withdraw or introduce public power as it suited industrial needs. Thus, the liberty advocated by Locke was not so much a freedom from the shackles of government as it was a desire to give license to embryonic business so that it might flex its muscles over the rest of society, particularly over a declining feudal order. (3) Likewise, as industry matured, the positive state was called in to stabilize competition and steer commercial development toward a more orderly course.

American history is replete with public intervention put to the use of private interests, once that became necessary. The great "robber barons" of the industrial era, who epitomized capitalist individualism, made ample use of government to exact private fortunes. Laws of incorporation which protected entrepreneurs from personal liability while also giving them the opportunity to build their own empires were made possible by actions taken at the public level. New Jersey was the early starter in this field, and enacted a series of corporate laws which nurtured these enterprises. In 1866, it permitted corporations to hold property and do business outside of the state. Some years later, it dispensed with ceilings placed on capital investment and, in a critical move, allowed for the creation of "holding companies," permitting corporations to retain and dispose of the stock of their subsidiaries. Only after these measures were taken could Standard Oil of New Jersey grow to dominate almost three-fourths of the national business in petroleum products at that time and give its investors handsome profits of 30 to 48 percent in dividends. (4)

New Jersey was, however, to be outdone by Delaware, which competed for the favor of having corporations chartered within its boundaries by allowing generous discretion to corporate directors, including the rights to issue and retire stock, hold meetings anywhere they chose, and change the firms' bylaws - all without shareholder consent. A boasted fact in both states was that corporate legislation was in safe hands, since all laws considered at the statehouse were also written or reviewed by attorneys who were employed by the leading businessmen. (5)

The railroads were the beneficiaries of direct public subsidies when outright grants were made to them in land as well as cash. Over 130 million acres, valued in 1890 at $190 million, were awarded to railways so that they might lay open the western frontier. (6) Government loans were made to rail companies for each mile of track put down, and construction companies extracted inordinate profits from the inflated costs. On an investment of $121 million, two Central Pacific construction companies earned $63 million in profit, most of which went to men whose names are prestigous in the West today - Leland Stanford, Charles Crocker, and Mark Hopkins (7)

Washington was especially active when it came to stabilizing the impact of private enterprise on the nation. The Hepburn and Mann-Elkins Acts were essentially pieces of legislation to regularize a railroad monopoly across interstate lines, and the former is acknowledged to have been drafted by a lawyer for a major railroad who also had close connections to J. Pierpont Morgan. (8) Gabriel Kolko's ground breaking work on the "progressive era" illustrates how antitrust legislation and banking acts were introduced to actually salvage private enterprise. Prior to the establishment of the Federal Reserve System, the central problem of large banks was monetary chaos caused by the inelasticity of the currency, the absence of funds in the event of panic, and the instability created by small proliferating banks. After nearly two decades of lobbying by leading financiers, including J. P. Morgan, the Federal Reserve Board was created under national sponsorship to serve as "a bank for the bankers." (9) By contracting or expanding the supply of money and credit, and by providing a supply of ready reserves when needed, the Board was able to make financial life more predictable as well as safer for American bankers.

Public policy shapes every nuance of private life - from tariffs and quotas which increase the costs of the goods we buy, to the underwriting of defense contracts to bolster local industries, to investment credits for manufacturers, and mortgage policies for builders to provide jobs for workers - with such frequency that we are often oblivious to its sweep. The routines of our lives, whether it be the highways we travel, the radio stations we tune, the food and drugs we imbibe, or the use to which we are able to put our bodies, are determined, in one way or another, by the power of government. It is ironic indeed that most Americans, who think of themselves as well educated, would recite the standard definition of "totalitarianism" as the control by the state over "nearly every aspect of an individual's life" (10) and hardly ever think of their own captivity.

Should we, by chance, ponder our own subjugation, we would
more than likely point to the oppressive features of government,
rather than to the particular chemistry which is brought about when
public and private power mesh with one another. Ideally, government
ought to consist of "us," as the commonwealth, and instead of recoil-
ing from its abuses we should value it as a representative of our
liberty. But we do not, and there may be good reason for our apprehension because, rather than reflecting the commonweal, the state
embodies a fragment of it, called privatism, which gives public policy
its direction.

The Push of Privatism and the
Inverted Liberal State

Public power is the collective ability of governments to utilize their
monopoly on resources and coercion in pursuit of a given policy.
Privatism is the term used here to encompass nongovernmental organizations of individuals in the upper reaches of society and the
process whereby these organizations expend energy and resources in
quest of profit and the fulfillment of their own objectives.

Nothing so much characterizes American privatism as the scope
and concentration of its corporate organizations. In 1969, the five
largest industrial corporations, with combined assets of $59 billion,
had just under 11 percent of all assets in manufacturing. The 50
largest corporations accounted for 38 percent of all assets, while the
500 largest corporations held 74 percent of industrial assets.

Looking at the progressive size of corporations and its relationship to the industrial market bears out the pattern of large organizational control. Again, in the year 1969, the 87 corporations with
assets of more than $1 billion possessed 46 percent of all assets used
in manufacture; corporations with more than $100 million had about
four-fifths of the assets; and those with more than $10 million had 86
percent of all assets. (11)

From a chronological perspective, concentration has been increasing steadily over several decades. The 100 largest firms in
1968 had a larger share of manufacturing assets than the 200 largest
companies in 1950; the 200 hundred largest companies in 1968 controlled as large a share as the 1000 largest in 1941. (12)

The pattern of concentration is held up even more strongly if we
turn to select industries on a category basis. In 1966, the top four
firms in each industry accounted for the following percentages of all
output: (13)

Aerospace	67%
Motor Vehicles	79
Computers	63
Tires	71
Cigarettes	81
Soap/detergent	72
Photographic Equipment	67

Turning from heavy industry to corporate finance there is a similar concentration which is matched by size. In 1972, out of approximately 14,000 banks in the United States, the top ten controlled more than 25 percent of all assets and deposits. In the field of trust management, which entails the power to invest and determine industrial movement, the top 26 banks account for close to two-thirds of all assets. Pension funds also constitute an important financial core for industrial development and over half of these are managed by 20 banking firms. (14)

Size and concentration are only a part of the makeup of privatism; what counts also is its "push," or those factors which determine the movement (i.e. the investment) of industry in some areas and not in others. The most prominent factor of this push is the simple lure of profit. Private enterprise exists to maximize its monetary return on work and investment so that its gravity is where the opportunities lie. These opportunities are conditioned by the potential for the cross fertilization of capital with cognate enterprises; or, in the case of smaller business, its potential for profiting from the commercial overspills created by major corporations. Cross fertilization between different enterprises has a tremendous capacity to generate a commercial dynamic within a particular area, as well as surplus for "export" elsewhere. These profits are, in turn, plowed into other lucrative fields stimulating a process which is inherently expansionary and ever mobile, since new outlets must always be found for additional capital investment and higher profits. Jane Jacobs, for example, points out that the city of Detroit began as a flour mill town. These mills needed machinery and parts, so small mechanical businesses arose to equip them. Gradually, mechanical enterprise erupted into the production of steamship engines and shipbuilding to export local merchandise. As capital accumulated within the city, mining was undertaken in the outlying countryside to feed this industry, and the basis for automobile manufacture and export was created. (15) Cross fertilization served Detroit well until the cycle ran out and that city began to die.

While there is a certain spontaneous generation to the dynamic
of privatism, a benign exercise of public power is indispensable for
its continuance and expansion. The employment of public power is an
intrinsic part of this process and encompasses a wide range of supportive policies. The most passive of these policies consist of low
taxes and lenient zoning laws, which enable corporations to easily
establish their operations and accumulate capital for further investment. Government policies which are more activist provide corporations with a ready-made infrastructure for better transportation
(canals, highways, bridges), with cheap electric supply to encourage
production, and manpower training to take advantage of new innova-
tions in technology. The most active public supports are made
through loans, contracts to carry out work for the government at acknowledged high costs which underwrite any risks, and subsidies of
various sorts. Usually the more sophisticated the industry, the more
elaborate are the uses to which public policy fosters this privatism.
Also, the longer the history of public support, the more complex it
becomes with clauses to manage special constituencies and other
inducements.

The city of Houston, a mainstay of the booming sunbelt, is a
contemporary exemplar of all three ingredients of privatism - profit,
cross fertilization, and benign public policy. Houston's privatism is
based on the major industries of energy and petrochemicals, the agribusiness, and space technology. As the petroleum capital of the nation, it is first in the manufacture of oil field equipment, refining,
and gas transmissions. It is also the home of several hundred oil
companies, whose concomitant needs for headquarters and living
space have put the city in the vanguard of a construction industry,
with over $670 million spent each year to build the tallest skyscrapers
in the southwest. Its role as a city of agriculture is also unsurpassed,
and it is a leading producer of fertilizer, a market for cattle and
other livestock, and a major port for farming commodities. Houston
also goes by the accolade, "Space City: USA" and is the site of the
Manned Spacecraft Center and space shuttle project. Space technology has not only made the city a major producer of scientific instruments, but has brought a scientific community to it and made it an
academic center, with Rice University being the host to the nation's
first Space Science Department.

Houston's offshoot enterprises feed on this considerable base.
The city has become a major tourist attraction (Space Center, Astro-
dome, Astroworld). The University of Houston is fast becoming a
research institution to fill the needs of energy production, and a convention center brings businessmen and scientists from all parts of the

country to its hotels and restaurants. Also, professional sports
(teams in football, baseball, hockey, basketball, tennis) have been
drawn to the city as big entertainment to absorb its bountiful capital
and the leisure time of its increased population. (16)

Houston's big gain, however, is Detroit's continuing loss. For
if it is in the nature of privatism to gravitate toward opportunities, it
is also in its nature to evacuate older cities once they are, in effect,
used up. The parlance used to describe these older cities betrays the
current prejudice against them and the contrasting admiration with
which private enterprise is regarded. Thus, traditional cities are
described by negative adjectives such as "obsolete," "lagging behind,"
or as suffering from "hardening of the arteries" because of costly
municipal services; while business enjoys laudatory descriptions of
being "forward looking," "flexible," and responsive to the "free market." (17) Yet, questions rarely arise as to who shaped these obsolete
cities, as to who profited from the services and costly infrastructure
they provided, and as to what capitalism required in the way of cheap
labor and glutted housing which wrecked the urban environment.

One of the great advantages of privatism is its ability to move
away from an area when conditions are no longer suitable for exploitation. Indeed, public policy encourages this by providing corporations
with tax relief through provisions for amortization over a period of
time and tax writeoffs for losses.

Another great advantage for privatism is that public power must
compete with itself in order to curry the favor of giant corporations.
Thus, while Detroit must stay on a thin line between higher taxes and
maintaining schools for the children of unemployed migrants, Houston
freely holds out its ecological and social terrain to privatism. Houston is a new city created out of emptiness with a vast amount of unused acreage, so that corporations can build at low costs (it is cheaper to build anew than to rehabilitate or demolish) and spread out
through extensive freeways, thereby accommodating future requirements for mobility and expansion. It is also a city with no corporate
or personal income taxes and with property taxes far below the national average. Extraordinary as it seems, Houston has no zoning
laws, so that corporations can build where, and as often as, they
like.

The upshot of this push can already be seen in Houston's appeal
as a residence for corporate concentration. It is the fastest growing
city in the nation and projected to be the second largest city by the
end of the century. No fewer than 550 of the nation's million dollar
corporations have located there, and more than 150 moved to the city
since 1950. Today, nine of the largest 500 companies in America
are in Houston. (18)

What the comparative positions of these cities tell us about the liberal state is intriguing. Returning to our earlier observations, conventional thought presents the state as something apart from or above private groups, often acting as a broker between them. Professor Theodore Lowi moves a step away from this conception in his classic, The End of Liberalism, by contending that the state has parceled out its sovereignty by allowing all kinds of groups to penetrate "the interior processes of policy formulation." (19)

Yet, these accounts miss the mark about what moves public policy, by lumping all groups together, as if they were roughly comparable, and by losing sight of the broader picture and its most persistent patterns. Furthermore, by endowing public power with a sovereignty which it might even be able to relinquish, these theorists are assuming what they should set out to prove - that government is indeed sovereign and can embark upon a sociopolitical path through its own power. Public power in America comes in many parts, through both the structure of federalism and the actualities of proliferating smaller governments (municipalities, special districts, counties, townships) as well as bureaucratic fragmentation. It is not possible to make judgments about our national sovereignty unless we examine it first through the perspective of its individual parts.

These parts of public power are so numerous and lacking in direction that they are governed by the far greater concentrated push of privatism. In short, the liberal state is inverted, with corporate privatism choosing between its competing parts, extracting benefits from them, and compelling them to behave in particular ways. It is not the state which acts as "arbiter" or even "mediator," but privatism which conditions the choices and forces the bidding to move in prescribed directions.

Comparing the statistics on these public parts and the trends in relation to private corporations leads to some interesting implications. There are about 80,000 local governments in the entire United States, which elect over 500,000 local officials. (20) Within metropolitan areas, this figure amounts to 20,000 such governments, for an average of 91 per area. The average metropolitan area contains, in addition to the county itself, 12 school districts, 12 incorporated municipalities, 7 townships and 16 special districts, which conduct a variety of functions including water supply, sewerage, housing, parks, and the like. (21)

High as these averages are, they conceal the discrepancy between metropolitan areas and the fact that more congested and traditional cities are likely to contain an even higher proportion of proliferating governments. The six county areas surrounding Chicago, for example, contained more than 1,100 governments, or about one government for every 6,344 persons. Of all the incorporated municipalities in the United States, one-third had less than 1,000 residents and two-thirds less than 5,000 residents. The majority of these municipalities presided over a land area of less than two square miles - most of these contemporary municipalities are a fraction of the political size of ancient Athens.

Despite the efforts and recommendations of experts in the field, this trend toward government proliferation continues and is likely to do so in the foreseeable future. Table 2.1 lays out this long-term proliferation in counties, townships, municipalities and special districts from 1952 to the year 2000. The figures are portrayed as absolute increases, growth per metropolitan area, and increases in total (nonschool) governments over close to half a century.

As the table illustrates, the total number of governments has been doubling for the periods 1952, 1967, and estimates for the year 2000. Of particular consequence is the very appreciable multiplication of special districts, while municipalities are also rising in numbers. The number of local governments saturating each metropolitan area is also growing, with special districts again accounting for a good deal of this proliferation. Nearly three-fifths of the actual change in numbers of local governments, involving some 2,000 municipalities and almost 7,000 special districts, reflects the establishment of new units within existing metropolitan areas, while the remainder will take place in newly created metropolitan areas.

The consequences of this splintering are serious and will exacerbate the plight of older cities, like Detroit, in the future. This prevents cities from tapping larger resources and gives rise to fiscal inequities, which reinforce their colonial status and cripple their own capacity to raise revenues. Serious inequities between local governments already exist, and studies have shown per capita differences in taxable property to vary by 15 to 1 in the Chicago metropolitan area, 10 to 1 in the New York area, and 18 to 1 in the Cleveland area. The state of New Jersey tops the list with discrepancies running as high as 32 to 1. (22)

Proliferation also makes local government highly vulnerable to the push of privatism and corporate dominance. This sometimes occurs when tiny jurisdictions believe they can surpass sister cities by making appeals to corporate wealth through "defensive incorporation." (23) Such an incorporation, which splits off a small sector from the large area around it, allows municipalities to do for privatism something akin to what Houston offers in the way of zoning and tax accommodations as well as specially constructed water lines,

Table 2.1. Government Proliferation: 1952 and Projection to Year 2000

Item	U.S. total	Numbers of Governments per county in metropolitan areas	Change in the Number of (non-school) Governments during intervals	U.S. total increases
Year 2000, total	31,645	39.7	Projected increase, 1967 to 2000	15,545
Counties	751	0.9	By geographic growth of SMSA's	6,786
Municipalities	9,112	11.4	1967 to 1980	4,650
Townships	5,351	6.7	1980 to 2000	2,146
Special Districts	16,431	20.6	By creation of new units total	8,759
1967, total	16,100	35.8	Actual increase, 1952 to 1967	7,241
Counties	419	0.9	By geographic growth of SMSA's	3,107
Municipalities	5,031	11.2	By creation of new units	4,326
Townships	3,458	7.7		
Special districts	7,192	16.0		
1952, total	8,859	32.1		
Counties	255	0.9		
Municipalities	3,144	11.4		
Townships	2,537	9.2		
Special districts	2,923	10.6		

Source: Adapted from Allen Manvel, "Metropolitan Growth and Government Fragmentation," Commission on Population Growth and the American Future: Research Reports, Vol. IV, Governance and Population, ed. A.E. Keir Nash (Washington, D.C.: U.S. Government Printing Office, 1972), pp. 207-08.

sewerage, and roads. There are, in fact, municipalities possessing the attributes of public power which consist almost entirely of private corporations. Teterboro, New Jersey is one example of a "city" which holds within its boundaries 50 industries employing 40,000 workers, while the total population of Teterboro is 22. (24) Industry City, located in the Los Angeles area, has a population which just about equals its 600 manufacturing firms, but is nowhere near the 40,000 people who travel to the plants each day.

At other times, corporate advances have been successfully carried out by private companies against local opposition. In the case of one suburb of New York, this literally resembled a white collar invasion conducted by a superior power against a weaker side. Teams of lawyers and public relations firms were deployed to first smooth the way for rezoning and public acquiescence, and the town was saturated with an advertising campaign. The township was later confronted with manipulation of a referendum and alleged voting improprieties. The corporate move succeeded by a slim two votes. (25)

Putting aside for a time this naked exercise of corporate power, it can be argued that the structure of public/private relationships makes the application of raw power frequently unnecessary. What matters most in this relationship is the compulsion of necessity which confronts almost all public policy. (26) By compulsion of necessity we mean roles and needs which are defined by the situation itself so that patterns of action are reflexive and limited by the available choices. In this case, local government is faced with accumulated pressures to provide services, raise revenues, and help create jobs, as well as feed a phychology which values indiscriminate growth. On the other side, privatism controls the wealth and, through its aggressive push, can distribute its benefits to many different publics. Coupling these factors against fragmented local government and the sheer weight of privatism makes independent choice almost a moot issue.

To appreciate the weight which corporations can wield in the making of public policy, we might examine the relative strengths of public and private organizations. Table 2.2 includes the 25 largest organizations (excluding the federal government) in the United States along two dimensions (1) employment and (2) general revenues or sales.

No public power can be found within the five wealthiest organizations in America. Eight out of the top ten organizations are in private hands, largely unaccountable to the wishes of the electorate. If we move to the top 25 organizations, only seven are governments (California, New York City, New York State, Pennsylvania, Illinois,

Table 2.2. Public and Private Power: Compared by Sales/Reve-
nues and Employment for 1974-76*

Organization	Sales/Revenues Thousands of $	# of Employees	Rank	
1. Exxon	44,864,824	137,000	1	
2. General Motors	35,724,911	681,000	2	
3. Texaco	24,507,454	75,235	3	
4. Ford Motor	24,009,100	416,120	4	
5. Mobil Oil	20,620,392	71,300	5	
6. Standard Oil of CA	16,822,077	38,801	6	
7. California	16,507,414	276,000	1	(State)
8. New York	16,010,816	200,000	2	(State)
9. IBM	14,436,541	288,647	7	
10. Gulf Oil	14,268,000	52,100	8	
11. New York City	13,845,830	348,000	1	(City)
12. General Electric	13,399,100	375,000	9	
13. Chrysler	11,699,305	217,594	10	
14. Inter. Tel. & Tel.	11,367,647	376,000	11	
15. Standard Oil	9,955,248	46,808	12	
16. Pennsylvania	8,286,099	147,000	3	(State)
17. U.S. Steel	8,167,269	172,796	13	
18. Sheel Oil	8,143,445	32,496	14	
19. Atlantic Richfield	7,307,854	28,080	15	
20. Illinois	7,254,548	139,000	4	(State)
21. continental Oil	7,253,801	44,028	16	
22. E.I. duPont deNemours	7,221,500	132,235	17	
23. Michigan	6,874,158	140,000	5	(State)
24. Western Electric	6,590,116	152,677	18	
25. Ohio	6,109,499	128,000	6	(State)

* For corporations, figures have been calculated as of 1975.
For states, revenue figures have been taken as of 1974 and em-
ployment figures as of October payrolls for 1976. Figures for
NYC for the year 1975 and the October payroll of that year.

Source: Fortune, May, 1976; U.S. Department of Commerce,
Bureau of the Census, State Government Finance, 1974; and City
Government Finances, 1975-76. Also, Department of Commerce,
The Statistical Abstract of the United States.

Michigan and Ohio), while the rest are private powers. Three giants
of industry (Exxon, General Motors, and Ford) well exceed the combined revenues and employment of the top six states in the Union.
Had we doubled the list to 50 organizations, only four additional states
and no additional cities would have been included, and they, too, are
dwarfed by IBM, U.S. Steel, and duPont.

It is an ironic testimony to the influence of these corporations
on public beliefs that many Americans have expressed concern about
the growth of big government, but are seldom aware of the size and
dominance of these other powers. One of these, Mobil Oil with sales
over $20 billion and employing 71,000 workers, has quite skillfully
deflected attention from its own size by leading a media campaign
against "big government. "

Placed against the compulsion of necessity felt by governments
to bolster their local economics, corporations pick and choose from
competing locations. Impending shifts of plants out of an area are
enough to ring alarm bells in city halls and statehouses about why
business is being "driven out;" corporate specualtion about where to
place future investments can precipitate a shower of competitive bids
from middle governments. This is particularly acute in the northeast, which is experiencing a decline through the 1970s, and where
economic crises have sparked infighting between the states. Thus,
with New York on the brink of ruin, the state of New Jersey began to
raid New York's shrinking base by publicly advertising the advantages
to be gained by moving across the Hudson River. The appeals to corporations read, in part, as follows: (27)

> Profit from free, customized training of your work force. We'll
> survey your needs, plan the training, secure the funds and faci-
> lities, screen and recruit workers - and train the workers pre-
> cisely to your needs.

> Profit from tremendous bargains in buildings and land. Right
> now there are 650 buildings in our computerized file, ready for
> occupancy, complete with utilities, roads, everything... at
> prices you couldn't duplicate anywhere... If you want to build,
> we'll put you together with architects, engineers, contractors,
> and realtors.

> Profit from long term, low interest loans. New Jersey's suc-
> cessful new economic development authority sells tax exempt
> bonds and passes on the favorable interest rates to you...

Profit from the end of government red tape. Our Office of
Business Advocacy handles all the details of taxes, environmental laws, community relations, zoning, licenses, and
permits for you. You're into profitable operations fast, with
no hassle.

Profit from New Jersey's economical government operations...
We have the lowest state government cost per capita and the
lowest number of state employees per capita of any state. In
fact, New Jersey actually cut its budget this fiscal year!
Imagine what all that does for your tax burden.

Not to be outdone by New Jersey, New York took measures to
amend its constitution so that it, too, could offer low interest loans
to firms and expand the prerogatives of its development agency. It
also reduced or repealed stock and bond transfer taxes, under the
threat that brokerage firms would cross state lines to New Jersey,
and began a campaign under the banner, "If you think New York State
has not done anything for business, there are 22 reasons why you are
wrong". (28) For conversationists, the most disappointing consequence of interstate rivalry was the suspension of major provisions
of New York's environmental laws and the resignation of an energetic
environmental commissioner. The most intense phases of the rivalry
within the tri-state area of New York, New Jersey, and Connecticut
occurred while all three of these states had shifted to Democratic
governors. In New York, the Rockefeller-Wilson administration was
replaced by Democrat Hugh Carey; in New Jersey Republican Thomas
Cahill was succeeded by Democrat Brendan Byrne; and in Connecticut,
Thomas Meskill was succeeded by Democratic Governor Ella Grasso.
The significance of this is not that it belies the conventional belief
that Republicans are "kinder" to business than Democrats, but that all
governors must conform to a compulsion of necessity by yielding to
corporations when their states are in difficulty. The problem is
rooted in a structural and systematic relationship and is not a matter
of individual belief or the will of a political party.
  The theoretical difficulties this case presents for an empirical
and realistic measurement of power are extraordinary. Looking at
some of the theoretical explanations of the problem, taken from the
literature on power structures, the two most common interpretations
of this event would be posed as one of the following alternatives. (29)
Either (a) the states of New York and New Jersey made these concessions under conditions of duress, in which threats or influence
were exerted on officials, thus requiring a researcher to turn up

evidence of intimidation, inducements, lobbying, etc.; or (b) there
was no duress found when these states decided upon the concessions
to be offered, and public policy was voluntarily made in which the
states decided from among a number of options.

The truth of the matter is that neither explanation nor a combination of them can sufficiently explain public decisions without accounting for the undersurface of the situation and making an elaborate
evaluation of the definition of alternatives. (30) Because neither state
had sufficient capacity to control the production and distribution of
wealth, they were severely circumscribed in the measures they could
take. For New York, the only recourse was the unacceptable choice
of economic collapse, unless they did something to stem the tide of
commercial exodus. For New Jersey, the alternatives were somewhat larger, since hypothetically it could elect a "no growth" strategy,
but given the race across the nation to lure industry to other states,
and the pressures to enlarge the tax base, this seems hardly feasible.
The upshot was that necessity predominated simply because, in the
words of French poet Jacques Prevert, "the game is rigged."

The most valuable lesson to be drawn from New York's fiscal
crisis of 1975-76 was not so much that a city and state could be driven
to bankruptcy, but that the control of wealth - hence power - was with
private finance. For months, stories in the media were captioned,
"Demand By Banks Perils City Plan," "Top Bankers Say State Must
Raise Its Taxes at Once," "Credit Rater Warns State On Additional
Aid to City," and the public accepted them with passivity. When
leading financiers held surreptitious meetings at the Rockefeller
estate to negotiate the "rescue" of the city, few persons recognized
how preposterous this political relationship had become. Only after
the velvet glove was removed, and financiers were appointed to extra
governmental boards to iron-fist the city into budget cuts, did some
rumblings begin. However, necessity prevailed and these boards
continued to rule. If anything, New York's fiscal crisis was portrayed as an urban aberration, brought on by a swollen bureaucracy
which spent itself into ruin ("profligate" was the popular adjective).
Only as Philadelphia declared its own financial emergency, and
Chicago and Detroit showed similar symptoms, were serious questions raised and the Conference of Mayors issued a report showing
the fiscal malady to be widespread. Nonetheless, with this experience as a prologue to the urban future, cities continue to be dependent
upon private banking for financing and these banks will continue, no
doubt, to use intercity competition over funds to control urban policy.
Today, U.S. banks hold approximately 48 percent of the total municipal debt of $208 billion, while insurance companies control another

15 percent. (31) A major portion of control over the municipal purse is not with city hall nor with the statehouse, but in the boardrooms of private finance.

PUBLIC POWER AS A CONDUIT FOR
PRIVATISM

The game is rigged also in ways which structure the rewards to be gotten through public policies and the primary role to which the liberal state has been consigned. Contrary to myth, that role is not to redistribute wealth, but to serve as an instrument for the private production of it and to shield privatism by absorbing the abuses and costs of its excesses.

Data on the control and distribution of wealth and income (32) in America during the last 50 years provide us with hints on the function of government and its relation to privatism. In 1922, the top one percent of the adult population owned 31 percent of the wealth; 34 years later that same stratum controlled 26 percent of the wealth. If we move to broader divisions of quintiles and count income only, the inequity is also borne out. In 1947, the highest quintile obtained 46 percent of the income, while the lowest had five percent; in 1972, those same quintiles had not appreciably changed, and their respective income shares were 41.6 percent and 5.5 percent. (33) We should remember too that these were mostly years in which the Democratic Party held power and championed the cause of income redistribution, accusing Republicans of being only for the rich and wellborn. They were also years in which positive government was heralded and the state took a more activist role in the economy and the regulation of private enterprise.

Why there has been no change in the distribution of income, granting the best of intentions by positive government, is a curiosity. As a beginning, it might be useful to take a closer look at the process of positive government - its role and how that role has matured through the years. Figure 2.1 illustrates how public power works with private power in carrying out policy. Like most flow charts its different-sized boxes and oblique arrows may not be readily grasped. A few interpretative steps, then, are in order:

In conception, the chart is triangular with mass stratified society and public power at the two bases of the triangle and privatism at the apex. Public power (divided into cities, middle governments, and federal government) functions as a conduit through which taxes are collected and policies are created. Taxes are taken from mass society and funneled up to privatism in the form of public policies (darkly striped arrow).

In flow, after taxes are paid to various public powers, and are converted into public policies, they bestow advantages (loans, manpower training, industrial parks, etc.) upon privatism. The anticipation is that these advantages will reach the neediest segments of the society. The process of carrying out these policies is known as a trickle down effect and operates on the assumption that as corporate business is stimulated, jobs and productivity will accrue to the population at large. In the lexicon of the systems analysts, the taxes, the policies, and the advantages are inputs, which lead to stratified jobs and earnings (darkly striped arrow to mass society).

In flow, and ramification, these inputs yield reinvestments (lightly striped arrow to public power). The reinvestments come from profits derived from mass society and along with salaries, wages, and dividends are put back into any of the domains governed by public power (cities, middle governments, and the nation at large). Reinvestments are essentially uneven, usually avoiding older cities or giving short shrift to classes at the bottom of mass society. This results in corporate flight, sunbelt booms, and a varied gross national profit.

In ramification, public policy and its advantages are distributed unevenly, causing grievances by the various strata which make up mass society. Grievances are illustrated by a shaded arrow at the bottom which is directed back onto the various forms of public power.

Flow and the Uneven Extraction of Society's Resources

The box at the left base of the triangle in figure 2.1 portrays a social order which is stratified into a handful of different classes. These classes are largely segregated by the locations in which they reside, the work they do, and sometimes by their ethnic or racial identification. This is not to say that one cannot move out of a social class, but once consigned within a notch, other features insulate that position.

The figure also intends to show that middle and lower middle strata bear a disproportionate tax burden. The tax believed to be the most equitable, the income tax, is only moderately progressive, and

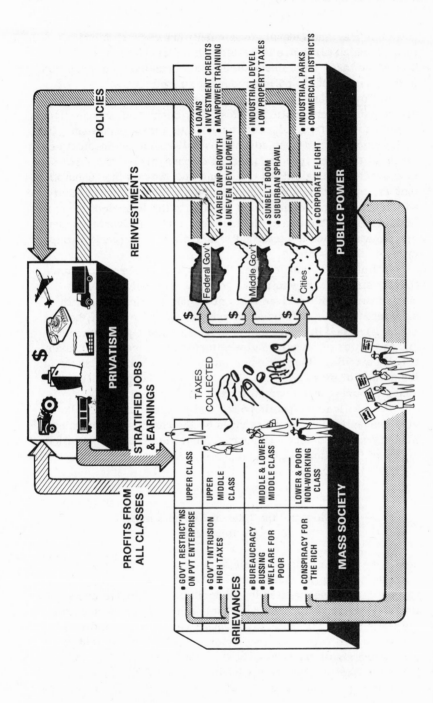

Fig. 2.1. How public and private power interact to implement policy.

counterbalanced by other levies which are regressive, such as consumption (e. g. sales) taxes, user charges, and property taxes. (34)
Moreover, there are so many income tax shelters ("tax escape" is
just as suitable a term, but hardly used) that it has been possible for
millionaires to avoid paying a single cent to the government. Tax
laws are extremely complicated and lawyers specializing in the field
disclaim a full knowledge of their intricacies, but the commonest
opportunities for escape include: accelerated depreciation allowances
given to businessmen; tax-free income from investments in special
bonds; tax options given in lieu of salary to corporate executives; and
payments to businessmen or professionals which are underreported
or never declared at all. The capital gains provisions of our laws
which allow income from investments to be taxed at a lower rate than
salaries are another means for avoiding full payment to the government. (A discussion of how this affects cities and suburbs can be
found in Ch. 8.)

Needless to say, these are advantages which are enjoyed by the
rich. Workers who earn weekly or hourly wages cannot easily avoid
declaring their incomes, nor do they usually obtain stock options or
have the capital to make lavish investments. The actual amounts in
taxes paid by social classes belie the assertion that we have a progressive tax system.

Flow and How Public Policy Works to
Bolster Privatism

Once collected, taxes are transformed into expenditures through the
adoption of public policies. Different levels of government are likely
to adopt different public policies and these are linked directly to private power as shown by a darkly striped arrow leading from public
power up to the apex. The listings of policies in the figure are not
exhaustive, nor is any single policy unique to a particular level of
government. Most policies are shared by three or four governments.
For example, low interest loans to corporations may be furnished by
cities, states, counties, or the federal government - all in different
degrees and under different conditions. Having acknowledged this, it
should also be pointed out that some levels of government favor certain kinds of policies over others because they are more easily
carried out. Older cities favor industrial parks or commercial
districts for business because they can make blighted land available
to industry at bargain prices. Affluent suburbs are prone to offer
low property taxes so they can compete with nearby cities for white

collar corporations. On the other hand, rural towns and counties
favor Industrial Development Bonds (IDB's) because of their need to
raise fast and substantial hunks of capital in order to draw industry
from a greater distance. IDB's are issued in the name of the local
government to finance the construction of industrial plants for private
use. Because they are issued under public aegis, they are exempt
from taxation and have been a boon to investors, underwriters, and
commercial banks. What usually occurs is that a local government
issues the bonds and builds a plant to a company's specifications with
the capital received. It then agrees to lease the government-owned
plant to the private firm, with rental payments used to defray the
interest and principal. In effect, the exemption from taxation constitutes a government subsidy for the underwriters by allowing them
to camouflage an investment for private purposes as a public one,
and gives the industrialist a facility at a cut rate price.

IDB's originated in the South during the depression so that areas
which were destitute could attract business. By 1967, the practice
had spread from coast to coast, with the combined value of new issues
exceeding $1 billion. This reached absurd proportions when sleepy
southern hamlets of a few thousand people began selling bond issues
for $50 million, an amount they would obviously not be able to repay
in the event of default. Eventually, the abuses of IDB's became so
great that the municipal bond market itself was threatened and the
practice was restricted by Congress. Organized labor also panicked
at the fear of industries moving en masse out of industrialized states,
and the AFL-CIO conducted an intensive lobbying campaign to restrict
the use of IDB's. (35)

Because their policies have a greater magnitude, federal and
state governments favor extensive loans, manpower programs, and
tax credits to corporations. The best known tax credits which have
been offered are oil depletion allowances. These allowances permit
petroleum companies to deduct substantial amounts from what they
owe in taxes, on the assumption that they are using up an irreplace-
able product. Investment credits for new plants and machinery as
well as manpower programs were the hallmark of the Kennedy/John-
son/Carter plans for economic recovery. In the case of manpower
policies, payment was direct, and government defrayed part of a
worker's wages if he was engaged in on-the-job training. Both tax
credit and manpower policies rested on the anticipations of a trickle
down effect. Corporations were supposed to save dollars through
government relief, and this money was to be invested in further production, putting idle laborers back to work. For the economy as a
whole, the strategy had marginal results, and pockets of poverty

spanning generations have persisted despite the optimism of trickle down strategists. For the corporations, this strategy had substantial benefits, since business was at the top of the aid funnel and enjoyed discretion on how benefits were passed down.

The Flow of Reinvestments and its Ramifications

Whether or not trickle down policies are used, corporate action has profound ramifications for the social order. These consequences are shown in figure 2.1 by lightly striped arrows leading back to public power which are labeled as "reinvestments." Profits which are made out of the chemistry of social classes, consumer habits, and public policy are fed back into mass society or territories governed by public power.

Tracing this dollar flow back to public power, reinvestments are channeled into many parts of the nation and shape development. Corporate reinvestment fulfills the expected push of privatism by distributing its resources differentially, depending on the profits to be made. In traditional cities, the opportunities for profit are declining and reinvestment is exceeded by corporate flight. There are exceptions to this rule, and some parts of some central cities (the golden nuggets) are enjoying large influxes of capital (see Ch. 1). In the middle government category of the suburbs there are profits to be made in real estate and construction. There, the push of privatism is dependent on the consumption of land, and reinvestment manifests itself in suburban sprawl, corporate parks, and shopping chains. This suburban sprawl is thought to be spontaneous and unplanned, but is very much prepared for by privatism (see Ch. 7). In the other middle government category of states, opportunities are skewed toward the West and the Southwest. This has brought on a vast boom in the sunbelt states (especially Texas, California, and Arizona). In those states reinvestment is based on the new industrial technology of aerospace, electronics, and energy. Finally, for the nation as a whole, privatism continues to move on a checkerboard. Parts of that checkerboard get a large infusion of cash while others are left with nothing. The guiding G's of national wealth - growth and the gross national product - are uneven and disproportionate.

Another way corporate profits are used to duplicate uneven investment is by feeding lopsided monetary earnings back into mass society. A system of stratified occupations leads to stratified earnings and stratified classes. Thus, extreme differentials in income are apportioned between corporate heads, middle management,

clerks, and workers. Those at the top of the class pyramid take in
extraordinary sums in salaries and profits. Those in the middle and
lower middle strata earn substantially less, while those at the very
bottom are employed intermittently and live at the margins of the
economy.

Grievances and Ramifying the Circle Back
Onto Public Power

Given the dual proposition that government is the conduit for funneling
policies between mass society and privatism, and the rewards of
public policy are disproportionate, another proposition follows that,
intense grievances must erupt and spill out onto the most visible institutions. These grievances are shown by a shaded arrow at the
bottom of figure 2.1 where the policy circle is closed and its ramifications pressed back onto public power. Despite all the convolutions
of policy, it is the liberal state which is at the forefront of adjustments and at the cutting edge of class discontent. Classes respond to
those discontents differently.

Not recognizing the political complexity which is required to meet
the needs of privatism, upper and upper middle classes reproach big
government for interference with the free market. The middle and
lower middle classes, which are pressured from above by spasmodic
growth and squeezed from below by racial fears, lament against
public spending, bureaucratic coercion, and handouts for the poor.
At the lowest rungs of the social structure, the poor look upward and
perceive a conspiracy on behalf of privilege, while they encounter
daily the most coercive apparatus of the system - police, welfare,
investigators, and the courts.

These reactions are, in reality, a product of the position in
which the liberal state has been placed through the allocation of
public and private functions. Government is left with the task of
dredging the backwash left by privatism and salvaging its remnants
without being able to control or countermand its push. In the meantime, the state is blamed for the inadequacy of its performance and
the abrasive ramifications of its roles. An army of the poor are
made wards of the state because structural unemployment has ren-
dered them jobless; children are bused from slums whose condition
is so ill starred that judges deem it a matter of equal opportunity
that they get an education elsewhere; housing which is no longer profitable or is too costly to rehabilitate is maintained by public agencies
or guaranteed by government dollars.

That government is also held responsible for these problems is
attested by the public reaction to it in recent years. Survey research-
ers assessing contemporary attitudes report that "trust in government" has for a time replaced "peace" and "prosperity" as a salient
issue. Over a period between 1964 and 1970, the proportion of those
in the population who had confidence that government would "do what
was right" declined by over 22 percent, and on other questions concerning competence and waste there were similarly negative results.
(36) Dominant themes in opinion polls and the political literature
harped on "alienation," "distrust," and "cynicism," long before
Watergate arose as a national issue. Out of almost a dozen aspirants
for the Democratic nomination in 1976, Jimmy Carter was distinguished by his disassociation with Washington and his sensitivity to
the raw nerves of the public on the issue of "trust." A study of
American opinion in 1976 showed a national expression toward privatism which was quite different. Asked how they rated various organizations for "honesty," "dependability" and "integrity," banks were at
the top of the list with 41% of respondents giving them a rating of
"high." At the very bottom were politicians and the federal bureaucracy which received high marks from only 1% and 4% of the sample.
(37)
  The great subterfuge made possible through the governmental
conduit is that is enables privatism to dodge criticism for its own
incompetence (Lockheed bailouts) and corruption (graft paid by oil
companies) and permits corporations to be intimately involved with
public power without being consigned to the same accountability or
held to similar opprobrium.

THE CUMULATIVE POWER OF PRIVATISM
AND ITS CULTURE

It is in the nature of private power to cumulate, to build upon each
achievement and establish the conditions for its continuous enhance-
ment. If we refer back again to figure 2.1 and contemplate the reinvestment patterns of privatism into its emerging markets - the
suburbs, sunbelt, and unexploited terrain - what also comes to the
fore is the beginnings of a massive power shift based on industrial
and cultural expansion. Corporate moves into the former deserts of
the sunbelt or the farmlands of suburbia create a constituency of its
own which reflect the values and needs of its commercial progenitors.

These changes are fraught with political consequences. At a
formal constitutional level, demographic changes mean that legislative seats will be reapportioned at the end of each decade, giving
new constituencies additional power in Congress and state legislatures. Together with this, changes in the electoral college and the
nominating procedures of both political parties will give these constituencies additional weight in the selection of future presidents. The
rising tide of suburban power has already been made evident in the
census outcomes of 1960 and 1970, and 1980 will signal the matura-
tion of political power from the sunbelt as well. At a minimum,
public policy follows votes; votes reflect the size and income of a
population; the distribution of that size and income is contingent upon
private investment.

It would be a mistake, however, to assume public policy is solely
a product of the vote any more than this new industrial base is a
natural or inevitable expression of growth. As in the earlier examples of New York and New Jersey competing for corporate investment,
the important question is how and in what manner are the choices
framed? In this case, the alternatives are limited by two imperatives: the utilization of human and mechanical energy in filling the
needs of industrial production; and the omnipresent force of the automobile in American society. (38) These are the factors which shape
the new constituencies being formed outside of traditional cities and
which help compose their political strength.

In older traditional cities, the utilization of human and mechanical energy was designed to enable factories to rely on central sources
of supply. Much of the power was generated by a single steam engine
or water mill, and a complex system of belts and gears transmitted
energy throughout the factory. Production also was labor intensive
and required a large pool of cheap, usually unskilled, manpower to
work the machinery. It was quite logical, therefore, that factories
would be multistoried and built to accommodate a concentrated productive power.

Nowadays, privatism has changed the utilization of productive
power to emphasize heavy consumption and inexhaustible supply.
Resources are scattered and there are elongated lines between various facilities. Labor, too, has become less intensive and a greater
stress is placed on skilled or semi-skilled white collar employment.
Examples of the new style production are electronics plants, airplane
manufacturers, and the white collar factories of IBM. They are built
low to the ground, consume large stretches of land, and are situated
to reflect human and material movement, rather than conservation of
resources.

Obviously, traditional cities are not hospitable environments for the cultivation of this productive power, and its growth might have been seriously hampered had it not worked so symbiotically with the advent of the automobile. In this instance, that technology of transportation was fashioned to accommodate new productive power and employed all the tools at its disposal to cumulate an industrial, cultural, and political momentum. Once roads were built, automobiles and trucks could be sold in profuse numbers, enabling corporations to locate in sparsely inhabited areas. Once these firms were resituated, populations pursued them and, with the help of the gas combustion engine, were able to sprawl through the countryside. Once families changed their habitat and occupied the open spaces in sufficient numbers, retail outlets trailed after them and developed along the same architectural patterns as the new industry, consuming land and emphasizing individual and private movement through the automobile. Once the entire environment is carved out to suit automotive traffic, the motor car becomes indispensable, literally governing the lives of the population. One needs an automotive vehicle to travel to work, visit friends, see a movie, or do the household shopping. Fast food restaurants, drive-in theaters, tire shops, and even drive-in banks dot the roadside, making everyday business reliant on the motor car. Cut away the automobile (as did the gasoline shortage of 1974), and everything will be brought to a standstill in many parts of the country.

The automobile is more than a means of transportation, it is the gestalt for the new urbanization which provides its privatism with employment, profits, outlets for capital investment and a conducive cultural style. If public policy were used to seriously undermine or damage it, the reverberations would throw the nation into depression and social chaos. It is estimated that approximately 18 percent of the gross national product goes directly into motor vehicle transportation, excluding buses. (39) This includes the production of cars, trucks, repairs, gas, insurance, tolls, and highway construction and maintenance. According to this estimate, with an impact multiplier of two or so, over one third of the gross national product depends upon the automotive complex for its sustenance. (40) Glancing back to table 2.2 the top three organizations in America (General Motors, Standard Oil, and Ford) derive either all or a major portion of their income from the motor car. A further perusal down this table to include related industries (steel, electric parts, petroleum products) shows how extensively the auto influence runs through the economic fabric of our society.

The automobile also shapes the sociocultural aspects of life in
the suburbs so that privatism can draw on an effective labor pool.
Social classes can be segregated in terms of their ability to afford
two or three cars for a family. Companies which establish themselves in the suburbs can locate their professional and managerial
employees in varied places, since an extensive road network (provided by government) makes transportation very flexible. Much of
this plays to the most educated and skilled clusters of the labor force,
which is also convenient for a new industrial order based on brain
power. Even semi-skilled labor, such as typists and key punch operators, can be hired at relatively inexpensive cost from the wives
of middle managers and technicians anxious to return to commercial
work. In many instances, these trained women, as second income
earners in a family, are employed at wages which a single wage
earner could not accept, or are used sporadically at peak seasons
and then released with little or no repercussion against the corporation.

With the assistance of the automobile, the most private aspects
of life are made possible and accentuated. Material and goods are
consumed at an extraordinary pace; families, though segregated
along class lines, are also divided from one another by the private
utilization of the household; and there is a considerable amount of
duplication. As Larry Sawyers points out:

> ... consumerism and privatization of life under capitalism reach
> their quintessential expression in the modern American suburb.
> Every family owns thousands of dollars worth of appliances that
> it uses only minutes a day. Each family has its own lawn mow-
> er, its own indoor and outdoor recreation space, its own auto-
> mobiles and its own children. A castle in the suburbs, sur-
> rounded by a moat of grass, is the nightly destination of millions
> driving home through the rush hour in the absolute privacy of
> their very own motor car. (41)

Still, the only way these things are made possible is through a
well-defined class structure. What may be considered a rational act
for a select number of people would be a catastrophe if everyone attempted it, and the only way it is limited is by sorting out the less
wealthy and leaving them behind in older cities. In fact, we can explain the colonial status of traditional cities as a simultaneous exodus
from the city coupled with an effort by those who are left to control
those parts of it which are still vital. The exodus on one side involves
a transition of wealthier classes and capital out of traditional cities to

suburbs and newer cities of the sunbelt, and on the other side entails
an extraction of profits from existing assets through the commuter
trail. In short, traditional cities are being used so long as they still
retain something of value - if their depletion continues they will be
reduced to reservations for the poor.

The transformation of America to an auto ridden society did not
come about without a dosage of corporate manipulation. Monopoly
control over the technology of transportation, as well as some illegal
methods, were parts of the drama, with the first acts ironically opening in major cities. In the 1930s, General Motors formed United
Cities Motor Transit, later National City Lines, whose "sole function
was to acquire electric streetcar companies, convert them to GM
motorbus operation, and then resell the properties to local concerns
which agreed to purchase GM bus replacements." (42) Years later,
Standard Oil of California and Firestone joined in the enterprise, and
the corporations together managed to destroy more than 100 trolley
systems in some 45 cities, including New York, Philadelphia, St.
Louis, and Oakland.

The most intensive attacks came on Los Angeles, which today is
the mecca of the freeway system. There, over 700 miles of trolley
track serving 80 million fares a year were ripped up, scrapped, and
replaced by lumbering, odorous buses. In 1949, some of these companies were convicted in federal court of conspiring to replace trolleys with buses and monopolizing the industry. General Motors was
fined $5,000 and its treasurer, who led the campaign, was fined one
dollar for their endeavors.

General Motors was also active in the interurban freight and
passenger business, and conspired to change the mode of transportation from electric rail to trucks, buses, and diesel locomotives. The
giant automotive producer helped form the Greyhound Corporation,
which, in turn, pressed railroads to drop large portions of their commuter service. GM also used its market power to deny business to
railroads which were tardy in converting to diesel locomotives.
Needless to say, most of the locomotives and buses in the United
States are General Motors products.

It is no coincidence, either, that after the automotive complex
became rooted in American society, public power was enlisted to
complete its dominance in what cost-conscious President Eisenhower
called "the greatest public works program in history." (43) The
National Defense Highway Act, begun in 1956, has expended a total
of $60 billion on interstate highways, creating over 41,000 miles of
road, and it is still incomplete. Subsequent low budget and veto-
prone Republican administrations have been spendthrifts when

highways were involved, with former President Ford authorizing the
unprecedented amount of $8 billion in 1976. (44) Today, approximate-
ly 20 percent of the nonmilitary budget is destined for highways, and
this does not touch the amounts spent by middle governments for
local roads. (45)

Since nearly all the costs for the interstate system are borne in
advance by the federal government (90 percent) and the states (10 percent), the direct price per mile for automobile travel is comparative-
ly inexpensive once a vehicle is purchased. In effect, public power
is used to hide the real cost for automotive traffic by furnishing it
with a giant subsidy in highways, while mass transit is derogated for
not being able to operate in the black. The hidden costs of the automobile conceal the high price America pays for its transportation.
In the United States, 20 percent of the gross national product is spent
on transportation because of high capital requirements (an estimated
$13 million per freeway mile) and poor utilization. (46)

The automobile is an illustration of how privatism augments
power to its cumulative advantage. The recipe is made up of a combination of ingredients using as a base market and monopoly power to
enhance the product, mixing it thoroughly with the push of privatism
to make it indispensable, leavening it with ample government funding
for seeming efficiency, and curing it, allowing it to ripen, until it
becomes the nation's industrial staple. Once this is understood, the
turns of public policy toward the left or right can also be explained
in its fullest perspective. In the next chapter we will examine these
turns as they occurred in the White House and explain them as meliorist (left) and reinforcing (right) policy efforts to cope with the imperatives of privatism.

II

Exterior Cities in the Arena of National Government

3 Reinforcing and Meliorist Prototypes: The Long but Withered Arms of the White House

Scene: The White House, April 19, 1971. A conversation between President Richard Nixon, John Ehrlichman, the chief domestic affairs adviser and Deputy Attorney General Richard Kleindienst, concerning the antitrust prosecutions against International Telephone and Telegraph.

NIXON: (Picks up telephone and speaks with Dick Kleindienst) Yeah Fine, fine, I'm going to talk to John tomorrow about my general attitude on antitrust, and in the meantime, I know that he has left with you, uh, the IT&T thing because apparently he says he had something to do with them once.

Well, I have, I have nothing to do with them, and I want something clearly understood and, if it is not understood, McLaren's ass is to be out within one hour. The IT&T thing – stay the hell out of it. Is that clear? That's an order.

The order is to leave the God damned thing alone. Now, I've said this, Dick, a number of times, and you fellow apparently don't get the me –, the message over there. I do not want McLaren to run around prosecuting people, raising hell about conglomerates, stirring things up at this point. Now, you keep him the hell out of that. Is that clear?

Or either he resigns. I'd rather have him out anyway. I don't like the son-of-a-bitch.

The question is, I know, that the jurisdiction – I know all the legal things, Dick, you don't have to spell out the legal –

That's right.

That's right. Don't file the brief.

Your – my order is to drop the God damn thing. Is that clear?

81

Okay. (Hangs up)...I hope he resigns. He may.

EHRLICHMAN: We'll try to make it as tight as we can, and indicate why it is.

NIXON: Good.

EHRLICHMAN: That the Federal Government cannot be intervening in every way.

NIXON: We have no discipline in this bureaucracy. We never fire anybody. We never reprimand anybody. We never demote anybody. We always promote the sons-of-bitches that kick us in the ass. That's true in the State Department. It's true in HEW. It's true in OMB, and true for ourselves, and it's got to stop. This fellow deliberately did not - I read the memorandum - he did not carry out an order I personally gave. I wrote the order out (unintelligible). And, the son-of-a-bitch did not do it. Now, I don't care what he is. Get him out of there. Get him out of there. Get him out of San Francisco, if he's, he's - the head is got to roll....this guy, in San Francisco, was the head of the Office. He was incompetent. I'm sure it wasn't deliberate. He was either incompetent or deliberately just didn't do it. So - but, the main point is, and I like, as I told Haldeman, it's got to be done with publicity. And, let him roll. So that - as a warning to a few other people around in this Government, that we are going to quit being a bunch of God damn soft-headed managers. I really think you got to do it.

EHRLICHMAN: Yeah.

NIXON: You've got to do it. That is the trouble with McLaren. McLaren thinks he's going to do everything. To hell with him. I mean, we, we're willing to go along with it, but he cannot deliberately just thumb his nose at everything that comes from this office, John. He is not that big, and of course, if John Mitchell won't stand up to him, I will. I don't want to, but I'll have to. We are not going to have it. All that they have to do in this case - I know what the procedure is - is that the Justice Department decides whether or not it's going to continue to fight the case. Isn't that what it is?

EHRLICHMAN: Right.

NIXON: Then - well, God damn it, they lost the case before. Lose it. Lose it for once. They fought the good fight, and they lost. And, let the little bastards work on something else. Work on the study that you've asked them to send us. That would be very good. (1)

REINFORCING AND MELIORIST TYPES

For all the shock which the Nixon presidency conjured up in the public
mind after 1974, Richard Nixon was not an aberration but rather a
caricature of the office to which he was twice elected. The Nixon tale
of bureaucratic recalcitrance is not novel. Political writers have always lamented the existence of a "permanent government" of civil
servants who have ignored presidential directives. Franklin Roosevelt's most sardonic remarks were made against those bureaucratic
nooks and crannies which thwarted his programs. Roosevelt is reported to have complained:

> The Treasury is so large and far flung and ingrained in its
> practices that I find it almost impossible to get action and the
> results I want - even with Henry (Morgenthau) there. But the
> Treasury is not to be compared with the State Department. You
> should go through the experience of trying to get any changes in
> the thinking, policy, and action of the career diplomats and then
> you'd know what a real problem was. But the Treasury and State
> Department put together are nothing compared with the Na-a-vy.
> The admirals are really something to cope with - and I should
> know. To change something in the Na-a-vy is like punching a
> feather bed. You punch it with your right and you punch it with
> your left until you are finally exhausted, and then you find the
> damn bed just as it was before you started punching. (2)

Nor were President Nixon's comments about halting antitrust
action against corporate conglomerates particularly new. The ups and
downs of government antitrust suits are well known to historians and
for every president who achieved a reputation as "trust-buster" there
was also one who went largely unnoticed as a trust-buttresser. Richard
Nixon preferred to protect rather than prosecute monopolies, and our
outrage at this behavior is as much a presumption of a nonexistent in-
nocence as it is an attempt to lash out against abuses which always
seem to be with us. The significant issues raised by these post-Watergate revelations are not the conduct of one man's presidency, but why
the White House appears to alternate between pro and anti corporate
policies without effecting much change, and why the most powerful
office in the land must resort to elaborate schemes in order to control
its own underlings.

The reason why all presidents manifest similar patterns of political response can be found in the pressures which emanate from privatism and in the organizational mechanics of responding to those

pressures. Privatism is an intractable environment and contains the
elements of concentrated power, a substantial latitude enjoyed by corporations in exercising that power, and the utilization of public policy
to maximize private gain. The uses to which these complex private/
public relationships can ultimately be put is described in a previous
chapter containing a graphic portrayal of the "government conduit"
(fig. 2.1). A variety of inducements are provided to the private sector in return for its cooperation and investments. The organizational
mechanics of working with privatism are extremely complex and shape
the conduct of the White House. How a president chooses to cooperate
with privatism can only be done by manipulating the bureaucratic arms
of government - to paraphrase Emerson, the federal bureaucracy is the
extended shadow of a president's policy preference. A president's
reaction to the push of corporate power affects his behavior toward
the organization of government. Franklin Roosevelt wanted government to intervene more vigorously with the push of privatism, and so
he complained about bureaucratic lethargy. Richard Nixon wanted
greater control over the extent and manner of government intervention,
and he complained about bureaucratic recalcitrance. Contrary to the
public perception of Nixon after Watergate, he was not a man drunk
with the power of the office, but a president making a somewhat con-
torted and desperate response to the imperatives of the system.

In this sense, Richard Nixon was participating in the tradition
of his predecessors whose personalities were probably less abrasive
(though not always) and whose private conversations were rarely exposed. That tradition divides itself into types of presidents who have
adopted policies to suit either a reinforcing or a meliorist orientation.
(3) Reinforcing presidents encourage the unhampered push of privatism
by giving vent to its natural directions and by allowing maximal leeway
for private growth. Though cloaking themselves in the economic garb
of laissez-faire and the political cloth of local responsibility, reinforcing presidents use the allocation of federal dollars to spur privatism.
Instead of social-programmatic policies, reinforcers rely on budget
policies which cut business taxes, advocate investment credits which
increase profits, build highways to promote business expansion, and
allocate large sums for defense spending to advance heavy industry
and technology.

By comparison, meliorist presidents recognize the virtues of
corporate enterprise but see the need to enlist it for public purposes
by building in the opportunity for profits. Meliorists use policy to tilt
privatism toward objectives into which private corporations would not
normally venture, as in constructing homes for the poor or investing
in neighborhoods which have long since been depleted of their profit-
making capability. Meliorists bring private businesses into public

programs by guaranteeing them against risks, matching their capital
investments, or providing them with profitable markets. Ironically,
it is the meliorist who suffers the barbs of the corporate world for
being "antibusiness," though meliorism has brought privatism into a
profitable partnership with government and even saved it from collapse
during the Great Depression. Meliorist presidents - Roosevelt, Truman,
Kennedy, and Johnson - built the government conduit and pumped it
with their policies to meet the crises of their age. Reinforcing presidents - Eisenhower, Nixon, Ford - diverted, cut off, or rechanneled
the flow of beneficence so that privatism might flourish at a greater
distance from government.

Domestic life in general has been dominated by reinforcing and
meliorist policies, and cities constitute a critical aspect of that life.
As the concentrated repositories of the nation's economic cycles, cities
refract these policies in the extreme and, like Alice in Lewis Carroll's
story, now find themselves at odds with some of their once desired
policy aims - first being made nine feet tall, then weeping about their
awkwardness, and later shrinking to the size of a mouse to almost
drown in their earlier begotten tears. The following pages will trace
these cycles from the perspective of the White House and the cities as
its policy target.

ROOSEVELT AND EISENHOWER AS
MELIORIST AND REINFORCING PROTOTYPES

The sting of the Great Depression was felt in Detroit and Chicago
earlier than most other places in America. As exemplars of the
"Roaring Twenties," both cities personified the business boom of the
time, built on stock margins, consumer credit, and the outpouring of
heavy industry in automobiles and other manufacture. Detroit and
Chicago also portrayed the seamier side of that prosperity which was
fed by the sale of bootleg whiskey, corruption, and the organizing
abilities of big city criminal syndicates (Detroit's Purple Gang and
Chicago's underworld led by Al Capone).

Prosperity came to a grim halt in Detroit even before the stock
market crashed. As early as 1927, production began slipping in the
Motor City and unemployment became commonplace. By 1930, over
14,000 families were without subsistence and had to be placed on local
relief roles; one year later that number climbed to over 40,000 families, with one-third of that city's work force unemployed. "I have
never confronted such misery as on the zero day of my arrival in
Detroit," one social worker commented. "The only worst [sic] thing

I've seen was the look in the faces of a company of French poilus who
had been in the trenches four years; all hope seemed to have been
wiped out and an intense weariness had taken its place. " (4)

Unlike most cities during the prosperous 1920s, Detroit had dug
into its own treasury to supply relatively bountiful services. Sums
were spent on health, recreation, planning, and the city even operated
a loosely structured welfare program. As it was ahead of sister cities
in municipal services during the 1920s, so too would it be ahead of
them in coming to a financial calamity during the 1930s. After the
crash, Detroit's assessed property valuation fell by over 40 percent,
tax delinquencies were running above 25 percent, and the city was unable to pay off its bonded indebtedness or meet a payroll. It was apparent that, during 1930-31, Detroit was teetering at the edge of bankruptcy, if not already in that de facto condition. In a series of shuttles
to banking firms, Detroit's Mayor Frank Murphy managed to convince
investors to lend his city additional money - their price in return was
a 50 percent cut in welfare roles of the city and a drastic reduction of
services. (5)

Detroit, however, could not do enough to fend off bankruptcy.
With city payrolls already cut in half, workers were eventually paid in
scrip, and at times welfare was cut to bread and flour. Debt repayment reached upwards of 70 percent of the municipal budget, and Mayor
Murphy put in his plea for federal help, proclaiming that Detroit "has
reached its limit. " (6) In terms strikingly similar to the New York experience over 40 years later, Murphy and his city were denounced for
their earlier spendthrift ways and reproved on the need for local "initiative and responsibility. " (7) President Hoover, on two occasions,
turned a deaf ear on Mayor Murphy and a host of other big city mayors
who had come to Washington to seek aid. The first was Hoover's veto
of a public works bill designed to put idle labor to work on municipal
projects. That rejected bill would also have mitigated the problem of
municipal debts which were piling up in city halls across the country.
The second Hoover rebuttal to the cities came on an amendment to the
Reconstruction Finance Corporation (RFC) which was sponsored by
Democrats in Congress and a good many influential mayors. RFC was
intended to place federal loans and credit at the disposal of banks, insurance companies, or railways, and was supported by the Hoover
administration. Hoover's thinking on RFC was to protect the machinery of private credit in the country and prevent its liquidation through
a psychological panic. Why not, then, asked the Democrats and their
city hall allies, do the same for public institutions by permitting loans
to cities which had good financial records. The President's answer
came in an angry veto, with Hoover calling the proposal a dangerous
suggestion and denouncing it as opening the way for states and localities

"to dump their financial liabilities and problems upon the federal
government. " RFC eventually did pass, but without loans for the cities,
and a mayor's conference the following year warned that the continued
failure of Washington "to do for municipal corporations what they have
done for private corporations" would bring "chaos to the cities. " (8)

As Chicago accented the "Roaring Twenties, " so, too, would it
enlarge the events of the Great Depression. There, the unemployed
took to the streets and marched, demanding three meals a day, free
medical attention, tobacco twice a week, and the right to organize.
When, as in Detroit, relief was cut in half, Chicago's destitute refused
to accept it and took to the streets again - the cuts were rescinded.
Chicago was also the scene of "rent riots, " expecially in black neighborhoods of the city where unemployment was reported as high as 85
percent. Frequently, groups as large as 100 persons, often led by
Communist Party members, would stand in the way of tenant eviction
and sometimes forcibly put a dislodged family's furniture back in their
apartment after it had been set in the street. These actions had an incendiary effect, and violence erupted on the streets of the Windy City.
As one witness described it:

> By '31, thousands of Negroes had been laid off. They were the
> first to go. Scores of them were evicted from their homes in
> the winter of that year... That's when the Communists came in
> ... They had parades and organized a riot. The police shot down
> six or eight Negroes on the street. This flared up the whole
> community. I spent the next forty-eight hours in the streets
> down there trying to quiet things down.
>
> I went down to see... the committee of leading businessmen.
> They were much disturbed. I said the only way to stop this
> business is to put these evicted men to work at once. This was
> Saturday. They said, "We don't have the money. " I said, "You
> better get some. " By Monday morning, they had the money, and
> we put three hundred of those men to work in the parks that
> day.... (9)

Street demonstrations in Chicago were not limited to the ghetto
poor. School teachers, one of the more staid occupations at the time,
also marched and others joined in. By the summer of 1932, with municipal employees not having been paid for months, Chicago's Mayor
Anton Cermak intimated to a congressional committee that violence
could be expected on the streets of Chicago in a short time. "It would
be cheaper for Congress, " he suggested, "to provide a loan of $152
million to the City of Chicago, than to pay for the services of federal

troops at a future date." (10) With the help of a Democratic Congress,
Hoover's opposition to loans for municipalities was cracked and a
trickle of federal money to localities was begun. Hoover's actions
were a response to pressure - ad hoc gestures of restricted federal
loans made under the threat of mass insurrection. It remained for
the next president to begin the task of building a durable nexus which
would connect the cities to Washington, D.C.

Roosevelt's New Deal: The Early Machinery

Franklin Roosevelt's New Deal was not an encompassing blueprint for
domestic policy in America. Roosevelt was a pragmatist whose mind
worked along tactical lines. He conceived of national policies which
were flexible and changed with the turn of events. As Roosevelt, himself, told a press conference at the beginning of his administration,
"If the play makes ten yards, the succeeding play will be different
from what it would have been if... (we) had been thrown for a loss. I
think that is the easiest way to explain it." (11) The main goal for the
new president lay in some nebulous vision of national recovery, and he
might move in any number of ways across the political field to reach
it. So it was, too, for Roosevelt's policies toward the cities. In a
real sense, the New Deal never contained an "urban policy" but rather
a series of measures for people and institutions which happened to inhabit the cities. This distinction is not superficial, for it represents
the difference between policies developed out of a holistic conception
of cities as uncommon areas of the nation which spawn uncommon
problems, as compared to measures derived out of the sweep of national needs and applied to urban dwellers. In contrast, Roosevelt did have
a rural or at least an agricultural policy. He talked about the needs
of the farmer qua farmer and seemed to romanticize the return of
people back to the land. It is not an accident that Arthur Schlesinger's
authoritative history of the New Deal contains several chapters on
Roosevelt's efforts to develop "rural policies" but none on "urban
policies" per se. (12)

Roosevelt was battling the Great Depression, and his actions on
behalf of city dwellers took place because they were the people who
most avidly voted him into office. His first priority was to provide
them with relief and jobs, and he accomplished this by undertaking
what Herbert Hoover had stubbornly refused. He put the direct and
irrevocable presence of the federal government into the cities. The
early measures of the New Deal put the cogs of a rudimentary machine
into motion for immediate relief, followed by public jobs - hence the
terms "work-relief" or "public-works." (13) Through a Federal

Emergency Relief Act (FERA) passed during Roosevelt's famed "first
one hundred days," grants were made to the states for relief to the
poor, and the tradition of welfare as a strictly local matter was broken.
Since the states could distribute funds to their localities as they saw fit,
their rural disposition was soon apparent. Over the two and a half year life
life span of FERA, cities found themselves contributing a disproportion-
tionate share of matching funds than their rural counterparts while the
monies were funnelled unfairly toward smaller communities. Roosevelt attempted to correct this, first administratively through the intervention of one of his top domestic chiefs, Harry Hopkins, and later by
converting outright payments to the unemployed into work-relief projects. This Roosevelt did by creating a number of governmental agencies to select public works projects and directly employ workers.
Within months after the start of his administration, four million people
who were on government charity lines were back at work. For the unskilled, projects were begun on roads and heavy construction; for trades-
men, there were opportunities to erect or refurbish city halls, court-
houses, and other public buildings; while white collar workers wrote
guidebooks for the conduct of municipal functions, indexed newspapers,
or classified local archives. Work was also found for artists to dec-
orate public buildings with murals and for those in the theater, and
Hopkins could be heard exclaiming, "Hell,... they've got to eat just
like other people." (14)

    Significantly, Roosevelt took precautions to make sure that cities
received their share of public works by placing the administering agencies in the hands of his closest advisers. Public works agencies also
bypassed the states in favor of direct contact between offices in Washington and the recipient localities. An advisory committee was set up
for a mushrooming public enterprise and to make recommendations on
the allocation of projects. Along with representatives from labor and
industry, the mayors were accorded a voice in the decisions, and they
chose as their spokesman the fiery Mayor of New York, Fiorello La-
Guardia. This structure of policymaking, placed in the hands of men
close to the president and centered in Washington, worked reasonably
well for cities. By one account, a major government agency, the
Works Progres Administration (WPA), spent half of its money in the
50 largest cities, containing 25 percent of the nation's population.
New York City alone accounted for 14 percent of WPA spending through
the end of 1936, and six industrial states absorbed over half the funding. (15)

    This was the early face of meliorism, and Roosevelt brought it
about because he ventured where his predecessors either refused or
dared not go. Meliorism also began as an effort in federal intervention
conducted on a one-to-one basis between Washington and local govern-

ments to alleviate the misery of the Great Depression. As such, it
proclaimed that government, and through it public policy, had a role
to play in providing direct public employment for people through socially useful labor. Public works began the task of chipping away at grimy
slums in the inner city with cheap but adequate public housing. Public
works also made it possible to put up the Triborough Bridge in New
York; it gave Chicago a new sewer system; Kansas City a great municipal auditorium; and it began to sketch out the framework for an organization which would integrate national and city planning.

Chip away and sketch out plans to meet urban problems was all
public works could do before the New Deal's experiment was brought
to a halt. In the Senate there were charges of presidential abuse, usur-
pation of the Constitution, or worse. "Is there anything left of our
federal system?" asked one Senator, rhetorically. "It is socialism,"
said a Senator from Massachusetts, adding with a suggestive glimmer,
"Whether it is communism or not I do not know." (16) Not unexpectedly, there was major opposition from business. The best the New Deal
could muster was from a liberal businessman from Sears-Roebuck,
who called relief a "serious mistake," but who conceded that with safeguards a "bare subsistence allowance" could be given. Out of the
Rockefeller estate, Winthrop Aldrich of the Chase National Bank called
for the outright elimination of work relief. After talks with business
leaders, a summation was reported to Hopkins of complete "opposition
to work-relief, not only because of its cost but because all work projects - even ditch digging - were deemed competitive with private industry." (17)

By the time World War II had broken out and soaked up employment, the pressure for public works was gone and so were the rudimentary parts of the federal-to-city machinery. For the time being,
urban poverty had receded as a national concern and, with it, so had
the problems of the city. What remained undisturbed were other more
intricately designed parts of the New Deal's meliorist machinery. These
parts retained the principle of federal intervention, but applied them to
a foundering private corporate structure; for all the opposition to government intervention, there was little to be found once privatism discovered
that it needed the steady hand of Washington to regulate monetary flows
or stimulate the economy.

When it came to urban matters, federal intervention might also
be retained but circuited so that it invariably operated on cities through
private enterprise. The city became a subsidiary part of a more complex apparatus which was set to work pumping up the private sector
with government finance. The essential parts of this apparatus were
created in the 1930s and in 1949, but refitted by meliorists in later decades. It consists of agencies which adjust credit markets for privatism

- as the Federal Home Loan Bank Board and the Federal National
Mortgage Association - as well as devices which assure a stream of
business for mortgage bankers and the housing industry - as the Federal Housing Authority and urban renewal projects. (18) This was a
side of meliorism kept under a tight lid during the New Deal by Roosevelt's managers; as it grew in size and complexity, its purposes were
inverted, putting the state at the service of privatism.

The Federal Home Loan Bank Board: The Stabilizer

A major stabilizer within the government conduit is the Federal Home
Loan Bank Board which accomplishes for mortgage and home loan
banks what the federal reserve system does, in part, for other American banks. Under the terms of the 1932 legislation, the Board works
through 12 regional banks. Private financial institutions are able to
join as members. The Board serves as a mega bank for its members
by allowing them loans and accepting their deposits, as they pursue
profitable investments in the housing market. In effect, the Board puts
the financial strength of the federal government behind its private
members by allowing them to borrow cheaply and maintaining a steady
flow of dollars to them. It also guarantees to their depositors the sol-
vency of savings and loan associations and has helped these associations increase their working capital over 20-fold since 1945. By per-
forming these functions, the Board ensures that private money will
continue to be lent at prevailing rates of interest which helps stabilize
the mortgage market. It also makes this market more predictable and
reliable as a source of profit.

The Federal Housing Authority: Brace and Pump

Functioning as a brace should default occur and sometimes as a monetary pump for the housing industry is the Federal Housing Authority
(FHA), established by the nation's first Housing Act in 1934. FHA is
essentially in the business of insuring against the risks of mortgage
nonpayment and, therefore, encourages banks to lend money at reasonable interest rates over lengthy (20 to 40 years) periods of time. To
do this, a premium is built into the conditions of the mortgage which
pays for the insurance, and, in return, FHA guarantees the lender
that the approved mortgage will be backed by the credit of the federal
government. The theory is that if banks can be prompted to engage in
liberal lending policies, builders will be more apt to build, and consumers (borrowers) will be provided with more units of shelter -

hence, benefits "trickle down" from government to banks, to builders, and ultimately to the household consumer.

FHA "risk insurance" is an example of how meliorism uses the government conduit. In the event that a householder can no longer meet his mortgage payments, the bank need only call in its governmental guarantees in order to be repaid the balance of the loan (plus outstanding interest), and Washington is left holding the abandoned property. Thus, it is the consumer who pays for the costs of the insurance, the government which bears the risk, and the mortgage bank which receives the benefit.

Through the 1950s, FHA had been a resounding success, and, since it was geared toward middle income groups, there had been relatively few mortgage defaults. Another reason for this success was that the FHA operated like any other business and avoided declining neighborhoods in the inner city, concentrating instead on lucrative open land in the suburbs. In total, FHA programs have done more damage to the city than its advocates care to admit. It has encouraged middle class flight from stable urban neighborhoods, it has fostered the growth of row by row "cracker box" housing in hurriedly built suburbs, and it has brought central cities and suburbs into an unnecessary struggle with one another over the issue of growth.

While the consequences of FHA's operations during the 1950s may not have been foreseen, its day-to-day objectives were intentionally oriented toward fast profit making, single family dwellings. In the decade after World War II, while housing could still be built cheaply, it was possible for single family builders to be reimbursed easily and quickly by cash from the down payment and proceeds of a guaranteed mortgage. This is why so many "Levittowns" could dot the rural landscape in so short a period of time. Those contractors who wanted to build apartment houses faced prospects which discouraged new construction in the city. If apartment buildings were eventually constructed below original cost estimates, builders had to run a bureaucratic hurdle by filing "cost certificate" forms. The rents landlords could charge were also regulated - and, most of all, their profits were delayed by requirements that they manage the building for a minimum number of years. (19)

The precise impact of FHA on the cities is inordinate and difficult to measure. What scanty information does exist, however, corroborates the charges of FHA's critics. Approximately one half of Detroit's districts and one-third of Chicago's have been ruled ineligible for this kind of federal aid. One systematic survey found that of 374 FHA mortgages in the Chicago metropolitan area, a total of three were in the central part of the city, the area most in need of investment. Looking at the impact from the perspective of before and after shows

a similar theme of disinvestment in center city Chicago. In 1927, before the advent of FHA, 74 percent of the new construction was inside
the city and 26 percent in suburban parts of the metropolitan area. By
1954, the figures were nearly reversed: 28 percent of new housing was
built in the center city while 72 percent rose in Chicago's suburbs.
While FHA financing of single family homes (mostly in the suburbs)
was dramatically up in the 1950s (about 20 percent of total construction),
similar financing for multi-family homes, which is the mainstay of the
city, declined steadily and hit a low of three percent in 1955. (20) Surveys over a later three-year period during the 1960s, after there were
attempts to correct city-suburban imbalance, show that between 1964
and 1966 about two-thirds of FHA sponsored housing within SMSA's
were in the suburbs. (21)

Having created this machinery to do something for their urban
constituents, meliorist presidents were disappointed at its unanticipated
effect on the city - even to the extent of laying the fault at the doors of
the Eisenhower White House. To offset what was interpreted as a
faulty direction of the machinery, the Johnson administration tried to
use the FHA for the urban poor by injecting federal dollars into the market in the form of subsidies. Instead of merely guaranteeing mortgage
payments to banks, the machinery was set to work funneling actual payments to private firms for rent or home ownership on behalf of low income consumers. The upshot of this redirection was discouraging both
for meliorists and the lower income groups they were supposed to help.

The Federal National Mortgage Association:
Converter and Liquidator

Private finance is engaged in the business of selling one major commodity, money. Obviously, when this commodity is in short supply, business can founder and profits often fall. Tying up large sums of capital
in long-term mortgages can, therefore, be stultifying to banks, especially when higher interest rates can be obtained for shorter lending
periods by investing elsewhere. A rule of thumb for financiers is to
"turn money over quickly" and keep it "working," particularly during
periods of inflation, when the value of a dollar can decline from year
to year.

The problem for mortgage banks is a very real one of not being
able to convert their long-term investments in home mortgages into
cash when new investment opportunities arise. To overcome this difficulty, the Federal National Mortgage Association ("Fannie Mae") was
established in 1938 to convert mortgage investments into liquid cash
for banks by providing a national secondary mortgage market. What

"Fannie Mae" does, in effect, is to provide a government demand for mortgages already held by banks by agreeing to purchase them at a price above their original cost, thereby converting paper assets into liquid cash. This liquidity means that banks can "turn their money over" into additional investments and keep the home purchasing and construction industry active.

Additional features of "Fannie Mae" make its operations as a liquidator helpful to firms seeking the security of a market sponsored by Washington. In purchasing mortgages from banks, "Fannie Mae" permits these firms to continue to "service" the original loans and to receive a fee between 0.25 and one percent for doing so. (22) "Fannie Mae" also sells shares of its own stock to private investors who wish to place their capital in a national pool of mortgages, rather than singular loans, and take advantage of buying and selling on short term opportunities. We have, then, a part of the government conduit which performs the double-edged task of providing the financial community with cash when it desires it, while also affording that community with profits after it has sold off paper assets.

The Housing Act of 1949:
Transmission and Connecting Linkages

Up until 1949, meliorism largely furnished private enterprise with various props in the form of guarantees, opportunities for risk-free investments, and regulations to control an erratic market place. The connections between government and privatism in this area were still tenuous, and a full "partnership" between the two was undeveloped. This changed with the Housing Act of 1949, which established the links for a kind of collaboration in housing and community development.

Slum clearance had been a high priority for early meliorists and government planners, who wished to replace dilapidated tenements with sound public housing. During the 1930s these liberals had some success in pressing their claims, and through the Housing Act of 1937 managed to promote low rent public housing. Some public housing was built prior to the war, and this provided public housing enthusiasts with a wedge in what, heretofore, had been a private preserve.

With the cause resuscitated in 1946, and Harry Truman in the White House, liberals began to lobby Congress for new housing legislation. After several years of acrimonious debate in both chambers of Congress, and one fist fight in the House of Representatives, public housing was passed under the sponsorship of three of the most prestigious names in Congress - Senator Robert Wagner, a Democratic hero of the cities during the New Deal, Senator Allen Ellender, a senior

member of the southern Democratic bloc, and Senator Robert Taft,
who was so revered within his own party he was given the accolade,
"Mr. Republican."

With this support and the signal of victory from a Democratic
White House, the Housing Act of 1949 was heralded as a breakthrough
in national policy for the cities. Emblazoned on the face of the act was
an unequivocal declaration that "housing production and related community development" be undertaken to eliminate "substandard and other inadequate housing through the clearance of slums and blighted areas."
The declaration concluded with a ringing statement of public responsibility by setting a goal of "a decent home and living environment for
every American." (23)

On the face of it, pro-city forces and liberals had won the day.
Those lobbying for the legislation were groups of the left of center
coalition put together by Roosevelt - the AFL and CIO, organizations
of social workers and planners, the U.S. Conference of Mayors, and
other "public interest" associations. Those opposed to it came largely
from the upper ranks of privatism - the Mortgage Bankers of America,
large home builders, real estate boards, and big business. As with
the initiation of the New Deal, these groups punctuated the introduction
of the Housing Act with verbal opposition and apocalyptic visions of
the future. The U.S. Chamber of Commerce called the act "creeping
socialism;" and echoing the socialism theme, one Congressman claimed
that "no home in America will be free" from the invasion of government
"or sacred from its trespass." Senator Ellender, who sponsored the
Act and who few people would ever label a socialist, saw a different
purpose in it, "The most realistic way to defeat Communism, Fascism,
and any other ism..." (24)

Ellender may have exaggerated the ideological potency of the new
legislation, but as one of its progenitors he could discern that it was
hardly "socialism." He recognized it, instead, as an affirmation of
private enterprise which, like other parts of the government conduit,
business would, in time, come to appreciate. Provisions for public
housing, for which liberals fought so hard, were limited, and even its
method of finance was circuited through private investors. Rather
than tapping directly into the federal treasury to support public housing,
local governments were to raise funds on their own by selling federally-
secured, tax-exempt bonds to private investors. The circuit between
private investors and local governments would be complete when Washington made a payment of interest and principal to the bondholders.

For all the controversy about government sponsorship of low
rent and decent public housing, that component turned out to be only
one feature of the Act. Another part of it was concerned with land
clearance and community redevelopment, and with its linkages to pri-

vatism. Again, a three terminal circuit was arranged between local governments, privatism, and Washington in which each fulfilled its own function. Local governments, or their designated renewal agencies, purchased the land to be redeveloped, cleared or bulldozed it, assumed the costs for planning and code enforcement, and paid for capital improvements to streets, electric lines, and water supply. After these preparations were complete, a site was let out for bid or negotiated with a private contractor for development. In the vast majority of instances these sites were sold to private developers for a fraction of the total cost, usually amounting to 30 percent of the local government's outlay. The federal government then assumed its function as the major subsidizer of the project. This it did by agreeing to pay or "write down" two-thirds of the difference between what a local authority spent on a redeveloped area and what it could receive from a private developer. To illustrate, if a redeveloped area were acquired by a local authority for $1 million and it received $300,000 from a private contractor, Washington would pay $466,666 or two-thirds of the $700,000 balance. In fact, the federal government frequently paid more than a two-thirds "write-down" because local governments counted ordinary capital improvements as part of their contributions or took advantage of bookkeeping techniques to reduce their actual expenditures. (25)

Only after the smoke of federal intervention had cleared some years later could the real tradeoffs between the interests of the city and those of privatism be evaluated. To be sure, meliorists had, regardless of its shortcomings, gotten a commitment for public housing and the reduction of slums. They had also managed to establish an important pipeline of federal dollars to the cities which might not only be a great benefit but enable Washington to assist cities in the conduct of planned community development. This was one interpretation of the law made by meliorists who read it broadly and envisioned a full partnership between Washington, the localities, and private developers. Another rendition of the same Act placed the center of gravity with local authorities and private interests which were apt to have a great deal of influence in those localities. The underlying structure of the Act and the division of functions between Washington, the localities, and private interests boded well for its Republican supporters who were anxious to see the federal government reduced to the role of disbursing agent while planning and construction were carried out elsewhere. The Housing Act recognized this viewpoint in its text when it instructed localities to give "maximum opportunity for the redevelopment of project areas to private enterprise." (26)

Senator Taft and a number of his followers in Congress were especially insistent on the major role to be played by private enter-

prise, and there was little Truman could do, despite his interest, to
bring about more forceful steps toward national planning. Taft even
refused to acknowledge the Act as an effort at urban rejuvenation and
commented that it made no difference to Washington "what a city looks
like, or whether it has a lot of tumbled-down structures around a railroad yard." (27) With the help of lobbyists working for realtors and
bankers, Taft's philosophy found its way into tangible fiscal mechanics
of the Act. Instead of a payments plan advocated by federal planners,
which would spread contributions over as long as 45 years and ensure
periodic reviews, a system of "lump sum" awards was decided upon
which would be made at the onset of development. As in good business
practice, investors and the localities wanted their benefits "up front"
with a minimum of bureaucratic meddling.

Eisenhower in the White House:
Bolstering the Push of Privatism

If Roosevelt came to the presidency as a meliorist - to reconcile the
drives of privatism with the injuries done to the urban poor - Eisenhower, as a reinforcing president, used the White House to bolster
those drives, regardless of their consequences for the city. As meliorists, Roosevelt and Truman sought to harmonize incentives for profit
with the necessities of reemploying idle labor and eliminating urban
slums. Eisenhower held few of these hopes; or, to put it another way,
chose to equate the pursuit of private profit with the realization of public goods. Thus the remark made to an inquiring congressional committee by Eisenhower's Secretary of Defense, Charles Wilson, that
"what was good for General Motors was also good for the country as a
whole" was crass, but, nonetheless, one of those unvarnished truths
which exposed the bald motives of White House policy. As a former
head of General Motors and member of Eisenhower's "inner cabinet, "
Wilson was in a better position than most politicians to appreciate
how this perception of the national interest might be realized - which
was to enable privatism to harness the energies of big government.
     The image of Republican/conservative administrations as being
"anti big government" is too facile and debunked by their actual behavior when in office to warrant credibility. If Republicans do reduce
the role of government, it is a selective reduction and one which relies
on the meliorist machinery to support privatism but eliminates the
meliorist habit of prescribing national ends. As reinforcers, the
Eisenhower White House chose to allow corporate enterprise to determine those ends and, in doing so, encouraged it to shape the configuration of the national encironment. This is what Secretary Wilson intended

to convey to unsympathetic Democrats in Congress when he equated the national interest with that of General Motors, and what Eisenhower really meant when he campaigned in 1952 on a platform of "modern Republicanism," which absorbed New Deal reforms but imparted them with conservative tones. Each of these men, in their own way, spoke for a philosophy which wanted privatism to use government, much as a hiker uses his walking stick - to clear a path for himself, to lean on it when needed, to even protect himself from uncertain dangers, but to determine his own course of travel in his own interest.

In the two policy areas of housing and transportation, where cities had planted nearly all of their stakes, the reinforcing presidency marks a departure from its meliorist predecessors. For a good part of its formative years, the Housing Act was administered and amended by the Eisenhower White House and cities did not fare well - not solely because the Act was never able to deliver on its stated promise, but also because of the active harm its administration engendered within both poor and stable middle class neighborhoods.

Eisenhower's strategy for carrying out the Act was to retain the provisions for public housing, but starve it of funding so that public housing could not compete in quality with the private sector. That fragment of public housing which was funded was conspicuously inferior to privately built multifamily housing and an unmistakable mark of degradation - high rise monoliths, segregated from the rest of the city, with elevators designed to stop only at every other floor, exits which lacked doors, and growing progressively black. In 1949, the Housing Act anticipated the construction of 810,000 housing units within a six year period - 20 years later that hope was still unfulfilled. (28)

Land clearance for commercial use was the administration's urban priority, and it accomplished this by cooperating in the reduction of provisions in the law which specified that a certain proportion of redeveloped land had to be set aside for residential use. This exacerbated rather than relieved the housing crisis and failed to stem urban decay. Target areas which were selected for bulldozing were chosen because of their attraction as sites for luxury apartments or as commercial centers - not for their fitness as a potentially decent neighborhood for the urban poor. In many instances, these areas were located in or near the strategic downtowns of the cities, so that levelling them brought about a chain-like contagion of disarray in adjoining neighborhoods. The chain began with the clearance of a blighted area's residents, followed by its displaced residents searching out housing in adjoining neighborhoods, later overcrowding these neighborhoods or straining their facilities, and eventually bringing about the panicky flight of the middle class. Slum clearance did not eliminate the slums; it merely shifted and spread them to once desirable communities.

From its inception up through the opening months of the Kennedy White House, slum clearance, or, as it came to be called after 1954, "urban renewal," destroyed 126,000 low rent homes and replaced them with 28,000 homes. Significant tracts of land were reserved for business or industry which often moved from older parts of the city. Of those homes which were constructed to replace the slums, only six percent enjoyed public subsidy. Of the remaining homes which were built, the great bulk of them, upwards of 90 percent, commanded monthly rentals which were prohibitive for most of those who had been displaced. (29) There was, then, little else the displaced could do, but move to the next vulnerable community within the city.

Urban renewal also took its toll directly on thriving ethnic neighborhoods and small businesses. Anxious for the chance to enlarge their tax base and bring in large corporations, local officials by their own fiat declared neighborhoods to be "slums" and ripped up the community fabric. In one study of an Italian-American community in the west end of Boston, families and friends were uprooted from familiar surroundings and scattered throughout the city. Subsequently, there was a rise in the incidence of suicide among these people and a heightened fear of personal desolation. (30) In other cities, small businesses were closed; and, while landlords received government reimbursement for their property, shopkeepers who had little but their neighborhood reputation lost everything. Of those small businesses which were forced to shut down because of urban renewal, an estimated quarter of them never opened again. One study conducted in Providence, Rhode Island, showed that 40 percent of those affected by renewal shut their doors permanently. (31)

The Eisenhower White House was significant for what it refused to do for cities as much as for what it did do to them. It is in the nature of a reinforcing presidency to retain the supportive features of meliorism, but to decline to furnish privatism with direction toward socially desirable ends. Eisenhower's method for bringing about the release of federal responsibility was to establish a Joint Federal-State Action Committee, a group which was to examine Washington's relations with local governments but from which mayors were excluded. By 1958, the President was ready with his recommendations - the cessation of federal grants to cities for water treatment facilities, the discontinuance of similar aid for waste disposal, and a veto on federal programs for the construction of airports. "I assure you," the President told a group of governors, "that I wouldn't mind being called a lobbyist for such a worthy cause." (32)

At the same time, the White House kept the machinery of FHA, the Federal Home Loan Bank, and "Fannie Mae" intact, but resisted attempts to consolidate them under the admistration of a cabinet level

department which might give stronger representation to the needs of
cities. Big city mayors had complained that these were separate fiefdoms which catered to private interests. They argued that these agencies could better serve their purpose if they were reorganized under
strong control from the Housing and Home Finance Agency (HHFA),
which was initiated under Truman to put through the New Deal's public
housing efforts and which they judged to be sympathetic to city hall.
There were also proposals from Congress and from a special advisory
group for a new cabinet post with an assortment of title recommendations ("urbiculture," "urban affairs," "community development") to
provide urban-related programs with a common chord.

All of these suggestions failed. It anything, the White House was
disposed to moving in the opposite direction. Eisenhower's special
assistant for intergovernmental relations, former Governor of Arizona
Howard Pyle, had told an official meeting of municipal officials some
years before that they should work through their individual congressmen and exhaust all other possibilities before coming to the White
House. (33) Pyle believed that any relations between the cities and
Washington should be carried out through the Department of the Interior,
a cabinet post known for its good work in conserving forests and mineral
resources, but hardly for renovating tenement buildings. The White
House chief of staff, Sherman Adams, (34) had strong reservations
about a department of urban affairs and feared it "would imply the potential assumption of increased federal responsibilities with regard to
urban areas." Another strong voice in the White House came from the
budget director at that time, Maurice Stans, who objected to strengthening HHFA to cabinet status because it could "become a clientele oriented agency, concerned exclusively with the municipality and the urban resident..." (35) Eisenhower finally did move in the opposite
direction organizationally by permitting the savings and loan associations to have their way in giving the Federal Home Loan Bank "independent status" and severing its ties with HHFA. By the end of Eisenhower's tenure, HHFA was weaker than it had ever been and a bureaucratic nightmare.

One urban historian suggests that the Eisenhower White House
not only erred in its opposition to a cabinet department for the cities
but "turned (its) back on almost three decades of federal-city ties..."
(36) But had it, really? Eisenhower had not dismantled the machinery
built by Roosevelt and Truman, he merely refused to augment it, and
he chose to adapt what he had inherited from the New Deal to a private
clientele rather than toward public ends. This is why neither Pyle,
Adams, nor Stans saw the inherent contradiction of accepting cabinet
status for a Department of Commerce to serve a corporate clientele,
or a Department of Agriculture to serve a large farming industry –

while at the same time objecting to a department to serve "the municipality and the urban residents."

Moreover, Eisenhower and the men around him held few such reservations when it came to committing the federal government to a
cause they believed was worthy. The National Interstate and Defense
Highway Act of 1956 was considered an urgent national priority for a
number of reasons, not the least of which was that it would bolster the
push of privatism and hasten its expansion through America's heartland. (Besides, anything which had the word "defense" appended to it
was considered an urgency during the 1950s and won the approval of
the White House and Congress.)

Eisenhower's reasoning on this tells us something about the motivations of the reinforcing presidency. Referring to the Highway Act
he explains:

> The reasons for urgency were incontrovertible. Ours was
> a nation on the move. Much of our merchandise moved by truck.
> We took to the roads for recreation. And we needed roads for
> defense. The weight of the nation was shifting. More people
> were moving westward. From coast to coast people were leav-
> ing the farms, and flocking to the cities (those who stayed behind,
> it was obvious, could produce more food and fiber than we knew
> what to do with). And the rush carried people not only into the
> cities but out into the areas just beyond them, creating great
> suburbs. With these movements and the burgeoning automobile
> population, the requirements for an efficient arterial network of
> roads, a true concrete and macadam lifeline, had become acute
> ... Our roads ought to be avenues of escape for persons living
> in big cities threatened by aerial attack or natural disaster; but
> I knew that if such a crisis ever occurred, our obsolescent
> highways, too small for the flood of traffic of an entire city's
> population going one way, would turn into traps of death and de-
> struction. (37)

The twin strands of a possible nuclear attack and the actuality of
private expansion are pressed further by the President:

> ... The total pavement of the system would make a parking
> lot big enough to hold two-thirds of the automobiles in the United
> States. The amount of concrete poured to form these roadways
> would build eighty Hoover dams or six sidewalks to the moon.
> To build them bulldozers and shovels would move enough dirt
> and rock to bury all of Connecticut two feet deep. More than any
> single action by government this one would change the face of

America...Its impact on the American economy - the jobs it
would produce in manufacturing and construction, the rural areas
it would open up - was beyond calculation. And motorists by the
millions would read a primary purpose in the signs that would
sprout up alongside the pavement: "In the event of enemy attack,
this road will be closed..." (38)

Eisenhower, the fiscal conservative, was not averse to using
federal money so that people and business might leave the city for
reasons of catastrophe or profit. This becomes all the more stark
when placed alongside other features of the President's policy toward
the city. While federal aid for urban renewal was given to the city on
a two-thirds for one-third matching basis, with Eisenhower attempting
to reduce it to a fifty-fifty sharing, the interstate highway system was
funded on a ratio of 90 to 10 percent. This was a time, too, when the
nation's commuter passenger service was falling off badly, from over
23 billion in 1946 to 11 billion in annual passenger rides in 1956. Two
years later, the Transportation Act of 1958 was passed, allowing railroads to drop their less profitable passenger lines. "Among U.S. industries," observed a prescient Business Week, "none had a darker
future than municipal transit." (39)

President Calvin Coolidge's dictum that "The business of America
is business" had never been put to better use by the White House. For
Eisenhower, the business of America was to assist corporations and
the middle class to move from the city and discover the suburbs and
the sunbelt. Urban centers were allowed to lapse after they had sacri-
ficed their water frontage to industrial yards, remade their rivers
into sewers for factory waste, and used their land for dingy multistoried towers. The reinforcing presidency had belittled urban housing and discarded mass transit as improper activities for Washington,
while it indulged in the largest private works highway project in history;
and, through FHA, "Fannie Mae," and the Federal Home Loan Bank,
continued to underwrite the drive toward open land.

COMPARING MELIORIST AND
REINFORCING PROTOTYPES

Presidents Roosevelt and Eisenhower represented prototypical policy
orientations for how the White House was to respond to the cities of
the nation. Each of these presidents epitomized differing policy responses to urban problems.

For Roosevelt, that response meant augmenting the machinery of government with elaborate plans to reinvigorate the city with private investment. Mortgage guarantees, "easy money," public works, and slum clearance (carried through by Truman, who took up the Rooseveltian mantle) laid the foundations for meliorist policy. Eisenhower typified the reinforcing orientation not so much for what he actively undertook, but for the fact that he inherited the Roosevelt/Truman machinery and chose to steer it in a different direction. Privatism was not something to be prodded toward nationally valued ends, but something which was "freed-up" by allowing it greater discretion in areas like urban renewal. Eisenhower's refusal to establish a cabinet level department for the cities, much as his refusal to strengthen the HHFA, was his way of encouraging corporations to pursue their own ends. And, still, these ends demanded a huge public investment in interstate and local highways, for which the Eisenhower White House proudly claimed credit.

The next four presidents were to manifest one or the other of these orientations, and slowly construct the history of how the White House coped with America's failing cities. Two of these Presidents - Johnson and Nixon - took their respective traditions in hand, and, with startling initiative, surpassed the record of their predecessors. Two others - Kennedy and Ford - remained cautiously within the bounds set for them and administered rather than initiated urban policy.

4 Kennedy and Johnson: The Meliorist White House and the Politics of Urban Promise

In the absence of visible crisis Presidents had to wait for some event to pierce the apathy and command the nation's ear; experience was more a potent teacher than exhortation. At moments one felt that it was nearly impossible to change people or policies in advance...

> John F. Kennedy and the problem of social change, quoted in Bruce Miroff's, Pragmatic Illusions

One of the groups I had asked to investigate this perplexing problem... on urban employment (was) chaired by George Schultz... the Shultz committee concluded that "the major objective... must be to provide the urban disadvantaged with meaningful job opportunities in the private sector." I had... that report before me when I received (another) proposal from Secretary of Labor Willard Wirtz that we launch a public works program to produce new jobs. I was far more attracted to the idea of accomplishing the objective through private industry, since six out of every seven jobs in our economy were in the private sector. Moreover, private enterprise had been demonstrating responsiveness to the needs of our times, as evidenced by a billion dollar insurance fund for housing and the so called turnkey approach to public housing... Working virtually around the clock (we)... hammered out a program the following week. The government would undertake to locate the jobs in test cities and selected industries would hire them and train them for jobs... It was unfair to expect

industry to pay the bill for all of this. The government's share
of the bargain would be to underwrite the expenses of the training
operation.

Lyndon Johnson, The Vantage
Point.

THE SPUTTERING CHALLENGE OF
JOHN F. KENNEDY

For the cities, there was great hope when Kennedy came to the White
House. As a senator with his eye on the presidency, Kennedy had
presented a seven point "urban Magna Carta" which would give cities
greater political power and guarantee them fair treatment in representation, taxes, and appropriations. As the Democratic nominee for
the presidency, he campaigned on pledges to help the cities; he told
audiences that urban problems were essentially national problems;
and he vowed to do something about urban crime, slums, and mass
transportation. Kennedy also won the White House because city
dwellers believed him. Six big urbanized states - Illinois, New York,
Pennsylvania, New Jersey, Massachusetts and Michigan - supplied
him with half of his electoral votes. Of the 39 largest cities, 27 voted
for the Democratic candidate, and a jubilant Mayor Richard Lee of
New Haven declared that "Kennedy more than anything else is the
President of the cities." (1) The bad news for cities, which would
hinder the Kennedy challenge for a new urban policy, could also be
found in the circumstances of his election. Kennedy won the presidency by a razor thin margin. With him at the top of the ticket, his
party lost 20 loyal seats in the new Congress; and, though Congress
was nominally Democratic, Kennedy realized he lacked a working
majority in both houses and would have to bargain for 40 to 60 votes
from either the southern conservative block or the Republican side.
(2) There was, in the White House, a personal impediment to the
anticipations of men like Lee, who believed cities had arrived at a
new age. The Kennedy charm and rhetoric of hope could be misleading, for the new president was at heart a cautious man who disliked
taking political chances.

Perhaps because Kennedy exemplified the style of a crisis president without a national trauma to perceive that crisis, the new president never adopted the bold, irregular tactics of Roosevelt. He preferred, instead, to rely on government levers which were familiar

to him, and to work gradually. This predilection was strengthened
by Kennedy's intuitive belief that the core of national power lay with
privatism and that he needed to work his policies through the corporate sector. Attempting to disabuse corporate leaders of his antibusiness image, Kennedy addressed the National Industrial Conference Board at the very onset of his administration and candidly
told them:

> Our revenues and thus our success are dependent upon your
> profits and your success. Far from being natural enemies,
> Government and business are natural allies... We know that your
> success and ours are intertwined - that you have the facts and
> knowledge that we need. Whatever past differences may have
> existed, we seek more than an attitude of truce, more than a
> treaty - we seek the spirit of a full-fledged alliance. (3)

With those remarks, Kennedy showed these businessmen that though
they had not voted for him they need not fear him. The new president
understood the meliorist tradition and was willing to remain within its
bounds - he could induce corporate enterprise, at times give it a
forceful governmental nudge, and might even denounce it, but he
would now disown it. (4)

Before any new policies could be undertaken for the cities, Kennedy worked on the broad plain of national privatism to invigorate a
somnolent economy. He attempted this by using cautious economic
policies to promote industrial expansion. Depreciation allowances
were liberalized so that manufacturers could, for tax purposes, write
off heavy, long-term investments at a faster rate and use these extra
dollars to employ additional workers. An investment credit of seven
percent was enacted at Kennedy'a urging to promote the purchase of
new equipment; and an Area Redevelopment Act was inspired by the
White House, which gave corporations choosing to locate in depressed
sectors of the nation a number of government subsidies.

Kennedy's promise for the cities was incorporated into his theme
of economic expansion, and he began cranking up the machinery built
during the Roosevelt and Truman years. Housing and home construction became the synonymous and encompassing rubric for the panoply
of urban problems that Kennedy had detailed during his earlier cam-
paigns - the tool by which these malfunctions were to be corrected.
At the President's behest the HHFA put together a bundle of directives
through the Housing Act of 1961; "Fannie Mae" was put to work to invest over $1.5 billion in the secondary mortgage market to free up
private money for home construction; and the FHA pumped up its

subsidy programs for low interest loans for home purchasing to families in medium income brackets. Lending policies of the Federal Home Loan Bank Board were also liberalized to increase housing production. Added to this were full loans to non-profit organizations, cooperatives, and public agencies for construction and rehabilitation of multifamily housing. As a sequel to the Housing Act of 1949 (which had been amended during the 1950s), the Kennedy White House boosted the commitment to public housing with additional funds, increased matching funds for urban renewal for certain cities, permitted urban renewal agencies to sell redeveloped land to nonprofit organizations, and raised the lending amounts that cities could spend on water and sewage treatment. Contained within the urban renewal title of the Act was something of a first for urban transportation - $25 million was set aside in federal matching grants for localities which wished to start "demonstration projects" for mass transit. The equivalent to the amount Washington spent to put down approximately 2 miles of interstate highway $25 million was not very much for mass transit but it seemed like a beginning.

Though hailed as a milestone, as "the most extensive piece of housing legislation for a dozen years", (5) the significance of this legislation was overstated. The Housing Act of 1961 may have seemed dramatic in the context of the Eisenhower drought - a drizzle of rain on the desert may seem like a torrent - but that measure was on the moderate side of the meliorist tradition. There were some helpful signs for public and nonprofit housing as well as for urban renewal, but much of the assistance (water and sewage treatment) was given through modest loans and the bulk of the aid package depended on the stimulation of private investment. By relying on the judgments of mortgage bankers, the activities of "Fannie Mae" and FHA might just as well quicken the flight from the cities as help them. Demonstration grants for mass transit turned out to be a diversion and a ploy to prevent stronger measures from being enacted in the Senate. Senator Harrison Williams, a Democrat from New Jersey, had a bill pending for mass transit which would have provided three times that amount for demonstration projects, plus $350 million in loans. Kennedy feared that passage of the Williams bill would do violence to his domestic budget and wanted to be spared the embarrassment of a veto. To avoid this, he instructed HHFA to incorporate a token amount for mass transit which would take the urgency out of the Williams measure. (6)

Kennedy did wage a strong but curious fight to fulfill his campaign promise for a cabinet level post to manage urban affairs. The struggle for an urban cabinet post began during Kennedy's fall

campaign for the White House. A number of urban leaders - men
like Ed Logue who was a major renewal planner in New Haven, and
Robert Wood, a political scientist from MIT - conspired with Kennedy's staff to plan the organization for such a department. By the
time of the inauguration, the participants had mushroomed to include
professionals within the Bureau of the Budget (BOB), lawyers within
HHFA, Kennedy's own advisers (Theodore Sorenson, Lee White,
Richard Neustadt), and influential bankers. The plan which emerged
was to opt for a relatively strong department and one which would
give its secretary authority over the paraphernalia of the government
conduit which had arisen to foster the housing market. FHA and
"Fannie Mae," together with the Veterans Administration which
managed loans for exservicemen, were incorporated under one urban
roof. Even the Federal Home Loan Bank Board was to be reinte-
grated into the federal structure, though with the knowledge that it
might constitute a bargaining chip for prying loose reluctant congressional votes and could regain its independence. (7)

On the delicate subject of the title for the proposed department,
the White House agreed to "Urban Affairs and Housing. " The words
"urban affairs" were chosen as both a symbol and an intent of the
Kennedy administration to serve the cities and their mayors, who had
lobbied hard for the department. "Housing" was included in the title
to assure lobbyists for the banking and home building industry that
their interests would be safeguarded within the new department. Despite this, the White House expected industry opposition to the reorganization and was prepared to concede further ground in winning
congressional approval if that became necessary.

Waiting as one of the "logical candidates" to fill the post as
Secretary of Urban Affairs and Housing was Robert Weaver, a black
who held a Ph.D. from Harvard, an "egghead" who also had considerable experience as a housing administrator in New York City.
Weaver, who had a reputation as a strong advocate of integration,
had already been appointed by Kennedy to head HHFA and was re-
hearsing this preliminary bout before moving into the main event.
As a black intellectual from New York City, an outspoken integration-
ist, who was already a Washington bureaucrat, Weaver loomed as a
challenge - a taunt - to conservative southerners whose votes Kennedy
needed for his new department. Why it was that the politically cautious president chose to show his colors beforehand and unfurl all the
symbols of big city liberalism to a conservative and heavily rural
Congress is still a mystery. Perhaps, as is claimed, Kennedy believed that one way or another, a cabinet department for the cities
would be approved and he wanted both the symbol and the substance

of victory. Perhaps, also, the President wanted to sharpen the dividing lines between his friends and his enemies and use it as political ammunition in subsequent elections. Whatever the case, Kennedy was confronted with a serious obstacle to his urban program, for without congressional approval he could neither obtain his mandate for an urban policy nor his Department of Urban Affairs and Housing to implement it.

Essentially, the Kennedy White House had a choice of two routes it could use in transmitting its proposal through the Congress. It might seek congressional approval for the department by submitting it as a piece of fresh legislation, which would require the normal congressional process of passing a bill through both Houses, a conference committee, and a presidential signature for passage into law; or it could satisfy itself with congressional acquiescence by submitting the proposed department as a measure of executive reorganization, which would take effect automatically unless stopped within 60 days by a resolution of disapproval from either House of Congress. The legislative route was the more dramatic and high keyed, since it would entail a broad statement of the department's purpose and highlight the controversies of earlier years. Such a route would probably result in a secretary who could work more forcefully for the cities because a brand new law would give him greater appointive power and control over subordinate units like FHA. Executive reorganization was a safer path toward the establishment of a new department, but, as an administrative measure, would have a weaker statutory base and limit the secretary's power of appointment. There was also the problem of giving the cities badly needed priority which only would come with prestige. As one Senator and former mayor of Philadelphia said, "... the importance of status cannot be ignored. A major, no matter how able, cannot do a general's job." (8)

Uncharacteristically, the Kennedy White House decided to load one daring gesture upon another and opted for the legislative route. The more conservative chamber of Congress, the House of Representatives, reciprocated when its Rules Committee by a vote of nine to six just as defiantly refused to allow the legislation to be considered on the floor. Kennedy lost the first skirmish but sensed an opportunity to turn it around by pursuing his secondary road to triumph. On the very afternoon of the vote by the Rules Committee, the President held a news conference and announced a plan for executive reorganization which would create a Department of Urban Affairs and Housing. Kennedy was now turning the initiative back on certain members of the Congress and saying that if they would not take the positive step of enacting his proposal, they would have to face up to

a negative recourse of disapproving it, if they wished to defeat him.
In response to planted questions by newsmen, Kennedy later put the
issue of race at the feet of his congressional opposition, explaining
that Weaver's selection was well known on "the Hill" and that "the
American people might as well know it. "

Rather than rally liberals to the cause, Kennedy's statement
brought a counter reaction and raised Republican tempers about the
impropriety of mixing the question of race with the merits of an urban
department. Chances for Kennedy's "safe route" for a department
through reorganization became bleak when the Senate refused to consider it on the floor, before the House had a chance to vote on it.
Shortly after, the House took up Kennedy's challenge and blocked his
route to reorganization by voting its disapproval, 264 to 150. (9)

Kennedy had lost both the battles and the war. "I played it too
cute," he told Tom Wicker of the New York Times. "It was so obvious it made them mad. " With an apparent sense of regret, the
President gave his Department of Urban Affairs and Housing its epi-
taph: "There will be an urban department some time... There isn't
going to be one now, but there's going to be one sooner or later. It
is as necessary as the Department of Agriculture or HEW. " Robert
Weaver, he added "will get along all right; it is the people in the
cities who have been defeated. "

For the time being, the Kennedy challenge was stopped in its
tracks. All the President could do was work from the solitude of
his office by issuing a limited decree banning discrimination in housing and planning for a future urban policy in the hope that the political
balance in Congress would change. The President had begun to do
this by assigning a number of task forces in the White House to work
on problems of poverty, juvenile delinquency, and community rejuvenation. Before his administration was brought to a precipitous
end, he told his chief economic adviser, Walter Heller, to put together a comprehensive plan for an attack on poverty. On November
22, 1968, the day of his assassination in Dallas, the beginnings of
that plan were on his desk in Washington in anticipation of his return.
One day later, as one of his first acts as President, Lyndon Johnson
after perusing that document would look up and say, "That's my kind
of program... Move full speed ahead, " (10) and the nation would get
to experience meliorism working at its most rapid pace.

LYNDON JOHNSON: THE QUINTESSENTIAL MELIORIST

Lyndon Baines John perfected meliorism by mixing its policy content with the fine art of politics. Johnson did this by the meticulous care he gave to negotiating these policies with Congress and with the interest groups which had a stake in them. Every measure which earned the Johnson imprimature was first forged in an apolitical context by one of the ad hoc task forces which stalked the White House. Johnson frequently instructed them to "forget politics" and deliver the "best proposal" they could put together - "leave the driving (i. e. the political problems of passing legislation) to us" was a precept given by Johnson staffers to professionals and businessmen who made up the task forces.

After the proposals were prepared, the President preferred to do much of the driving himself - cajoling, flattering, and pleading with key members of Congress and interest groups to agree to his programs. Johnson was, above all else, a legislative president who conferred to an extraordinary degree with legislators, briefing them on the substance of his policies, bargaining with them so that they would be acceptable, and selecting allies who would sponsor his bills. The legendary "Johnson treatment," by which the President would manipulate the sympathies of prospective supporters ("They tell me you did a helluva job up there...," "You did the U. S. a great service. "), was only a part of the Johnson style. Another part of that style was to expand the scope of participation to a select clientele that would play a vital role in framing the substance of policy. This had a great deal to do with Johnson's legislative success - 57. 6 percent of his proposals passed into law in 1965, rising to 68. 9 percent one year later, and climbing continually, so that over one four-year compilation it reached an average of 92 percent. (11) No American president had produced so profuse a stream of legislation over as long a period with such success; yet with all that motion, the movement to rejuvenate cities was sparse.

Johnson succeeded politically in almost every way that Kennedy failed because, while appreciating the need for privatism, he also had the tactical wherewithal to convince corporate enterprise that his needs were also theirs. He would frame his policies so that they were highly inclusive, and he managed to assure even those interests which contested the legislation that they all stood to gain something from its passage. If this did not succeed, he would bargain on the points at issue, always keeping his politically attuned mind on the ways he might engorge his program with concessions to increase its chances of passage. This method of operation put a sharp accent on his meliorism so that it pressed the ideas of "consensus" and "full partnership."

Where Kennedy had failed with his Department of Urban Affairs and Housing, Johnson showed his "upsmanship" by toying with the title and reversing the word order to read "Housing and Urban Development" (HUD). The change was as real as it was symbolic, for in it he was giving a secure place to the housing industry and mortgage bankers. The text of the legislation underscored the role of privatism by directing the secretary to achieve the "fullest cooperation" with private enterprise in meeting departmental objectives. (12) Moreover, the use of the words "Urban Development" instead of "Urban Affairs" as a designation for the department denoted its industrial focus at the expense of an integrated approach to the problems of the city.

For a department which was supposed to emphasize the needs of cities, HUD's creators went to some length in purging its statutory basis of the urban concept. There was no definition of what was meant by an urban area, and neither the size nor the qualitative characteristics of the areas which might benefit from HUD programs were made clear. Even the word "urban" was deleted at key points within the Act and replaced by the term "community."

The concessions given to lobbyists on who would control the machinery of government beneficence were considerable. The Federal Home Loan Bank Board was not included in the Johnson legislation creating HUD, and "Fannie Mae" was included only as a "constituent unit," giving it quasi independent status within the department. At the insistence of mortgage bankers, FHA was also treated as a separate entity, with prime responsibility for private mortgage problems. As a way of assuring that private interests would not be slighted, FHA was given its own commissioner who also had a dual title as Assistant Secretary of HUD.

Three years after Kennedy's debacle with Congress, Lyndon Johnson managed to get a seat at the cabinet table for the cities amidst smiles and complacency. HUD was enacted by solid majorities in both houses of Congress, two key interest groups (the National Association of Home Builders and the Savings and Loan League) had switched from vocal opposition to support, and Robert Weaver was appointed as Secretary - but were the concessions worth it? The new department turned out to be a potpourri of its old fiefdoms with nominal cabinet status; its new secretary was frequently undercut by his assistant secretaries contradicting him before Congress or whispering rumors to the President. The White House itself became so disenchanted with HUD as a captive of housing interests and as a hawker of "FHA commercials," that the President came to ignore it when major problems arose. (13)

Of all the bureaucracies in the government, save perhaps HEW, Housing and Urban Development would become a hornet's nest, and its secretaries would scramble from its stings by seeking refuge elsewhere. The effort to establish HUD and use it to implement urban policy reads like Washington had been invaded by characters from a Kafka novel. In order to overcome both the diffusion and inattention which meliorist presidents believed hindered the cause of cities, a cabinet level department needed to be created. To create this department quickly, it needed to be politically palatable. To be politically palatable, HUD needed to confine itself narrowly to the housing industry and the interests which had grown up around it. In confining itself too narrowly and to special interests, HUD was ineffectual in meeting urban difficulties and unable to control its member units. Inevitably, the White House was caught in the same trap from which it had sought to extricate itself, by having a department which was more of an embarrassment to it than a help.

Nothing better illustrates the shambles HUD would make for cities than the housing policies of the Johnson White House, which were conceived and operated through meliorist machinery within the department. These policies attempted to correct the negligence of the Eisenhower years by shifting government subsidies to the inner cities and to low and moderate income families. The thinking behind this scheme was that since FHA mortgage subsidies and "Fannie Mae" activities worked so well for middle income groups in the suburbs, why not apply the same treatment to "higher risk" properties within the cities by increasing federal guarantees to them.

In typical Johnson fashion, a spate of housing legislation was enacted in 1965 and 1968 for multifamily housing, calling for rent supplements and rental assistance (Section 236, 1968 Housing Act) as well as special provisions for "high risk" home ownership (Section 235, 1968 Housing Act). The rent supplements were designed for low income groups, segments of the population which would ordinarily be eligible for public housing. The advantage of the program was that low income families could blend into private apartment buildings and avoid the stigma of segregated public housing. These tenants would be required to pay one-fourth of their income toward rent, with the government making up the difference between the tenant's share and the total rent cost with cash supplements. There were limitations on the rent to be paid, and the total costs charged could not exceed fair market value. Under this program, too, a family need not move if its income rose, but would simply have its supplements gradually reduced. New families just beginning to receive benefits could mix with older ones on their way up the income ladder, poor families on supplements could mix with middle class neighbors who were entirely self sufficient, and blacks and whites could live side by side. Rent supplements might be a flexible tool which could be used to build, as one writer put it "nests of economic diversity." (14) The cash nexus of the program, however, took place between the federal government and the housing contractor. HUD would agree with the contractor to make rent supplement payments at a stipulated maximum per year for forty years. Having secured this commitment, the housing developer began construction and the supplements started only after the units were completed and occupied. At the time rent supplements were being considered by Congress, Robert Weaver testified that, if they were adopted, HUD hoped to secure the construction of 500,000 units within four years; nearly five years after its enactment only 46,000 units were begun. (15)

Rental assistance (Section 236, 1968 Housing Act) and assistance for homebuyers (Section 235, 1968 Housing Act) attempted to use the governmental conduit in much the same way as rent supplements - by funneling federal dollars through private enterprise which in turn would pass the benefits on to needy recipients. Section 236 was a successor to an earlier and less than successful program passed under Kennedy, where nonprofit or limited dividend corporations could obtain loans at very minimal rates of interest from banks, which had assurances from "Fannie Mae" that the government would immediately repurchase their low interest loans at the prevailing market rates. In effect, "Fannie Mae" was the real lender, while the banks acted as brokers and collected a service commission. This was found to be too indirect and cumbersome a way to stimulate moderate income housing, and in its place Section 236 established direct subsidies to builders and banks which would sponsor low income housing. Provided by FHA, these subsidies meant that the government would pay interest charges above one percent on loans taken under the program. This means that the federal government subsidizes the interest on these loans "down to one percent," with the borrower paying as little as one percent interest and Washington picking up the remainder. Thus, at an interest rate of eight percent, Washington would be paying seven percent to mortgage banks on behalf of the builder. Over a 35 year period, compounded annually these costs can be quite hefty and can double the total cost (i.e. principal plus interest) of building a house. In return, the contractor agreed to rent units to tenants at a rate which was not to exceed 25 percent of their income. Since costs and income could be calculated beforehand, and tenants selected according to preestablished criteria, there would be no loss on the project. In conception, the program assured all parties something - mortgage banks received their full interest, developers got a major portion of their buildings subsidized, and tenants could presumably live in decent rental housing.

Assistance for home buyers (Section 235) also applied the government conduit to low income families and to inner cities via private mortgage banks. In this case, FHA would go beyond conventional guarantees and subsidize a portion of the interest on a home mortgage. These subsidies varied on a sliding scale, depending upon the income of the home owner, with those at the lower end having their interest payments reduced to as little as one percent. If a homeowner's income rose, the amount of government assistance gradually decreased. As in other assistance programs, subsidies were not given to the ostensible recipient but to private enterprise, which, under Section 235, was the bank. Thus, a person whose income fell within a prescribed range went to a lending institution and obtained a mortgage loan for a home to be repaid over a 35 year period. HUD then drew up its contract directly with the bank for payment of a monthly interest subsidy on the mortgage with the individual also making his share of the payment to the bank. Assuming a market interest rate of eight percent, an individual in the lowest income bracket would pay the principal of the mortgage plus one percent interest, while the federal government paid the remaining 7 percent. Should a family default on its mortgage payment, the bank was insured against its losses and could apply to HUD for the remainder of the interest and principal on the mortgage.

This kind of meliorist assistance to the cities was well intended and should have contributed to their rejuvenation, albeit with considerable gains for private investors. In reality, however, its implementation and center of administrative gravity, like in urban renewal, was oriented toward the maximization of profits, and there was bound to be an excessive and abusive impulse toward that end. Once HUD, through FHA, combined unlimited guarantees with subsidies for profit, the floodgates against extortion were opened and so, too, was the trail toward neighborhood ruination. Realtors simply turned on its head, the idea of communities being improved through private investment. Now, handsome profits could be made from communities as their condition grew worse.

Real estate dealers, derisively called "suede shoe operators" or "block busters," would enter a stable neighborhood and convince its residents that the area was "changing," with the aim of inducing a sale at the lowest possible price. Frequently it was easier for one

of these realtors to buy whatever abandoned houses existed in the
area, together with occupied housing, so that a psychology of anxious
selling could be inculcated. After these houses were bought, "cosmetic" repairs would be made - dirty walls covered with a thin coat
of paint, spot plumbing replaced with cheap pipes, or inadequate
flooring and roofing used to cover up empty spaces. The house was
then ready for presentation and sale to an unsuspecting low income
buyer who could purchase it with as little as a $200 down payment
under the rules of the program. Since these houses were resold at
enormous markups (a house could be bought for a few thousand dollars by a realtor and resold for six or seven times the original price)
the realtors had little hesitation in furnishing the down payment
themselves or as a "loan" to the home buyer. HUD officials and
banks would subsequently be contacted and the house inspected - often
as a "windshield assessment" because it was so brief or made from
the inside of a cruising automobile which canvassed blocks of available housing. Contracts would then be drawn primarily between the
home buyer and the bank which awarded the mortgage, and between
the bank and HUD, which provided the guarantee and the subsidy.
The realtor would depart with a handsome profit and within a year or
two the house would begin to crumble - pipes would burst and flood
the house, paint would chip profusely, and incidents were reported
of family members falling through inadequately supported floors.
Mortgage default would soon follow, and the banks, only too anxious
to collect their loans and reinvest their capital into a rising interest
market, would make their claims to HUD. (16) Ultimately, the
federal government would be left with the title and ownership of an
abandoned building. HUD became the largest slum owner in the
country. (17) Figure 4.1 illustrates graphically how under meliorism the government conduit works in this aspect of housing policy.

By the mid 1970s, officiel HUD records indicated that it had
taken title to 65,000 single-family houses which had defaulted on
mortgage payments, and another 35,000 multi-family units of housing. All told, this was enough to house 260,000 people, comparable
to the population of a small city. The scandalous proportions of the
program did not begin to surface until the Nixon years at the White
House and was a serious embarrassment to the Secretary of HUD,
Goerge Romney. Whole neighborhoods were destroyed in Chicago
and Detroit, and the sight of abandoned houses often ripped up by
vandals provoked demonstrations against HUD itself as the one responsible for these eyesores. In Detroit, Mayor Coleman Young
threatened to take matters into his own hands and order the bulldozing of federally owned slums. The President of Detroit's City Council

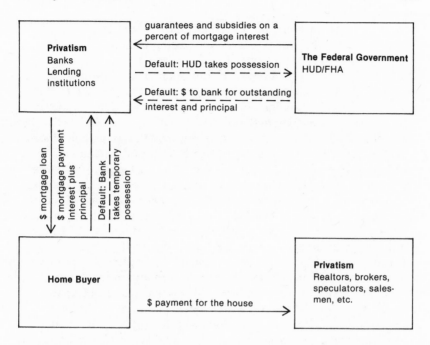

Note: all lines entailing the transfer of dollars ($) and profit lead to privatism, as represented by banks, lending institutions, realtors, brokers, etc. Broken lines denote the eventuation of risk-loss, or default.

Figure 4.1.   Another version of the government conduit: housing assistance under the Johnson White House.

had another suggestion, and proposed that the city go to court in order to appoint a receiver for all HUD properties. "If someone's mentally incompetent," he mused, "you have a receiver. I have believed for years that HUD is incapable. The failures have been too vast for me to have any faith whatsoever." (18) The conduit had run its full course - rather than stimulate private investment in the inner city, there was a faster exodus out of it. Neighborhood organizations poured out their grievances against those left in possession of the ruins, and feelings against Washington's incompetence intensified.

Broadening the Urban Commitment Through
the War on Poverty: Bigger is Better

If nothing else, Johnson's brand of meliorism brought cities to Washington's attention. Serious people might argue that the White House
was handling urban problems in the wrong way, or that the war in
Vietnam was sapping domestic priorities, but they could hardly claim
that Johnson ignored the cities. At first, the President had pieces of
legislation enacted which made adjustments to past policies in order
to relieve urban burdens. Beginning in 1964, measures for better
planning and stronger code enforcement were tacked onto "omnibus
housing acts." For those who had been caught in the path of the renewal bulldozer, there were loans and grants to reestablish small
businesses, and there were measures to relocate displaced families
in alternative housing. Grants were also enlarged for cities which
sought to create "open spaces," or undertake repairs to public works,
and small amounts were allocated for expriments in mass transit.
     Getting legislation passed was Johnson's metier, but what he
needed was volume which would dramatize his commitment to the
poor and which would make him Roosevelt's rightful heir. For the
first time, spokesmen for the administration began talking about the
quality of urban life, stressing a new ethic of "urban conservation."
Johnson himself followed these themes before academic audiences
with references to Aristotle's maxim that "Men come together in
cities in order to live," and remain together in them "to live the good
life"; but in practice he gave it the Johnson imprint of bigness and a
Texas panache. The President was no dabbler in the nuances of
living, and "goodness" was not enough - his society would have to be
the "Great Society." America was to be a grandiose society. While
Kennedy hesitated on his urban challenge, Johnson embraced his own
urban commitment, declaring that American society "will never be
great until our cities are great". (19) He went beyond the problems
in housing or community development to the social, the human, condition of cities. Like the rest of the Johnson schema, the Great
Society was all inclusive and there was no credence given to the possibility that the prosperity of one segment of society might hinge on
the misery of another. If there was urban blight, it was due to past
negligence or a lack of commitment; if families lived in poverty, that
was due to individual misfortune and a lack of life's chances. Building the Great Society, then, entailed dealing with "pathologies" which
were atypical of the American condition, and overcoming disadvantages
which prevented the poor, or the cities they inhabited, from becoming
full members of it. In short, the problem was defined as belonging
to people who were unsuccessful in life, not to structural elements

within society which perforce wasted parts of itself. The distinction
constitutes the difference between an apologia for the ongoing social
order and a critique of that order. It does not belittle or deride
Johnson's urban commitment, but it does point up the reason why it
was a "conservative" effort designed to preserve the social order by
attempting to adapt its outcasts to it. (20) Because of this, Johnson
was bound to move things about a great deal, causing a political
frenzy, but change conditions very little.

To make a Great Society, Johnson needed to launch a crusade,
an all out "War on Poverty," and the army and material for it were
gathered through the Economic Opportunity Act of 1964. This was a
commitment which was to match and, especially for the cities, exceed Roosevelt's New Deal. It was constructed on the foundation that
America's sore spots, its pathologies, were brought about by ignorance, low motivation, and political apathy. The reason why slums
became slums was that people with poor habits lived in them - they
threw garbage out of windows, allowed their children to urinate on
stairwells, and were on welfare because they lacked proper skills.
With an original appropriation of $947.7 million, the mission of the
Economic Opportunity Act would be to strike "at the main front of
poverty" through its transmission of "hoplessness, from one generation to another." Its "weapons" were "directly aimed at improving
human motivation and performance" (21) by educating the poor. A
phalanx of titles within the Act (see fig. 4.2) stood poised to attack
squalor in America.

A portion of the War on Poverty was to be administered by a
special Office of Economic Opportunity (OEO), its head directly responsible to the President. Also, through the years, changes were
made to the original legislation which added "Project Head Start" to
assist underprivleged preschool children to begin their education
ahead of their middle class peers, "Upward Bound" to prepare older
ghetto youths for college, and "Legal Services" to provide neighborhoods with free legal centers. For cities, the heart of the war effort
was to be made through Title II, the Community Action Program
(CAPs) which was administered by the OEO in Washington. On a
national level, over 75 percent of the funding for CAPs was spent in
urban areas, which were to cope directly with the social environment
of the city by lifting the human element to a new dimension - investing
in people rather than exclusively in "bricks and mortar" were the
watchwords of the White House's "poverty warriors." Over 900
CAPs were set up in urban neighborhoods throughout the country by
1967, and that number later swelled to over 1,000. Over the first
four years of its life, CAP grants averaged roughly $97 per poor

Title I

Job Corps - intended for school
drop-outs that were felt to
need a total change in environment to improve their way of
life. Volunteers would live
away from home, either as members of a "Youth Conservation
Corps" in special camps where
they would gain training, or
in urban areas, where they
would learn job skills.

Work-Training - authorized
federal assistance for state
and local programs which would
enable underprivileged youths
to do beneficial work in their
own communities. The ultimate
aim was to encourage participants to resume schooling

College Work-Study - aid for
low income students, where the
government pays up to 90 percent of the costs for part-
time work on or off campus

Title III

Loans - authorized to make 15
year loans of up to $2,500 to
low income rural familieis who
could not get credit elsewhere.

Migrant Workers - loans and
grants to aid migrant workers
in housing, sanitation, education, and day care for children.

Title V

Work Experience Programs -
pilot projects to employ and
train heads of families receiving welfare payments

Title II

Community Action Programs
(CAPs) - government t o provide funding for the establishment of local nonprofit organizations conducted by local
governments to operate a large
number of discretionary projects within local communities.
Such organizations or CAPs are
to be administered by community
elected or appointed "governing boards" and by staff hired
primarily from within a community. These CAPs could conduct a variety of self-initia-
ted programs - trips for slum
children, remedial reading,
job counseling, tenant counseling and training, educational intervention, voter information, etc. Emphasis was
to be put on "helping the poor
to help themselves" by encouraging community participation
and self motivation.

Adult Education - grants to the
states for local programs to
teach persons over 1 8 how to
read and write.

Title IV

Business Incentives - loans to
strengthen small business and
help them employ long-term
unemployed workers. Borrowers
were required to participate
in management training programs.

Title VI

Volunteers in Service to
America (VISTA) - recruitment
and training ov volunteers to
combat poverty on the local
level. A kind of "domestic
peace corps," heavily drawn
from middle class, college-
educated youth, who would work
in rural or urban areas to aid
the underprivileged.

Fig. 4.2. Titles under the Economic Opportunity Act of 1964.

person, while the largest cities in America (New York, Chicago, Los Angeles, Detroit, Philadelphia, Boston) received nearly three times that average. (22) These programs were run out of shabby storefronts and abandoned buildings of the inner city, with full-time staffs and community residents conducting their day-to-day activities.

Precisely what CAPs were supposed to do or how they were to undertake the Herculean job of reweaving the social fiber of cities was not made clear. (23) Motivation and training can be very fuzzy when they have to be undertaken in a vacuum. Motivate toward what, when there was little prospect of reacting toward something tangible? CAPs did not possess the resources to build parks or reconstruct buildings. Train for what purpose, when skilled jobs were not abundant and·trade unions had frozen their ranks? The failure that the job corps would shortly experience was that it was unable to place its trainees in positions which would give them a living wage.

One primary mission of the CAPs was the acknowledgedly political one of providing for "the maximum feasible participation of residents" in a community in its activities. This, too, was all process without substance, since it posed the question of participation for what goal. Were the poor to participate in their own motivation or their own training for imprescribable ends? The entire reasoning behind the CAPs seemed circular and without specific cause, yet somehow the Johnson White House felt that the urban poor needed to be the makers of their own rehabilitation. One theory for why CAPs emphasized citizen participation was that the White House deliberately wanted to build the political muscle of the urban poor and use it as a ramrod against lethargic urban bureaucracies. (24) If the poor could be taught to act and scream politically, went the theory, they could apply pressure to city halls and get more accomplished on their own behalf. (25) This line of thought had a corollary assertion that Johnson wanted to build a strong voting coalition of urban blacks and Hispanics against old line political machines, and needed to redistribute power to maintain his leadership in the cities. The idea has a certain charm for those who discern an omni-manipulative White House, and does coincide with Johnson's own desire to have the poor act for themwelves and learn middle class mores of political participation. Johnson's own publicized hopes for the CAP experiment were mild, and while he conceded that the plan was "faintly radical," he also equated it with the classic tradition of the "New England town meeting - self determination at the local level." The President was also thinking of his own experiences with Roosevelt's New Deal, where, as an administrator in the National Youth Administration, he helped involve the local citizenry. (26) A bit of pressure on local ward heelers might serve him well, but he got far more than he anticipated.

Before long, CAPs had dispelled concerns in the White House that urban ghettos were politically moribund. "Maximum feasible participation" turned out to be an incendiary idea which inflamed neighborhoods in unexpected ways. Rather than a gradual, tutored activism which could be channeled through conventional institutions (like voting booths), CAP workers grew radical and began hacking away, directly or indirectly, at the foundations of the social system. Tenant counseling brought about rent strikes against landlords; educational experimentation led to demands for community control of schools; legal counsel for the poor brought challenges to welfare regulations; cultural programs for blacks and Hispanics ignited a surge of nationalism. Johnson's concern for the human condition brought radical challenges to the most visible agents of authority within the city itself - landlords, teacher unions, school boards, city bureaucracies, and whites frightened by the angry rhetoric of black militants - yet there was little these ostensible power holders could do except become self protective. Instead of furnishing tangible ends which would enlarge the possibilities of reward, the War On Poverty concentrated on activity for the sake of activity and parts of the city were turned against other parts. It was as if too many contestants were on a carousel with too few horses, each contestant fighting with one another for a better seat, but all going nowhere.

The War on Poverty's scheme for welfare reform is a case in point. Welfare recipients were either trained for nonexistent positions (except perhaps a job within a CAP itself, counseling other community residents) or, more often, they received counseling and legal advice about obtaining welfare aid. This exercise in self-help caused a ballooning of welfare applications, rising after 1964 in metropolitan areas by 105 percent, and by a much faster pace in New York and Los Angeles. (27) There was also an added stridency about the "right to welfare," and some antipoverty radicals moved to an outright intent of putting so many families on welfare that the entire fiscal structure of local government would collapse. The best way to change, they believed, was to bring down the entire rotten system by bloating it with beneficiaries.

This may have sounded like a simple and effective road to change, but it caused a violent counter-reaction among other sectors of the city. Local officials chafed at the abrasive demands of radicals and threats to their power; taxi drivers earning wages not much above a total welfare check sneered at the entire Johnson effort and could be seen with bumper decals reading, "Fight Poverty and Work for A

Living. " A popular journalist, writing for a newspaper in New York City, portrayed the sentiments of the city's working class:

> "I'm going out of my mind, " an ironworker friend named Eddie Cush told me a few weeks ago. "I average about $8,500 a year, pretty good money. I work my ass off. But I can't make it. I come home at the end of the week. I start paying the bills, I give my wife some money for food. And there's nothing left. Maybe, if I work overtime, I get $15 or $20 to spend on myself. But most of the time, there's nothin'. They take $65 a week out of my pay. I have to come up with $90 a month rent. But every time I turn around, one of the kids need shoes or a dress or something for school. And then I pick up a paper and read about a million people on welfare in New York, or spades rioting... or some fat welfare bitch demanding--you know, not askin', demanding - a credit card at Korvette's. . . . I work for a living and I can't get a credit card at Korvette's. . . . You know, you see that, and you want to go out and strangle someone. " (28)

The problems of Johnson's War on Poverty were compounded by the rise in mass disorder and collective violence after 1964. Concomitant with the growth of CAPs "riots" erupted in America's major cities - in Rochester (1964), Los Angeles (1965), San Francisco (1966), Neward and Detroit (1967), and Washington, D.C. (1968). With each year of the Johnson tenure, collective rioting mounted, with four major riots reported in 1965, 21 in 1966, 83 in 1967, and another 80 large scale disorders in 1968. (29) Rightly or wrongly the blame was put on community activism, and politicians who had been amongst the strongest boosters of the War on Poverty took steps to clip its political wings. Johnson himself confided to a friendly senator that Community Action had hardly become his favorite program and he used the Bureau of the Budget to cut CAP funding. Mayors all over the country protested that CAPs were undermining city halls, and sent a delegation headed by Chicago's powerful Mayor Daley to make their feelings known in Washington. Vice President Humphrey was quickly assigned to settle the matter, and, addressing a meeting of urban officials, assured them of White House support. "I can tell you now..., " he said, "I'm your built-in, special agent to make sure that you are represented in this program 24 hours a day, 365 days a year. I've been hired for you. "

If Lyndon Johnson ever entertained thoughts of stirring the ghettoes against big city machines, they vanished quickly under a tide of public and official revulsion. Congress soon followed the White House retreat from community activism by passing amendments

to the War on Poverty which barred CAPs from engaging in political
activities, provided that one-third of the governing boards of CAPs
be appointed by the local city hall, and gave local officials the option
of placing CAPs under their control. As a reminder to unruly CAPs,
the OEO Director in Washington was empowered to overrule local
CAPs and administer programs directly. Also, legal services within
the poverty program were prohibited from defending persons charged
with civil disturbance, and ceilings were placed on both the number
and salary of staff who occupied supergrade positions. Washington
may not have been able to launch a War On Poverty very effectively,
but it could discipline its overzealous soldiers and their CAPs with
just a whiff of political clout and a chokehold on the purse.

Trying to Catch the Urban Commitment Through Model Cities: More is Better

Between the Kennedy and Johnson White Houses, cities experienced a
profusion of categorical grants and programs to bolster their sagging
social structures. At the end of 1962, the number of grant authorizations from Washington was 160; from 1963 to 1965 an additional 170
programs had been authorized, and the numbers and regulations continued to climb. The Johnson programs alone read like a laundry
list without an end. For the poor, there were Community Action
Programs, neighborhood health centers, Upward Bound, Legal Services, Jobs Corps, VISTA; in education: assistance to elementary
and secondary schools, bilingual teaching, vocational training; in
health: medicare and medicaid assistance, mental health and rehabilitation for drug addicts; in labor and commerce: manpower
training, special legislation for depressed areas, fair hiring practices; and in housing: assistance for low income families, grants
for community development, and revisions to urban renewal.

Still, cities seemed to be making little headway, and denuncia-
tions by conservatives who cried that Washington was doing too much,
and by radicals who charged it was not doing nearly enough contributed to the babble of political confusion. The White House came to believe that what its urban commitment badly needed was coordination
and a clearer focus. Johnson assigned one of his innumerable task
forces to work on the problem, and within a short period had whipped
up a policy consensus - its solution was a proposal for a limited
number of "demonstration" or "model" cities, which could pull together a potpourri of federal grants and apply them to a select
neighborhood. The strategy of the "model cities" proposal was to

single out a critical area within a particular kind of city and concentrate all available federal programs within it, so that it could serve
as a prototype for future programs in sister cities. The strategy
was supposed to have other advantages, not the least of which was to
compensate for the neglect and damage done to the poor by previous
policies. Urban renewal had not only side-stepped the difficulties of
hard core slums, but it had reduced the quantity of low-cost housing
for the poor and failed to integrate human needs (health, recreation,
education) with the physical design of an area. "Model cities" was
supposed to correct that by shifting federal priorities to the most
devastated neighborhoods, foster citizen participation in community
planning, and augment existing grants with an inducement bonus.
Cities which could best coordinate, concentrate, and redirect federal
goodies would be designated as the models. For the White House, the
problem was not to be found in the substance of past urban policy but
in its faulty application - if earlier medicine did not work, increase
the dosage and change its method of administration.

The specifics of model cities followed its general conception. (31)
As proposed, the program called for cities to compete for a broad
supplemental grant which would provide the winners with 80 percent
of the cost of their "model cities" project. A city that presented a
plan to Washington which demonstrated how grants for health services, open spaces, educational assistance, and drug rehabilitation
might be pooled together and properly administered could be awarded
a general purpose grant for 80 percent of the additional costs involved. These costs might stem from hiring planners, supporting
citizen participation, or supplementing projects like methadone
maintenance. Essentially, the ambiguity of model cities was supposed to be its strength, because localities were free to use it for
their own self conceived needs. Nowhere did the model cities bill
stress what must be done, but rather emphasized how to do it through
organizational change and better planning. Like the War on Poverty,
model cities was largely process without substantive ends.

The attention given to process was not entirely vacuous, and
some of the original proposals submitted by the White House task
force turned out to be heady political stuff. To deal with Washington's
bureaucracy, a special council consisting of relevant cabinet departments (Commerce, Labor, HEW, HUD, Defense) headed by the
Secretary of HUD, was suggested as a "coordinating mechanism" so
that grants administered by the separate cabinet departments could
be applied in tandem. It was an open secret that "coordination" at
the top was a euphemism for extending HUD's purview over urban
policy and a way of giving its secretary leverage over his peers, so
that he could knock recalcitrant heads together.

For the cities, the task force proposed the introduction of a
federal expediter for each locality, who could find a way through the
red tape and mounds of regulations that were churned out by the federal bureaucracy. Bureaucratic flexibility was an idea prized by the
task forces and one which meant that the job of urban rejuvenation
should circumvent formalities but not relinquish White House control
over the process. An expediter appointed by Washington could do
both. He could familiarize himself with the special needs of a city
and tailor grants to fit those needs, while also holding onto how and
where the dollars could be spent. Deep down, too, the White House
staff had no faith in the capacity of urban politicians to find their own
solutions. They wanted the guiding presence of White House emis-
saries within the city halls.

In keeping with the strategy of making localities compete for
model cities' funds, the task force at the White House wanted to limit
the number of awards to a select few. Walter Reuther, who was
President of the United Automobile Workers and sat with the group,
preferred to start with one single demonstration and, not surpris-
inly, suggested Detroit. Six other cities were suggested, and the
number later mushroomed to some 50 municipalities, reflecting different numbers and densities of population. When the bill was finally
written, the total number of cities to be included cam to 66, the great
majority of which had populations below 200,000.

President Johnson lavished his attention on the model cities bill
with a lofty message to Congress calling its inception "the year of rebirth for American cities." (32) In chauffeuring the bill through the
Congress, the President had shortened some turns on his own and,
deft legislator that he was, allowed the congressional committees to
do the rest of the driving for him. The concept of a federal expediter
was, with presidential assent, watered down so that it hardly resembled the daring machinations of the task force. As a final insult
to the idea, funds were never appropriated for an expediter. Coming
in the wake of a sour experience with the CAPs, Johnson became
cautious about getting entwined in the mire of neighborhood problem
solving, and told one advocate of the plan "you're out of your mind.
The mayors will take me apart" with your proposal and, "you'll make
me the mayor of every city in America." (33) Johnson may have
been willing to take model cities to the water's edge and throw a line
out to sinking city halls, but he was not anxious to dive in after someone who might refuse to come ashore.

With the help of Congress, which, by this time was also wary of
local entanglement, the original plan was changed to stipulate that
only cities which requested a metropolitan expediter would be granted

one, and that this function would be purely technical, "limited to
providing data, information, and assistance to local authorities...."
The idea of an interdepartmental council of the cabinet, led by HUD,
was dropped entirely, and HUD was left by itself to implement a program which was supposed to cut across all lines of the federal
bureaucracy.

Moreover, once the proposal for model cities was put into the
congressional hopper, the resources for it were bound to be spread
more thinly and for different purposes. The White House itself had
expanded its own list of cities from a half dozen to over 60, and
Congress piled on still more by adding a second round of competition
for model cities' funding. The number under this second round could
amount to well over 100 localities. Senator Edward Muskie of Maine
put in his own invitation for rural hamlets to join by insisting that
"cities of all sizes" be eligible for funds. Senator John Tower of
Texas, concerned that the largest metropolitan regions would get
too much money, limited the allocation that any one state could receive to no more than 15 percent of the total authorization. A House
committee heard a statement from Secretary Weaver that categorical
grants would not be diverted from one part of a city to help another,
more needy section. (34) Exactly where additional grants could be
gotten, if they were needed, remained something of a mystery right
through to the end of the congressional hearings on the bill. By that
time, too, the idea of a "demonstration" or "model" project to concentrate, redirect, and reorganize federal efforts within a neighborhood was much more illusive. Quite obviously, the program the
White House task force had in mind was not the same as the one
Johnson finally presented, and still more different was the one which
was enacted. Commenting on this metamorphosis, HUD staff members reported:

We keep telling Congress that Model Cities is a demonstration
program, not a program program. At least part of Congress
does not understand that. Do we understand what we mean by
it?... Do we hope to demonstrate 70 approaches or one approach
70 times?... As it is the program is of sufficient magnitude that
Congressmen tend not to treat it as a demonstration and continually expect it to operate like a categorical grant-in-aid program.
KEEP ON JIVING, BUT KEEP IT COOL. (35)

Johnson's Meliorism: Something For
Everyone May Not Be Enough

President Johnson added another point to an impressive legislative
score when he signed model cities into law on November 3, 1966, but
he never witnessed pangs of urban revival, much less its full rebirth.
Acting in near isolation, HUD was slow to crank up guidelines for
model cities until the last year of the Johnson White House. Despite
presidential declarations that the nation could afford both "guns and
butter," an expected budget windfall never materialized due to the
war in Vietnam, and other departments were reluctant to give up
older programs for the sake of an experiment. OEO, which was still
managing an attenuated War On Poverty, held on dearly to its remaining prerogatives; the Department of Labor refused to integrate its
manpower programs into model neighborhoods; and HEW was split
into too many fiefdoms, each catering to its own clientele, to cinch
them together.

With no single hand at the tiller in Washington, the competition
and ambiguities of model cities translated down through the localities. Scarce resources within urban neighborhoods prompted inter-
ethnic rivalry between blacks and Hispanics. Squabbles erupted between neighborhood groups and officials at city hall over controlling
what had, in effect, become a grant on top of existing grants, a kind
of petty cash fund given out on a competitive basis. Nor was it very
clear about where CAP, urban renewal, and model cities lines began
or ended. Each program had its own crisscrossing priorities and
regulations, all of which appeared very confusing to ordinary citizens.
Each program, too, had its own methods of citizen participation or
public review which bombarded local residents with propaganda,
but did little to ease hard problems. Citizen participation was supposed to sensitize local officials to the needs of the community, but
participation meant different things to different programs in different
cities. For CAPs, it entailed elections to governing boards, which
by law had to comprise a certain percentage of community residents.
For model cities, there was no clear definition, except that residents
should be given a "meaningful dialogue" with officials. Precisely
what this meant was left for local officials to decide. To city officials in Dayton, citizen participation was interpreted as citizen
control through election to policymaking boards. In other localities,
participation was reduced to going through the motions of informing a
preselected number of residents what was being undertaken; and in
still other places, it was interpreted as obtaining inputs, seeking
advice, or manipulating public approval. Urban renewal projects

were an entirely different matter and were usually channeled through official city councils or boards of elected representatives. (36)

Because each of these programs was devoid of tangible outcomes which could change the neighborhood environment, citizen participation turned out to be a frustrating and demoralizing experience. CAP elections were dismal affairs, and the voter turnout proved it: 2.7 percent in Philadelphia, 0.7 percent in Boston, and 4.2 percent in Cleveland. (37) Model cities offered little better in its elections, and citizen interest rarely matched voter turnout in a boring, off-year, political contest. This combination of heightened expectations and disappointing results exacerbated community tensions to the point where the less substance over which to fight, the more local people engaged in a protracted conflict over outer and superficial vestiges of power. Who held office was more significant than what was being done; how consultation was carried out was of more concern than what was being discussed; which people received benefits was more significant than what changes were being made.

The White House unwittingly encouraged this kind of empty strife within the cities by first holding out the promise of great expectations, only to fall short on hard dollars or on decisive, focused administration. The budget for the War On Poverty took a roller coaster course, up-down, down-up, with fluctuations bringing on panicky demonstrations by community people over the possible loss of their newly found jobs. OEO lost favor as the supreme administrative organ for the urban poor, and its programs were parceled out to other federal departments, blurring their intent and diluting their impact. Despite the initial enthusiasm for model cities, the actual money spent for it during its first three years was nowhere near the anticipated amount of $1.3 billion; yet the demonstrations continued to sprinkle droplets of dollars over hundreds of areas. If the meliorist commitment to the cities could not be effective, the White House believed that it might at least be kept in existence.

After 1969, when Richard Nixon took over the presidency, Washington began to reverse its efforts on behalf of the cities. Budgets were held down, the OEO was stripped of its remaining power, and model cities was converted into a management project rather than an arm for a new social order. Nonetheless, to contend, as many liberals did, that Nixon dashed the hopes of the cities requires either a notable capacity for escapism or for extended seclusion in a glass jar. Johnson's urban commitment failed as it began, and continued to fail as it was being implemented. Nixon may have delivered the coup de grace, but this could well be judged as an act of untender mercy, not an execution.

The reasons for Johnson's failure might better be found in the structure and relationships that meliorism builds upon than in searching for personalities who contrive to destroy it. That is, there is a quality to meliorism, and particularly to Lyndon Johnson's brand of it - quick, rash, and given to voluminous activity - that disposes it to circumvent hard choices in order to win indiscriminate acceptance by supporters, fence sitters, and opponents alike. Pork barreling describes Johnson's tactic of spreading legislative benefits, but instead of dividing up aspects within one bill, he did so with a proliferation of bills. Meliorism also brought Johnson to practice the art of the legislative presidency and to equate legislative volume with policy accomplishments. As Johnson himself put it:

...the books were closing on our campaign to take action against the most pressing problems inherited from the past - the old agenda. The War on Poverty was more than a year old. The landmark Elementary and Secondary Education Act had become law in April... In all thirty-six major pieces of legislation had been signed into law, twenty six others were moving through the House or Senate, and eleven more awaiting scheduling. (38)

Quoting approvingly from Tom Wicker of the New York Times, the president added:

They are rolling bills out of Congress these days the way Detroit turns super sleek, souped up autos off the assembly lines. Could that pace be sustained? I urgently wanted to continue... (39)

For Lyndon Johnson form equalled substance, and he perceived his task as adding new titles and more bills, as if stating the objective was the same as changing the condition. Form also substituted for substance as Johnson used meliorism to draw everyone into his fold - bankers, the poor, builders, unions, businessmen, and idealists. Where productive capacity and hard services were needed, the government conduit was cranked up or new gears and cogs added, so that relief could be given to the inner city. Economic development in depressed areas and housing were instances where Washington worked through privatism to drip benefits down to the poor. If slums continued to fester within central cities, urban renewal stood intact, but redoubled its effort by concentrating on better planning and grants for public works. If additional housing units needed to be built within central cities, FHA ventured into the thicket of high risk investments by inducing banks to give mortgages. Similarly, "Fannie Mae" sped up its liquidating operations by increasing purchases of mortgages from banks, so that looser money could flow into urban neighborhoods.

Johnson's meliorism was aimed primarily toward the satisfaction of groups, not conditions. Conditions were the rationale for policy; groups were its beneficiaries. This, too, was a meliorism which calculated its benefits and losses to its clients, and tried to make good on each. Possible losses or an attrition of benefits to private enterprise were readily absorbed by Washington. Subsidized housing was a blatant example of Washington taking all the risks, and the blame, for private investors. However, even when government operations were doing well, Washington sloughed off the fruit of its meliorism and held onto the remains. As "Fannie Mae" reaped profits from earlier investments in middle class suburbs, the Johnson White House transferred it out of HUD and placed it in private hands. The organization is now managed by a 15 member board of directors, with a minority of five appointed by the president and, by necessity, other directors appointed from the home building industry, the mortgage lending sector, and the real estate business. In place of "Fannie Mae" the White House organized the Government National Mortgage Association, or "Ginnie Mae," which is relegated to risk investments and mortgages which are not".... readily acceptable to such (private) investors". (40) "Ginnie Mae", which is outfitted to shore up housing industry losses by subsidizing borrowers and lenders, is wholly within the federal government and appropriately placed within HUD.

Where productive capacity was not involved, or privatism could not absorb the energies of the poor, motivational politics was employed. Motivational politics encouraged the unemployed to become involved in the decision and administration of urban policies which poured down from Washington by building subgovernments (model cities, CAPs) within the city. These subgovernments were linked directly to Washington and obtained their political and budgetary power largely from the White House. They could be used for or against the official power structure at city hall and contributed to the internecine strife which plagued the cities during the 1960s. CAPs, model cities, and other special programs used political motivation to fill a conspicuous idleness within communities, which lingered even after the governmental conduit was accelerated. Political motivation was justified on the grounds that the poor could not be assimilated into the private sector until they gained the necessary initiative and training.

Between the applications of the government conduit and the motivational politics of the poor, Johnson built a new kind of federal relationship he called creative federalism. This was a federalism which put Washington at the interstices of the fragmented parts which went into carrying out urban policy. Disputes between community-based subgovernments and the city halls were arbitrated by the intervention of Congress, the White House, the bureaucracy, or the combined practices of all three institutions. Relationships between privatism and city halls were mediated through Washington, as were arrangements between local governments and the states. A tangled web was woven through the agglomeration of one policy upon another, with Washington at its nexus. To decide on a matter of subsidized housing entailed an extended number of communications between HUD, local authorities, and private sectors, with the federal government acting as mediator or arbitrator. Manpower training or the Job Corps brought in a long line of contracts and subcontracts between community agencies, cities, and private firms, with OEO or the Department of Labor signing on the last line of these elaborate agreements. In the event of breakdown or should one group want to veto a project, Washington functioned as a court of political appeal and if this should fail, there was the judiciary to interpret and interpolate legislative fine print.

Franklin Roosevelt may have been the trail blazer for meliorism; Harry Truman and John Kennedy widened its path; but Lyndon Johnson cut new roads at a frenetic pace. In the space of little more than five years, Johnson compounded meliorism by knitting privatism inextricably into the government conduit and adding a new dimension to city politics. Johnson's course, however, did not continue without interruption. It was left to Richard Nixon and Gerald Ford to find out whether the White House could apply brakes to it and set it into reverse gear.

5 Nixon and Ford: The Reinforcing White House and the Politics of Urban Disengagement

When Nixon's guys came in here, the thing they were concerned about was who would get the office with the private "John." After that, they really got heated up about the rat extermination bill we got passed.... Ehrlichman was outraged at the federal government intervening in the "rat problem." He really thought people should take care of their own rats. "Schmuck," I said, "have you ever seen rats in a big city?"

A former high level official in the Johnson administration describing the transition to the Nixon staff

The President's interventions are minor until the discussion of the Democrats' big bill to provide jobs. Here his only interest is in keeping spending down. He proposes the preparation, as quickly as possible, of "an updated scoreboard" on the budget, reflecting Congressional proposals to spend more and more and Congressional refusals to rescind or defer spending already authorized. He stresses more than once the need to dramatize "their" additions to the deficit.

Why am I shocked? Because in this discussion I have seen a glimpse of another side of the man who has been so considerate, so open and so kind to me as an individual - what seems a deep, hard, rigid side. Talking here, he has seemed a million miles away from many Americans who have been hardworking people all their lives and are now feeling the cruel pinch of hard times.

What is it in him? Is it an inability to extend compassion far
beyond the faces directly in view? Is it a failure of imagination?
Is it something obdurate he was born with, alongside the energy
and serenity he was born with?

John Hersey observing Gerald
Ford in the White House.

RICHARD NIXON'S NEW FEDERALISM
AS THE WAY OUT

Start a new job and the best impression you can create is to have
people believe that you have had to begin at the very bottom, clearing
up the rubble left over by your predecessors.

Presidents who take over the White House from an opposition
party try to impart that impression to the public, and as one of the
shrewd runners on America's political track, Richard Nixon set a
pace that was uniquely his own. Upon taking office, Nixon announced
on nationwide television that the social order and, particularly, the
cities were in danger of collapse. "We face an urban crisis," con-
fessed the President, "a social crisis - and, at the same time, a
crisis of confidence in the capacity of government to do its job." (1)
Backing up Nixon, a group of intellectuals gathered in New York City
to elucidate a version of the urban crisis, intoning about its violence
and mass turmoil. Paul Weaver, a political scientist and writer,
recounted events in American cities in a manner reminiscent of
Edmond Burke describing the fall of the ancien regime during the
French Revolution. Weaver informed his audience that the "social
fabric" of the city was "coming to pieces" and, "like a sheet of
rotten canvas," was beginning to rip and disintegrate. The "pathology," according to Weaver, was most acute in black and Puerto
Rican communities, where a large part of those populations were becoming "incompetent and destructive" and were given to an infectious attitude of indolence, or, as Weaver phrased it, "parasitism."
(2)

Nixon read Weaver's analysis, presumably with approval, and
while intellectualizing that the turn of events might provide insight,
the President was not one to remain passively reflective about anything. The White House needed to find a way out of its entanglement
with city halls and the disruption which was gripping the neighborhoods, and in the mind of the President they were linked together.

In Nixon's opinion, Lyndon Johnson's urban commitment had led the federal government into an endless labyrinth, filled with political embraces which laid waste the treasury and social experiments which could yield no practical solutions - a thankless venture which, if allowed to continue, would weaken the credibility of national institutions and spread the dissolution to the rest of society.

Nixon had made frequent remarks about the need of the nation to "lower its voices," to expect less from Washington and to make government lean but still strong. Tangible policies had to follow conservative precepts, and the President set about promoting a "New American Revolution," or, as it came to be called, the "New Federalism." There were many Democrats who contended that calling a halt to Johnson's meliorism and putting parts of the government conduit into reverse was a move backward and a counter revolution. But Nixon recognized, as few Republicans did, the need to inaugurate reinforcing policies under the appellation of innovation and to suffuse well worn practices, like federalism, with the vitality of a revolution.

How to do this was a tricky political affair, requiring a compromise on parts of Nixon's goals without losing their essence, and convincing others that giving up material and immediate benefits for principled and eventual rewards would be good for them. Under Lyndon Johnson's tutelage, meliorism had acquired a following of powerful interests. Financiers, builders, associations of all kinds had learned to thrive in an incubated market place, and not all of them were anxious to trade it for pioneering in what might be an unknown direction. Groups at the bottom of the economic pyramid had also become accustomed to scraps of government subsidies which trickled through, and since they had everything to lose from the New Federalism, they became the underprivileged defenders of meliorism.

The defensive bulwark for meliorist policies was lodged in Congress and the bureaucracy, the institutions most responsible for the passage and implementation of Great Society programs. Not surprisingly, the adherents of meliorism cocooned themselves within these structures by their influence through and over congressional committees and strategic offices of the federal bureaucracy. Interest groups, like the National Association of Home Builders, had an especially tight relationship with leading staff and committee members on Capitol Hill and within HUD; lobbyists for the health industry (doctors, hospitals, insurance companies) exerted a comparable pressure on Congress and within HEW: and the roster of influentials extended out to the fields of labor (AFL-CIO), and commerce (National Association of Manufacturers).

Clearly, the Nixon White House had a job for itself if it planned
to bring the nation back to reinforcing policies, where privatism
could free-wheel again. Through both of his terms, the President
faced a Democratic Congress, and though the legislature had tilted
rightward as a result of his victory in 1968, the Senate lineup was 58
Democrats to 42 Republicans, while the House contained 243 Democrats and 192 Republicans. Even disregarding party lines, Nixon had
some difficulty in counting on the conservative coalition of like-minded
Democrats and Republicans. The first Congress the President confronted, the 91st, lost about 10 meliorist seats in the House of Representatives, but the lineup on hard votes for meliorism was still 160
against 85 solid reinforcers; the rest of the House, which held the
decisive balance, favored a middle ground. (3) In the Senate, the
meliorist/reinforcing dichotomy was not too dissimilar but not encouraging for Nixon staffers, who wanted a sweeping reversal of the
Johnson era. Three meliorist Senators had been replaced, while 36
Senators remained committed to more aid for the cities, and 22
Senators (mainly from rural states) held up the reinforcing line.
Like the House, a middle group of 42 members held the balance of
power, which could swing either way, depending on the President's
persuasion and the stakes to be decided for their constituencies. (4)
    Contrary to the political advantages which incumbency is sup-
posed to confer, Nixon's future with Washington's legislators never
brightened. The 92nd (1970) and 93rd (1972) Congresses brought no
dramatic changes, and were perhaps slight reversals for the White
House; and after 1974, Richard Nixon was consigned to the role of a
Sisyphus pushing up the rock of Watergate, as it ultimately came down
upon him. Nixon's reinforcing policies, then, must be examined in
the context of what he hoped Congress would buy, and we should
distinguish between proposals which emanated from the White House
and their modification or rejection by a resistant Congress. Richard
Nixon was not only poles apart from Lyndon Johnson in temperament
(he was not a gregarious congressional gladhander), but he was also
never given an equal number of political chips in the Congress, and
this made a difference in his behavior. (5)
    The federal bureaucracy was also a different matter for Nixon
than it was for Johnson. Though nominally under the White House,
it is not a malleable institution. It is run by career administrators,
wedded to habits which they acquire over the years. Since meliorist
White Houses contributed to and presided over bureaucratic growth,
these agencies reflect the complexities and circumventions of the
conduit system. Turgid in its process, the work of the bureaucracy
is carried on by callous pettifoggers whose conditioned reaction to a

problem is to strangle its perpetrators in triplicate forms. Being
cumbersome is not, however, equivalent to being passive, and parts
of the federal bureaucracy are activist and interventionist. Many of
its most ambitious workers (especially in HEW, the OEO, and Justice)
are motivated by the desire to bring about social change and became
involved under meliorist presidents for that reason. Many firmly
believe in what they are doing, and if they entertain strong doubts,
they either convince themselves of the righteousness of their action
or fail to muster the incentive to advance to positions of importance.
The bureaucracy and its thousands of administrators was a real problem for Nixon, who, as a reinforcer, wanted less intervention in local
affairs and thought he could defuse the urban time bomb by simply
ignoring it. This is an unnatural reaction for government social
planners, whose first instinct is to get at the root of the problem
before it explodes, and who are not inclined to believe that time
bombs fizzle out.

Hedged between the walls of a suspicious Congress and an un-
wieldy bureaucracy, the Nixon White House needed to devise a plan
which would deal with each of these institutions and at the same time
disengage Washington from the deepest problems of the city. The
approach which evolved was an ingenious one which mixed political
necessity with desirable policies and applied a variety of carrots and
sticks to win its acceptance. All of this, too, was packaged within
the New Federalism for electoral consumption and in the hope that a
new coalition of voters would later emerge to give Nixon a real majority at the polls.

The policies of the New Federalism were not constructed with
precise chronological or conceptual demarcations, though there are
discernible patterns associated with each of them, and they are consistent with one another. Urban policy is not thought out in one week
or four years, and emerges, instead, over a period of time. Despite
these qualifications, the Nixon White House did have a clearer notion
of what it was doing than its predecessors and was guided by a roughly
hewn approach to the cities. These policies are not unrelated,
though they are divisible and are presented here as 1) policies of
reciprocity, 2) policies of refusal, and 3) policies of reorganization.

Policies of reciprocity represent the Nixon efforts to deal with
the former makers and beneficiaries of Johnson's urban commitment - members of Congress, interest groups, and the mayors of
exterior cities who relied so heavily on categorical grants. These
policies were reciprocal because they attempted to exchange the
categorical grant system with broadened categories of assistance or
revenue sharing type programs.(6) Revenue sharing type programs

eliminated specific definitions of purpose as well as the meliorist
method of targeting federal grants on the most desperate problems
and, instead, framed grants for general purposes, which were to be
decided by the states or localities themselves. The revenue sharing
approach varied in scope from general revenue sharing, which was
very close to awarding undefined lump sum payments to be spent by
states or localities, to programs of a more defined scope called
special revenue sharing and block grants, which were grants channeled into functional areas (education, housing, and community
development) but which allowed maximum latitude to the recipients
on how funds were apportioned. In addition, policies of reciprocity
followed the logic of allowing recipients "maximum discretion" by
attempting to replace specific "social programs" of the Johnson
White House with what Nixon policy thinkers called "an income
strategy," designed to put money directly into the pockets of intended
beneficiaries to be spent in the market place as they wished. To use
a hypothetical example, instead of federal dollars going directly into
the construction of public housing via the government conduit (which
was one meliorist solution to inadequate housing), government housing
allowances could be given to qualified families who would then shop
around for housing in an exclusively private market (a reinforcing
solution, relying on conditions of supply and demand). (7)

The Nixon White House sensed that it could not simply withdraw
federal aid from cities - that would have only led to unnecessary em-
bitterment and confrontation in which the President would be cast in
the role of an arch reactionary and placed on the losing side of a
political battle. Revenue sharing type programs were the expedi-
tious way out of a dilemma which posed either an unacceptable political alternative of feeding the city through the government conduit with
more dollars or an unacceptable political alternative of being identified with Herbert Hoover and Calvin Coolidge. With the revenue
sharing approach, the President could retain a type of broad assistance to the cities by giving them swatches of federal dollars, with
few or no strings attached, and without specifying objectives or
commitments. At the same time, it was an effective approach for
disengaging and minimizing Washington's obligation for "solving the
urban problem." Revenue sharing also indirectly conplemented the
need to give fuller vent to the push of privatism by enabling the White
House to claim that cities could spend federal dollars as they saw fit
and curtailing the role of an interventionist federal bureaucracy.
Failure, then, could be attributed to a failure of efficiency within
city halls and a failure to be competitive with suburbs and newer
areas of the sunbelt in attracting private investment. The ecopolitical

framework which reinforcers prize, competition between local
governments which maximizes the freedom of privatism, could be
invigorated - under the name of something new and revolutionary.

If revenue sharing programs were the carrots of the New Federalism, offering to substitute the categorical grants of the 1960s with
an allegedly rewarding flexible system of aid, the Nixon White House
also carried some heavy sticks, under its policies of refusal. These
policies reflected the negative and punishing Nixon, and were attempts
to reject the Great Society by slashing directly away at it. Impoundment of parts of the federal budget, a moratorium on government-
assisted housing, efforts to dismantle OEO and model cities, and the
use of "law and order" to quell disruption in the cities were all a
part of Nixon's strategy to take a hard line against stubborn dissidents.

Impoundments of authorized and appropriated spending were
actions taken against recalcitrant congressional meliorists who refused to heed the warnings of the White House on uncontrollable expenditures. When the White House was unable to trade on parts of
its program or arrange policy compromises, Nixon simply said "no,"
in open defiance of the legislature, and a court fight ensued over the
constitutional question of executive prerogatives.

The Nixon moratorium on housing was a similar refusal directed
primarily against the HUD bureaucracy and interest groups which
relied on the government conduit to stimulate construction and reno-
vation. The moratorium on government-subsidized housing construction was sparked by the scandals of Sections 235 and 236. As the
corruption associated with the program reached the notebooks of investigating journalists and the hearing rooms of Congress in 1973,
Nixon used the occasion to halt further funding by government. Os-
tensibly such a moratorium was to give White House policymakers
time to review the difficulties of housing subsidies for poor and
moderate income families, but the programs never again saw the
light of day.

Efforts by the Nixon White House to dismantle Great Society
leftovers - OEO, model cities, and the restiveness of the ghettoes -
were directed against the bottom of society, the underprivileged defenders of meliorism, and their allies in Congress. The efforts
themselves met with mixed success - OEO was never completely
disbanded due to its congressional supporters, but it was shattered;
model cities was collapsed into a block grant; and the Law Enforcement Assistance Administration emerged to cope with the problem of
urban disorder.

Overall, the strategy of disengagement, which like a thread ran
through the policies of the New Federalism, was most effective when

it came to quelling protest and disorder. The Nixon White House
reasoned correctly that if the organizing cadres of the War On Poverty could be extricated from their positions, or at least pacified, the
potential for disorder would decrease. The presumption in this instance is that the removal of the organizing base within the ghetto
would also remove the catalyst for action - douse the rest with policies for "law and order" (which were popular across the congressional
spectrum), and the slums of the city can be quiet once again.

Liberal and radical critics of Nixon may deny it (because of ro-
manticized ideas that unrest spontaneously arises from the grassroots, or that repression never works), but these policies of refusal
did work to quiet the cities. Mass rioting and disruption decreased
after 1969, ending a previous period of linear and continual rise. The
urban time bomb that civil rights leaders predicted would explode
without additional meliorist programs did in fact fizzle out - what remained was its cannister which festered with urban wreckage.

Finally, policies of reorganization represented efforts by the
Nixon White House to deal with almost everything and everybody,
including itself. These policies revolved around the President's
effort to establish a mechanism within the White House to develop and
manage urban policy. More than any other president, Nixon attempted
to define in advance just how policy would be made at the top and how
it was to be managed as it wended its way through the bureaucracy.
He engaged in a number of experiments he hoped would give the White
House control over this process. During the opening years of his
term, the Urban Affairs Council was formed, under the guiding aegis
of Daniel Patrick Moynihan. Later, that converted into a Domestic
Council, tightly centralized and tied to Nixon through John Ehrlichman, who became part of the President's inner sanctum. On top of
this, Nixon initiated dramatic changes in 1971, when he took steps to
reorganize the entire executive structure of the presidency. The old
budget bureau was expanded to exert stronger control over the apparatus of government and was renamed the Office of Management and
Budget (OMB), and a two-tiered, super and super-super cabinet was
created to lord over other cabinet members. Though Nixon ushered
in this reorganization saying that "the age of centralization in American government is ending," (8) he had by this stroke accomplished the
most thoroughgoing centralization of the presidency in contemporary
history.

The reason for centralizing the White House and the executive
branch was to gain control over those things which mattered most to
the President. This included control over the bureaucracy and some
members of the "outer cabinet" who Nixon felt had been thwarting him.

It also meant control over the flow of communication from the White House to Congress and to the public, concerning the intent of Nixon policy. Most of all, reorganization meant a greater effort by the White House to gain control over itself by centralizing policymaking. The job of disengagement required an active and vigilant White House - active, because only a strenuous search for alternatives could reverse the government conduit - vigilant, because Nixon knew there would be a bureaucratic drag on any reversal he attempted. "Don't let the bureaucracy fuzz it up" (9) was the admonition given by Nixon to trusted administrators.

Taken together, the Nixon White House and its New Federalism comprised a curious blend of decentralization at the bottom and centralization at the top. Policies of reciprocity and refusal were designed to deactivate Washington in local affairs and decentralize the public sector at that level, so that privatism could move uninhibitedly through it. Simultaneously, power was tightened at the top to control Congress and the bureaucracy so that reinforcing policies could work properly. Put another way, suctioning off the presence of government at the local level required superior and concentrated power at the national level - the Nixon White House saw that decentralization and centralized power were not necessarily antipodal ideas, but could be joined to complement one another in order to invigorate the push of privatism. Movement and the presumable initiative that comes with "freeing up" private enterprise, coupled with a vision supplied by the White House, would make the "New American Revolution" possible.

Policies of Reciprocity: Smaller Packages in Shinier Wrappings

General and special revenue sharing were twins born of the New Federalism and presented to assert a reinforcing thrust throughout the nation. As a political strategy, revenue sharing was above all a replacement for categorical grants and a gambit for disengaging Washington from the quicksand of the inner cities - let the cities keep the dollars which stemmed from Johnson's urban commitment, but not hold Nixon responsible for the commitment itself. This idea was not presented in the bald lexicon of urban withdrawal, but had a positive tone of "sharing" the tax dollars collected by Washington by "returning" those dollars to the localities. In this way, New Federalism could be furnished with a popular following at the grassroots (mayors, voters, congressmen) and the White House could enjoy the benefits of that new strength.

The largest carrots were shown to Congress and the public at
the very beginning of the Nixon administration in 1969, and, in 1971,
when general and special revenue sharing were held up together.
General revenue sharing was the return to the states and local governments of $5-6 billion annually, with no strings attached, with no
narrow-purpose guidelines, and with a promise of no red tape. As
presented by the President, general revenue sharing was a bonus of
leftover tax dollars, oriented toward the states rather than their localities. Under his proposal, 90 percent of the annual total would be
allocated on the basis of each state's population as a percentage of
the total U.S. population, with an adjustment made for a state's tax
effort. The remaining 10 percent was to be made available for states
that had negotiated their own formulas for mini revenue sharing with
their own localities. Essentially, Nixon was seeking not only to provide an alternative to categorical assistance, but to unhinge the relationship between Washington and the cities built during meliorist
years by replacing it with a simpler cash nexus that would take place
exclusively between Washington and the states.

In an earlier period, bypassing the cities in favor of the states
would have evoked immediate apprehension among urban mayors,
and fears that cities would never see their just distribution of federal
aid. Statehouses and most governors have not traditionally been
sympathetic toward the needs of the unwashed ethnic and racial
minorities of their big cities, and frequently mixed federal assistance
into the state's treasury to the advantage of rural and suburban hamlets. This, however, was a different period when cities were still
reeling from the riots and disruption of the 1960s and were beginning
to feel pressure on their expense budgets and cash flow. Nixon's
message on revenue sharing was greeted as fiscal relief for city halls
which were exhausted from a decade of carrying bureaucratic and
financial burdens. Besides, city mayors knew they had meliorist
friends in Congress and the twists and turns of the legislative process
would eventually redound to greater benefits for the cities than Nixon
had originally proposed.

The mayors were correct - by the time general revenue sharing
had found its way out of the congressional labyrinth, local governments had grabbed a greater portion of the package, leaving only
one-third of the dollar total for the states, while local general purpose governments (municipalities, counties, townships) received
two-thirds of all revenue sharing funds. (10)

With the enactment of general revenue sharing in 1972, the
positive themes of the New Federalism were paying off politically.
(11) Nixon's earlier declaration that the time had come to "start

power and resources flowing back to the states and communities"
aroused the nation, and he was near the apogee of his popular appeal -
a good harbinger for a strong rush to the White House a second time.
Nixon had even disarmed the mayors of central cities by winning an
endorsement from the Democratic mayor of Philadelphia, Frank
Rizzo. The black mayor of dilapidated East St. Louis commented
that the Nixon White House had "been good to the city" and wondered
aloud if "a Democratic administration would be any better". (12)
Another black Democrat, Kenneth Gibson, who was mayor of Newark,
one of the fastest evacuating cities for the middle class in the nation,
could not find fault with the President's urban policy, and announced
that his city was being given "special help" from the White House.
Quite naturally, the President's most enthusiastic following came
from the newer and booming cities of the south and southwest, where
mayors from Houston and San Diego along with officials from affluent
suburbs expressed their pleasure with the White House. For them,
revenue sharing was a bonus of federal tax monies for which they
would not ordinarily qualify under standards of need or deprivation.
However, skewed revenue sharing was toward failing areas, taking
federally collected taxes, and not pouring them down another categorical grant ("rathole" was the favored description by conservative
congressmen) turned out to be an unexpected bonanza for all localities which was to be repeated and guaranteed for five running years.
The comparative data on revenue sharing funds received in the 1970s
between older central cities of the northeast and midwest and those of
the south and southwest are as follows:

Exterior or Central Cities (Revenue Sharing per capita)	Newer Cities ("sunbelt") (Revenue Sharing per capita)
New York ($31.34)	Houston ($11.38)
Chicago ($20.62)	Dallas ($11.49)
Detroit ($24.15)	San Diego ($9.36)
Cleveland ($18.79)	Phoenix ($15.96)
St. Louis ($20.41)	Miami ($20.78)
Pittsburgh ($22.46)	Tulsa ($9.12)
Newark ($22.09)	Oklahoma City ($18.39)

Making comparisons between states is far more difficult
because of the internal variation between them. Nonetheless,
the per capita differences in revenue sharing funds received in
the 1970s between some of the more urbanized states and the less
urbanized states show a very mixed picture which does not establish that urban states gained any advantage.

Less Urbanized States	More Urbanized States
(Revenue Sharing per capita)	(Revenue Sharing per capita)
Alaska ($20.97)	California ($27.87)
Arizona ($28.35)	Illinois ($27.92)
Idaho ($27.92)	Massachusetts ($28.65)
Kansas ($23.50)	New York ($32.42)
Nevada ($22.71)	Pennsylvania ($23.23)
Oklahoma ($23.21)	Ohio ($19.43)
Utah ($29.64)	Michigan ($25.00)
Wyoming ($29.18)	New Jersey ($22.82)

General revenue sharing was only half of the Nixon package which also contained special revenue sharing. Like its twin, special revenue sharing was also sold as a return of federal dollars to the states and localities to be used as they pleased, though it was far more transparent and withheld more than it gave. While general revenue sharing was, on its face, a straight bonus on top of existing programs, special revenue sharing sought to eliminate older categorical grants, and Congress was not readily buying Nixon's argument for the proposed trade.

The President had actually presented his argument for special revenue sharing twice - once in 1971, when he asked for the consolidation of 105 categorical grant programs in an $11 billion package of unrestricted monies to be used by localities for six broad purposes; and again, in 1973, when he presented a similar plan, which was pruned down to $6.9 billion covering four broad areas of education, manpower, law enforcement, and urban community development.

In each of these special revenue sharing proposals, the driving political motives were similar - hold back the rising tide of funds that flowed from Washington to the cities and release the federal government from its self-imposed obligation of remedying urban ills and alleviating pockets of crisis. In education, the Nixon White House sought to do this by abolishing 30 categorical grants which were aimed toward impacted areas and remedial education. Compensatory educational allotments for states which were the most deeply struck by poverty were also to be reduced. In their place, funding was to be more broadly defined and used or distributed at the discretion of the governor of each state. Under this kind of special revenue sharing, the "poverty index" was redefined so that states with a large concentration of welfare families (New York, New Jersey, California, West Virginia, or Washington, D.C.) would incur substantial cutbacks in assistance.

Special revenue sharing struck similar chords when it came to
the President's proposals for manpower. The potpourri of efforts
begun by Kennedy and Johnson were all cast into a "no strings" allocation made available to the states. Meliorist programs, like the
Neighborhood Youth Corps and vocational training for the unemployed,
were either repealed or converted into discretionary projects, directed by the localities and monitored at a distance by the Department
of Labor. Special revenue sharing for law enforcement was also
part of the Nixon logic of enlarging the local role by removing matching fund and maintenance of effort requirements. Law enforcement,
though, enjoyed the exceptional status of being a popular campaign
promise. On this issue, the President cited the need for more, not
less, expenditures, pridefully pointing out that he had already spent
"more than 67 times as much" money in this area, than did Lyndon
Johnson. (13)

Above all, it was Nixon's plan for urban and community development which evoked suspicions and stripped the revenue sharing stratagem of its fanciful wrappings. The proposed legislation for this,
known as the Better Communities Act, called for "folding in" a large
number of meliorist grants in aid - from urban renewal through water
and sewer loans to model cities - and encompassing them within one
$2.3 billion allocation for the cities. (14)

On its face alone, Better Communities was enough to turn the
earlier plaudits heaped on general revenue sharing into jeers and
lamentations. Better Communities might have projected a handsome
$2.3 billion for the cities to spend as they wishes, but Nixon invited
hundreds of additional localities to share in the federal cornucopia.
After counting up the numbers of newly invited guests, mostly small
cities and suburban counties, big city mayors discovered that the
federal horn of plenty was filled with only half rations.

A large part of this disillusion was also due to the funding levels
of Better Communities and the paucity of housing and development
monies that cities found were available to them as the New Federalism took root. Under the Better Communities formula, cities were
to be gradually phased into their special revenue sharing dollars and,
for a period of time, could receive "hold harmless" funding, which
was equal to the average amount they received for a period of years
under meliorist grant programs. After taking the opportunity to
compare older categorical dollars with their entitlement under Better
Communities, big city mayors began to change their minds about the
President's intentions. Older and larger central cities, which were
on the decline, saw their funds shrink, while many newer cities,
which were experiencing impressive growth, stood to receive

increased federal aid. Thus, of the group considered as exterior
cities, only New York would gain substantial federal aid, while
Chicago would receive only modest increments. Of this group, cities
on the losing side of the Better Communities ledger were far more
numerous (Baltimore, Detroit, Cleveland) and almost as sore to the
eye as were their slums. By contrast, those cities on the profit
side of Better Communities (Dallas, Pheonix, Houston) were in unprecedented booms and growing stronger with each passing year.
Table 5. 1 indicates how twenty cities would have fared under Nixon's
proposal. Ten are exterior cities while the other half are growing
and prosperous cities.

Running one's finger down this list of twenty cities, we might
ask ourselves which cities are the comparative "losers" and "gainers" and how do they divide themselves on matters of age, growth,
and prosperity. On the whole, Nixon chose to give seven out of ten
exterior cities (Cleveland, Baltimore, St. Louis, Detroit, Philadelphia, Boston, and San Francisco) fewer federal dollars than they had
received under a five year average of categorical grant aid. Only
three exterior cities (New York, Chicago. and New Orleans) came out
ahead or broke even under Better Communities. The proportion was
exactly the opposite for "prosperous" cities with seven of those gaining federal money or breaking about even (Omaha, Dallas, Houston,
Pheonix, El Paso, Tampa, and Long Beach). Only three prosperous
cities could be counted as "losers" (Norfolk, San Diego, and Seattle)
and for one of those (San Diego) the loss was quite negligible.

"Loser" cities were mainly clustered in the northeast or north
central states, and only San Francisco could be classified as a far
western city. "Gainer" cities were mainly located in the sunbelt or
far west and were relative newcomers to an urban status.

Why it was that the Nixon White House chose to give prosperous
cities more federal money and declining cities less can best be explained by the modus operandi of a reinforcing presidency. Nixon
was not a fiscal conservative in the sense of being frugal and wanting
to spend fewer tax dollars. Under the Nixon administration, national
budget spending continued to soar to higher peaks, while budget deficits ground the treasury into a deeper hole. (15) For reinforcers,
the question is not one of fiscal conservatism, which is long dead as
a budget reality, but one of how, for what pruposes, and where federal dollars will be spent. For the reinforcing president pursuing policies, slashing federal dollars in one area means increasing the dollar flow into another area, by one means or another. The overriding
objective is to strengthen and reinforce the inherent disposition of
corporate enterprise. Since the sunbelt was booming and its spread

Table 5.1. Nixon's Better Communities Plan: Exterior and Prosperous Cities Compared

Exterior City	Average Hold Harmless over 5 years (thousands)	Entitlement Under Better Communities (thousands)	Prosperous* City	Hold Harmless Over 5 Years (thousands)	Entitlement Under Better Communities (thousands)
Cleveland	14,656	8,025	Omaha	1,437	4,315
Baltimore	33,471	15,834	Dallas	4,224	12,684
Chicago	42,549	54,199	Houston	12,935	19,375
St. Louis	15,061	12,898	Phoenix	2,710	8,138
New York	91,305	132,460	Norfolk	12,589	5,075
Detroit	30,347	22,874	El Paso	2,350	7,058
Philadelphia	52,991	28,942	San Diego	9,616	8,782
Boston	21,507	10,073	Seattle	12,134	5,801
New Orleans	14,114	14,693	Tampa	4,768	4,876
San Francisco	28,524	10,803	Long Beach	1,514	4,425

* It is difficult to define what constitutes a "prosperous" city. These cities have been selected on the basis of their newly developed infrastructure vis a vis exterior cities and partially from a composite list of "non-hardship" cities developed by Richard Nathan. Nathan used a "hardship index" based on unemployment, dependency, educational level, per capita income, crowded housing, and poverty. Most of the cities in the "prosperous" category appeared on Nathan's index as "non-hardship" cities. See Richard Nathan and Charles Adams "Understanding Central City Hardship," Political Science Quarter-ly 21, 1 (Spring 1976), 47–62.

Sources: HUD and U.S. Bureau of the Census.

cities, designed by the architecture of the automobile and petroleum, were on the rise, Nixon's urban policy was bound to follow the investment patterns of private capital.

As a reinforcing policy, general revenue sharing performed much the same function for privatism as did Better Communities, by providing cities and suburbs with undesignated funding. Data on how general revenue sharing funds have been spent is fuzzy, but studies indicate that a portion of this money has been used to either cut local taxes or keep them from rising. Given the tax reducing consequence of general revenue sharing, benefits directly or indirectly redound to private enterprise. Tax reductions within localities lessen property and other tax obligations and stimulate business activity - tax reductions across local governments prompt competition between them to entice private investment. Thus, when government funds are not applied toward a public purpose and are left to ambiguous discretionary use, they are likely to find themselves serving private purposes or relieving private obligations.

At any rate general revenue sharing never aroused the anger of big city mayors, while Better Communities did and helped tip Nixon's urban hand. With Better Communities waiting to replace meliorist policies and the President's order to cut back on urban programs during the transition to New Federalism, big city mayors began to feel the pinch of the reinforcing presidency and made their pains known. San Francisco's colorful Joseph Alioto grieved that his city was "being hit from all sides" and brought in the figures to demonstrate it - $17 million was being lost in manpower programs, $15 million in housing subsidies, and $44 million cut from community development. Former Nixon champions, joined by the mayor of East St. Louis who once gave the President high marks, called general revenue sharing "a hoax" and admitted, "Boy, they really led us down the path on that one." Better Communities was dubbed by some to be a "Bitter Communities" act, and Milwaukee's veteran mayor Henry Maier denounced revenue sharing as a "gigantic double cross." "The mayors of America," he said, "...certainly would not have campaigned for general revenue sharing in a form which simply further enriches the wealthy suburbs of America had we known that later the categorical cuts were going to be designed to make the inner cities and the rural poor areas poorer." (16)

Richard Nixon's policies of reciprocity had their successes and failures. General revenue sharing was passed into law but failed to eliminate the meliorist conduit or pave the way for special revenue sharing. Special revenue sharing was not enacted as a hard line reinforcing measure, though truncated versions of it were passed in manpower, law enforcement, and in minor areas. Probably the most significant consequence of Nixon's special revenue sharing proposals was that they set out a bargaining position for the introduction of block grant legislation, which was a middling path between the meliorist categorical grant and the reinforcing revenue sharing approach. This was particularly true for urban policy, and while Better Communities did not get through the Congress as a special revenue sharing act, a block grant version of it did get enacted into law during the early days of the Ford administration.

Meandering along a legislative side road toward the New Federalism was, nevertheless, tedious and uncertain, encouraging Nixon to take a shortcut through the congressional thicket by wielding his presidential machete. The executive power to cut and slash at meliorism could be quicker and far more decisive than dithering with a Democratic Congress; and after his landslide reelection in 1972, the President felt a greater liberty to do this.

Policies of Refusal: Hunkering Down on the Cities

As history, the image of the "hunkered down" Nixon, the sullen President who punished his enemies rather than come to terms with them, will probably be written through the prism of Watergate. As a matter of political style, Nixon hunkered down on his opposition before Watergate burst his Presidency, because Nixon could tolerate a dissident Congress for just so long before he lost patience with it and went on the attack. Richard Nixon the "dragon slayer" (the "new" Nixon, circa 1968), and Richard Nixon "the dragon" (the "old" and disgraced Nixon) are one and the same President. The punishing, negative Nixon is the other side of the reciprocating, positive Nixon, and his policy of refusal was a harpoon he kept at his side when subjects refused to bite for the bait of revenue sharing.

That harpoon was applied to meliorist policies as early as 1970, when HUD took budgetary and procedural steps to pull in some of Lyndon Johnson's favorite programs. Urban renewal, model cities, and neighborhood development were the first programs to be curtailed. Philadelphia had hung its hopes on a continuance of these older policies, expecting $40 to 50 million in "new money" for urban renewal - it wound up with substantially less than half that amount. San Francisco had also expected a continuance of past practices and began a massive 72 block renewal program, only to be slowed as HUD constricted the federal pipeline. St. Louis, Detroit, and

Atlanta faced similar episodes of bureaucratic paralysis, as funds
for neighborhood development or model cities were reduced. (17)

Some of these curtailments were due to decisions taken at the
White House to spread smaller federal pots of money between more
cities. Most of the newcomers were small municipalities, less experienced in the political finesse required for categorical grants, and
they had sympathetic ears listening to them at HUD. Thus, big cities'
losses might mean marginal gains for smaller ones. Another reason
for slashing at big city programs was a general deemphasis and
souring on the idea of neighborhood or ghetto redevelopment. Nixon
policymakers saw black deprivation not as a problem requiring collective rejuvenation but as something to be managed by easing the
chances for individual mobility. The black ghetto was not to be
treated in the meliorist mode, as a community afflicted with atypical
hardships or as a pathology, but as a place from which its most enterprising inhabitants should be given the opportunity to escape. The
idea of "black capitalism" via loans and investments outside of the
ghetto was closer to Nixon's preference and part of the reinforcing
gestalt.

These ideas were underpinned by Nixon's perception that the
Great Society was a gross failure, and by the unwillingness of meliorists to move toward different solutions. By the beginning of 1973,
Nixon had begun to cut and slash at meliorist programs with a ven-
geance. As the 93rd Congress opened in January, 1973, Nixon had
already impounded $12 billion appropriated by the previous Congress.
Half of this amount was for sewage treatment voted by the Congress
over the President's veto, so that the issue stood as a contest over
whose policy preferences would ultimately prevail. Through 1973,
Nixon brought all of his legal powers, plus some others, to bear in
this contest. Impoundments were made to stop already-appropriated
funds from going into food stamp programs, water pollution projects,
highways, and environmental assistance. Vetoes were exercised on
legislation for social welfare; and where executive budgetary priorities needed to be set, Nixon reduced or eliminated over 100 categories that were slated for federal funding. (18)

Launching a political attack through executive vetoes and budget
submissions was one thing, and considered within the rules of legitimate opposition. The use of impoundments was another question and
clearly appeared to be in unconstitutional defiance of the Congress,
which had enacted appropriations over Nixon's veto. Nixon justified
the impoundments by either papering over the real totals with fiscal
technicalities or by claiming that he was acting within a tradition set
by other presidents by merely holding funds in "budgetary reserves".

Meliorists in Congress, however, did not share that interpretation
and an outraged Speaker of the House, Carl Albert, vowed that his
colleagues "will not permit the President to lay waste the great programs which we have developed during the decades past". The President's action, Albert declared, "was nothing less than the systematic
dismantling and destruction of the great social programs and the great
precedents of humanitarian government inaugurated by Franklin Roosevelt and advanced and enlarged by every Democratic President since
them." (19) Of course, Congress ultimately prevailed when the courts
ruled against the President's impoundment of funds.

Policies of refusal and policies of reciprocity could be mixed to
intimidate or induce cities to fall in line with the broader objectives
of the New Federalism. As a professional politician, Nixon knew that
he should avoid making unnecessary enemies and used punishment
sparingly, often for its value as a threat to gain compliance for other
priorities. Slinging a whip for a brief period and then offering to stop
the pain is an effective way to confuse and divide the opposition. This
was poignantly conveyed during the opening days of Nixon's second
term, when, flushed with confidence and facing a stubborn Congress,
the President resorted to sterner measures of refusal.

Acting through George Romney, the Secretary of HUD, the White
House began to send out inklings that it was rethinking existing policies toward urban housing. Romney chose to deliver the opening
salvo before a convention of the Mortgage Bankers Association of
America, at which he claimed that housing programs were in crisis
and that drastic changes would be needed to avoid further mistakes.
Romney also let it be known that the White House hoped to avoid future
errors by ending subsidies to low income families, and suggested that
the government "privatize" the FHA. (20) In January 1973, Romney
(who was by this time an outgoing Secretary) took the cutting axe in
hand and, in a speech before the National Association of Home Builders, announced an immediate moratorium on all further commitments
for government assisted housing. At the butt ends of the moratorium
were Sections 235 and 236 of Lyndon Johnson's Housing Act which
provided subsidies for housing the poor, and which had been suffering
from revelations of corruption and inefficiency. The moratorium was
more extensive than Romney had originally let on, and it was apparent
that Nixon was using the subsidy scandals to shut down the entire conduit for both housing and community development. Included in the
ban were rent supplements, public housing, urban renewal, open
space preservation, and many more programs. As it turned out,
Nixon had combined the moratorium on housing with drastic federal
budget reductions in community development so that freezes cut

across the flow of all money going to cities. "The time has come to
pause, to reevaluate and to seek out better ways," commented Romney, who added that he was delighted that there was going to be a
total review of the "entire Rube Goldberg structure" or urban policy.
(21) The words "review" and "reevaluate" were White House euphe-
misms (a communications technique which was to mark the administration) for Nixon's intention to abolish and replace past policies.
This was acknowledged as such by a top White House staffer, who
dismissed any ideas that a "simple retooling" or "cosmetic change"
would follow these actions.

What was to succeed this "Rube Goldberg structure" was, of
course, Better Communities which Nixon was about to propose some
months later. In the meantime, Nixon intended to let cities feel the
sting of federal withdrawal so that they might fully appreciate the
salve of special revenue sharing. The predicted agonies came from
all over the country and from a good many former supporters of the
New Federalism. Roman Gribbs, the "law and order" mayor of
Detroit, whose city was about to be cut by $250 million protested
these tactics, saying "We cannot wait two years for new tools....
Problems, programs, and people do not stand still for deliberation
and negotiation.... We support restructuring, we support efficiency...
but we cannot tolerate the human misery and suffering while we wait
for that new day." (23) Surprisingly for the Nixon White House, conservative business groups before which Romney had made his an-
nouncements also voiced their protestations. A coalition of bankers
and builders, led by the Mortgage Bankers of America and the National Association of Home Builders, turned to Congress to oppose
Nixon's cuts, showing their ideological affection for meliorism.
Joined by unions and other interest groups, the coalition urged Nixon
to "honor the promises of a few short year ago" and dedicate himself
to the objectives of "decent shelter" and greater opportunities for all
Americans. The coalition did not consign its opposition to nostalgic
praise of Johnson's social philosophy. The head of the home builders
association went before a congressional committee to denounce the
cuts as "disastrous and catastrophic"; and his colleagues raised some
threats of their own, urging sympathetic Democrats to delay confirmation of Nixon nominees until the President lifted the freeze. (24)

Despite the protests, the White House was convinced that its
supporters outnumbered its resisters, and enlarged the scope of its
refusals from housing and development to poverty and the role of the
OEO. As an issue, poverty held a certain attraction for Nixon who
quite accurately sensed it to be the meliorists' Achilles heel. Nixon
knew the difficulty of attempting to filter benefits to the poor through

the double mesh of bureaucracy and privatism, and for a while had
been infatuated with the thought of outdoing meliorists on the issue
they preached about so smugly. In 1969-70, the President had been
persuaded by Daniel Moynihan, an iconoclastic Democrat who was a
member of Nixon's closest circle, to back an alternative plan for
dealing with the welfare population. The Moynihan plan, or the
Family Assistance Plan (FAP) as it came to be presented, was a
complex but dramatic proposal for making an end-run around the
Democrats' favorite issue by using reinforcing methods to settle the
problem of skyrocketing welfarism. FAP called for a modest income
floor of up to $2,400, to be placed under families which had little or
no income, and coupled this floor with a sliding scale of welfare payments to be paid to eligible families while they worked at low paying
jobs. For a family which earned a marginal income, welfare payments would continue, but would be phased out gradually at a reduction of fifty cents on each welfare dollar for every dollar earned in
wages. After a welfare family reached an income ceiling of $4,000,
welfare payments would cease entirely, since the wage earner(s)
would presumably be strong enough to survive without government
help on the labor market.

This ingenious plan contained a mild strain of a minimum national
income for all families, which was hedged by a proviso that they be
willing to work should employment exist, a much stronger dosage of
work incentives, and a "negative income tax," (25) which made it
more profitable to work and simultaneously collect a smaller welfare
check, than not to work at all. To illustrate how work incentives
would operate, a family of seven which could not find employment and
had to rely totally on government support might collect as much as
$2,400 in annual welfare payments. The same family of seven which
could find employment and managed to earn $2,000 over a year could
continue under FAP to collect a small welfare stipend of $1,400, cal-
culated on the basis of a fifty cent reduction on each welfare dollar
for every dollar earned in wages. Thus, the welfare/working family
of seven would have a total income of $3,400 (i.e. $1,400 in reduced
welfare payments plus $2,000 in wages) while the welfare/non-working
family of seven would only receive the maximum income floor of
$2,400. (26)

Moynihan and other Nixon policy thinkers liked to call FAP the
beginning of "an income strategy", because it moved away from the
government injecting itself into the resolution of social problems,
toward one of enabling individuals to settle their own problems by
giving them cash assistance. Peter Drucker has referred to these
kinds of policies as a "reprivatization" of decisions because they

reduce the reliance on government bureaucracy and increase the role of individual discretion within the market place. While FAP fell conspicuously short of the individualistic ethic, it was a significant accommodation to it; a sort of post-New Deal effort to restore the values of Social Darwinism, while, at the same time, recognizing the benign influence of government in making social competition possible.

The Nixon administration knew that it was not feasible to deal with welfare dependency by abolishing programs or reducing payments to starvation levels - that was an idea entertained by diehard reactionaries and would certainly not fit with American politics after the New Deal was so firmly legitimized. How else, then, could the President deal with welfare dependency without increasing the role of Washington and diminishing the value of self reliance? The answer for Nixon was to accept the fundamental premise of New Dealism - that it was the responsibility of government to provide something for the indigent - but after accepting that role, to turn responsibility back on the individual and to play on the inherent forces of the market place. As a national policy, FAP accomplished this amazingly well by allowing a minimal income for all indigent families and not going any further with meliorist penchants for vocational training or neighborhood planning. After Washington put a floor under the poor, they were free to explore the market place without bureaucratic guidelines to tell them that if they worked they would be ineligible for welfare. Federal pipelines to lure private enterprise into investing in unattractive ventures were no longer necessary. In short, FAP was a way of defanging social planners who wanted to continue with the Great Society. It was Nixon's way of saying that the poor might have some cash, but not a federal pledge to cure their condition. Any such cures would have to be self discovered, but the cash that welfare families received could easily be spent in the market place, and the jobs they took with privatism need not be fully supporting. Migrant laborers could work seasonally, as corporate farming required them, and still collect a welfare check. The inner city poor could work on and off as domestics or factory porters and still receive a welfare subsidy. In the tradition of reinforcement, there was, too, an invisible subsidy for the employers of welfare/working families since they could more easily hire or lay-off workers and justify lower wage scales. This occurred without government intervention, bureaucracies, or elaborate conduits and with private parties making private decisions in their own interests.

In style and substance, FAP was, perhaps, Nixon's earliest experiment with policies of reciprocity, since it attempted to exchange a decidedly reinforcing approach, a la an income strategy,

for older meliorist policies. Like other policies of reciprocity, FAP
fell flat politically when it failed to gain passage in the Senate. Having failed with the carrot in 1970, Nixon began to take a stick in hand
sometime thereafter. Without a comprehensive welfare change, the
White House was constrained in moving toward the introduction of a
new system, but it could work around the periphery of meliorism by
containing it and, upon occasion, chop away at large hunks of it.
Nixon first began to do this by pressing for a ceiling on federal expenditures for social services (child care, family planning, etc.),
most of which were being piled up by HEW. By late 1972, a lid was
placed on HEW social service programs, just as general revenue
sharing was being passed by Congress.

Once again, the harshest policies of refusal surfaced as Nixon
entered his second term and launched his own attack on poverty - only
this time it was against the poverty warriors themselves. Almost
immediately, the President announced that after June 30, 1973, no
further funds would be made available to OEO and he placed the agency
in charge of an acting director, Howard Phillips, whose acknowledged
purpose was to eventually administer himself out of the poverty business. Asked why he was reluctant to appear before a congressional
committee for confirmation hearings, Phillips responded with the
candor of a political novice, "I'd have to spend all my time up there,
getting confirmed and I'd never get the place dismantled." (27)

The effort to dismantle OEO had its moments of political intrigue,
which typified the Nixon style, as did its lapses of leaked information,
which typified the Nixon blunders. After the appointment of Howard
Phillips, a "secret memo" was obtained by the press which outlined
dispersing Johnson's warriors on all fronts by abolishing their central
office (OEO), destroying the CAP organizations in the field (referred
to as Community Action Agencies or CAAs), and encapsulating their
legal arm into a "Legal Services Corporation." The secret memo,
unsigned and undated, is interesting for what it reveals about how the
Nixon White House sought to deal with the urban poor and its perception of the political opposition. Part of it reads as follows:

> ... At this point, there probably is not much fight left in congres-
> sional supporters of OEO and Community Action. (Legal Services
> is probably another matter.) That does not mean that the liberals
> may not subsequently decide to coalesce around the "save OEO"
> issue prompted either by a decision to concentrate on the Presi-
> dent as "weak-on-poverty/hunger," or else in response to suc-
> cessful grassroots organization by the Community Action

Agencies. Thus, unless the administration decides that such a
confrontation would be a desirable trap for ensnaring the opposition, everything would point to completing the disagreeable business as soon as possible. That probably means prompt transfer
of all surviving programs to new agencies, and then completing
arrangements for the GSA receivership by the end of this fiscal
year. Under such a timetable it is unlikely that the opposition
could muster enough strength (or will) to put humpty-dumpty together again. A swift and successful dismemberment of the rest
of OEO would also strengthen the administration's hand in pressing for its Legal Services Corporation. Disappearance of its
present home would reinforce the Hobson's choice between the
President's corporation or oblivion. The more delay, the more
opportunity for congressional opposition to gather and develop a
legislative counter-strategy. Unless there is stronger-than-
expected grassroots opposition, (or the administration blunders),
it is quite possible that the OEO/CAA actions could go through
with little more than rhetorical opposition, while the Congress
concentrates its fire on Legal Services. (28)

Nixon and the men around him gauged that when confronted with a
political attack, street support around the War On Poverty was likely
to swing between the extremes of volatility and indifference. If the
attack was going to be successful, it should be quick and decisive in
cutting off grassroots organizations (like CAPs or CAAs) which had
the potential of activating nasty protests within urban ghettoes. The
White House wanted no replay of the urban riots of the 1960s and was
aware that a president, perceived as a "conservative" Republican by
the inner cities, could be a provocative target for demonstrators.
Should protests or riots erupt, Nixon's men were prepared to bring
in a vast reserve of public antipathy against the poor - the "silent
majority," which the White House believed constituted an overwhelming undercurrent of Nixon sympathizers. Hence, in other places, the
secret memo discusses the possibilities of urban protests and urges
the President to appeal to his latent support and "develop an adverse
public reaction to... scattered and angry demonstrations" which could
follow his decision to obliterate the OEO. (29)
   At the same time, the White House was not ready to pursue its
policies of refusal by solely relying on a cutting axe when sedation
could neutralize the opposition. This was especially so with OEO's
legal services, which had a political mooring in the Congress. Legal
services had taken its original mission seriously and was filled with
activist lawyers who were in it to litigate social causes, rather than

process mundane legal problems. Nixon would let Democrats in
Congress have their legal program for the poor if they would agree
to purge it of its activist elements and quit stirring up inner city
populations. The price for congressional Democrats was the sever-
ance of legal services from a defunct OEO and its conversion into a
supposedly apolitical corporation which was indirectly controlled by
the President.

Like other Nixon initiatives, policies of refusal yielded a mixture
of outcomes. Vetoes, selective budget cuts, the housing moratorium,
and impoundments had serious short-term consequences for the cities.
The precipitous withdrawal of federal funds exacerbated the fiscal
plight of cities and contributed to higher local budgets, often camou-
flaged deficits, and onerous charges for borrowing. The attack on
the War On Poverty also had mixed results. Meliorists in Congress
resisted the Phillips appointment and managed to have him removed
on the grounds that he never received Senate confirmation. With that
maneuver against the White House, Congress followed up by salvaging
CAP agencies and their numbers continued to hover at around a thousand. Nonetheless, for the greater period of the Nixon-Ford tenure,
OEO and its CAPs toed a narrow line between life and death. Their
budgets were restored only through the constant intervention of Congress and the courts which rescued them at the eleventh hour. This
on again, off again status of OEO/CAPs was enough to provide the
White House with its minimum goals, since it paralyzed the most
aggressive poverty warriors and tamed the remainder. Moreover,
the sheer quantity of Nixon assaults was bound to hit some marks and
bring down whole sectors of the War On Poverty - and it did. Through
executive action, Nixon further defused the OEO by scattering programs to the Departments of Labor or HEW. OEO's legal arm was
finally severed in 1974, after some wrangling with Congress, through
a compromise plan which made it an independent corporation.

The "scattered and angry demonstration's" feared by Nixon's men
never did materialize to any appreciable degree, and through the
Nixon period the political surface of the inner cities remained quies-
cent. The evaporation of mass protest and insurrection during these
years is probably due to a number of complex factors. For one, the
Nixon White House did succeed, at the least, in "lowering voices"
for a certain number of groups in the nation. Bloated expectations
for the cities and their poor were punctured and so was the hope that
collective outbursts might convince power holders of the righteousness of the urban cause or the fulfillment of national promise.

Nixon's policy of refusal was a political demurrer on past promises and this had a tangible effect on leadership through every rung of

society. Budget cuts of one kind or another and the pullback on categorical grants dampened the urban tinder which might have ignited
sparks of political activity. In effect, the leadership cadre of inner
cities which emerged during the Johnson years was decapitated. The
withdrawal of Washington's commitment also entailed a withdrawal of
idealistic social workers, planners, and lawyers who had begun to
take root in the soil of urban deprivation. Private foundations followed suit and put a halt to the neighborhood experimentation and
social programs which they had once enthusiastically funded. At the
moment funds were drying up, many of the most ideological activists
believed they could do just as well without support from the "establishment"; but without resources to organize the poor, or the skills
to battle the opposition, or the money needed to buy manpower time,
grassroots activism began to wither, and one social experiment after
another died for lack of financial nourishment.

The most volatile and radical of inner city organizers were
handled in an altogether different way. Here, government organized
counter-violence was used to turn radical activists into fugitives and
drive them underground. In some instances, radicals were appre-
hended, sent to trial, and jailed; in one cause celebre, local police
in Chicago shot to death two members of the radical Black Panthers
Party under circumstances which reeked of political assassination.

On the surface, it appeared as if hounding insurrectionist radicals was an isolated activity carried out by disparate local police
forces. In reality, local and national police had teamed up to combat
violent radicalism as well as some lesser forms of political protest.
Their efforts were underwritten by massive amounts of federal monies
and cooperative programs to deal with a broad range of illegal activity. Through the Omnibus Crime Control Act of 1970, over $3.5
billion was made available to local governments over a three-year
period for a new "war on crime." (30) The program was managed
by the Law Enforcement Assistance Administration (LEAA) which
gave substance to the "law and order" abstractions of Nixon speeches.
In budget dollars and rhetorical pronouncements, law enforcement
and "peace in the streets" had begun to rival housing, transportation,
and manpower training as top national priorities. What was lacking
in resources for law enforcement was made up by a tough and aggressive Attorney General, John Mitchell, who directed the FBI and
Justice Department to apprehend and prosecute political dissidents.

The curious paradox of Nixon's emphasis on "law and order" as
a substitute for meliorist social policies was that it did not lead to
any diminution in non-political or common crimes. The more the
White House took action to fight common crime, the less effect those

actions seemed to have on its reduction. This was true in nearly
every category of common crime against persons (murder, rape,
robbery, assault) and every category against property (burglary,
larceny, auto theft). With every passing year of the Nixon administration, common crime statistics rose; yet, as mentioned earlier,
there was a drop in mass political protests. (31) No doubt the relationship between the rise in common crimes, the fall in mass protests, and Nixon policies is complex and difficult to unravel. One
tentative explanation, however, is that sunk in despair and without
expectation of better things, the ghettoes turned away from political
consciousness toward the self destructive poisons of violent crime
and narcotics addiction. Indeed, many of the black leaders who
turned to radical politics during the 1960s had been former convicts,
so that there seems to be some evidence of a linkage between a background of criminal behavior and a conversion to radical political protest. With avenues of policy closed off and the organizational base of
the ghetto snuffed out, many individuals returned to predatory crimes
for profit, instead of collective political protest.

Policies of Reorganization: The Pitfalls of
Lording Over the Imperial Presidency

While Nixon was attempting the most thorough pullback of social policy
in American history, he was also pulling in and tightening his control
over the government. Nixon's troubles stemmed not only from the
depths of a recalcitrant bureaucracy, an organization he complained
was governed by the "rule of no one," but from many of the cabinet
appointments made in his first term of office. Through his first
term, the President and his closest staff advisers, H. R. Haldeman
and John Ehrlichman, increasingly felt that the cabinet members had
gone astray "to marry the natives" and could not be trusted to hold
back special causes within their departments. (32)
     The darkest clouds of suspicion gathered around Interior Secre-
tary Walter Hickel, who became a convert to the environmental cause.
Soon after his appointment, he opposed the construction of a giant
airport near the Florida Everglades and cracked down on petroleum
companies responsible for oil spills off the coast of California.
Hickel's unpopularity with the White House grew as he stretched his
liberalism to include criticisms of the administration for its conduct
of the war in Viet Nam and its attitude toward youthful protesters.
After an interlude of punitive ostracism from White House deliberations (on one occasion he was disinvited to a Sunday prayer service,

hosted by the President), Hickel was forced to resign. Secretary of
Transportation John Volpe had similar problems with the White House,
as did other cabinet luminaries, who either resisted White House
commandments to cut their departmental budgets or insisted on following an independent line of policy.

One celebrated case of Nixon's difficulties with the rest of the
executive branch was that of HUD Secretary George Romney. Romney
came to the Nixon administration as a liberal and a champion of the
cities. As Governor of Michigan during the 1960s, he bore witness
to the plunder of Detroit by both industrial exploitation and rioting
mobs, and had trumpeted the idea of saving the cities through a national urban policy. Romney's appointment as the head of HUD was
hailed in 1969 as a sign of the "new Nixon" and as a move to give
"moderate Republicanism" a voice in the White House.

Taking his cue from press interpretations of his appointment,
and what some claim to be an exaggerated sense of self importance,
Romney came in to the Nixon administration as a meliorist. Much to
Nixon's dislike, he argued for the retention of model cities and, as
one official stated, "went production crazy" when it came to fueling
the government conduit with more housing. So long as Nixon was
currying favor with congressional Democrats and promoting his policies of reciprocity, the over-zealous Secretary might be tolerated.
Once Romney allowed his zeal to trespass into the sacred territory of
Nixon's election strategy, he became more than a minor irritant and
a threat to the President's chances for reelection. The violation
occurred as Romney presented plans for the construction of interra-
cial housing in the suburbs. That was more than just a political embarrassment; it was equivalent to launching a kamikaze raid against
the home base. Nixon was pinning his chances for a major realign-
ment toward conservatism on the 1972 elections, and a vital part of
that strategy depended on offsetting Democratic strength in the cities
with big gains in middle and working class suburbs. Clearly, Romney's proposal to build federal housing projects for blacks in the
midst of white suburbia did not enhance his reputation with the President or with Haldeman and Ehrlichman, who were gaining increasing
influence in deciding on domestic priorities. (33)

Like Hickel and other Cabinet members, Romney was falling
into disfavor, yet zealotry in service of duty does not surrender
easily, and if Romney could not distinguish himself as a spokesman
for Republican moderates, he thought he might do it as a Nixon stal-
wart. When Nixon told his Cabinet about his plans for special revenue sharing for the coming years, Romney protested that he was
never included in the original planning. Having expressed his

indignation, the Secretary soon "took his marching orders" like
everyone else and proceeded to vigorously defend the administration's
suspension of housing aid and its proposal for Better Communities.
In a reversal of his earlier meliorist style, Romney went on to do the
administration one better on each of its policies. With Romney zest,
he denounced "big government" as the plague of the cities, and time
and again laid the blame on "GS 7's who work in the bowels of the
bureaucracy." (34) If the White House insisted on cutting government costs, Romney would over-cut his own department to demonstrate his frugality; if the President wanted to decentralize government administration down to a regional level, Romney would devolve
it down to individual states.

    With all the overcompensating that Romney did, his actions went
for nought at the White House. Each action was interpreted not as a
desire to become an accepted member of the team, but as a concession on his earlier stance and a sign of weakness. This was not only
a specific reaction to Romney but a general perception of Nixon's
first term Cabinet (John Mitchell, the Attorney General, was an exception), and a reflection of the deep suspicion that Nixon had of
government as an intervener in the market place of society. As
Nixon himself told the nation in a radio address, likening government
to the family and to a business:

    ...In a family, when a father tells the rest of the family what to
    do, that's called paternalism. In a business when an employer
    tells the workers he knows what is best for their future, that is
    called paternalism. And in government, when a central authori-
    ty in Washington tells people across the country how they should
    conduct their lives, that, too, is paternalism.... It is time that
    good, decent people stopped letting themselves be bulldozed by
    anybody who presumes to be the self righteous moral judge of
    our society. (35)

    To prevent paternalism, the President was determined to cut
away at a heavy-handed bureaucracy which, through its intervention
and red tape, had squelched the impulses of the private sector. For
Richard Nixon, governmental cuts did not mean an absence of activity
or "do-nothing Republicanism." On the contrary, such cuts would
release pent-up private initiatives within society which were capable
of limitless innovation and productivity. Nixon had also calculated
the tradeoffs that would result from diverting government dollars to
privatism, and explained this to the nation in another radio address.

But after talking about these cuts, let's get one thing straight.
Cutting back on Federal programs does not mean cutting back on
progress. In fact, it means a better way to progress. When we
cut a million dollars from a Federal program, that money is not
lost and its power to do good things eliminated; rather, that
money is transferred to other budgets where its power to do good
things is multiplied. (36)

At first sight, it may be difficult to reconcile what appears to be
classic laissez faire doctrine with Nixon's actual behavior in augmenting his own power, and we might dismiss his speeches as mere
cant. After all, "sincere conservatives" like Presidents Taft or
Coolidge shunned the concentration of presidential power and preferred government to be a passive instrument. Yet there is a consistency to what Nixon said about the desirability of less government
intervention and his own behavior in magnifying the power of the
White House. Quite logically for Richard Nixon, less government
intervention did not also mean less government power - and particularly not less presidential power. Nixon was neither a "conservative" nor an old fashioned laissez faireist; he was a modern reinforcer who was enthusiastic about using the supplemental force of the
White House to speed up the self directed capital flows of private
enterprise. Denouncing government paternalism and federal cutbacks
was one way of speeding up these flows - or, as Nixon put it, transferring "that money... to other budgets. " (37)
Another and indispensable path toward the same end was to concentrate presidential power by means of reorganizing the executive
branch of government. Clear and precise policy ends demanded decisiveness, and Nixon could have no cabinet members sniping at his
policies with heavy spending programs, or bureaucrats spoiling
the enterprising spirit of the American people. Every meliorist
program was regarded by the White House as a parasite which sapped
the strength of America to feed its weakness. To counteract this,
Nixon needed to build an internal source of policy controls which he
could trust and rely on for direction - and this he found in the form
of a sophisticated domestic (and foreign) policymaking machinery.
It is one of the ironies of White House history that Richard Nixon, a
president who sought to do less for central cities, should distinguish
himself by creating his own staffing organizations for a national urban
policy whose alleged purpose was to do more for cities.
Nixon's urban policy apparatus evolved by a process of feeling
out what staffing arrangements worked best for him. At first, Daniel
Moynihan played a leading role in organizing the Urban Affairs

Council (UAC) - a loosely combined group of Cabinet members and leading advisers who clustered around problematic policy areas, and used specialized task forces to turn out options for presidential decision. The UAC functioned as a kind of high council on urban policy and, after refining options down to a narrow range of plausible choices, made its arguments before the President himself.

The White House pyramid was formalized in an executive reorganization, which like most of Nixon's drastic measures, was taken just after his reelection. The idea called for tying together in a hierarchy all the instruments, domestic and foreign, of White House policy. At the peak of the hierarchy were John Ehrlichman's Domestic Council, Roy Ash's Office of Management and Budget (OMB) plus three other members of the Nixon team (H. R. Haldeman on politics and staff, George Shultz on economics and finance, and Henry Kissinger on security and foreign affairs) who occupied positions of preeminence. Collectively, these five men constituted a Super-Super Cabinet, acting as White House vicars in five general areas, and were frequently at the President's ear. A member of this inner circle, like Ehrlichman, might oversee domestic policy responses, varying from welfare to revenue sharing or a general strategy for transportation. Descending downward to the second tier were three Super Cabinet members who directed composite aspects of domestic activity (James Lynn on Community Development, Earl Butz on Natural Resources, and Casper Weinberger on Human Resources) plus four other regular Cabinet members who were in charge of major departments (Defense, State, Treasury, and Justice). Two of these three Super Cabinet members were directly in charge of their own departments and coordinated one other related department. This meant that each Super Cabinet Secretary held a rank just below the first tier, but had an appreciable influence over more narrowly gauged policies. Someone like James Lynn, who was HUD Secretary and oversaw the cognate area of transportation, might make recommendations on how mass transit assistance might be intelligently linked with housing development, normally confining his observations to these two areas. At the bottom tier were cabinet secretaries without privilege, who administered the day-to-day affairs of their departments and had to make their influence felt by reporting to a member of the tier above them. Figure 5.1 portrays how the Nixon reorganization patterned this hierarchy of relationships.

Notwithstanding the limitations of trying to read relationships through organizational charts, the Nixon reorganization did achieve a certain neatness. It centralized and concentrated power around Nixon and placed the broadest contours of policymaking in the hands of like-minded men.

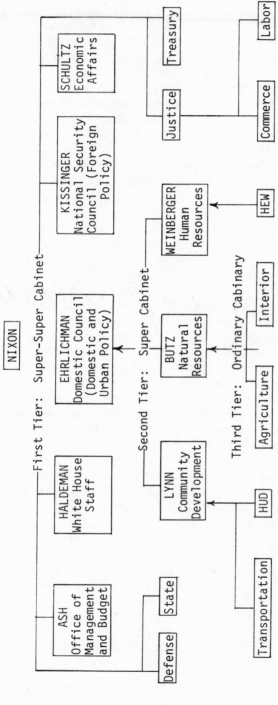

Fig. 5.1. Nixon's reorganization: the pyramid of White House policymaking.

164

The Domestic Council was established as part of an executive reorganization in 1970. At the same time the Bureau of the Budget was converted into the Office of Management and Budget (OMB). Between the Council and OMB, Nixon developed the organizational mainsprings for deciding on and carrying out urban policy. Nominally, the Council consisted of domestic cabinet members (Treasury, Labor, HUD, HEW, etc.) and comparable officials from other parts of the executive branch who worked with a Council staff. Under John Ehrlichman, the Domestic Council was very different from its predecessor, the UAC, and it seldom met as a formal body, deferring instead to its working staff. It became a tail of Ehrlichman's personal assistants which wagged the dog of the executive branch.

The staff of the Council, whose numbers varied from a high of 70 down to 30 workers, functioned as an intercessor for domestic policy and did the backup research for winnowing down policy choices. Information and options would then pass through Ehrlichman's fine screen and then to Nixon in the form of a thick notebook of "option papers." In reality, Ehrlichman's Domestic Council had interposed itself between the President and most of the departmental bureaucracies. At first, according to Ehrlichman, Cabinet Secretaries had a difficult time believing "that the president actually did not want to hear their oral arguments on policy disputes," but the power of the process showed itself to be irresistible and subsequent resignations took care of the remaining disbelievers. (38)

What also made the increasing enclosure of the Nixon presidency possible was the increasing prominence of the OMB. Its predecessor, the Bureau of the Budget, had always been a highly regarded elite organization of professionals who oversaw spending and kept scrupulous watch over departmental programs. However, it was constrained by what it could do to initiate policy, and its heat was more often felt in the afterglow of decisions than in their generation. Once Budget became Management and Budget, the line between policy formulation and its implementation blurred and OMB played an unusually heavy role. OMB began to decide, along with Ehrlichman's Domestic Council, what policies were desirable as well as feasible. It was instrumental, for example, in developing the specifics of an "income strategy" for a broad number of areas and, when special revenue sharing was bogged down in Congress, it quietly came up with a plan to order federal departments to implement the idea as far as possible by administrative means.

The role of OMB as a policymaker was also enhanced by Nixon's changing priorities as his presidency wore on. His policies of refusal required that a strong grip be placed on spending and on the

bureaucracies - a job which OMB was superbly equipped to do. Nixon
had infused OMB with an additional coterie of his own appointees, and
its new directors and second-tier managers set about putting the
brakes on the rest of government. Working closely with the President, these officials designed the moratorium on government-assisted
housing after 1973, prepared the cutbacks for program freezes, and
arranged the impoundments which sparked a furor in the halls of
Congress. Through his second term, Nixon's steady reliance on OMB
made it a major exponent of refusal policies and a juggernaut for their
implementation. The White House used its personnel to invade the
most stubborn bureaucracies and conduct the firing of subcabinet
members who persisted in hanging onto their posts. Men like Roy
Ash, the former head of a giant conglomerate which did a multimillion
dollar business with the Defense Department, and James Lynn, a
Nixon protege, were recruited as its Directors and, together with
Ehrlichman, were brought to the pinnacle of the White House pyramid. (39)

Between Ash, Haldeman, Ehrlichman, and the others, Nixon was
not as likely to get caught between quibbling crossfires of jealous
lieutenants or between polarized objectives. The President could rule
with decisiveness. This consistency could also be translated down to
a second tier of men Nixon could trust for an undistorted follow
through. James Lynn, who was at the command posts of housing and
transportation, had been politically weaned by Ehrlichman and Haldeman and was determined to minimize federal intervention in urban
programs; he subsequently negotiated a bill through Congress which
did just that. As Romney's replacement at HUD, he was a stark contrast and showed little interest in getting HUD to produce more housing, pushing instead for direct cash payments for recipients to purchase their own housing. Casper Weinberger, a fellow Californian of
Nixon's, came to HEW with a reputation as a "cutter" and where his
predecessors had fallen into sympathy with activists, he was more
successful in curtailing that department. To automate policy compliance down the line, Nixon placed trusted White House staffers in
critical subcabinet positions throughout the federal bureaucracy.
Three staffers from the Domestic Council were placed at the under
or assistant secretary level in Transportation, Interior, and Treasury. Other unknown aides were put in charge of the Urban Mass Transportation Administration, the Federal Trade Commission, and in
vital positions at HEW and HUD. (40) Reorganization, then, could be
used not only to command the bureaucracy, but to infiltrate it at
upper and middle management positions.

Finally, the Nixon reorganization was fraught with political consequences which ultimately turned out to be fatal. When the

reorganization was presented to the nation in the early days of 1973, it was touted as an efficiency measure, an act to streamline the government. (41) The truth of the matter was that reorganization was accompanied by massive firings or reshufflings and was a way of solidifying a new order of White House politics. With power lodged in a handful of trusted overseers, reinforcing policies could be executed automatically, without a loss of precious presidential time. Reorganization was also the formalization of the "imperial presidency" and the finishing blocks put on the "Berlin Wall" of Haldeman, Ehrlichman, and Kissinger (add, Ash and Shultz) that was to enclose Nixon. Thus, policy was the necessity that brought Nixon to seal off the White House - Watergate and its cover-up were but political symptoms of an enclosed presidency which was driven by domestic and substantive ends.

   Whether or not Nixon accomplished much through policies of reciprocity, refusal, and reorganization depends upon one's expectations and one's partisanship. Policies of reciprocity and refusal had a mixed record and reorganization was scuttled after the Watergate revelations came crashing down on Ehrlichman and Haldeman (though Lynn and Kissinger maintained their power base and the Domestic Council survived as a White House institution after Nixon fell from office). Whatever the substantive results, Nixon was bound to put the best face on them and pronounce his urban policy to be a success. By the same fiat that Nixon declared at the start of his first term, that "we face an urban crisis," so did he announce to the nation in his second term, that "the hour of crisis has passed," as if proclamation would change reality:

   A few years ago we constantly heard that urban America was on the brink of collapse. It was one minute to midnight, we were told, and the bells of doom were beginning to toll. One history of America in the 1960s was even given the title "Coming Apart." Today, America is no longer coming apart. . . . City governments are no longer on the verge of financial catastrophe. Once again the business world is investing in our downtown areas. What does all this mean for community life in America? Simply this: The hour of crisis has passed. The ship of state is back on an even keel, and we can put behind us the fear of capsizing. (42)

The worst was yet to come.

THE FORD WHITE HOUSE AS A SEQUEL TO
THE REINFORCING PRESIDENCY

When Gerald Ford took over the presidency in August, 1974, he was
hailed in national exultation. Newspapers across the country glowed
with print that he was the "people's man" and would be an "open" and
"honest" leader. Congress greeted him with even greater enthusiasm
and broke into cheers when he told a joint session of the House and
Senate that "it's good to be back in the people's house." Members of
Congress from both political parties interrupted his speech 32 times
with applause, and after he finished, they warmly patted him on the
back as he strode down the aisle. The relief that Ford's personality
brought to Washington was such that he would have been cheered and
applauded had he read his speech out of a local telephone directory.

Personality and integrity are undeniably essential qualities of
leadership and ought not to be slighted. Policy, however, is the
ultimate scorecard, the tangible measure of how a president distrib-
utes and uses national wealth; and, from the perspective of public
policy, Ford was another installment on the Nixon White House - a
sort of Nixon without Nixon. Even before he was cast into the presidency by Nixon's breach of trust, Gerald Ford as a congressman
showed all the inclinations of a reinforcer. Congressman Ford's
voting record showed a strong aversion to federal intervention for
social welfare but scant laissez faireist attitudes against using the
federal arm for the benefit of big business. During the 1960s, Ford
opposed federal aid for education, voted against the creation of OEO,
Medicare, and most of Johnson's Great Society legislation, and during
the Eisenhower years, took a stand against federal aid for water pollution programs. When Ford was still in Congress and Nixon took to
the cutting axe in 1973, he voted to sustain nearly every presidential
veto on grounds of fiscal responsibility. As a legislator from the
auto dependent state of Michigan and as House Minority Leader, Ford
took the lead in opposing the diversion of highway trust fund monies
to support mass transit. Apparently, Ford saw some beneficial uses
for federal tax dollars and wanted to preserve them for more highways. He also found positive reasons to spend federal dollars on
agricultural price supports, he voted for federal loan guarantees to
the foundering Lockheed Aircraft Corporation, and he favored federal
funding for private enterprise to develop a supersonic transport plane
(SST). (43)

When Ford testified before a congressional committee for his
possible confirmation as vice president, he claimed to be a "moderate

on domestic issues. " After his confirmation, one congressman, Don
Edwards (D-Calif.) commented on Ford's ideology and his potential
as president saying, "They'll rue the day" that he was confirmed.
"He's more conservative than Nixon and his judgment's not as good. "

Once he became president, Ford continued along the reinforcing
trail and to a remarkable extent emulated the Nixon policies - even
down to compacting policies of reciprocity, refusal, and reorganization within the time frame of his 29 months of office. Ford modified
these policies somewhat; he substituted block grants for special
revenue sharing, used the idea of budget "recisions" and "deferrals"
instead of impoundments, and injected his personal informality into
the organization of the White House. Still, the basic contours of
White House policy remained unchanged after Nixon's departure.

Thirteen days after that departure, one of Ford's first policy
steps as President was to sign into legislation the Housing and Community Development Act of 1974, or HCDA. HCDA was the block
grant successor to Better Communities and had been negotiated with
the Congress mostly by the Nixon team. Though it was not all that
Nixon had been asking for, it was a step in that direction and one of
the more significant pieces of urban policy legislation since 1949. In
one fell swoop the act digested all of Lyndon Johnson's ploys in the
area of urban housing and community development. The word "digested" is used advisedly and with intentional ambiguity, because
HCDA neither obliterated the Johnson influence nor kept that influence
intact. Rather, HCDA absorbed past programs and pointed the way
for carrying them out through a reinforcing mode, using that mode to
apportion federal dollars and divert them from the inner cities. Like
most measures arrived at through congressional bargaining, HCDA
was a hybrid of meliorist and reinforcing approaches which retained
some continuity with the past - though it was not an act which Lyndon
Johnson would have promoted.

HCDA did away with the meliorist principle of targeting federal
money into the neediest communities, and rejected the compensatory
notion that Washington could best do that job by directly involving itself in local affairs. Along with this, the idea of categorical assistance, where needy communities could appeal directly to Washington
through subgovernments, was also abandoned in an effort to unravel
the tangle of intergovernmental relationships that had agglomerated
during the Johnson years. In their place, simplification was sought
and for this HCDA relied on the revenue sharing approach which
accented local discretion and official multipurpose governments.
Specifically, this meant that seven different programs, each with
its own complicated application and review procedures, would be

terminated and incorporated into HCDA for possible resurrection by
the localities themselves. The seven program casualties were similar to the targets which were supposed to be hit by Better Communities, namely: model cities, urban renewal, grants for open space,
programs for housing rehabilitation, and assistance for community
facilities, water, and sewers. Under HCDA, local multipurpose
governments could apply for a lump sum award from Washington and,
if a local government elected to start up or continue any or all of
these programs, they were free to do so - if not, their extinction
would be a matter of phase out time.

Allowing local governments the freedom to choose whether and
how to spend federal money can be a deceptive kind of freedom.
Typically, lower income minorities within localities have less influence and power than their more affluent neighbors; their rates of
political participation and organizational membership tend to be lower; and when they do attempt to partake in local decisions, they are
frequently precluded by discriminatory norms and political blockages.
(44) Thus, the seemingly absolute question of freedom of local choice
is, in reality, a relative question of which particular group within a
locality is strong enough to exercise that choice, and whether federal
assistance will be given to the needy or to those powerful enough to
articulate their need.

This was precisely the kind of question which bothered meliorists
in the Johnson White House and which prompted Johnson to take a
strong interventionist hand through elaborate procedures and direct
liaison with subgovernments, which handled problems peculiar to
inner city ghettoes. Less than a decade later, the Ford White House
was undoing this by placing the choices back on official powerholders
and established multipurpose institutions.

The upshot of this "fewer federal strings" approach within localities was a noticeable shift of federal assistance away from the most
poverty-ridden populations. Early studies conducted on the first year
or two of HCDA's implementation show that, when local officials were
given wider discretion to identify their own needs, they frequently
mixed political pressure into policy options. As one local development official put it, "you can't divorce politics from that much
money... we must remember the needs of the people who vote... because they hold us accountable.... Poor people don't vote. " (45)

Statistics which have just begun to appear on the Act's implementation bear out, with some modification, these observations.
One study surveyed 86 entitlement cities and found that only 12 percent
of their community development funds were headed for low income census tracts where median incomes were less than half of the cities' median

earnings. According to this study, the bulk of the funding (almost 40 percent) was headed for households in the "moderate" income range. Furthermore, when money was spent on low income communities, nearly half of it was used for land clearance and the continuation of urban renewal commitments made prior to HCDA. Urban renewal and land clearance have hardly been omens of progress for the poor, often resulting in their removal from existing communities and hardship relocations to other parts of the city.

Expenditures for the continuance of urban renewal portend a pattern within HCDA to move away from the "soft service" approach (education, health) of model cities to one of providing more "hardware" (land clearance, flood control) for localities. Under approved first year applications, some 42 percent of the total funding went for "clearance related" activities, while only 12 percent was used to sustain the "soft services" of model cities. (46) Clearly, in the battle between the policy offsprings of the last 30 years, model cities is the stepchild, while commercially oriented renewal programs are becoming favorite sons of HCDA. (47)

Another blow to the formal theme of model cities has been a decided thinning out of funds across more urban neighborhoods and a rejection of any idea that funds ought to be concentrated in communities with the greatest ruination. To the contrary, something like a triage philosophy (48) has been adopted, where salvageable neighborhoods are divided from utterly devastated areas and funds are applied to communities which, in the judgment of local officials, are capable of surviving, leaving the most destitute to linger through an inexorable death. While not explicitly mentioning triage, HUD is aware of its role at the local level, and in its study of 151 sample cities observes that "Recipients are placing greater emphasis on activities in neighborhoods beginning to decline.... Those neighborhoods accelerating into major decline and nonviable, heavily abandoned neighborhoods receive less emphasis." (49) Though triage or a modified triage seeped into local implementation practices during the Ford administration, some neighborhoods in the largest central cities managed to fend it off. Significantly, poverty neighborhoods which had the greatest success in winning a large chunk of HCDA funds were politically active during the 1960s and had organizational experience with model cities programs. Once having begun and thrived, these neighborhoods are better able to function politically, under the pressure group sensitivity of a block grant.

From the perspective of national trends looking toward 1980, HCDA took a giant step toward fulfilling the reinforcing objectives of its Better Communities forerunner. Here the strategy of spreading

and diverting urban assistance was more conspicuous. Under the
compromise worked out between the Nixon/Ford White House and
Congress, a somewhat larger amount of funding would find its way to
a much greater number of urban jurisdictions. These run a gamut
from small cities with populations exceeding 50,000 to urban counties
which are frequently suburbs lying at the outskirts of some central
cities, to tiny urban communities which have populations of less than
50,000. All in all, HUD funded over 3,500 of these urban multipurpose governments in the first year of HCDA's operation, more than
twice the number under three years of categorical grants. Through
1977, that number proliferated to over 7,500 localities which qualified
as urban trouble spots.

    In its unamended 1974 version, HCDA also protected central
cities for a time with a "hold harmless" clause, so that central cities
could receive no less than a stipulated average amount of what they
obtained under the older categorical grants. After 1980, these protections were supposed to cease and the familiar pattern of increased
aid for prosperous cities and decreased aid for most exterior cities
would have begun to shape the reinforcing tide. Using the "hold harmless" averages as a yardstick for determining relative shares or
urban aid, declining central cities would drop from 71.8 percent of
federal dollars down to 42.2 percent by 1980, with the newer cities
of the sun belt and the suburbs ultimately receiving the largest slice
of the federal pie. (50) Translated into raw minus and plus percentages of community development aid, this means that by 1980 relative
loser cities would include Baltimore (-44 percent), Detroit (-22 percent), Philadelphia (-44 percent), and Boston (-63 percent). The
gainer cities were already at the peak of Moody's listings and high
among private investors. They include Dallas (+549 percent),
Houston (+69 percent), Phoenix (+726 percent), Fort Lauderdale
(+436 percent), and San Diego (+12 percent). Applying a more systematic listing to this data, if we were to plot out 10 exterior cities
and 10 prosperous cities, precisely seven exterior cities lose money
while six prosperous cities gain federal dollars (see table 5.2).
Thus, under HCDA the proportion of losers and gainers between exterior and prosperous cities would not be very different from that
under Nixon's earlier proposal for Better Communities. By clear
standards, the Ford administration was following the lessons of
Better Communities and, by demonstrating a willingness to compromise, was getting some of its urban proposals enacted. Ford
helped give a new ring to urban policy and a predictive reality to a
rather dismal Biblical prophecy: "For whosoever hath, to him shall
be given and he shall have more abundance; but whosoever hath not,
from him shall be taken away even that which he hath!"

Table 5. 2.   The Losers and Gainers after
Hold Harmless (51)

Exterior City	Prosperous City
Cleveland (-11%)	Omaha (+637%)
Baltimore (-44%)	Dallas (+549%)
Chicago (+45%)	Houston (+70%)
St. Louis (-3%)	Phoenix (727%)
New York (+50%)	Norfolk (-67%)
Detroit (-22%)	San Diego (+13%)
Philadelphia (-45%)	Seattle (-42%)
Boston (-64%)	Ft. Lauderdale (+436%)
New Orleans (+13%)	Greensboro (0%)
San Francisco (-56%)	Salt Lake City (-30%)

Note: The percentages for all of the above cities are rounded.
For the prosperous cities, Ft. Lauderdale, Greensboro, and Salt
Lake City have been substituted for El Paso, Tampa, and Long Beach
which were used earlier in table 5. 1.

The Ford Transition: From Special Revenue
Sharing and Impoundments to Block Grants and Vetoes

HCDA was an initiation rite for Gerald Ford, a first shovel of earth
toward building an urban policy according to Nixon's specifications of
federal disengagement and a stronger reliance on privatism. The
major steps toward that policy occurred as President Ford submitted
his State of the Union and Budget Messages to Congress in 1976.
Those documents ensconced the philosophy and policy of the Ford
White House by calling for lowered spending on domestic programs
for education, manpower, and social services; and, at the same
time, asked that stimulants be applied to the corporate sector through
tax shifts and increased spending on military hardware. (52)
    For the cities, the not so novel news was that the President was
asking for the abolition of almost 60 different categorical grants in
education, health, social services (day care, aid for the disabled and
elderly, etc.), and child nutrition and replacing them with four block
grants to be administered by the individual states. Consolidation and
cutting federal string was not the only aim of the block grant proposals
for when all the accounting was done, Ford's suggestions contained

a total only about $2 billion less than the categorical grants had provided. In education, the reduction amounted to $500 million less than Congress had provided under previous programs, and Ford asked that a major portion of the remaining funds be turned over to the states for internal distribution. In health, there was a $600 million reduction and a call that the federal government turn over to the states some $10 billion to replace separate spending categories for Medicaid, health planning, community services, and mental health centers. Much the same patterns were suggested for the utilization of block grants in social services and child nutrition, although the White House bandied about the idea that upon receiving its block grant each state should be required to publicize a plan on how federal funds were going to be distributed, before the governors made final selections. Most of the block grant proposals were devoid of outright requirements that states or local governments match the federal dollar contributions, though built into the formula for appropriating block monies there was a proviso for "maintenance of effort" by the states. In spite of this provision, feelings ran high in Congress that, with the exception of a handful of big states, the real gainers would be those states in the south and the southwest. (53)

Aside from the obvious effort to continue the strategy of disengagement, a clue to Ford's motivations could be found by comparing the context of budget reductions with Ford's policy on individual and corporate taxation. The White House press office bannered the promise that if the President's budget were passed by Congress there would be a $10 billion tax cut. Who was to enjoy the benefits of tax relief was another question. Ford had placed priority on a decrease of one or two percent in corporate taxes, coupled with sizable depreciation write-offs and investment credits for businessmen. There were also tax reductions for individuals, but for those monies which would not be going to the federal government or to its social programs, Ford proposed an inducement for individuals who invested in corporate common stock. That inducement consisted of an additional tax cut which allowed certain income earners to invest in common stocks, with the income so invested to be non-taxable.

Quite naturally, these proposals had the consequence of reducing federal revenues and creating the need to generate alternative sources of income - at least to make up the gaps not bridged by social program cuts. Ford turned to the wage earner by proposing increases in social security taxes and unemployment insurance payments. What gaps remained after exactions were made on these wages were bridged by putting the squeeze on recipients of medicare, food stamps, and an assortment of retired federal workers.

Like the pieces of a jigsaw puzzle being slowly assembled,
Ford's entire domestic policy began to fall into place, and so, too,
did a rather dire picture of his urban policy. Block grants were a
compromising substitute for special revenue sharing, much as HCDA
filled many of the objectives of Better Communities. Like the Nixon
strategy, there was a recognition by Ford that once federal money
had been pledged and given, it could not be retracted; losses could be
cut by restricting the federal commitment and unloading major portions of it on the states. This approach to the cities was rooted in a
jaded belief amongst Ford's closest aides that most big cities were
irretrievably on the road to destruction, if not already there. What
else could they do? As one aide mockingly put it, "What do you want
us to do, save the cities? Do you really believe we should go in there
and run them? Why, that would be a political joke with the biggest
laughs made on us by the Democrats. " (54)

Ford's budget and tax policies were a way of transferring the
public's dollars from a government and social program kitty to a
private and corporate one. Where meliorist presidents wanted to
raise public funds and apply more of them to sore spots in society
through the workings of privatism, reinforcers took the converse
position by encouraging the intrinsic expansion of privatism to condition the flow of public dollars. In the former case, we have an
attempt to "governmentalize" privatism, while the latter illustrates
an effort to "privatize" the government. In neither case did public
or private power step aside to make way for the other and, depending
on who happened to be president, domestic and urban policy tilted in
on direction or the other. But always, each sector operated within
safe boundaries of mutual tolerance and in an uneasy partnership with
the other.

To be sure, reinforcing presidents like Ford had a deeper respect for the capacities of privatism and a stronger skepticism about
what Washington could do, even if it wanted to act to change the plight
of cities. One top Ford adviser likened this task to "turning a government spigot on into the ocean. It just won't make a difference, " he
added, "you can't overwhelm market forces with just a little stream
from Washington. " (55) Ford burrowed through his political life and
made it to the White House by adhering to that principle, and, as
President, he was determined that an opposition Congress would not
violate it. While he may have been handcuffed in what he himself
could do to reinforce privatism, he could wield his veto against irresponsible meliorists who presumed they could overwhelm it - and
this he did more than 60 times in just over two years. (56) Between
Nixon's and Ford's executive axe, and the attempt to withdraw

Washington's urban commitment, the psychological optimism upon
which cities build their future began to darken and a storm of fiscal
crises hit cities throughout the nation.

The Reinforcing White House and the Fiscal Crisis:
New York Was and Is Not Alone

In December 1974, some of the most powerful financiers in America
went to Gracie Mansion, the residence of New York City's mayor,
who at the time was Abe Beame, to tell him they were no longer eager
to invest in the city's notes and bonds. New York had been running
up tremendous expenses with its operating budget soaring by over 300
percent over the previous ten years and its short-term debt multiply-
ing by over 500 percent in the last five years. By virtue of these
costs, the city was sponging up an investment market that was becoming arid, and the financiers were worried about the prospects of
selling additional securities. Their apprehension was aggravated by
what they charged was inefficiency and profligacy by the city, most
particularly by the politicians who surrounded "hizzoner" Beame.
Moreover, investors no longer needed tax-free municipal bonds when
they could make lucrative and less risky investments elsewhere.

Springing this upon a mayor with the second largest budget in the
nation, growing in billion dollar multiples, made a worrisome situation a calamitous one, once the word echoed through the financial
caverns of the investment world. Many cities need money in advance
in order to float their payrolls and meet daily expenses. Their usual
practice is to borrow from private sources in anticipation of funds
which are due at a future date, and later pay back the borrowed principal plus a handsome interest dividend. As political and economic
pressures mounted in New York, the mayor resorted to bookkeeping
contortions to keep the city vital and borrowed against "semi" or,
in fact, non existent funds. This entailed juggling revenue anticipations so that next year's income was counted as the current year's
income, and juggling expenses so that the current year's expenses
were "rolled over" to the next year. Anything that jeopardized the
city's money supply would also suffocate its very life, not to mention
Beame's administration; he needed to keep all arteries of support
flowing.

Beame knew what he was doing, but also realized the world's
largest bankers were not naive. They had been more than glad to
buy New York's securities so long as they could make a large profit
by easily reselling the merchandise at sizable commissions. Now

that the purse strings were tightening among buyers, he was incensed at what he regarded as precipitous panic mongering by the bankers. Unable to change their minds, he first denied the charges that his city was in fiscal straits and countered that it was a technical difficulty of cash flow - meaning that the funds for paying off past loans were imminent and all that needed to be done was for the city to continue borrowing on the securities market. When facts and the city's own comptroller contradicted this wishful thinking, Beame turned on the tap of populist, anti-Wall Street feeling, and accused the largest banks of "poisoning our wells" with their dismal talk. He appealed to the public and to medium-sized investors, telling them that New York had been exposed to a "corrosive negativism" that was unjustly tarnishing the credit rating of the city. When all this failed to bring forth the necessary cash for New York, Beame turned to the President of the United States.

In May of 1975, the Mayor of New York City, accompanied by the Empire State's Governor, Hugh Carey, went to the White House to plead for help in meeting $1.5 billion of debt obligations which were coming due within the next month and a half. Ford conceded that he was deeply impressed by the city's need for cash, but rejected any kind of federal help, even if the plea was only for temporary loan guarantees. To provide any kind of federal backing for the city, Ford said "would merely postpone, for that period, coming to grips with the problem." The President and his advisers were of a mind that New York City's plight was not, and ought not to be, a matter for the federal government, and that the city should be facing up to its self created predicament by curtailing its "less essential services." Lending an "amen" to the President's rebuke was his Secretary of the Treasury, William Simon, who feared a Pandora's box of other distressed cities prying at the federal vaults for money as their overdue debts matured. "Where does this stop?" asked one official, "We'd have Newark and Detroit and 10 or 12 other cities lined up here if we do this for New York." (57)

In a way, the White House had a fuller grasp of the potential of the urban fiscal crisis than did the media, whose accounts were largely confined to a profligate mayor with a reputation for fiscal chicanery crossing swords with a callous and sometimes bumbling president. For the press, it was New York as an outcast city dueling with an anti-urban Republican White House. The White House knew, despite political disclaimers, that the urban crisis had not ended and that its fiscal dimensions were just beginning to show. As early as January 1975, a delegation from the U.S. Conference of Mayors told a Senate committee that many, if not most, of the major cities would

soon be confronting deficits between the level of services they needed
to provide and what they could afford to pay. They reasoned that if
something were not done to reverse Nixon/Ford policies, these cities
would be heading toward a drastic economic slide. Within two months,
survey data from 67 cities confirmed the prognosis, and revealed that
a major number of them were planning to hold off on capital improvements, lay off municipal employees, raise taxes while simultaneously
reducing public services, and, even then, more than two-thirds were
anticipating budget deficits. (58)

In some instances, at least, the reality for individual cities was
harsher than aggregate data conveyed. Newark, New Jersey was already at the point where New York City dreaded being. Heavy demands were placed on it by poor persons filling the void left by an
exiting middle class; its tax base was eroding as its industry fled;
and it simply was not able to pay its bills or continue functioning as a
whole city. The only recourse left to its mayor, Kenneth Gibson,
was to retract on the city's obligations, and in January of 1975, well
before New York publicly acknowledged its crisis, Gibson announced
substantial layoffs of public employees in an effort to reduce a $35
million deficit. A short time later, Gibson announced that the public
schools would be cut by 20 percent with administrators, teachers,
and workers dismissed.

Cleveland followed the Newark example and was facing a $16
million deficit. To meet its crisis, the mayor had laid off approximately 1100 city workers, reduced garbage collection, and closed
four fire stations. As a proportion of its budget, Cleveland's annual
debt repayment to its private lenders exceeded New York's and consisted of a whopping 17.9 percent - a figure municipal investment
analysts said, "warrants concern." The apprehensions materialized
in late 1978 and early 1979 when Cleveland defaulted on outstanding
bank notes. The air of default lingered over Cleveland throughout
this period. It is important to recognize that though cities like
Cleveland may temporarily balance their books, the structural factors
of urban decline persist.

Other cities in similar financial crises during the early months
of 1975 were Philadelphia, Buffalo, Boston, and St. Louis - all with
the telltale signs of budget deficits, declining tax bases, and shrinking vital services. Detroit was, perhaps, the most severely affected,
and nearly one-quarter of that city's employees had to be laid off in
order to make up for a $65 to 85 million budget deficit. Its out-
spoken mayor, Coleman Young, bridled at the interest charges of
9.9 percent being levied on his city's tax-free bonds and labeled
them "extortion." Allying himself with Beame, Young took a swat

at the Ford White House and declared that "New York's problems are symptomatic of a national urban crisis that has been overlooked in Washington." (59)

Meanwhile, having returned to New York City empty handed, Beame reluctantly began to make cuts and layoffs of his own. Over an eight month interim - beginning with the time he was confronted by the city's private financiers in December, 1974 up to September, 1975 - the mayor had been forced to reduce the city's payroll by over 31,000 jobs, or over 10 percent of the municipal labor force. This included 4,000 policemen, more than 3,500 firemen and sanitation workers, and 7,000 educators. In addition, transit fares were hiked up, hospitals and fire stations shut down, and preparations made for imposing tuition at the once-free City University. Sundry other closings were made in the city's public housing repair services, in its libraries and museums, and in child care centers.

The biggest blow to the city and to the mayor's political stature was in the forced surrender of New York's self governance. In exchange for financial help given by the state, Beame was humiliated into firing key members of his administration and a sizable part of the city's right to self governance was abrogated by nonelected panels. A Municipal Assistance Corporation (dubbed Big MAC) was given the chore of marketing the city's securities and virtually given a lien on certain taxes to ensure the city's repayment. An Emergency Financial Control Board (EFCB) functioned as an overseer of all revenues coming into or out of the city, and was given the prerogative of approving or disapproving labor agreements and other major transactions. Each of these panels was heavily weighted with members from business or investment circles, and no popular representation could be found on them from labor, consumers, or the neighborhoods. So far as New York was concerned, by September 1975, private finance had removed its velvet gloves and had iron fisted the city into handing over some of its tax collections and relinquishing its right to make its own decisions.

With all of this, New York still could not raise enough money to meet its short- and long-term debts. By October, Beame was back in Washington, this time lobbying at both the White House and Capitol Hill for some $5 to 9 billion in loan guarantees. Alongside of Beame and testifying before a congressional committee which was considering the loan guarantees was a golden trinity of New York Bankers - David Rockefeller of Chase Manhattan, Walter Wriston of First National City, and Elmore Patterson of Morgan Guaranty Trust - who warned of national and possible worldwide reverberations should New York default on its loan repayments. The bankers felt that the

"disruptive effects of default" were "potentially large. " How large
those effects might be, they cautioned, "is a matter of judgment. "
(60)

   In the White House, the view was substantially different. William
Simon was claiming that there was a limited number of holders of
New York securities and that a default by the city would not cause
financial havoc but could be contained. Simon was backed up by
Arthur Burns, a former adviser to Presidents Eisenhower and Nixon.
As head of the Federal Reserve, Burns was at a command post of the
money supply to the nation, and by opening or shutting its valves he
could let it flow down certain channels or away from others. Burns'
plan to contain the city's fiscal crisis was to make ready credit available to banks caught in a "liquidity squeeze" by "opening up the federal
discount window. " This meant that in the event that New York could
not pay back its loans, leaving banks with cash shortages, they could
take all eligible paper obligations (notes, drafts, securities, and
financial instruments) and exchange them for cash from the federal
government at the prevailing discount rate. In short, Burns was
willing to lend taxpayers' money to private banks in order to insulate
them from New York City's problems, but not support the idea of
allowing the city to get the money itself.

   The Burns plan was a pinpointed, albeit an imperfect and risky,
solution to handling the "domino consequences" that a New York default could bring on the economy. Over the years, the city had in-
conspicuously sold billions of dollars of notes to bankers and underwriters, who, in turn, resold them to smaller investors, fanning
these securities throughout the nation and the world. Such was the
magnitude of fanning out New York City's monetary promises that it
was something of a mystery about who actually possessed all of them.
Default or nonpayment would block cash which noteholders were expecting, causing a shrinkage of investment dollars, worsening the
recession which was already hurting the economy, and possibly
precipitating a financial panic which some feared would lead to a
massive depression. Like a row of dominoes, the fall of New York
would make its weight felt on the banks, which could collapse rows
of industrial enterprises. Just where the most likely rows were or
how hard they would fall was not known, so that Burns was working
in the dead of night with only a few rays of light to guide him.

   Nonetheless, the Ford administration had a plan for curbing the
ramifications of default. On October 29 Ford told a news conference
that he would veto any loan guarantees passed by the Congress, and
that he would rather have New York default and go bankrupt than
provide it with a federal "bailout. " The headline in the newspaper

with the largest circulation in the country was bluntly memorable -
"FORD TO CITY: DROP DEAD. " Below that was a little-noticed
subheadline which, in the same staccato form, said: "Stocks Skid,
Dow (Jones) Down 12 (points). " (61)

During the news conference, Ford accused "a few desperate New
York officials and bankers" of "stampeding" the American people and
Congress into "panicky support of blatantly bad policy. " The President's alternative to this bad policy was that the city, should it have
the need, could file a petition of bankruptcy with the federal courts
and place itself in receivership. (62) Bankruptcy and the consequent
delivery of the city's existing assets for distribution and division between its private creditors was Ford's answer to New York City.

When Ford was asked by a reporter what the difference was between the federal government's rescue of the Lockheed Aircraft
Corporation with public loans and its refusal to bail out New York
City, the President replied that, since Lockheed held a large number
of contracts with the Defense Department, "a very substantial portion
of the revenue that comes to the company" comes from the federal
government anyway. (63) This difference, claimed Ford, gave Washington a "capability of maintaining control precisely without other
public officials being involved. " One might have asked Ford why,
since the federal government was supporting Lockheed with contracts,
it was also necessary to feed the corporation still more public dollars after it had shown itself to be inefficient and corrupt? (64) Or
why it was more preferable to deal with corporate officials than
public officeholders. Were New York City's residents any less
worthy than Lockheed stockholders? Indeed, the case could have
been made that New York was more deserving because it was not
nearly as dependent upon Washington as was Lockheed, 75 percent of
whose revenue was obtained from the Defense Department. But the
President was not listening, and his mind had been made up by the
precedent of Washington "bailing out" other private corporations such
as the Penn Central Railroad and the Franklin National Bank.

What did change Ford's mind eventually was the mounting evidence that default might not be contained to just New York City. A
study by the Federal Deposit Insurance Corporation, which insures
private bank deposits, revealed that should a default occur there
would be "serious consequences" for 271 banks spread throughout
34 states of the Union. These banks held New York securities equal
to at least 20 percent of their net worth. Another 56 banks in 18
states held securities equal to 50 percent of their net worth and were
even more vulnerable to a New York collapse. (65)

Up until November 1975, it was hoped that these institutions could be protected by the Burns plan, but later studies indicated that these few hundred banks were only a tip of the fiscal iceberg. Two-thirds of New York's securities, or some $4.9 billion were held by a multitude of large and small investors - insurance companies, annuity funds, widows, and retirees. According to these last minute surveys, as many as 160,000 investors could be left with nonusable paper if New York failed to pay its debts. This did not include $3 billion of securities held by private commercial banks. Foreign banks were even more gravely concerned about the possible reverberations of a New York default, and one survey indicated that an overwhelming majority of international investors felt that a default would have "a major negative impact on international financial markets." (66) By this time, too, Treasury Secretary Simon was talking more openly about the possibility of a psychological ripple effect accompanying a default, and Arthur Burns, while holding to his position, was saying that if Congress was planning to help the city it ought to do it quickly.

In the end, under this consistent pressure, Ford relented and agreed to a $2.3 billion loan to New York City, plus interest, to terminate in 1978. The terms were barely sufficient to avert a local crisis which could have mushroomed to a national one. New York still had a massive debt accumulation and borrowing needs which, by 1980, would total over $8 billion. In an age of billion dollar governments, $8 billion is easy enough to roll off one's tongue, but by any standards, it is a huge amount of money. The conditions of the loan, the nature of White House assistance, and the fiscal health of the city prompted one sympathetic congressman to predict that the fiscal "problems will come back to haunt us" - and they may very well. (67)

New York City is not alone and while its bookkeeping practices may have been a fiscal novelty, the dynamics of its decline were not unusual. Within two years of Jimmy Carter's administration, the federal government had to extend loan guarantees to the city through 1982. Loans and loan guarantees may help a city bridge temporary gaps between revenues and expenses, but they do not rebuild slums nor do they create jobs.

6 Rowing with Muffled Oars: Making Urban Policy on Capitol Hill

Scene: Patricia Roberts Harris appearing before the Senate Committee on Banking, Housing and Urban Affairs to testify on her nomination as Secretary of Housing and Urban Development.

THE CHAIRMAN (Senator William Proxmire, Democrat from Wisconsin): ...Now let me ask you about this. Among your corporate director-ships you list Chase Manhattan Bank. The Chase Manhattan Bank is the third largest bank in the country. It's located in the heart of our largest urban area, New York City. The committee has been very concerned about the impact of bank lending practices on cities, on housing investments in low and moderate income neighborhoods, and business investment in the inner-city, and so forth. As the director, have you taken any steps to make Chase Manhattan more responsive in its lending policies to the needs of urban areas, parti-cularly New York City residents?

MRS. HARRIS: ...I would say this is among the concerns that I have had and it's one of the things we have talked about. We have a divi-sion of the bank that is a lender to real estate and that, if my memory serves me right, is one of the areas of best performance.

THE CHAIRMAN: That's right. The difficulty is... Chase has not done well. It's made investments in condominiums in Florida and else-where. It's made very little investment in the northeastern section of the country and practically none in New York City; Chase Manhat-tan itself has only about 2 percent of its assets in mortgages com-pared to smaller banks which have 30, 40 and 50 percent typically. It seems to me with that colossal conglomeration of capital and with a very good record in mortgages of being sound investments, Chase has followed a bad social - bad economic as well as social policy.

Chase should have found a way to have had a better record of making mortgage loans, housing loans in New York City.

MRS. HARRIS: Well, I'm not prepared to concede, Senator, that its record, given the nature of this bank which is a lender to really large businesses, international and national businesses... is a bad one...

THE CHAIRMAN: ...I see you're also a director of IBM and Scott Paper. Have you taken any steps to encourage either of these companies to be more responsive to urban problems.

MRS. HARRIS: As a matter of fact, IBM has been one of the leaders in dealing with the problems of the inner city. I'm not terribly familiar with Bedford Stuyvesant activity by the corporation, but it has been there. IBM, through its contributing process, has made contributions to institutions which had a deep concern with urban development. It is a socially responsible corporation.

THE CHAIRMAN: I realize it is. It's a fine corporation. Of course, it's a very successful corporation. My question, however, related to whether or not they had followed a policy of trying to provide jobs in the inner cities where jobs are so urgently needed. With that enormous track record of success in business and so forth, they might have been able to pioneer and be very helpful.

MRS. HARRIS: Yes. I think they have [been helpful] with their employment policy [and] with respect to minorities.

THE CHAIRMAN: Let me ask you about the Community Development Act. I don't share the views some other members of the committee have expressed that it's been a success. I think it's been very bad. I'm glad to hear you say you want to improve it. You apparently recognize it can be improved.... In 1975 only 51 percent of the funds granted to cities were spent in low and moderate income areas, barely half. In 1976, that slipped to 44 percent, less than one-half. In both 1975 and 1976, more was spent in the highest income city areas than the lowest income areas. This is a massive urban problem, a multibillion dollar program and it seems to me it's outrageous that this isn't concentrated in the areas of obviously the greater social need; that is, where you have low and moderate income...

MRS. HARRIS: As I said in my statement, Senator, it seems to me the Department of Housing and Urban Development has a responsibility for making certain that the standards set in the legislation are adhered to by local communities...I think there has been a failure on the part of the agency (HUD) to implement the policy of Congress.

THE CHAIRMAN: That's good. You understand the problem because the mayors and councilmen, of course, are susceptible to pressures from the most articulate and powerful people in the community and those people don't live in the low and moderate-income areas; they live in the upper-income areas. (1)

THE FLATTENED PYRAMID OF CONGRESS
AND ITS CENTRIFUGAL PULLS

The Changing Shape of the Congressional Pyramid
Through the 1970s

Congress, in its hearings, quite rightfully points accusatory fingers
at the failings of American society, but rarely ever includes itself as
a contributor to those failings. Investigations are held by our national
legislature to unearth the culprits in the banks, in the bureaucracy, and
elsewhere. Aside from castigating its members for personal misconduct, Congress rarely takes aim at its own structural defects and at
legislative practices which yield hazardous results. When things fall
apart, it is assumed that the will of Congress was thwarted by the permanent government of bureaucrats, and that urban failings were abetted
by "special interests" who rode herd over local public officials. This
observation can be gleaned from the interchange, noted above, between
Chairman Proxmire and Mrs. Harris, and the Senator was no doubt
correct in his assertions. (2) Proxmire, however, neglected to mention that it is his Senate committee which is responsible for legislation
which regulates banks and which also helped design the community development provision, of which he was so critical.

The difficulties in making urban policy touch all parts of public
and private sectors ; they are more than personality-deep and seep to
the institutional marrow of our government. This is particularly true
of Congress and the enduring qualities which condition its behavior.
It is an institution comprised of two houses and 535 members who
draw their status and power from singular constituencies, in the respective states of senators and the districts of congressmen. More
than this, 535 people trying to legislate for the nation can be unwieldly
unless they are organized hierarchically. Invariably, some legislators
have been more equal than others and this has been and will continue to
be the case in both the House and the Senate.

In the past, the congressional pyramid was steeper and only a few
men sat on or near its summit. Both the House and the Senate experienced a period of centralized leadership during the latter part of the
nineteenth century and early years of the twentieth. House Speaker
Joe Cannon ruled with an iron grip until he was faced with a revolt by
his colleagues between 1909-11. In the Senate, William Allison of
Iowa and Nelson Aldrich of Rhode Island held the majority Republican
Party in their grasp during the 1890s, and lesser senators beseeched
them for political favors.

Over a time the pyramid of congressional power became less steep
and more of its members shared in the prerequisites of the institution.

Presidents Kennedy and Johnson faced congresses which were said to be
decentralized, meaning that power had spread to the committees, their
chairmen, and their most senior members. (3) This was a broad pyramid of multiple elites (committee chairman) ruling over islands of
functional autonomy (committees) which were capable of making or destroying policy within areas of their jurisdiction. The House Committee
on Ways and Means reserved substantial autonomy for itself on taxation
and health care for the elderly, the Committee on Agriculture did the
same for itself on supports for cotton and tobacco, while Armed Services built exclusive bridges between itself and the Pentagon on which
outsiders and junior legislators dared not tread.

As the 1970s wear on the political pyramid of Congress has continued to flatten, especially in the House, and power has spread to additional clusters of new legislators. One major reason for this has
been an influx of new congressmen brought to office on successive
surges of antiwar (and antiestablishment) feeling and post-Watergate
reformism. Realizing that the path to congressional power lay in the
manipulation of organizational rules, these newly arrived congressmen
set about changing those rules and showed their prowess by deposing
some of their elders.

The movement to change organizational rules in both the House and
Senate began roughly in 1970 and carried on for the next five years. It
began innocently enough with procedural modifications to record teller
votes on the House floor and was extended to a requirement that roll
call votes be taken in closed committee sessions and made available to
the public. The move to open up these closed proceedings to public
scrutiny proved infectious, and by 1975, the House and Senate had
adopted "sunshine laws" which made most committee hearings and
"mark up" sessions available for attendance by the public and the press.

Public exposure, however, was but a means toward the end of
spreading power and by the mid-1970s, younger Democrats had bored
openings into the rule of congressional elders. Committee assignments
were still to be made by House leaders, but they agreed to act in conjunction with other congressional delegations from geographical regions
or minority groupings (blacks, women, junior legislators). In addition,
committee members had recourse against abusive chairmen through the
adoption of a "subcommittee bill of rights" which guaranteed Democrats
adequate starring resources to carry out their duties as well as the
power to vote on the composition of subcommittees.

Having loosened the grip of senior authority, House Democrats
went on to modify the order of ultimate sanctions and, in 1975, decided
to make all nominees for committee chairmanships subject to a secret
ballot vote by the party caucus. A short time later, those sanctions
were applied and three powerful chairmen - of the Armed Services,

Agriculture, and Banking committees - were removed from their positions. There was little doubt of the role played by the younger membership which, led by the Class of 1974, had interviewed all nominees. The Senate also enacted measures to check the power of committee chairmen which, though more modest, served the needs of its smaller membership. (4)

What the reforms of 1970-75 accomplished was not to abolish the shape of the congressional pyramid, but to infuse it with new members and bulge it at its upper middle rungs. Instead of rule by an older, restricted, political sect, a new and larger group of influentials have risen through the congressional pyramid and taken over the committees (and subcommittees) which are the real workshops of Congress. Moreover, the reforms functioned as a check on arbitrary rule, but they did not do away with the routine exercise of power by committee chairmen or leading committee members. For some, the rise to influential seats has been rapid, and they are already on a whispering relationship with a new generation of Majority Leaders and Whips in both Houses who also tend to be younger than their predecessors. (5)

Politics was not the only pressure which prompted a further decentralization of Congress. The increasingly complex and technical content of legislative policy itself has created the need for a sharper division of labor and this will continue. No longer is it as easy for a handful of leaders to master the nuances of housing or taxation. Because of this, party leaders are not likely to be able to control their more specialized brethren. Knowledge is more than power, it furnishes the freedom to obfuscate and spread the uses for which policy can be made. This, as we shall see in later sections, is a major consequence of flattening out the congressional pyramid. The transfer of power to new pockets and the technocratization of policy has made Congress permeable to outside interests in special kinds of ways. The more elaborate a piece of legislation, the more numerous are the ways it can be broken down and subsequently spread out among multiple groups. This is especially true when its comprehensibility is limited to fewer legislators and its divisibility is shared by multiple partitions of labor. Negotiated bargaining and collaboration have for a long time been a trademark of Congress, (6) yet by now these traits have crystallized around selective groups whose deliberations are defined by meliorist and reinforcing alternatives to policy. Little or nothing on urban policy has been written outside this realm of expertise or outside of the bounds set by the meliorist and reinforcing debate. To understand how the flattened pyramid of Congress works to accommodate this process and shape the exterior city, we will examine these other participants.

Other Participants in Congressional Policymaking

Congress does not make policy in isolation. There is, instead, a continuum of organizations which join in making urban policy, and these
range from the representation of top public officials (the President,
governors, mayors) to collective organizations of public officials (U.S.
Conference of Mayors, National Association of Counties, National
Governors' Conference) and to private organizations (Chambers of
Commerce, National Association of Home Builders, American Truck-
ing Association). To say that Congress has been made more permeable
to outside influence by the changes of the 1970s, by no means implies
that every interest or organization has an equal seat at the legislative
table. How influential these seats may be is conditioned by three factors: 1) the intimacy and nature of the working relationship that key
legislators have with a particular organization; 2) the power of a given
organization to facilitate, obstruct, or veto a legislative policy; and
3) policy precedents or a cognition by legislators of how policy is supposed to function according to a ready-made governmental conduit with
privatism.

Organizational representation by other governments or branches
of government inside the legislature is commonplace. Though the Constitution decrees a separation of powers between the three branches of
national government and a federalist sharing of concurrent powers between the states and Washington, these prescriptions, for the most
part, disappear under mundane exigencies when policy is actually negotiated out. Separation of powers and concurrent federalism are, in
practical terms, replaced by a potpourri of bargaining, second guessing,
and collaboration among all the different parties. In reality, constitutional prescriptions only furnish cues about a person's role in the process and define his representative status, but they do not bar the White
House, the states, nor the cities from acting together, within a common
process, on a piece of legislation.

The White House's working relationship with Congress in making
urban policy is ever present but nonetheless variable. During the
halcyon days of Lyndon Johnson's Great Society legislation, the relationship between the President and Congress was extremely close.
Johnson quite literally injected himself into the legislature in the manner, as Bagehot described the British Cabinet, of "a buckle which fas-
tens the legislative part of the state to the executive part." "I learned,"
Johnson mused, "that the best guarantee to legislative success was a
process by which the wishes and views of the (congressional) members
were obtained ahead of time and, wherever possible, incorporated into
the early drafts of the bills. As President I went one step further. I
insisted on congressional consultation at every stage, beginning with

the process of deciding what problems and issues to consider for my task forces right up to the drafting of bills. " (7)

As minority party presidents, Nixon and Ford did not have the same kind of working relationship with Congress, but both maintained a constant interaction with particular members of Congress on pending urban legislation. Under Nixon and Ford, policy specialists on the Domestic Council conferred regularly with their staff counterparts and legislators on the Hill. Sometimes there were direct calls between presidential and congressional staffers working out an agreeable formula for revenue sharing, while at other times general feeling was solicited directly from legislators on whether rural congressmen would resist proposals to federalize the costs of welfare. When the Housing Act of 1974 was being written in House and Senate committees, White House staff and delegates from HUD were called up to the Hill frequently to confer on what provisions Nixon/Ford would accept or reject. Conversely, during New York's fiscal crisis, sentiments flowed from the Hill to the White House on whether to "bail out" the city. As the congressional tide of opposition moderated in favor of limited aid, so, too, did feeling in the White House. (8)

Whether the White House happens to be in physical contact with the Congress or not, it constitutes a presence through its sheer formal power to facilitate or veto legislation. Johnson, of course, was a great facilitator and actively promoted his legislation, but there was also an anticipation by meliorist legislators that the White House was fully behind them. Legislation for the War on Poverty sailed through the Congress in just five months and House Republicans were virtually locked out of the deliberative process by enthusiastic Democrats who were confident of its passage. Republicans complained that the Democrats, under the chairmanship of Representative Adam Clayton Powell, scheduled meetings at irregular hours without giving them proper notice and refused to hear hostile witnesses. At one point Powell simply dismissed them by declaring, "I am the chairman. I will run this committee as I desire. " (9)

On the other hand, the Nixon/Ford White Houses frequently evoked anticipations of a veto, and this had a dampening effect on quick legislative passage. Aid to mass transit was stalled for years in Congress because of apprehensions that reinforcing presidents would block any bill that included subsidies for the operating costs of buses and trains.

Chief executives at the state and local levels obviously have no such formal power of veto over Congress, but they do enjoy a working relationship with it, and at times can informally facilitate or obstruct legislation. This can be accomplished by collective pressure through the respective organization of governors, mayors, and county officials,

or by ad hoc representation such as testifying at hearings, strongly
worded letters, or by personally buttonholing influential legislators.
All of these means have been used by state and local executives to
press their claims on Congress. As problems with Johnson's War On
Poverty and its CAPs began to simmer in 1967, mayors from all over
the country pressured Congress to amend the program. Mayor Joseph
Durley of Providence arranged for a steady stream of his colleagues
to descend on the House floor during debate, and congressmen were
later called out to talk matters over with individual mayors. The upshot was House passage of the Green Amendment, which allowed city
halls control over the distribution of federal monies to local CAPs.
State governors, too, exacted their cut into the operation of the War On
Poverty by lobbying Congress to pass provisions for a "governor's
veto" over parts of the program. This resulted in a veto prerogative
given to governors to block either Job Corps or VISTA programs that
were scheduled to be located in their individual states. (10) In both of
these cases, Congress proved amenable to state and local officials who
could lobby their home delegations and gain sympathy from legislators
with similar constituencies; after all, local control over Washington-
based programs flattered the power of mayors and governors as well
as the legislators who made it possible.

The nation's governors used their collective power through the
National Governors' Conference (NGC) to promote revenue sharing and
to support provisions within revenue sharing which bestowed a great
deal of federal largess on the states and made them prime recipients
of the funds. Well before Richard Nixon became president, the NGC
set to work on revenue sharing proposals and conferred with Congress
and the White House on their enactment. Nixon later used the governors
to stimulate support for revenue sharing and, when meliorists in Congress resisted putting the states in a prime position, Nixon encouraged
a coalition of Republican governors to work their influence on important
legislators. When the Chairman of the powerful House Ways and Means
Committee, Wilbur Mills, balked at this idea and presented his own
plan for direct aid to the cities, the influential governor of New York,
Nelson Rockefeller, persuaded Mills to drop it. Rockefeller and others
at the Hill argued that the Mills plan would only cause states to retali-
ate by shrinking their own assistance to cities and would get states in
the habit of sending their urban problems to Washington, leaving the
cities as "federal reservations." (11) NGC and Rockefeller's personal
entreaties paid off, since Mills was instrumental in establishing a complicated revenue sharing arrangement which also benefited the states
(for a discussion on this, see Ch. 1, pp. 16-24). Not only did the
governors affect revenue sharing but county executives, through their
National Association (NACO) and mayors through USCM/NLC also levied
political bids on the plan and ultimately everybody obtained something.

As a rule, private organizations do not have a comparable political facility or working relationship with Congress, but their powers are formidable and they enjoy a different sort of collaboration with sectors of Congress. Contrary to the stereotype of private lobbyists winning legislation through campaign threats or perniciously luring congressmen with bags of gold, their influence is far more subtle. Actually, the more powerful a private organization happens to be, the less threatening or underhanded need be its tactics. Also, such organizations are less inclined to trade on political favors, which are a common exchange for governors and mayors. Influence among the most powerful private organizations thrives on mutual acceptability with Congress about common ends, and these ends are made possible by the precedents of the governmental conduit. Once the ends are agreed upon, the means for accomplishing them are reduced to technical questions of mortgage subsidy rates, matching fund requirements, or the legal obligations of federal guarantees. Illegal graft may still be plied by lobbyists, but it is a crude method of influence when there is abundant opportunity for honest favors established by precedent and force of habit.

The best example of how private organizations operate to shape urban policy can be found in the housing lobby which is active in the lower chamber with its Banking, Finance, and Urban Affairs Committee, and on the Senate side with its Banking, Housing and Urban Affairs Committee. It is more than coincidence that these committees jointly link in their titles the functions of "banking" with that of "housing" and both of these with "urban affairs." Housing policy rests on inducements provided to banking interests, and these in turn make up a substantial part of the nation's "urban policy."

The term "housing lobby" is a modest one and an abbreviation for a cortege of interest groups connected with the construction and banking industries. The spearhead of this lobby is the National Association of Home Builders (NAHB) which is a hybrid organization of small and large builders, mortgage bankers, and land speculators. (12) In total, NAHB has gathered into its fold over 50,000 of these individual members, but it also works with other composite organizations and keeps them alert to legislative possibilities through an "information group" which consists of the National Association of Real Estate Boards, the U.S. Savings and Loan League, Mutual Savings Banks, and the National Forest Products Association. These organizations encompass the landed and financial assets which are necessary to commit housing starts, the builders required to construct them, and the timber interests which are needed to furnish materials.

Since housing legislation eventually provides the stimulus for urban development and construction across the nation, private lobbying

can be very intense. But it is an intensity which is neither noisy nor
marked by signs of overt pressure. NAHB's first precept is to em-
brace the broadest housing goals and push for increased construction,
preferably with numerical targets, and a requirement that federal performance reports be issued annually to evaluate conformity with these
targets. By establishing this priority, the housing lobby gets the
broadest coalition behind it and obtains implicit support for stoking up
the machinery of federal credit and mortgage subsidies. "We keep
ourselves always on the side of the angels as far as issues are concerned," says one NAHB lobbyist. "Almost no one wants ever to tangle with us because then they'll end up looking like they're against
housing." (13)

After a substantial enough momentum is generated about the
need for increased shelter, the housing lobby moves quietly through
various congressional committees. One observor describes NAHB's
lobbying techniques as "rowing with muffled oars" because it prefers
to work with smaller sessions in either of the two housing committees
or at the conference stage, or makes its big gains in the post drama
of legislation during authorizations and appropriations.

"Rowing with muffled oars" also symbolizes the trust and team-
work in moving toward the same goal that has grown up between NAHB
and legislators in the House and Senate. NAHB is careful not to present too many demands, and to appreciate a broader perspective on
problems of housing and community development. The organization
which once opposed government interference in the housing market
now favors it, and takes pride in maintaining an image of empathy and
enlightenment. As one NAHB official comments:

> We let them know that we are trying to understand their problems
> and that's why we hold our fire whenever we see something in
> the press which could be interpreted as hostile to us. We always
> check it out with their people. And because we store up our
> credits, they know that when we do want to see them about some-
> thing, then there is an issue of real substance involved. (14)

Selectivity on issues and enlightenment of attitude is complemented
by solid influence with mayors and legislators alike. NAHB's influence
with the mayors stems from a mutual interest both parties have in
stimulating local construction, and the USCM/NLC have shared in the
homebuilders' "information groups." With Congress, there is a strong
element of personal influence which makes a difference. A large number of homebuilders are located in the south and, in the past, have
been in favor with southern legislators like John Sparkman who chaired
the Senate Banking and Housing Committee. NAHB's top lobbyists also

enjoy a personal familiarity with some legislators and move in close circles between government and private groups. One envious lobbyist emphasized the significance of personal contact by pointing out that, "This is where the influence is strongest and where they can make the most of Sparkman and Tower (the ranking minority Senator on the banking committee) who are their big housing-production allies. Let's face it, they have set themselves up to do this. Their number two lobbyist - Carl Coan, Jr. - is the son of Carl Coan, Sr., who is the staff director of the Senate Banking, Housing, and Urban Affairs Subcommittee. ...I'd like to have someone like that working for me." (15)

With all of these advantages plus a staff of 29 policy professionals who work in 12 specialized areas of urban development (apartment construction, land use, mortgage finance, etc.), it is not difficult to see why the homebuilders have so easily rowed through the difficult waters of Congress. NAHB's success is a ready demonstration of how lobbies have reached their goals by working through the government conduit and beefing up its capacity. The homebuilders' lobby played a vital role in persuading Congress to increase the special assistance available through "Fannie Mae" and "Ginnie Mae"; it prodded Washington into bolstering the borrowing authority of the Federal Home Loan Bank Board; and it managed to tilt congressional voting toward passing rent supplements and other housing bills during the 1960s (for a discussion on how these institutions work, see Ch. 3, p. 93-102).

It would be a mistake, however, to conclude from this that NAHB and its allies are sui generis or that they hold a position among private organizations which is atypical. NAHB is prototypical of major private lobbies in Washington. Whereas the homebuilders have considerable clout with the housing committees of Congress, the limestone, concrete, and highway interests exercise a similar influence with the public works committees; low tax business groups and petroleum organizations have inroads into the House Ways and Means and Senate Finance Committees; and big labor and professional organizations command an equivalent status on the welfare and education committees. All of these private organizations row with muffled oars through what have become well charted waters. Committees delimit the courses, and many years of experience with them have created an elite of expert navigators, making congressional lobbying a matter of technique and policy science. The next section will examine the composition and policy disposition of Congress and those committees most responsible for urban legislation.

A CLOSER LOOK AT THE FLATTENED PYRAMID:
URBAN-ORIENTED COMMITTEES AND
THEIR POLICY DISPOSITION

Organizational lobbying is but one factor in determining the outcome
of urban policy in Congress. Both the House and the Senate also respond to their inherent dispositions which are an admixture of constituent pressure and ideology. Ideology is treated here within a policy
context and as a choice between meliorist and reinforcing approaches
to urban problems, while constituent pressures are subsumed under
urban-suburban-rural dichotomies.

When all is said and done, aside from those exerted by lobbyists,
legislators respond to pressures exerted by those who are most responsible for their reelection, and they develop ideological rationales to
justify their behavior. Taking ideology and constituent pressure as
indicators of legislative behavior furnishes us with a picture of how
Congress has managed urban problems in the past and could respond
to them in the future. Common sense also dictates that meliorist
("liberal") proclivities are likely to be strongest among urban legislators; rural legislators usually have a stronger bent toward reinforcing
("conservative") policies; and suburban legislators often fall some-
where in between. One study of the House of Representatives confirmed
this observation and found that on a scale of increasing "liberalism"
ranging from zero to 100 percent, urban members were highest with
an average of 63, rural congressmen scored a low of 27, and suburban
members fell slightly short of the midway mark with an average of
40. (16)

More narrowly gauged data, limited to key urban votes and taking
party and region of the country into account, reveals a fuller picture of
just who votes for or against the city. As Table 6.1 shows, urban and
suburban Democrats from the North are most favorable toward the
city while rural Republicans are polar opposites.

These are logical enough deductions, but the table also provides
some useful facts regarding constituent pressure, party affiliation,
and the orientation of a new force of suburban congressmen. In some
cases, the relationship between affiliation and constituent pressure is
quite mixed. For instance, urban Republicans (both North and South)
and rural southern Democrats show a similar ambivalence in voting
either for or against legislative aid to the cities. Urban Republicans
took a more pro city attitude than southern rural Democrats on two
issues involving use of the highway trust monies for mass transit and
increased funds for urban renewal; whereas southern rural Democrats
did slightly better for the cities on the issues of mass transit operating

Table 6.1. Key Urban Votes in the House According to Party and Region

| | URBAN | | | | SUBURBAN | | | | RURAL | | | |
	All (78)	North Dems (52)	South Dems (12)	Reps (14)	All (88)	North Dems (28)	South Dems (3)	Reps (57)	All (92)	North Dems (17)	South Dems (30)	Reps (45)
					PERCENTAGE VOTING IN FAVOR							
1. Permit use of highway trust fund for mass transit	77	98	27	46	71	88	100	63	7	27	0	5
2. Authorize funds for mass transit operating subsidies	79	100	72	29	49	93	67	27	24	75	31	0
3. Increase funds for community comprehensive planning grants	81	93	44	33	44	83	67	24	24	36	36	12
4. Increase funds for urban renewal	70	93	25	8	28	73	67	6	12	64	4	0

Source: Congressional Quarterly, Weekly Report, April 6, 1974

subsidies and community planning grants. Thus, while the grip of
party affiliation may be important, its hold can loosen when constituent
pressure forces a vote in another direction. Urban Republicans, for
example, held a more favorable attitude toward the city on more issues
than suburban Republicans who were not as vulnerable to inner city demands for federal relief. The single pro city issue which received a
majority of suburban Republican support (63 percent) was the use of
highway trust funds for mass transit, and this offered obvious advantages to all suburban commuters regardless of party affiliation. (17)

Taking a closer look at the combined Democratic and Republican
suburban vote in the House, it can be regarded as neutral or slightly
negative toward the central cities. In three out of four key issues, the
suburbs could not muster a majority of congressional legislators to
vote on behalf of the cities, and the only issue which received majority
support (a whopping 71 percent) was the attempt to divert highway
trust funds. Other pro city issues declined down the line in total suburban support, with operating subsidies garnering close to a majority (49
percent) while planning grants (44 percent) and urban renewal (28 percent) lagged behind. Here, constituent pressure meant a great deal,
since transit issues touch directly on suburban commuters, while planning grants and urban renewal are perceived with little relevance, if
not with hostility. The stark exception to this pattern is among suburban Democrats whose votes have been favorable toward the city, though
not with the same consistency as their urban Democratic counterparts.
Whether this pro city vote among suburban Democrats is due to the
pull of partisanship, the proximity of urban-suburban problems, or the
simple fact that these congressmen are elected by former urbanites
who are sympathetic toward federal intervention is a difficult question
to answer. It may be that middle class migrants to the suburbs still
retain pro city attitudes and also tend to elect Democrats to represent
them. If this is true, the suburban pro city vote could be an ephemeral
one, which will dissipate as a new generation of "native" suburban residents reaches voting age.

The answers to these questions are important because of the
growing significance and number of "suburban seats." Already, suburban seats are the single largest grouping in the House, representing
131 districts compared to 102 urban districts, 130 rural seats, and 72
"mixed" constituencies. Moreover, suburban constituencies have been
the big gainers in past reapportionments, and this will continue after
the 1980 census is taken. Between 1966 and 1973, the number of suburban constituencies jumped by 39 districts while urban and rural districts
declined by -4 and -51 respectively.

With this continued pattern of suburban growth, cities will fare
slightly better with Congress because suburban expansion is occurring

at relatively greater expense to more hostile rural areas, leaving cities with the lesser of two oppositions. This assumes that the suburbs will continue to elect pro city Democrats to offset a less favorable Republican vote, that massive regional shifts toward the new sunbelt will not cripple the political strength of older areas, and that there will be some political convergence about urban-suburban problems. These caveats are noteworthy because much has been touted about an impending urban-suburban coalition as the suburbs experience similar problems. Any such coalition, however, will be fragile and either forged or shattered depending upon what issues are brought to the fore or are left buried. Questions related to mass transit, better planning, and more federal assistance for crime prevention may nurture that coalition. On the other hand, issues which underline the class or racial tensions of the urban crises, such as segregated housing, corporate flight, and unequal rewards will tear it apart.

The best predictions based on voting records and party have been thwarted because they could not account for issues which unexpectedly well up and receive attention. Agenda setting, who brings up the issues, and what issues are debated are keys to which way Congress will move. Sometimes, these issues are taken up by those in agenda setting positions within the flattened pyramid of Congress - the leaders, committee chairmen, and influential legislators. To find out who helps mold urban issues in Congress, we will need to examine its committees and the content of their leadership. These are the minilegislatures where policy is put together piece by piece or is manipulated at a later stage by specially formed conference committees. Who controls these minilegislatures, and their constituent pressures and ideological makeup are critical factors for determining the content of the congressional debate.

Demarcating and Packing Urban Minilegislatures

The nation's farmers have, for over 100 years, enjoyed the privilege of twin agriculture committees on each side of Congress, packed with rural legislators who are exclusively devoted to their problems. Urban problems are not as amenable to clear-cut committee distinctions and are dispersed between at least eight committees containing urban, rural, and suburban legislators, who are beset with a multitude of different problems. These eight committees, four on each side of Congress, consist of two in the areas of banking and housing, two on public works, two which handle broad policies of education/welfare/or labor, and two "money" committees.

Not all of these committees share the same relationship to the city, and some have aspects which are more uniquely urban than others.

Those committees on the House side which produce legislation having
a spatial relevance and direct impact on the city are the Banking,
Finance and Urban Affairs Committee and the Public Works and Transportation Committee. Their Senate counterparts have similar, though
not exactly the same, titles and consist of Banking, Housing and Urban
Affairs and the Environment and Public Works Committee. Both of
the banking committees deal with legislation related to mortgage and
housing subsidies of various kinds and are responsible for community
development assistance (housing rehabilitation, planning and code enforcement, water and sewer facilities). These were the committees
which put together the housing acts discussed in earlier chapters and
managed urban aid policies (including a loan negotiated during the
storm of New York's fiscal crisis) through the Nixon, Ford, and Carter
presidencies. The two public works committees are important to cities
because they are largely responsible for the nation's highway network
and for developing national transportation policies. Together with the
banking committees, they have shared a role in working out federal aid
for urban mass transit, though frequently that "sharing" turned into
clashes between public works and banking over the costs of mass transit. The issue of mass transit has provoked several conflicts and the
public works committees have been in the heat of the battle over use
of the Highway Trust Fund. Recently, the public works committees in
both Houses have functioned as minilegislatures responsible for funneling aid to the cities through public employment projects and through
counter-cyclical or antirecession funding.

Other committees whose legislative purview is of a national
sweep but, by virtue of their generality, also have a direct impact on
urban populations are the House Committee on Education and Labor and
its "money" committee, which has the deceptively modest appellation
of Ways and Means. On the Senate side, their counterparts can be
found respectively in Labor and Public Welfare (later changed to Human
Resources) Committee and the Finance Committee. The two education-
al/labor/welfare committees manage a large part of Congress' social
policies and played a central role in managing the legislative aspects of
the War on Poverty. If the two money committees (Finance and Ways
and Means) did nothing else but tend to revenue raising and taxation,
they would be indispensable to an analysis of urban legislation. Both
of these committees, however, played a key role in passing on legislation for welfare reform from the Nixon through the Carter White
Houses, and what they did or continue to do will shape the urban future.

Table 6.2 lists four of these urban committees on the House side
in terms of constituent pressure via their city/suburban/rural breakdowns. Each committee's membership is assessed as (a) a whole body,
(b) a total of its top five Democrats, and (c) a combined total of its top

three Democrats and top two Republicans. The House Committee on
Agriculture is included at the bottom in order to compare the makeup
of a committee handling rural as opposed to urban policy.

As of the 1970 census, approximately 31 percent of Americans
lived in central cities, another 38 percent lived in suburbs, and a remaining 31 percent lived in what can be described as rural areas or
small towns. These proportions are not frequently reflected in the
makeup of congressional committees, nor should they necessarily be
adhered to with exactitude. Congress is, and always has been, an
assemblage of interest groups and certain interests in the nation are
likely to show a marked desire to represent themselves on particular
committees rather than others. The makeup of the Agriculture Committee highlights this fact of political life. Over 60 percent of its
membership comes from predominantly rural constituencies, and if
we look at its most senior members this figure climbs to 63 percent
for Democrats and 68 percent for a combination of top Democrats and
Republicans. By contrast, the committee which comes closest to being
the House's urban policy specialist--Banking, Finance and Urban Af-
fairs--contains only 29 percent of an urban membership (somewhat
below the central city proportion of the national population) and is actually outweighed by the rural delegation. The suburbs are in the en-
viable position of having the largest delegation on the committee and
can serve as a strategic balancer in any standoff between urban and
rural congressmen.

The other committee which is spatially related to the city is
Public Works and Transportation. This committee also holds a plural-
ity of rural congressmen (44 percent) which neither city nor suburban
delegations can singularly overcome. Among the top two Republicans,
the rural delegation actually commands an absolute majority (71 percent) which, despite the committee reforms of the 1970s, still carries
appreciable weight.

These figures reflect more than just raw votes of congressmen
working in committees to report out a bill, and go beyond the simplis-
tic empiricism of counting numbers in order to ascertain the relative
strength of city/suburban/rural delegations. The ability to command
potential votes plus longevity in office are major ingredients of political influence. Each bloc of votes constitutes a potential veto, check-
point, or a reason to tack on or delete amendments to a housing or
mass transit bill. This is compounded by the skill (and power) which
comes with experience, and top legislators are in the best position to
slice up the provisions of a bill so that it is palatable to their colleagues.

In the instances of the banking and public works committees, a
fistful of suburban votes which can fall either way are bargaining chips

Table 6.2. Constituent Pressure and Urban Policy Committees in
the House: City/Suburban/Rural Breakdowns (94th Cong. 1975-76)

Committee	Membership	% Central City	% Sub- urban	% Rural
Banking, Currency	Whole	29	39	32
and Housing*	Top five Dems.	25	36	39
	Combined three Dems./two Reps.	29	39	32
Public Works and	Whole	24	33	44
Transportation	Top Five Dems	30	28	43
	Combined three Dems./two Reps.	8	22	71
Education and	Whole	34	41	25
Labor	Top five Dems.	22	44	34
	Combined three Dems./two Reps.	10	42	48
Ways and Means	Whole	39	42	20
	Top five Dems.	38	36	26
	Combined three Dems./two Reps	44	33	24
Agriculture	Whole	19	20	61
	Top five Dems.	20	17	63
	Combined three Dems./two Reps.	18	13	68

* Name changed to Banking, Finance, and Urban Affairs in the
95th Cong. 1978.

which can be used by a legislator to promote or eliminate a policy choice. The mere fact that both of these urban committees, unlike Agriculture, are so heavily laden with potentially unsympathetic votes is of enormous consequence to the central city. For the Banking Committee, this means that dollars for community development can just as easily be used for suburban or rural assistance as for rebuilding the central city. For Public Works it means that mass transit assistance is substantially influenced by how farmers feel about the issue. Most often, it is the senior members of the legislating committee who are appointed as conferees to iron out differences between House and Senate. Ironing out these differences can be more than twiddling with minor amendments, and conferees do more than a fair share of rewriting. These built-in dispositions manage to thin out the beneficial intent of urban policies; on some occasions they obstruct or delay those policies indefinitely.

The remaining two committees in the areas of education/labor/welfare and the single "money" committee deal largely with policy of national import and can be analyzed with that role in mind. Education and Labor is viewed by liberals as a safe harbor for policy advocacy and has attracted a good many social activists to it in recent years. Rural congressmen tend to be underrepresented, consisting of 25 percent of the entire committee, though their proportion climbs appreciably through the senior ranks. Quite the opposite is true of the urban delegation, which constitutes a little more than a third of the whole committee's makeup but drops dramatically through the senior ranks. The largest voting group in all ranks is made up of the suburban members who consistently hover at 40 odd percent of the committee's membership.

Historically, Education and Labor has had a reputation for ideological politics, and a bloc of liberals from urban and suburban constituencies have openly feuded with its conservative rural members. These divisions run deep, reaching into visceral animosities, which are regarded as unseemly conduct by other members of the House. Deservedly or not, the committee has been regarded by conventional observers as a "bunch of smart asses" who "don't do their homework" and as a playground for freshman legislators who just "sound off." (18) Education and Labor's credibility is low compared to other committees and so is its power to get its recommendations enacted into law. (19)

If Education and Labor is seen as a "wild" committee with a penchant for "irresponsibility," no image could be further from it than that of Ways and Means. (20) This is a committee which has a reputation for consensual politics and for getting its legislation passed on the House floor. As one veteran of Ways and Means is reported to have said, "I don't know of anyone on the Committee who wants to report a

bill that can't pass in the House. " And one student of the Committee
writes, "A good bill that can't pass the House is a contradiction in
terms for Ways and Means. " (21)

As Table 6.2 indicates, Ways and Means is largely in the hands
of urban and suburban congressmen and rural membership is lower
than its national proportion would warrant. Nonetheless, the committee is not particularly left of center and its city and suburban Democrats show little of the propensity for strong meliorism that can be
seen on Education and Labor or Banking and Currency. (22) Though
its ideology is "moderate" it is not overtly ideological, and it tends to
subordinate open debate to technical questions of revenue raising and
the mathematical implications of welfare policy. This style was particularly characteristic of Ways and Means when Wilbur Mills was its
Chairman. Mills was a cautious man who sought to bury heated debate
under a commonly understood desire to maintain the committee's
supremacy on certain House matters.

The Senate warrants a different procedure for analyzing its urban-oriented committees; first, because it is a smaller institution,
calling for a more parsimonious examination of its much smaller committee membership, and second, because states do not fall into the
same neat categories as do congressional districts. Being more heterogeneous than congressional districts, states are best broken down
on a continuum of possessing lesser or greater percentages of their
populations residing in central cities.

Figure 6.1 begins with three Senate committees which are rough
counterparts to those in the House. The first two are in the policy
areas of banking and public works and manage legislation which is
spatially related to the city. The third committee is Agriculture and
Forestry and is used for the sake of comparison. Each of these committees, and the ones which follow, are analyzed along a horizontal
dimension which indicates the percentage of a given state's population
which resides in its central cities, and a vertical dimension which indicates the number of senators on a committee shown by dots. In in-
terpreting this figure we should recognize that the national average of
the population for those living in central cities is slightly above 30 percent.

Note that the picture for these three committees is not too different from that drawn for the House. Agriculture is heavily loaded
with Senators from predominantly rural states, while its major urban
counterpart in Banking, Housing and Urban Affairs actually has more
Senators from states below the national average of central city populations than from urban states. The Public Works Committee also is
dominated by Senators from predominantly rural states, although it
should be granted that its legislative mandate stretches beyond urban
issues.

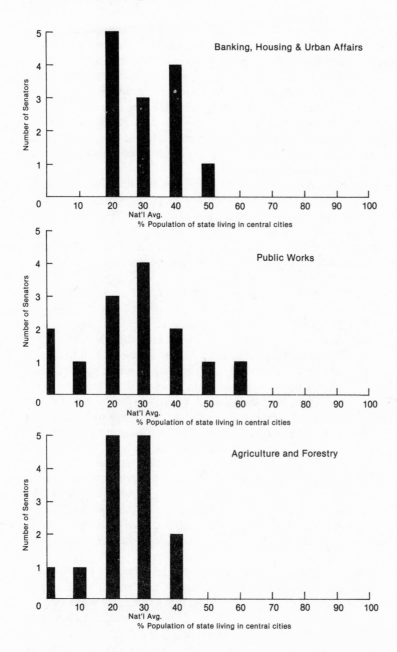

Fig. 6.1. Constituent pressure and the committees on Banking, Public Works, and Agriculture in the Senate: least and greatest central city populations (94th Cong. 1975-76).

Breaking this committee representation into hard numbers, on
the Agriculture Committee 12 out of 14 Senators, or about 85 percent
of its membership, come from predominantly rural states. By contrast, on the Banking Committee, only five out of 13 Senators, or about
38 percent of its membership, are elected from urban-oriented states.
Of the two urban committees, Public Works is more distant from urban
needs and only four out of 14 Senators, or less than 30 percent of its
membership, are drawn from urban-oriented states. On all counts,
urban constituencies are as poorly represented on the Senate's urban
committees as they are in the House.

The next two committees, like their House counterparts, deal
with broader constituencies than just those in the central cities, though
the direct impact of their legislation has a profound effect on the lives
of most central city residents. These committees are Labor and Public
Welfare and the Committee on Finance, both of which are examined in
figure 6.2 in the same procedural fashion as the previous three Senate
committees.

Like the Education/Labor Committee in the House, the Senate's
Committee on Labor and Public Welfare is also regarded as a liberal
maverick, though it does not share the same history of disapprobation.
The Committee played an important role in paving the way for meliorist
legislation during the Johnson era and acted as something of a counter-
weight to some of Nixon's proposals for special revenue sharing. In a
moment of uninhibited comment, one Democrat on the Committee attributed its rise to a desire by "the establishment" to "put all those
screwy bastards on Labor (and Public Welfare). Much to their surprise, however, the Committee took the bit in...(their) teeth" and began running away with Great Society legislation. (23)

The relatively high number of Senators from urban-oriented
states is, therefore, not surprising to see on this committee. Seven
of its 15 Senators come from urbanized states and compose close to
half of its membership. Another four Senators on Labor and Public
Welfare represent states which fall just short of the national average
for central city residents, while rural states hold the remaining four
seats.

The Finance Committee has an altogether different kind of membership and is a different kind of committee. Traditionally, it has been
given to a similar kind of fiscal prudence that existed in Ways and
Means. Its past Chairman, Harry F. Byrd of Virginia, was a conservative with the proper stripe of a southern Senator, who chose to wait
for legislation to come over from the lower chamber before taking initiatives on his own. Its current Chairman, Russell Long of Louisiana,
handles the Committee differently, although it continues to be a special
pleader for interest groups which oppose specific pieces of tax legisla-

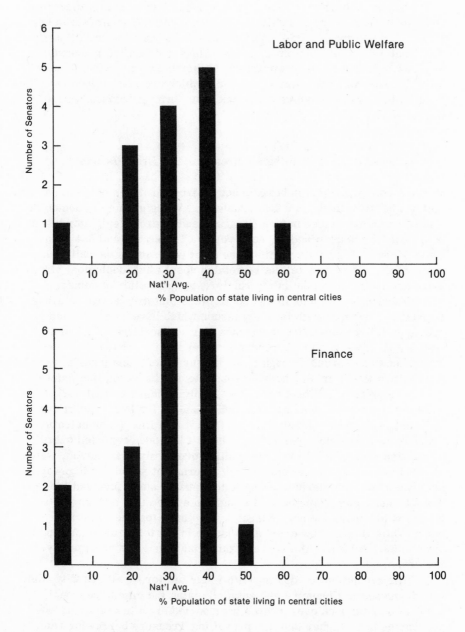

Fig. 6.2. Constituent pressure and the Committees on Labor, Public Welfare, and Finance in the Senate: least and greatest central city populations (94th Cong. 1975-76).

tion which have already passed the House. As one of the elite baronies of the Senate, the Finance Committee is high on individual preference lists for membership, and usually attainable only to Senators who have put due time on the job. (24) As a result, it inclines toward seniority and Senators who come from states with less competitive two party systems. Eleven of the Committee's 18 members, or nearly 61 percent of its membership, are from states which are predominantly rural, while seven Senators represent states with substantial urban populations.

Where Urban Minilegislatures Stand on Urban Issues

Where a committee's membership comes from provides only the barest hint of where it stands on urban problems. Votes ultimately decide the issues which are placed before Congress and where a legislator stands can usually be determined by those votes. Tables 6.3 and 6.4 unravel some of the voting habits within these eight committees as well as between them. They also tell us something about what ideological sides these key legislators take in the reinforcing and meliorist debate.

Table 6.3 lists four House committees that are central to urban legislation, together with four key issues which have been selected to provide a fuller context for discussion (for a description of all nine issues - H1-H9 - see the Appendix at the end of this chapter). These four issues are spread through the policy areas of mass transit, New York City's fiscal crisis, housing subsidies for the poor, and federal aid for older cities. The first issue, involving mass transit (H2), arose over a debate concerning an authorization for loans and grants to assist in the development of mass transit facilities (demonstration projects, construction, planning). The bill had been reported out of committee with a $5 billion authorization over a six year period, which is about one-sixth of what the federal government spends on highways over the same time period. Despite the modest sums involved for mass transit, some members of Congress argued that cities were not prepared to absorb the new federal dollars and, together with the Nixon White House, supported a reduction in the total authorization down to $3.1 billion. The reduced authorizations were accepted by the House.

The second issue, dealing with fiscal aid for New York City (H3), was discussed in Chapter 3 and entailed giving the city a "seasonal loan" to be paid back over a three year period at an interest rate one percentage point higher than the prevailing Treasury borrowing rate. This was legislation that President Ford eventually agreed to support after resisting any bail-out for the city, and which meliorist leaders

Table 6.3. Voting On the Cities: Urban Committees in the House

Committee	Vote	H2 Reduce Money Available for Urban Mass Transit (1970)			H3 Fiscal Aid For NYC Thru Loans (1975)			H7 Reduce Subsidized Housing (1976)			H9 Increase Aid For Older Cities (1976)			Committee Break-down	Urban Score (9 Issues)
		Dems	Reps	%T	Dems	Reps	%T	Dems	Reps	%T	Dems	Reps	%T		
Banking, Currency and Housing	For	6	0	54	14	5	61	17	0	50	23	12	79	Whole Comm.	62
	Agn.	1	4	46	7	4	36	7	8	44	7	2	20	Top 5 3D/2R	73
	Abst.	0	0	0	0	1	3	0	2	6	0	0	0	Top 5 Dem	87
Education and Labor	For	8	0	61	14	3	57	13	1	46	20	11	82	Whole Comm.	62
	Agn.	1	4	38	5	7	40	7	8	50	4	2	16	Top 5 3D/2R	55
	Abst.	0	0		1	0	3	0	1	3	1	0	3	Top 5 Dems	77
Public Works and Transportation	For	4	0	40	11	1	38	7	0	22	14	8	55	Whole	49
	Agn.	1	4	50	9	10	59	12	10	69	12	4	40	Top 5 3D/2R	45
	Abst.	0	1	10	0	1	3	0	2	9	1	1	5	Top 5 Dem	68
Ways and Means	For	5	2	46	3	4	21	8	0	24	13	5	49	Whole	44
	Agn.	5	0	33	17	8	76	10	12	67	12	6	49	Top 5 3D/2R	57
	Abst.	0	3	2	1	0	3	3	0	9	0	1	2	Top 5 Dem	67

Source: Compiled from Congressional Quarterly Weekly Reports, 1970-77.

207

in Congress uneasily accepted on the grounds that "half a loan is better than none." (25)

The third and fourth issues are both in the area of housing and community development. The reduction of subsidized housing (H7) came on an amendment to delete provisions for "set aside" funding to build additional public housing or undertake a substantial rehabilitation of existing dwellings. The issue was prompted by a slowdown in the Ford White House of construction starts for low and moderate income families, and was an effort to supplement laggard programs. Ford disapproved of this effort, and Republicans in Congress denounced the "set asides" as a "veritable minefield" of red tape for which Washington would be blamed. With both the Ford White House and HUD hinting that the "set asides" could not be put to efficient use, Congress finally voted to delete them.

Increases in community development aid for older cities (H9) were also discussed in Chapter 3. The issue was brought on as a result of funding inequities which would have occurred after "hold harmless" protections were phased out. These funding disadvantages came about as a result of a formula agreed upon under the Housing and Community Development Act of 1974 (HCDA), which supplanted programs such as urban renewal and model cities. Later the Carter White House worked with legislators from urban concentrations in the northeast and midwest to redress the imbalance.

All four pieces of legislation were reported out by the Banking Committee, which essentially wrote the original bills and, not surprisingly, took a pro urban position on all of them. While this Committee is not weighted with urban representatives, it does contain an adequate sampling of central city legislators in its upper ranks and its leadership is regarded as "liberal." For a dozen years, the Banking Committee was chaired by a populist rural Texan, Wright Patman, who brought to the committee the attitudes of a farmer who had lost his savings in a failing bank during the Depression. Though not particularly engrossed with housing questions, Patman spent a lifetime inveighing against the banks and flashing his committee's investigative spotlight on the Federal Reserve Bank. When freshman legislators in 1975 began a small reformation against the seniority system, the 82-year-old Chairman was among the first to go and was replaced by a liberal from Milwaukee, Henry Reuss. Reuss, too, believes in keeping a careful eye on the nation's banks, but where Patman had the eye of a farmer who learned to stow his money under the mattress, the new Chairman sees banks as playing a necessary role in the economy. Another important senior Democrat on the committee is Thomas Ashley who comes from a mainly urban constituency centered in Toledo.

In addition to the four issues just discussed, Table 6.3 contains an "urban score" based on an additional five key issues. This "urban

score" represents a percentage of each committee member's vote
cast "for" the urban position on all the nine issues. Each legislator's
voting percentage is then averaged into a total committee score or a
composite score for its top members. The score is also based on
committee members who voted on at least three of the key urban issues
and on members who were still serving in the House or the Senate when
the 95th Congress (1977-78) was in session. Also, the score is not
necessarily congruent with a legislator's "yea" or "nay" vote, since in
some cases a "nay" to reduce urban assistance was a vote "for" rather
than "against" the city. As with previous discussions on these committees, the top leadership among Democrats and Republicans is singled
out to underline their role as influential leaders who construct the
choices which are voted upon.

As the table shows, the Banking Committee has a relatively favorable record toward cities, and much of this is due to its "urban mandate" as well as to the personalities who have led it. The committee
voted the "pro city" position on all four issues, and only Education
and Labor rivals it in providing the largest majorities for the urban
position. When Patman was Chairman, he not only objected to a reduction of funds for mass transit, but argued that even the $5 billion
agreed on by his committee was inadequate to meet urban needs.
Reuss and Ashley followed the Patman stance of reporting out more,
not less, money for the cities and, like Patman, had their recommendations whittled down by the House. On fiscal aid for New York, both
of these men led the Committee to report out an aid package that was
more than three times the amount which the House ultimately passed.

The committee's urban score of 62 on all nine issues reflects
this disposition, and it is tied for the highest committee score with
Education and Labor. Banking, Currency and Housing has a higher
urban score, however, among its top leadership and this has added to
the meliorist quality of its legislation. The score is also a sign of
the Committee's willingness to pump federal dollars into subsidies
for housing and aid for community development - all of which are
objectives that the homebuilding lobby has come to endorse.

Neither Public Works nor Ways and Means show any such incli-
nation to meliorate urban problems. Public Works, which is an important committee for framing transportation policy, voted against the
city on three out of four issues selected, and its total urban score was
only 49. Its position on mass transit for the city was to opt for lower
federal funding, and half of its membership voted against higher authorizations. This was an issue that did not entail the diversion of funds
for highways, and posed little overt conflict between automobile and
mass transit users. On other issues which directly posed that confrontation, such as breaking into the Highway Trust, commuter taxes, or

higher taxes on gasoline, the committee's opposition is far more
steadfast. On another issue involving federal subsidies for the operating costs of public transit systems, members of the Public Works Committee voted against the city by 56 to 44 percent. On still a different
issue concerning commuter taxes, which would have allowed federal
agencies in cities over 60,000 to withhold municipal taxes for their
employees, the Committee also voted against the urban position by 53
to 40 percent. Its top leadership among the Democrats, however, has
a higher urban score than its bipartisan rank and file. This is probably
due to the partisan pull of Democrats usually taking a more pro city
position than Republicans.

On none of the four selected issues did Ways and Means muster a
a clear majority for the urban position, whether it involved housing,
mass transit, or aid for the cities. Apparently, in this case, neither
its Democratic membership nor the fact that 39 percent of its congressmen come from central cities has contributed to a pro city position.
Ways and Means has the lowest urban score of any of the committees
listed with only 44, though this score shoots up to 67 for its top five
Democrats. Here, too, the pull of partisanship must be strong. The
committee is regarded as a special plum for loyal party members, and
its most influential leaders cannot stray too far from the main pack and
still retain their standing. This may also explain why the issue of increased aid for older cities may have mustered as close to a majority
(49 percent) as it did. The issue affected the heaviest Democratic constituencies in the nation (i.e. the cities of the northeast and midwest)
and had a more universal appeal than the more narrowly functional
policies of housing and transportation or the ostensible parochialism
of New York City.

As a last note to this analysis of House committees, partisanship
plays an obvious role in which sides legislators take in the urban policy
debate. In going through each of the cells in Table 6.3 on those voting
"for" or "against" the city, partisan sides are sharply divided. On
all but one issue voted "for" the urban position, Democrats provided
the majority of favorable votes. The obverse, however, is not true;
Republicans did not provide the majority of "against" votes on each
issue, though, under the circumstances, this would have been numeri-
cally impossible because Republicans have been outnumbered in most
Congresses by ratios of two to one.

The specific issues listed for the Senate are similar to those
selected for the House, and are also a sampling of urban policy in the
areas of housing, community development, mass transit, and New
York's fiscal crisis (for a description of all 11 issues - S1-S11 - see
the Appendix at the end of this chapter). For the fiscal crisis, the
bills voted upon in each chamber were identical. The issue of expanded

subsidy programs for housing (S5), involved an effort by the Senate to
stimulate housing production for poor and moderate income families
after several years of a construction slump. The Senate bill required
HUD to place greater emphasis on public housing programs, and to re-
new support for greater mortgage subsidies. Part of this effort also
included a revival of home ownership for the poor through Section 235,
which had been discredited by scandal years earlier. Both the Ford
administration and HUD worked to convince sympathetic Senators to
block the bill, but the heavily Democratic Senate passed it by a comfortable majority.

The next issue on mass transit (S7) came on a move by Senators
Edward Kennedy and Lowell Weicker to force a confrontation between
highway and mass transit interests. When the issue arose, states and
localities had some narrow options available to them for converting
limited amounts of highway monies into some mass transit projects.
Kennedy and Weicker wanted to take this a giant step further by permitting the unrestricted use of the Highway Trust Fund for any kind of
mass transit or road building. Opponents of the amendment saw it as
an assault on the automobile and a drain on rural highway priorities.
The amendment was resoundingly defeated by a vote of 26 to 61.

The fourth issue specified (S11) deals with the question of "redlining" which is a practice attributed to banks of demarcating a depressed neighborhood with a red circle and barring investments in that
community. In most instances, "redlining" constitutes a form of disinvestment, since the deposits of local residents are diverted to more
prosperous communities. Sometime earlier, the Senate succeeded in
passing a measure to inhibit "redlining, " by requiring federal agencies
to investigage banks under their jurisdiction. Such investigations were
simple enough to conduct since they only required a comparison of
neighborhood deposits with neighborhood investments, but the law fell
short on hard sanctions which could be enforced against violators.
Despite the mildness of the measure, an amendment was offered by
Senator Robert Morgan of North Carolina to delete it from a larger
bill. Senator Morgan's amendment, however, was rejected by a vote
of 31 to 40.

Like its House counterpart, the Senate's Banking, Housing and
Urban Affairs Committee originally framed three out of four bills
listed in table 6.4. The single piece of legislation taken up by the
Senate which did not originate with banking was the mass transit issue,
which derived from a highway bill reported out by the Committee on
Public Works.

Until recently, the Senate's banking committee was regarded as
something of a secondary assignment by its senior members, and former Chairmen William Fullbright and John Sparkman pegged their

careers to the more prestigious Foreign Relations Committee. When
William Proxmire took over the Committee he imparted its activities
with an uncommon zeal, and this seems to have become contagious.
Proxmire prompted the Committee to recommend aid for New York
under the shadow of a presidential veto and the dismal conviction of
one colleague who opined that, "There ain't gonna be no loan guarantee
legislation. ... The fact of the matter is that New York City is going
into default and there is nothing we can do to prevent it." (26) Proxmire
went on to manage the floor fight for the legislation and helped fend off
a threatened filibuster to get it passed.

Chairman Proxmire has also had some acid remarks for "redlining" policies, arguing that financial houses are "chartered to serve
the convenience and needs of their communities" and that "does not...
(solely) mean drive-in teller windows and Christmas Clubs. It means
loans!" (27) The Senator from Wisconsin and former graduate of
Harvard Business School, however, hems his criticism to the point
where he can pressure banks to shift priorities and is by no means a
renegade from the traditions of private finance. Other influential
Senators on the Committee are Harrison Williams, a longtime advocate
of mass transit, and John Tower, who holds up a staunch Republican
minority.

Table 6.4 lists these issues and how members of four Senate
committees voted on them. The "urban score" is constructed on the
same basis as that of the House, except that an additional two issues
have been used, giving it a total of 11 Senate bills.

Quite expectedly, the Banking Committee voted for the cities on
three out of four issues and has the second highest "urban score" of
69 for the whole committee, next to Labor and Public Welfare. On the
thorniest of the issues listed, the Kennedy/Weicker proposal for mass
transit (S7), the committee failed to follow up on its pro-urban stance
and 60 percent of its members voted against it. Of the four Senate
urban-oriented committees, the only one that managed to squeeze out
a majority for Kennedy/Weicker was Labor and Public Welfare. Every
other committee buried it in an avalanche of votes against urban mass
transit users.

The vote on the Kennedy/Weicker proposal is significant because
it represents a cutting edge between city and suburb, urban and rural,
and mass transit versus auto users. It was also a proposal which was
not compromised out within a committee, so that the ultimate choices
were raw values made on behalf of one or the other side. (A fuller
account of what votes mean and how choices shape that meaning is discussed in the next section).

The Committee on Public Works, which has a good deal of responsibility for national transportation policy, voted against Kennedy/Weicker

Table 6.4. Voting On the Cities: Urban Committees in the Senate

Committee	Vote	(S5) Expand Housing Subsidy Programs (1975)			(S6) Fiscal Aid For NYC Thru Loans (1975)			(S7) Permit Use of any Federal Highway Monies to Mass Transit (1975)			(S11) Delete Measure to Combat Redlining (1977)			Committee Break-down	Urban Score (11 Issues)
		Dems	Reps	%T	Dems	Reps	%T	Dems	Reps	%T	Dems	Reps	%T		
Banking, Housing and Urban Affairs	For	6	1	70	6	2	80	3	1	40	6	2	53	Whole	69
	Agn.	0	2	20	1	1	20	4	2	60	2	3	33	3 Dem	76
	Abst.	1	0	10	0	0	0	0	0	0	1	1	14	2 Rep	86
														Top 5 Dem	
Labor and Public Welfare	For	6	3	82	8	3	100	5	1	55	6	3	60	Whole	89
	Agn.	0	0	0	0	0	0	3	2	45	1	2	20	3 Dem	87
	Abst.	2	0	18	0	0	0	0	0	0	2	1	20	2 Rep	89
														Top 5 Dem	
Public Works	For	5	1	60	6	2	73	1	0	9	5	1	40	Whole	59
	Agn.	0	2	20	1	2	27	6	4	91	4	4	53	3 Dem	67
	Abst.	2	0	20	0	0	0	0	0	0	0	1	7	2 Rep	58
														Top 5 Dem	
Finance	For	5	0	38	6	2	57	2	2	27	6	4	56	Whole	52
	Agn.	1	4	38	2	4	42	7	3	67	4	0	22	3 Dem	47
	Abst.	3	0	23	0	0	0	0	1	7	1	3	22	2 Rep	67
														Top 5 Dem	

Source: Data compiled from Congressional Quarterly Weekly Reports, 1966-77.

213

by a 10 to 1 majority. Milder remedies for urban transit ills have
failed to elicit a more sympathetic attitude, and that Committee has a
history of resisting legislation of this kind. Only two of the four issues
listed received a majority of pro-urban votes by Public Works and this
trend is consistent with its urban score of 59.

Of the four committees, the extremely influential group of Senators on Finance takes the least positive position toward the cities. Only
two of the four issues received a majority "for" the urban position and
the remaining two were unable to enlist a substantial percentage of its
membership. Its urban score for the whole Committee is 52 and jumps
around a good deal among its top leaders according to partisan divisions.

Overall, the four Senate committees have a more favorable voting
disposition toward cities than the House committees. Each of the Senate committees has higher urban scores than their House counterparts
and generally gave the selected urban issues higher majorities for the
city. Partisanship is a bit less sharp on these issues, but nevertheless distinct. In almost every cell containing votes "for" the urban
position, Democrats provided the majority. Like the situation in the
House, Republicans were too few in number to provide absolute majorities "against" the urban position and needed a substantial number of
Democrats to maintain this position.

Given the assumption that all eight committees on the House and
Senate are charged with making legislation for the nation's cities, their
combined voting record indicates that they are hardly advocates of the
urban cause. We should also recognize that most of these votes were
taken after committees consulted with the opposition and agreed to
weed out some of the more objectionable features of the legislation.
Of the four House committees two of them (Public Works and Ways and
Means) voted "against" the city nearly as many times as they voted "for"
it and held modest urban scores. On the Senate side, the same two committee counterparts (Public Works and Finance) also held a modest position in support of the cities. Such a record on farming issues within the
Agriculture Committees would be unusual and improbable under the
weight of their rural membership.

Significantly, on one of the few issues brought directly to the
Senate floor - the Kennedy/Weicker proposal - committee majorities
"for" the city all but disappeared, and even partisan Democrats de-
fected to take a stand "against" the cities. Such was the force of a
legislative proposal unadulterated by committee modifications, that
even Senators thought to be friends of a strong urban policy turned
against it. Thus, counting votes "for" or "against" the city reveals an
uppermost layer of a well tilled congressional surface. Deeper layers
are much rougher, and bear the scars of fights over how the issues are
to be framed, what provisions to include, and which interests are to be

assuaged. Counting votes may give us an outcome, but it tells nothing about what alternatives were quashed before the votes were taken, or which policies were manipulated to mislead the public. To get down to the undersurface of urban legislation, we have to reach beyond outcome to the infighting of how policy choices are framed.

TAKING MASS TRANSIT
ON A CONGRESSIONAL RIDE

The hypothesis of this book, that public policy is a response to the most dominant corporate needs, is well illustrated in the making of national transportation policy. In the United States, auto manufacture is its biggest business and is woven so centrally into our economic fiber that any jeopardy to it will tear through subordinate industries ripping away their profits and causing severe hardship. Like an elaborate tapestry, the automobile embraces 60 percent of the synthetic rubber produced in this country, 47 percent of the malleable iron we extract, and countless amounts of lead, aluminum, and electrical components go into it by the time it has made its final stop on the assembly line. Vast amounts of petroleum used in America are also consumed by motor vehicles and side by side the auto-oil complex upholds the prosperity of millions of Americans as well as their manner of daily intercourse. (28)

What keeps this industrial fiber together is the public primacy we give to our highway systems and the relegation to trivial status in which we place mass transit. It is not possible to discuss mass transit without including our policies toward all privately owned motor vehicles and the publicly supported roads on which they depend. Between the private motor vehicle and mass transit, different options are offered to the traveler, and heaping dollars on one mode of transportation detracts from the viability of the other. Plainly, the billions of dollars which underwrite automobiles and trucks also undermine the possibility of developing mass transit through trains and buses. The decades of habitual highway use and the immense concrete and commercial infrastructure which that use has generated, render mass transit a weak stepsister unless these two policy choices are joined into a comprehensive strategy. Defenders of the highways would have Congress maintain the separation not only because of the obvious threat a joint policy would pose, but because leaving the current method of financing untouched assures its dominance, regardless of what is done to develop alternatives.

Indeed, this argument has constituted a major component of the struggle in Congress between an anti-urban coalition of highway users and pro-urban groups which want to place greater emphasis on mass transit. Highway lobbies would reinforce the current movement of people and wealth out of the cities, while proponents of mass transit seek to meliorate city losses by attempting to shift some transportation subsidies back into it. At the heart of the controversy is the Highway Trust Fund, which is a replenishable federal account from which states and localities can draw allocated amounts. The unique features of the Fund are its relative exclusiveness - almost all of it is reserved for roadbuilding - and its relative longevity - it need not go through frequent congressional trials about where and how to obtain money. Instead, the federal government has given the fund its own fiscal cachet which is collected from various "user" taxes on gasoline, tires, licenses, and excise revenues. Money from the Fund can be used by the states and local governments either to construct their section of an interstate highway network, where 90 percent of the costs are paid, or for intrastate and local highways where 70 percent of the costs are now covered.

There is no gainsaying the considerable advantages that come with knowing how much money can be acquired for a project and the financial predictability of planning highways and being able to carry them through to completion. Most federal aid programs must defend themselves against the stringency of the national budget. The Highway Turst Fund operates outside of the national budget. Most programs, too, incur the frequent traumas of congressional authorizations and appropriations, and must stand for examination when they are due for renewal every two to six years. Since its inception in 1956, the Fund has rarely been compelled to endure these decisions about itself. (There are some highway programs that go through congressional authorizations and appropriations, but the bulk of highway funding is carried through an independent source of revenues.) If anything, the Fund has grown from the original estimate for the interstate segment from $41 billion to new estimates of over $76 billion and costs keep escalating. (29) By comparison, Washington's commitment to mass transit dates back little more than a dozen years and amounts to $6.4 billion in earmarked dollars with another $8 billion available for future use. Roughly estimated, for every $1 Washington has spent on mass transit, it has awarded $13 to highway building. (30)

Attempting to Break Through the Highway Trust

Rather than continue the onerous (and unpopular) job of trying to lift budget ceilings for a single program, proponents of mass transit began casting their nets toward the Highway Trust Fund. From an economic point of view, this made good sense since there were just so many

dollars which could be squeezed out of the budget and available amounts
came nowhere near meeting the problem. From the viewpoint of policy,
diverting money from the Fund held even greater merit because the plan
called for substituting highway money with funding for mass transit, if
local governments found it advantageous to do so. In this way, cities
which found highways to be ruinous or unnecessary could apply their
roadbuilding allocations to their sorest needs without losing federal aid.
Used wisely, these funds could go toward capital investments (subway
stations, railroad cars, buses) or toward daily operating expenditures
and keeping fares down. Mass transit ridership had decreased dramatically as private automobiles became popular and this has sped up, if
not precipitated, central city decline.

The real obstacles to modifying the Fund were political, and from
the perspective of what was legislatively possible, mass transit advocates faced a tough uphill climb. Highway interests were solidly en-
trenched within the public works committees of both Houses and these
committees held great influence over the bills they reported out. The
membership of these committees was mostly nonurban and their voting
records on more than one occasion were clearly anti-urban. Committee staffs were heavily weighted with highway engineers who spent their
careers devising bigger and safer roads. With some notable exceptions,
these were legislators and professionals whose politics depended on the
delivery of public works projects, and they would fight for more projects, even if they were ridiculed as the "road gang" by disdainful urban colleagues. Other barbs from the urban corner referred to the
public works committees as "captives of the concrete and limestone
lobbies" or as surrogates for the American Association of State Highway Officials (AAHSO). These characterizations may contain more
than a grain of truth, but they oversimplify the politics of the situation.
The fact of the matter is that highways enjoy a substantial measure of
support across the congressional spectrum because they stimulate jobs
and industry. Regardless of national or urban policy needs, pulling
out the highways from the federal coffer removed an important conduc-
tor of commercial energy to local economies.

Despite this, supporters of mass transit believed their demands
were not unreasonable. All they were trying to do was achieve consistency with good "conservative" principles by allowing localities to
decide their own priorities, without the imposition of big government.
They also argued that the release of highway monies in a few distant
cities could hardly jeopardize the nation's giant roadbuilding programs.
On political grounds, mass transit supporters had their own ploys to
use against defenders of the Trust Fund. While they could not easily
vault over obstacles to getting highway monies, they could make it difficult for the Fund to continue its operations. The Fund was due to

expire in 1972, and was coming up for one of its infrequent reviews by
the Congress. Urban forces sensed an opportunity to hold back approval
of the Fund as a wedge toward driving it open. Moreover, mass transit supporters had some friends in Congress, and believed they might
prevail if they could wage part of the battle in the more pro-urban banking committees or on the floor of each house.

Their first opportunity arose in the Senate, when its Public Works
Committee reported out a bill which was wholly committed to road construction, but contained a minor deviation for bus transportation on the
presumption that it was a legitimate highway related activity. At one
point, the committee had considered making part of the Fund available
for rail systems, but later changed its mind. Undaunted by the Committee's rebuff, several Senators pushed their separate proposals onto
different legislative ground. Senators Edward Kennedy and Lowell
Weicker offered one alternative that would reduce funding for highways
and make all the remaining money in the Fund available for either highways or mass transit at local option. The Kennedy/Weicker proposal
came closest to meeting urban transit needs, and was presented at a
hearing of the Banking and Urban Affairs Committee, which was considering the highway bill because of its relevance to mass transit. A
much milder alternative was offered by Senators Edmund Muskie and
John Cooper, which asked that only a part of the Highway Trust Fund
be available for diversion to mass transit. The Muskie/Cooper proposal (later to become the Muskie/Baker proposal) allowed $800
million of "urban systems" money, which is a select portion of the
Fund, to be used at local option. Because "urban systems" money is
alloted specifically for city highways or roads (not including larger
interstate links), allowing metropolitan areas to spend this small portion of the Fund as they saw fit was only a minor encumbrance on the
overall highway program. Each of these alternatives was seen in competition with the other, not only because passage meant prestige, but
because of the scope one alternative posed vis-a-vis the other in sug-
gesting a comprehensive approach to transportation. Friction between
the Kennedy/Weicker and Muskie/Cooper forces was an open secret
and there was some concern that it might spill onto the issue itself.
Whatever else might happen, the Muskie/Cooper proposal was on the
inside track since, as a halfway measure, it antagonized fewer defenders of the Highway Trust. Also, both Muskie and Cooper were members
of the Public Works Committee and were able to reach out to highway-
oriented legislators in fashioning a compromise.

In the fall of 1972, the issues of mass transit and the Fund came
to their first Senate decision. The Kennedy/Weicker and Muskie/
Cooper alternatives were set against one another and, not surprisingly,
Muskie/Cooper won handily. Far from being disappointed, pro-urban

groups saw the passage of the Muskie/Cooper amendment as a partial triumph, since there were other victory feathers which mass transit could have to plume its bonnet. For the first time, part of the Highway Trust Fund had been opened for rail transport and, in addition to "urban systems" money, there was a provision for transferring interstate highway funds to support it. Under the "interstate transfer" option, localities could apply to Washington for approval to exchange nonvital interstate links with mass transit investments. Like the "urban systems" idea, this enabled cities to place that portion of their highway money toward capital expenses. It seemed also that the hearings of the Banking and Urban Affairs Committee had yielded some dividends for mass transit when it slipped an additional title into the highway bill for aid toward operating expenses. Though this aid would not be drawn from the Fund, it was a recognition that transportation habits needed to be changed if the nation wanted cleaner air. Environmentalists joined with urban lobbies in hailing the bill.

Once the issues of mass transit and the Highway Trust Fund were joined, it was left to the House to cope with the matter. While the Senate had not gone the full route in opening up the Fund, it had delivered substantial promises. The House is a much larger institution, however, where hierarchical power and the manipulation of procedural rules is more vital to legislative outcomes. Committees also have a pervasive influence on pending bills after they have left its hearing rooms and mark-up sessions. In the House, committee power is far more stretchable, and it is difficult to amend legislation simply by changing the scene of battle.

Under the circumstances, breaking into the Highway Trust Fund was no easy job, particularly since highway legislation was tucked away within the Committee on Public Works. Like its Senate counterpart, the Committee was in no mood to modify the Fund, but there was a minority of pro-urban members who waged a skirmish over the issue. Led by Glenn Anderson, a Democrat with a working class constituency in the Los Angeles area, this group endorsed a measure similar to the Muskie/Cooper plan, which would have allowed up to $700 million from the Fund for possible application to public transportation. (31). Anderson and his allies were soundly defeated within the Committee by a 16 vote margin, amply supplied by a coalition of non-urban Democrats and Republicans. One atypical contributor to this coalition was John Kluczynski, a Chicago Democrat who was a neighbor of former Mayor Richard Daley. Kluczynski had been chairman of the important Subcommittee on Roads, and as a congressman with close ties to the highway lobby was instrumental in having Anderson's amendment defeated. With Kluczynski's help, the Committee succeeded in reporting out a highway bill which was unadulterated by mass transit needs.

Anderson's next avenue of appeal was to arrange for friends on
the powerful House Rules Committee to furnish broad enough guidelines
on the highway bill when it came up for a full vote, so that he could
offer his amendment on the floor. Although this Committee agreed to
waive points of order on other provisions of the bill (which allowed
additional freeway projects), it wound up rejecting broader guidelines
for the consideration of mass transit. This time the outcome was
closer, though no less decisive, and the door to the Trust Fund was
kept shut by a single vote.

Steadfast in the face of two consecutive defeats, mass transit
supporters continued their struggle. They turned to the House parliamentarian, Lewis Deschler, and secured assurances that they could
still have·an opportunity to bring the Anderson amendment up for a
full vote. Anderson and his cohorts believed they had taken a shortcut through the procedural maze of the House by getting the opinion
of its chief debating technician that their amendment would be in order.
Up until the morning of the vote, pro transit congressmen were optimistic that this stratagem had worked, but the cogs of legislative power
were operating in a different direction. Wilbur Mills, Chairman of
Ways and Means, announced that, because diversion of highway funds
touched on matters of taxation, the issue should have been taken up by
his Committee. Mills was telling everyone that he opposed consideration of the Anderson amendment. House Minority Leader Gerald Ford
was less circumventing in his opposition, and made a head-on attack
against the "trust busters." Arguing that this could be the beginning
of the end for highways, Ford said, "... if you start breaking faith
with the Highway Trust Fund, then pretty soon you will find some
people who will say, let us divert from the Airport Trust Fund....
Every member in this House has a highway project that needs to be
expedited. We in Michigan want U.S. 131 expedited...." (32) Ford
was one of the most energetic opponents of mass transit and lobbied
hard among his Republican colleagues to prevent, as he put it, "mass
transit people from getting their nose under the tent...." (33)

Within a short time, Anderson knew that his amendment would
not be considered, but he went through the sacrificial motion of offering
it. On his first try on the floor, he introduced a full-blown proposal
permitting local officials to use the Trust Fund for any mass transit
project including subways or rail. As expected, the chair sustained a
point of order against him on the grounds that the subject matter was
not germane to highway legislation. Anderson retorted, saying it was
germane because 51 percent of the miles traveled in the nation took
place in the cities which had different transportation needs. He added
that cities received only 10 percent of federal highway aid because
there were just so many roads and cars they could absorb. On the

question of taxation, the Congressman claimed his amendment did not
involve a question of whether to tax "but rather a disposition of taxes"
already collected. Each time Anderson was overruled and the amendment killed.

The Congressman then retreated to a lesser position and introduced an amendment to permit trust funds to be used for public transportation other than rail. Noting that this earlier effort had been ruled
out of order because it was not exclusively for "a highway purpose,"
Anderson contended that this amendment was germane because it dealt
with bus transportation and buses rely on highways. Again, the chair
ruled his amendment out of order, and the threat to the Fund was
silenced. Afterward, when Deschler was asked by a reporter why he
had changed his mind, the parliamentarian refused to answer. His
only comment was that he could not remember whether he had met the
previous day with the House leadership to discuss the matter. (34)

The House failure to consider, much less pass, the Anderson
amendment was a blow to mass transit supporters and increased the
chances for stalemate. With the Senate cranking through the "urban
systems plan," the "interstate transfer," or operating subsidies and
the House coming up with virtually nothing for mass transit, the chambers seemed hopelessly apart in drawing a common bill. House and
Senate conferees attempted to cross the chasm by trading on parts of
their bills - vainly, as it turned out that bridging one gap caused a rift
elsewhere. Thus, when senior members of the House Public Works
Committee (who were also serving as conferees) let it be known they
would allow operating subsidies if the Trust Fund were left untampered
with, the Nixon White House threatened to veto any subsidy plan. The
stalemate hardened and, as the differences between House and Senate
appeared uncrossable, the worn out conferees agreed to extend the Fund
for one year. Even this was viewed as a compromise of sorts - Trust
defenders got their highway projects through for one more year and
Trust busters played for more time, hoping to rouse a better fight the
next year.

Conference Politics - Halfway Resolutions as
No Way Resolutions

As the deadline year of 1973 rolled on, the House and Senate once again
came through with divergent interpretations of a highway bill, and conferees met for a second time. Although the conferees were drawn from
the Public Works Committees of both chambers, there were supposed
to be guidelines for them to take mass transit needs into account, lest
their agreements be rejected. The Senate had again included an "urban

systems" plan together with provisions for mass transit. Pressure
was also exerted on one important member of the House, John
Kluczynski, through the political might of Mayor Richard Daley. The
Chicago Transit Authority (CTA) was in financial trouble and, when
Daley went to the Illinois legislature for help, the cold response was,
"My God, you can't even control your own Congressman" who votes
against mass transit. A Chicago newspaper also played up the ailments
of the CTA and ran a letter writing campaign against Kluczynski's highway record. Kluczynski soon got the message, and announced that he
had decided to "step forward" and support public transportation, though
he hedged on just how far that support would go. (35)

Constraints of the kind expressed through Senate voting preferences or city hall pressures touch only the perimeters of power - they
are external in origin and, as such, set only the broadest bounds within which power over detail is exercised. The core of congressional
power reposes in the makeup of its decisive committees, and of the
16 conferees only two or three could be said to represent urban-oriented
constituencies. Even these had doubtful pro-city credentials. Senator
James Buckley, elected under a Conservative Party line with mostly
suburban/rural backing, represented New York State; Representative
John Kluczynski was an unwilling convert to mass transit and came out
of inner city Chicago; and Representative James Wright hailed from the
Dallas/Fort Worth areas. The rest of the conferees were elected from
states like West Virginia, Texas, Tennessee, Vermont, Maine - or
else from predominantly rural and suburban districts in Ohio, Kentucky,
Minnesota, and California. (36) Most of these conferees had voted
against breaking the Highway Trust, but they were charged with the
task of negotiating the issue.

Leadership was another crucial element in the Fund decision,
and conference politics is a good deal like congressional politics writ
small. Some conferees are more senior than others, some have more
power than others, and some are by expertise or interest likely to play
a more central role than others. In the resolution of mass transit versus the Highway Trust Fund, two Texas Democrats - Senator Lloyd
Bentsen and Representative James Wright - played the major cards for
their respective Houses. According to one account, Wright was the
"mastermind of strategy" in reaching the final accord, while Bentsen
was the "skillful counter-negotiator" who labored on the compromises.
Precisely what Senator Bentsen had to "counter negotiate" with Representative Wright and the other conferees is a puzzlement, because it
it difficult to discern honest polar differences between them. As the
chief conferees, Bentsen and Wright had political records which were
candidly opposed to breaking the Highway Trust (though not necessarily
opposed to aiding mass transit), and both came from a state which

gained acclamation through a potent blend of highways and oil. Politically, both men were very much on the same side, and the best that can be said about their role is that they acted as honorable surrogates for urban mass transit colleagues - the worst can be interpreted from the outcome of the bill they negotiated.

Popular and scholarly accounts of the day explained the Conference bill and the Bentsen/Wright role in the best of terms. The resolution of the Fund was applauded as a "breakthrough" for mass transit, albeit a "psychological" one, and as legislation which was "elephantine in... its potential significance to U.S. transportation policy." (37) Held to a critical light, the resolution of the Trust Fund may have resolved the problem of highway funding, but it was scarcely so for mass transit. Under Bentsen and Wright, the Conference attenuated the vital objective of building a policy link between highway construction and mass transit funding, and reduced it to a political mirage. The original Kennedy/Weicker amendment to allow all Trust Funds to be applied at local option, which had been trimmed to the "urban systems" plan using a part of the Trust Fund, was postponed so that it would not go into effect for mass transit projects until 1976. After that, it was held down to approximately 13 percent of the bill's apportionment. (38)

Where policy limitations left off, administration restrictions were inserted to muffle whatever independent use cities could make of the "urban systems" plan. Under pressure from the National Governors Conference (NGC), the negotiators agreed to eliminate "pass through" provisions adopted by the Senate so that cities with populations of more than 400,000 might receive their funding directly. In its place, all "urban systems" money was funneled through the individual states with approval required by their governor's office. The usual routing for a recommendation of approval took place through the state's department of transportation - a bureaucracy which quite often was a converted highway department run by highway officials. Many states did not even take the trouble of renaming these departments and highway personnel turned out to be the only reviewers of local requests.

Moreover, the "urban systems" plan gave localities only 70 percent of federal money for their projects. The remaining portions were decided by the states themselves, leaving state houses with a choice as to how high the local share would be. In Virginia, for example, localities must contribute 50 percent of the cost beyond the federal contribution, while California has the most generous formula allowed by law and requires localities to contribute 30 percent.

From its very inception, "urban systems" was littered with so many vetoes and qualifiers that its suitability for mass transit was questionable. Mistakenly, its sparse use was ascribed to the incompetence of local governments, yet in many cases the states were com-

petitors for the same funds and would rather continue to use these
funds for roads than permit their diversion for mass transit. By the
end of 1976, only $77 million, or 2 percent of available "urban sys-
tems" money, had actually been applied to mass transit purposes, and
these involved only a handful of the neediest large cities. Asked why,
mayors and transit administrators explain the discomfort of having to
make their requests to state highway departments, and the disadvan-
tage of relying on a 70 percent matching federal grant when 80 percent
can be gotten through other sources - leaving highway dollars untouched. (39)

Statistical findings also point to a legislative path which has pur-
posely veered away from big city mass transit projects. Up through
1976, over $2 billion had been appropriated to large metropolitan
areas, but they were allowed to spend just over half of that total.
Smaller, less populated metropolitan areas, which are not as likely
to assist rail transport, had a much better record of obligating their
funds. (40)

Where the "urban systems" plan preserved highways by subterfuge, changes in the "interstate transfer" protected them through legislative intent. These changes involved a shuffle and replenishment of
money from one federal kitty to another supposedly without any of the
contestants losing out. Under the shuffle, cities which wanted to replace their interstate links with mass transit could receive an equivalent sum from the general treasury. That portion of their interstate
funds not used would revert to the Fund for distribution elsewhere.
The plan was politically ingenious, since it assuaged mass transit
supporters with more money and protected interstate funding so that
more highways could be built. There was also a disincentive built
into the "interstate transfer" since cities that elected to use it received
only 80 percent matching allowance from Washington instead of the
customary 90 percent for interstate highways. What it did to the federal budget in bloated expenditures for the combined costs of transportation was a different matter.

With "urban systems" and the "interstate transfer" deleted as
threats to the Highway Trust, all that remained was to deal with the
non-highway related question of operating subsidies for mass transit.
Operating subsidies were crucial to mass transit advocates because
the costs of labor and repairs were driving up fares. Politically, the
subject was controversial because the Nixon/Ford White House had refused to bend on the issue, and it was a happy surprise when the Senate
had slipped subsidies into the highway bill. But even this remnant of
optimism was snuffed out when the conferees, while agreeing to more
funding through general taxes, stipulated that this aid could not be
used for operating costs.

In the end, the issue of mass transit and the Highway Trust
Fund was settled by a well-known congressional practice of splitting
differences – but with mass transit getting splinters, and highways en-
shrined in larger amounts of concrete. The conferees stopped any
chance for change by publicly stating there could be a limited tap on
the Fund, and privately burying the spigot in the offices of state highway departments and in the general treasury. Any opposition that remained was quieted with marginal amounts of federal money. Lloyd
Bentsen walked out of the Conference beaming and saying that a good
compromise is where "everyone comes out with something." In Congress, where some interests have a protected role, this is true, but
it leaves the mass of rail and bus riders who came out with nothing
wondering about the process.

APPENDIX: KEY URBAN ISSUES VOTED ON BY
HOUSE AND SENATE COMMITTEES

House

1.   Conference report on fiscal 1970 supplemental appropriations
bill appropriating $6,702,375,083. Cohelan (D-Calif.) motion to
agree to the Senate amendment reported in disagreement adding
$587.5 million for urban renewal grants. Rejected 137-236: R 14-151:
D 123-85 (ND 114-18; SD 9-67), June 25, 1970. A "nay" was a vote
supporting the President's position.

2.   Urban Mass Transportation. Boland (D-Mass.) amendment reducing aggregate authority to $3.1 billion from $5 billion for grants
and loans. Adopted 200-145: R 122-27 D 78-118 (ND 24-101: SD
54-17). Sept. 19, 1970. The President did not take a position on the
amendment.

3.   Aid to New York City. Passage of the bill to authorize federal
loans of up to $2.3 billion a year to help New York City meet seasonal
cash flow needs. Passed 213-203: R 38-100; D 175-103 (ND 160-32;
SD 15-71), Dec. 2, 1975. A "yea" was a vote supporting the President's position.

4.   Public Works Jobs. Passage over the President's veto of a
bill to authorize funding through fiscal 1977 of $2 billion for job creat-
ing state and local public works projects, $1.25 billion for anti-reces-
sionary aid to help state and local govt's maintain services and $700

million for waste and water treatment programs. Passed 310-96;
R 57-81; D 253-15 (ND 186-2; SD 67-13), July 22, 1976. A "nay"
was a vote supporting the President.

5.   Supplemental Appropriations, Fiscal 1976.   Michel (R-Ill.)
motion to recommit the bill (see vote 581 below) to the conference
committee with specific instructions to reduce appropriations for a
revolving loan fund to aid New York City to $1.3 billion from $2.3
billion.   Rejected 187-219: R 112-28; D 75-191 (ND 22-161; SD 53-30),
Dec. 15, 1975.

6.   National Energy Policy. Howard (D-N.J.) substitute amendment,
to the ad hoc energy committee amendment to increase the federal
gasoline tax by 5 cents, effective Jan. 1, 1979, with half the revenues
going to support mass transit programs and half going toward the repair of the nation's bridges and highways.   Rejected 82-339: R 6-135;
D 76-204 (ND 60-132; SD 16-72), Aug. 4, 1977.   A "yea" was a vote
supporting the President's position.

7.   Housing Programs. Brown (R-Mich.) amendment to delete provisions of the bill earmarking fiscal 1977 contract authority for public
housing, new construction of subsidized housing, and public housing
modernization, and to authorize $850 million in untargeted fiscal 1977
contract authority for subsidized housing programs.   Adopted 260-110;
R 120-1; D 140-109 (ND 77-97; SD 63-12), May 26, 1976.

8.   Fiscal 1977 Supplemental Housing Authorization. Adoption of
the Banking, Finance and Urban Affairs Committee amendment to increase the term of Section 8 assistance contracts from 20 to 30 years
for new or rehabilitated units financed conventionally or under the Department of Housing and Urban Development co-insurance program.
Adopted 323-87: R 69-71; D 254-16 (ND 183-2; SD 71-14), March 10,
1977.   A "yea" was a vote supporting the President's position.

9.   Housing and Community Development Programs. Hannaford
(D-Calif.) amendment to delete from the bill a new alternative formula
for allocation of community development block grant funds.   Rejected
149-261: R 45-89; D 104-172 (ND 32-156; SD 72-16), May 10, 1977.

Senate

1.   Passage of Model Cities. Vote on a report of the conference
committee to assist comprehensive city demonstration projects for

rebuilding slums and blighted areas and for providing public facilities and services in those depressed urban areas. The report also assists/ encourages planned metropolitan development. October 18, 1966. Adopted 38-22. A "yea" supported the President.

2.   Mass Transit. Passage of the bill committing Federal Government to $10 billion program for urban public transportation over a 12-year period, but limiting authorization to $3.1 billion in first five years. Accepted 84-4: R 37-1; D 47-3 (ND 34-0; SD 13-3), Feb. 3, 1970. A "yea" was a vote supporting the President's position.

3.   Highway Authorization. Muskie/Cooper amendment which would allow a limited amount of monies from the Highway Trust Fund to be used for mass transit projects, including subways. Approved 48-26, 1972.

4.   Highway Authorization. Muskie (D-Maine)/Baker (R-Tenn.) amendment to give states and cities the option of using $850 million a year of federal urban highway funds in the Highway Trust Fund for buses or rail transit (subway) construction programs as well as for highways. Adopted 49-44: R 23-19; D 26-25 (ND 24-12; SD 2-13), March 14, 1973. A "yea" was a vote supporting the President's position.

5.   Housing Programs. Passage of the bill to authorize fiscal 1977 funding for public housing construction, federal rental and homeownership subsidy programs and a number of other federal housing programs. Passed 55-24: R 10-21; D 45-3 (ND 33-0; SD 12-3), April 27, 1976.

6.   Aid to New York City. Passage of the bill to authorize federal loans of up to $2.3 billion a year through June 30, 1978, to help New York City meet its seasonal cash flow needs. Passed (thus cleared for the President) 57-30: R 16-16; D 41-14 (ND 35-3; SD 6-11), Dec. 6, 1975. A "yea" was a vote supporting the President's position.

7.   Federal-Aid Highway Program. Kennedy (D-Mass)/Weicker (R-Conn.) amendment to permit states and localities to use non-Interstate Highway Systems monies from the Highway Trust Fund for mass transit. Rejected 26-61: R 9-21; D 17-40 (ND 17-24; SD 0-16), Dec. 12, 1975.

8.   Revenue Sharing Extension. Passage of the bill to extend the general revenue sharing program for five and three-fourths years - to September 30, 1982, and to authorize as an entitlement to qualified state and local governments payments totaling $41,267,141,391. Passed 80-4: R 30-2; D 50-2 (ND 34-2; SD 16-0), Sept. 14, 1976.

9.   Urban Development Action Grants. Tower (R-Texas) amendment to allow cities which were basically prosperous but contained
"pockets of poverty" to qualify for special HUD grants designed to
stimulate employment and production. Opponents of this amendment
argued that HUD funds would be spread too far and wide and that passage would be harmful to "targeting" funds to cities which needed the
help most. Adopted 47-38: R 20-13; D 27-25. July 20, 1978. A
"nay" was a vote supporting the President's position.

10.   Housing and Community Development Programs. Passage of the
bill to authorize $12.45 billion for the community development block
grant program for fiscal years 1978-80 and to authorize more than
$2 billion for federally assisted, public and rural housing, to continue
Federal Housing Administration mortgage and flood insurance programs and to encourage financial institutions to invest in their service areas. Passed 79-7; R 25-7; D 54-0 (ND 39-0; SD 15-0), June 7,
1977.

11.   Housing and Community Development Program. Morgan (D-N.C.)
amendment to delete Title IV aimed at combating urban decay by encouraging financial institutions to invest in their service areas. Rejected 31-40: R 16-8; D 15-32 (ND 5-30; SD 10-2), June 6, 1977.

III

Exterior Cities
in the Arena of
Middle Government

7 Cities, States, and the Environment of Urban Policy

This city is ruled entirely by the hayseed legislators at
Albany. I've never known an upstate Republican who didn't want
to run things here, and I've met many thousands of them in my
long service in the legislature. The hayseeds think we are like
the Indians . . . sort of wards of the state who don't know how
to look after ourselves and have to be taken care of by the
Republicans . . . . We don't own our own streets or our docks
or our waterfront or anything else. The Republican Legislature
and the Governor run the whole shootin' match. We've got to eat
and drink what they tell us to eat and drink, and have got to
choose our time for eatin' and drinkin' to suit them. If they
don't feel like takin' a glass of beer on Sunday, we must abstain.
If they have not got any amusements up in their backwoods, we
mustn't have none. We've got to regulate our whole lives to
suit them. And then we have to pay their taxes to boot.

> George Washington Plunkitt
> complaining about state abuse
> in 1905.

URBAN POLICY AT THE JUNCTURE OF A
VEN DIAGRAM

The states are at the critical juncture of urban policy. Together with
federal and private action they have affected the exterior city to an
extraordinary degree. "Marble cake" federalism is a popular analogy

to describe a phenomenon in which "unexpected whirls" of federal,
state, and local governments merge with one another to formulate a
tri-institutional system for making policy. (1) The marble cake analogy broke the myth that federalism consists of separate actions by
separated realms of government. The abiding orthodoxy of marble
cake federalism was that however much governments might merge in
their deliberations, it was a merger by chance among political whirls
which might also run past one another. More importantly, it treated
federalism as independent of private power, and did not account for
the political mix between government and the corporation.

Like much of political science, marble cake federalism analyzed
policy as it was being carried out, as a fundamental process. Its field
of vision was basically from the top down or from the viewpoint of the
policymakers. A different field of vision might look at policy as it impacts upon the city, as an event analyzed from the bottom looking upward. Such a viewpoint suggests that federalism consists not so much
of separate policy streams which may converge at times, but as a juncture of a quadra circled Ven Diagram. At this juncture national, state,
and private power go through a kind of political coagulation with the
city to compose urban policy. The phenomenon is depicted in figure
7.1, where the meshed diamond represents the point of convergence
between these forces.

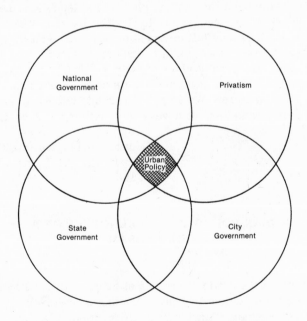

Fig. 7.1. The mesh of urban policy impacts.

The case of highway policy discussed in the preceding chapter
provides a scenario to explain the diagram. How cities were to develop
their mode of transportation was arranged in Washington. Also supplied
were the actors who would make policy at the local level. As may be
recalled, under the final compromise worked out by Congress, cities
could apply for a portion of funding available through either the "urban
systems" plan or the "interstate transfer" provision. In most instances,
though, the states were given the opportunity to approve such an application and the National Governors' Conference managed to veto a "pass
through provision" which would have allowed direct funding to the cities.
The concrete and limestone industry also played an important part in
lobbying for the protection of the Highway Trust Fund and established
clauses in the law (such as the prohibition against funding mass transit operating costs) which made it more attractive to build highways
than support mass transit.

Seen from the vantage of the law's impact on a city's effort to
improve its mass transit, a mesh of external powers condition the outcome. Applications must be sent to Washington for final approval, but
before that can be obtained state officials comment on the proposal and
help work out its details. This gambit brings in the private sector
(construction firms, labor unions) who lobby for or against the proposal
or seek to amend it. Urban transportation policy finds itself in a web
of interested parties, each tugging toward its own objectives. The resolution which follows almost always involves delegates from all four
arenas of power whose influences are exerted on this single urban issue.

This is classic pluralism compounded by the innumerable interests which hinge around the exterior city. Washington sets the pace
of activity and the basic rules. Privatism furnishes the industrial,
labor, and monetary resources for carrying out the project. Cities
administer, supervise, and run through a paper maze to complete
their projects, and yet incur the consequences of actions taken elsewhere. The question is how the states contribute to these consequences. Are they just another interested party? Do they fend for the
city? Do states pressure their exterior cities to induce certain outcomes? Or are states benevolent overseers cast in a constitutional
role in which they are uneasy and which they are unprepared to fulfill?

SETTING THE ENVIRONMENT FOR THE
EXTERIOR CITY

On the surface of things, states have immense power over the life of
cities and all local government. Technically, there is no such thing

as "the city" and as every professor is wont to admonish his beginning students, cities are "mere creatures" of the state. As a parent decides the rights of an infant, so, too, is the state entitled to decide the rights of local government. Legally, there is no such thing as an "urban citizen." Urban people are mere residents of a place they may call Philadelphia or New Orleans. They cannot be citizens of their cities because cities do not possess sovereignty and have always been treated in jurisprudence under the law of "municipal corporations" - not as sovereign policymaking entities, but as artificial beings given a limited grant from a superior body.

The limitations on local government have been pungently expressed through the opinion of Judge John Forrest Dillon, who, in a case in Iowa, declared that:

> Municipal corporations owe their origins to and derive their powers and rights wholly from the legislature. It breathes into them the breath of life, without which they cannot exist. As it creates, so it may destroy. If it may destroy it may abridge and control. Unless there is some constitutional limitation on the right, the legislature might, by a single act, if we can suppose it capable of so great a folly and so great a wrong, sweep from existence all of the municipal corporations in the State and the corporation could not prevent it... They are, so to phrase it, mere tenants at the will of the legislature. (2)

The judicial theories of John Dillon gave legal force to the realities of state/city relationships. Throughout the union, states have enormous latitude in setting conditions for local governments as well as carrying out hard, tangible policies. In doing so they let localities know what actions they can undertake on their own behalf and provide a yardstick for what they ought to be doing.

It is the state which establishes the condition for local boundaries, municipal incorporations, and regional agreements.

It is the state which formulates taxation and economic development policies for the region of which cities are an integral part.

It is the state which creates debt ceilings over which localities cannot legally rise and fixes their methods for raising revenues. Some cities, like New York, have managed to rise illegally above these limits, or at least quasi-legally, by resorting to fiscal devices of dubious integrity.

It is the state which can mandate that cities make payments toward certain services, such as welfare, and require that cities abide by certain standards in running schools or hiring policemen.

It is the state which has the capacity for functional ascendancy by
which it can take over mass transit systems, manage the libraries, or
impel the construction of low income housing.

Finally, it is the state which holds the ultimate power of intercession in municipal affairs. State governors have appointed police
commissioners (in Boston); they have investigated city officials (in
Chicago); and they have overridden district attorneys by imposing
"super prosecutors" (in New York).

The history of state/city relationships shows that states have
taken their prerogatives seriously. This was particularly true in the
late nineteenth and early twentieth centuries when interior cities had
much to lose by being denied self rule, and rural dominated state legislatures had something to gain by curtailing urban power. Interior
cities were, after all, desirable locations sought after by corporations
and an upper class establishment which set the cultural and economic
pace of the nation. Rural constituencies still controlled the state
houses through rotten boroughs and voting laws which made it difficult
for immigrant constituencies of the city to exercise their electoral
franchise. Since corruption was the major urban issue of the time,
the states were eager to teach city halls a lesson. State legislatures
in New York, Maryland, Illinois, Michigan, and Missouri abolished
police departments in their biggest cities, and decided instead to run
law enforcement through state boards. Big city politicians were also
replaced, and state houses created new positions within the cities,
ordered that salaries be raised for some officials, and passed bills
regulating every minutia of urban activity including the naming of
streets and the designation of magnificent plazas. In less than a quarter of a century (1885 to 1908) Massachusetts enacted 400 special laws
dealing solely with the city of Boston. New York State accomplished
the same feat in less than ten years (1880 to 1889). Louisiana took
steps in the nineteenth century to include a clause in its constitution
limiting the amount of representation that New Orleans could have in
the state legislature. Northern states were less circumspect in dealing with their major cities and allowed the governor to replace city
officials (Pennsylvania) or denied municipalities permission to operate
electric generating plants (New York). (3)

Dillon's Rule, For What?

Judge Dillon was yet to have his say on the prerogative of local governments vis-a-vis their parent states, and in 1911 announced very precisely what those rights were. These specifications, known as "Dillon's
Rule," appeared to come down harshly on the independence of cities:

It is a general and undisputed proposition of law that a _muni-
cipal corporation possesses and can exercise the following
powers, and no others_. First, those powers granted in _express
words_; second, those _necessarily or fairly implied_ in or _incident_
to the powers expressly granted; third, those powers _essential_
to the accomplishment of the declared objects and purposes of
the corporation - not simply convenient but indispensable. Any
fair, reasonable, substantial doubt concerning the existence of
power is resolved by the courts against the corporation and the
power denied. Neither the corporation nor its officers can do
any act, or make any contract, or incur any liability, not authorized thereby, or by some legislative act applicable thereto. All
acts granted beyond the scope of the powers are void. Much less
can any power be exercised, or any act done, which is forbidden
by charter or statute. _These principles are of transcendent importance, and lie at the foundation of the law of municipal corpo-
rations._ (4)

Dillon's rule seemed unequivocal and other decisions of courts
throughout the nation confirmed a very bleak outlook for the cities. In
Connecticut, the city of Norwalk was found to lack statutory authority
to establish its own law department. In Missouri, a statute conferring
authority to "regulate, suppress, and abate slaughterhouses" was held
not to authorize a local ordinance prohibiting the actual construction of
slaughterhouses. In Utah, a statute authorizing a city to operate street
railways was held not to authorize the operation of motor buses. (5)
    While systematic data on the results of Dillon's Rule are not
abundant, there is evidence of judicial prejudice against cities. In New
York State, a survey of court decisions between 1937 and 1939 found
a clear bias against its biggest city. The state's highest court reversed
New York City 33 percent of the time, and ruled for it only 13 percent
of the time. Smaller municipalities, which were often located in rural
upstate regions, had a much better reception. The state's highest
court reversed them only 18 percent of the time and ruled for small
municipalities 36 percent of the time. Flexing its political muscle
years later, the state legislature reduced New York City's ability to
raise taxes and threatened further reductions unless the city gave up
direct control of its mass transit facilities. The city capitulated and
gave control to an independent authority, free from the day-to-day
skirmishes of city hall. (6)
    The heavy handedness of the states was bound to cause a strong
reaction by the localities which eventually took hold. In the last 50
years, a movement for "Home Rule" emerged to counter the legal reverberations of the Dillon Rule and restrain the sweeping actions of

state legislatures. Incorporated in statutes or in constitutional revisions, "Home Rule" permitted municipalities greater freedom over
local matters, and cities took up the invitation by adapting their char-
ters to fulfill their new privileges. Today, most states of the Union
allow some kind of "Home Rule" for cities with populations over
200,000. By the mid 1950s, not only were cities being granted wider
discretion through express consent of the state, but the idea came into
vogue of giving them implied powers. The proposal first drafted by
Dean Jefferson Fordham of the University of Pennsylvania suggested
that cities be granted the right to adopt whatever legislation they
wished so long as it was not inconsistent with the state constitution or
denied by its legislature. New York, Pennsylvania, Massachusetts,
and Maryland have adopted some variant of these implied powers.
Moreover, complaints about "hayseed" legislatures running rampant
over the big city have all but disappeared since the Supreme Court's
"one man, one vote" rulings in the 1960s. (7)

Pushing the pendulum of legal authority further toward the cities,
legal revisionists have begun to scrutinize the Dillon Rule. Scholars
and judges began to pay more attention to the words "essential to the
accomplishment of the declared objects and purposes of the corporation" with an eye toward imparting the rule with a broader construction. What was "essential" to the "purposes" of a pre-industrial city,
might very well be different from that of the declining, exterior city.
Presumably, exterior cities have a larger number of purposes to fulfill
and need greater powers in order to ensure their survival. Words like
"fair, reasonable, substantial doubt" are also relative to the time and
circumstances of the case. Doubts as to the propriety of a city's action
may be linked to the complexity of its problems, and judges are prone
to account for the general welfare of a city when it carries out new
functions. Much as research into court decisions of the 1930s may
have shown a prejudice against cities like New York, the same survey
during the 1960s indicated that the restrictive effects of Dillon's Rule
are now overstated. (8)

As of late, the legal pendulum appears to have swung back toward more autonomy for the city. But does this reflect political realities? In fact, there are crisscrossing currents which obfuscate Home
Rule. For every increment of power given a city over parking ordinances, there is much more activity by the state in building toll bridges
which double the number of automobiles using city streets. Cities may
have expanded their autonomy, but states have also expanded their
activities.

Though cities may be free to take action not denied by the parent
body, the states are not averse to taking action where it really matters.
States need not use their powers fully or aggressively in order to be

heard. The mere fact that states possess ultimate power and can invoke it sparingly is enough to curb or expand the actions of localities.
It is the threat of latent power - the expectation of how the state will
react to a local decision - that influences big city mayors or suburban
supervisors. Put another way, there is no escape that exterior cities
or suburbs can have from the authority of their states, just as there
is no escape that crops can have from the soil in which they are rooted.
States furnish the milieu in which their offspring grow.

This can be elucidated as a basic proposition that once having
established the rules and conditions for the localities, it is not possible
for the state to abdicate responsibility. State non-intervention is itself a way of tilting the ultimate choice toward a small repository of
power which the state has created and to which it has given rights. On
the other hand, state intervention is a different way of declaring that
there are regional needs which must be met and this tilts the ultimate
choice toward a larger, interdependent constituency of state citizens.
For example, any state which sets permissive conditions for localities
to incorporate as villages or municipalities automatically biases the
outcome toward fragmentation and, hence, toward economic competition
between local governments. Another state which invokes a type of
regional governance tilts the ultimate decision toward comprehensive
planning and a regional sharing of revenues. Thus, most states of the
Union require that mergers between city and suburn be approved con-
currently by a majority of residents voting in their separate jurisdictions. Because of this, such mergers have been rare and difficult to
attain. At the opposite side, the state of Minnesota has taken an unusual step toward regional cooperation in the seven counties around
Minneapolis/St. Paul. Under one of its plans, a portion of the revenue
growth from increased property taxes on new industry is put into a
common regional pool and then redistributed. In each of these instances, whether the state does or does not intervene, it affects the
development of its progeny.

Another example of the inextricability of state power can be
found in tax and zoning policy. All states collect taxes while few states
set zoning requirements. (Alaska and Hawaii are exceptions.) If a
state offers special tax concessions for new real estate investments
and leaves zoning policies up to its localities, it is apt to promote
commercial development in its open spaces and give special advantage
to its suburbs. By contrast, if a state adopts tax concessions exclusively for the rehabilitation of old buildings and decides to establish
statewide zoning requirements, it is likely to encourage reconstruction
in the inner city. Even a total hands off attitude by the state has a profound effect on its localities. If a state does nothing on taxation (i. e.
pursues an across-the-board, low tax strategy) or nothing on zoning,

it then places a greater burden back on local competition. Cities, towns, or counties which can offer a lower array of taxes and easier zoning laws will be more attractive to commercial developers. Localities which either wish to discourage industrial development because they can afford to do so, or are compelled to raise taxes and maintain strict zoning laws because they have poor, densely settled populations will not attract new development. Even in this latter case, the state cannot help but involve itself because the financial capacity of localities is dependent upon aid given to them for education, welfare, or other services. The less a state does to directly affect local policy, the more it does to indirectly weaken these localities by causing them to become more reliant on external factors.

Once the real difficulties facing the exterior city were grasped, the controversy around Dillon's Rule and state intervention was a tempest in a teapot. By the time the argument reached the exterior city it was an exercise in triviality because more was happening to determine the urban future outside of city boundaries than within them. The bulk of remedial action for urban problems lay with the larger, comprehensive governments in Washington, in the state capital, or in the greater metropolitan region. What cities needed was more state intervention of a benevolent sort, not less. At some level, city halls around the country understood this and began clamoring for state regional transportation systems or for help in housing construction.

By this time, some states had shed their anti-urban bias and acted out of the best of intentions. These were meliorist states which embarked upon urban strategies of one sort or another. Other states simply let local autonomy run on its ideological steam and did little to relieve their big cities. These were essentially reinforcing states.

THE STATES AS MELIORIST AND
REINFORCING POLICYMAKERS

As policymakers the states have not been popular, either with their big cities or with the population at large. (9) According to one survey by the Senate Subcommittee on Intergovernmental relations, close to 75 percent of all mayors opposed the mandatory channeling of federal grants to the states. In Washington, individuals who seriously propose that urban policy should first be run through the states face the riposte, "And what will you tell the mayors as they're climbing over your back?" Indeed, the history of urban legislation, going back to Johnson's War on Poverty and through Nixon's general revenue sharing, is filled with mayoral opposition to a stronger state role and to a deepseated distrust

of most state governments. As one attuned to the sentiments of big
cities, HUD Secretary Patricia Harris showed skepticism about the
ability of states to deal with urban problems. When asked what role
she saw for the states in carrying out a national urban policy, Harris
replied, "We are focusing not on political aggregations known as states;
we are addressing our problems to... cities... and to regional concerns
which may stop at state lines, may cross states lines." (10)

This lack of enthusiasm extends down to the ordinary citizen and
to the perceived effectiveness of state policies. In a nationwide survey
conducted in 1973, the question was asked, "From Which Level of
Government do You Feel You Get the Most for Your Money - Federal,
State, or Local?" A partial listing of the results is in table 7.1.

Despite the many complaints about the federal government, it
fares better than any other level of policymaking. Across almost every
stratum of the American public, the perception is that national government does more than either state or local. In all but two cases (those
with incomes of $5,000 - $6,999, and non-whites) small localities fare
better than the states. For the population as a whole, only 18 percent
selected the states, while 35 and 25 percent chose federal and local
governments, respectively. Note, too, that states do poorly among
those with less than a high school education, among people who live in
the highly urbanized northeast and north central regions, among urban
dwellers, and among non-whites. One of the few sectors of the nation
where states do reasonably well is among farmers and farm laborers.
Clearly, those who live in the city and who are most in need of melio-
rative policies have a low regard for what states can do for them.

This is true at the level of perception, but there could be a difference between what people believe states have done for them and
what states actually have accomplished. Moreover, the 50 states in
the Union perform differently. Evaluating state performance is a hazardous task, because it is difficult to isolate states from the larger
complex of federalism and privatism. States compete with one another
for corporate firms and private investments. States also receive a
substantial part of their revenues from direct federal aid, and in
1973-74 over 20 percent of that revenue came from Washington. How
Washington dispenses direct aid and where it decides to place indirect
aid, such as military bases or aerospace contracts, has a tremendous
bearing on what states can do. During the mid-1970s, California received $396 in defense contracts awarded for each man, woman, and
child, while Illinois received only $60 in per capita income from this
source. Illinois did better in direct federal aid for welfare, collecting
$117 in per capita payments, but this sum still lagged behind Califor-
nia's $139 in per capita welfare aid. (11)

Furthermore, it is difficult to unravel the statistics of intergovernmental aid, particularly aid that states make available to their

Table 7.1. Level of Government From Which People Get Most For
Their Money

Sampled Population	% selected Federal	% selected State	% selected Local	% selected Don't Know
Total U.S. Public	35	18	25	22
(Education)				
Less Than High School	37	16	19	28
High School Complete	35	20	27	18
Some College	34	21	30	15
(Occupation)				
Professional	30	22	37	11
Managerial	34	19	30	17
Clerical, Sales	34	17	28	21
Craftsmen, Foremen	33	21	27	19
Other Manual	37	18	22	23
Farmer/Farm Laborer	23	28	20	29
(Location)				
Rural/nonmetropolitan	35	20	21	24
Urban	35	19	28	18
Northeast	34	16	28	22
North Central	37	16	26	21
South	37	19	21	23
West	30	25	26	19
(Family Income)				
Under $5,000	37	15	26	32
$5,000 to 6,999	38	20	18	24
$15,000 or over	33	18	33	16
(Race)				
White	35	19	27	19
Non White	40	16	11	33

Source: U.S. Commission on Intergovernmental Relations,
Significant Features of Fiscal Federalism, Vol. I, 1973-74,
Table 171.

exterior cities. States vary in the amounts of matching funds they require of their cities for highway programs or for welfare costs. There
are 13 states (among them California, Maryland, and New York) in
which welfare programs are administered by local governments.
Matching contributions from these local governments range from a
high of 25 percent in New York City down to 5 percent for the city of
Baltimore. The contributions are mandated by state law, and it is
difficult to encapsulate these features of state/city relationships in a
set of statistics.

There are other problems in making determinations about how
states treat their localities. The federal funnel does not work the same
way in all states, and some localities receive money directly while
others receive federal funds as a proportion of state aid. The jurisdictional status of a city has considerable implications on the state aid
it receives, and on the responsibilities it must absorb. A city may be
part of a larger county, it may be entirely independent of a county, it
may be coterminous with a county, or it may include several counties.
As a city which runs coterminously with a county, San Francisco receives state money because it is required to undertake services that
are expected of counties in California. Chicago, which is a part of
Cook County, has some of those services performed for it.

During 1975-76, San Francisco spent over $65 million in cash
assistance payments for welfare; Chicago spent nothing in this category.
The county status of the 10 exterior cities we are most concerned with
is as follows:

New York City: consists of five counties
Chicago: part of Cook County (county seat)
Philadelphia: coterminous with county
Detroit: part of Wayne County (county seat)
Baltimore: independent city
Cleveland: part of Cuyahoga County (county seat)
Boston: part of Suffolk County
St. Louis: independent city
New Orleans: coterminous with parish (county)
San Francisco: coterminous with county

Categorizing Ten Exterior/City States

Having made these caveats, an effort will be made to make something out of the complexities of fiscal urban policies. Any statements
drawn from these fiscal profiles should be taken as a first probe; as
an initial diagnosis of a broad problem which has as many qualitative
roots as quantitative ones.

Beginning with indrect urban policies, taxation and revenue
raising are critical factors in understanding the ground rules laid down
for exterior cities. As mentioned earlier, states with a stronger and
more progressive tax structure take some of the strain off their hard
pressed localities. There are several ways to measure revenue raising policy. One is to assess income and corporate taxes as a percentage of a state's total revenue collection (revenue effort). Revenue
effort makes a comparative distinction between a state's reliance on
individual or corporate income taxes as opposed to reliance on more
regressive sales taxes and user charges. Still another way to analyze
fiscal policy is to measure the percentage of taxes collected relative
to the population's personal income (tax effort). Tax effort asks what
is the personal income within a state and how much of that income is
being levied by taxes.

It should be pointed out, too, that there is a distinction between
an income tax which is relatively static and one which rises on a graduated basis. By now, every urbanized state has an income tax, but
not all of them are effective revenue producers. Pennsylvania has a
flat 2 percent levy on individual income, and Ohio's income tax begins
at .5 percent and rises very gradually to only 3.5 percent. By contrast, New York's individual income tax begins at 2 percent and rises
to 14 percent for unearned income at $23,000 or more. (In New York
State individual income derived from salaries, fees, or wages reaches
a high of 12 percent on incomes of $19,000 or more. As of this writ-
ing, the state is in the process of reducing taxes for upper income
levels.)

Table 7.2 presents these three measures for ten states in which
selected exterior cities are located. Most of these "exterior city/
states" are heavily urbanized, and some contain more than one major
city so that larger inferences can be made.

Massachusetts, New York, and California have the highest levies
in revenue effort. Maryland, Pennsylvania, Illinois, and Michigan
have higher individual income taxes than California, but their corporate
taxes are significantly lower. At the bottom end of this measure are
Louisiana, Ohio, and Missouri which are low on both the individual and
corporate sides.

The tax effort of these ten states approximates the previous pattern. New York, Massachusetts, and California make the greatest
effort, while Ohio and Missouri make the least (Louisiana does show
itself as an exception on this sole measure). In the middle are some
of the more industrialized states led by Maryland and followed in a dead
heat by Illinois, Pennsylvania, and Michigan. In fact if we were to
average out revenue effort with tax effort, the following ranking would
occur:

Table 7.2. Revenue Source and Tax Structure of Ten Exterior City/States: 1974-75

State (exterior city)	Revenue Effort individual income	Revenue Effort corporate income	Tax Effort
New York (New York City)	40.3%	10.3%	16.7%
Illinois (Chicago)	25.6	6.5	11.7
Pennsylvania (Philadelphia)	24.2	11.7	11.7
Michigan (Detroit)	26.2	8.4	11.7
Maryland (Baltimore)	36.3	5.7	12.3
Ohio (Cleveland)	15.0	6.8	9.7
Massachusetts (Boston)	44.0	12.9	14.2
Missouri (St. Louis)	22.5	4.3	10.4
Louisiana (New Orleans)	7.6	4.2	13.0
California (San Francisco)	22.6	13.1	14.6

Sources: The U.S. Advisory Commission On Intergovernmental Relations, Significant Features of Fiscal Federalism 1976-77, Tables 11, 29, and 32. Percentage of income and corporate revenue are taken for the year 1974, Tax Effort is assessed for the year 1975.

Massachusetts	23.7%
New York	22.4
Maryland	18.1
California	16.7
Pennsylvania	15.8
Michigan	15.4
Illinois	14.6
Missouri	12.4
Ohio	10.5
Louisiana	8.6

We should now hold this picture in our minds and turn to the more particular problem of how each of these states treats its cities after the revenue is collected. This can be shown by introducing a few facts of fiscal life which exist between exterior cities and their states. Table 7.3 contains some figures on the distribution of per capita aid to cities and on the percentage of urban revenues contributed by a state. The third column in this table shows the difference within an entire state between per capita aid spent on highways and on welfare assistance. Though this last column is a rougher measure of urban aid, it is useful. All ten exterior cities have a disproportionate amount of welfare recipients relative to their state populations. New York City, with 44 percent of the state's population, contains 70 percent of its welfare recipients; Philadelphia, with 18 percent of Pennsylvania's population, has 33 percent of the welfare recipients. For Baltimore, the figures are 27 percent versus 66 percent; for Boston 13 percent versus 39 percent; and for St. Louis 15 percent versus 25 percent. (12) Generally, the welfare burden that exterior cities carry for their states is twice their expected amount, and it is not unreasonable to assume that statewide highway assistance does not serve the interests of the central city. Just how urban interests are or are not served by state dollars can be seen in this table.

Again, the figures do not indicate a radical departure from earlier patterns. There appears to be a link between state revenue policies as indirect efforts to meliorate urban problems and state assistance policies as direct efforts to help cities. The one place which surfaces as a leading beneficiary of direct assistance is Baltimore, Maryland. Heretofore, the state of Maryland had been in the upper middle range of revenue raising policies, and well behind Massachusetts and New York. Under direct assistance policies, however, Maryland furnishes more to its leading city in two categories (percent of aid and per capita aid) than any other city listed. Part of this can be explained by Baltimore's jurisdictional status, i.e. the city does not rely on an encompassing county for its services. This is, however, only a

Table 7.3. State Assistance to Ten Exterior Cities: 1973-76

City/State	State Aid % of City Revenue	Per Capita State Aid to City	Per capita difference in a State Between Welfare & Highway Ass't ($)
New York, N.Y.	20%	.37	+100.44
Chicago, Ill.	12	.04	-1.38
Philadelphia, Pa.	15	.08	-1.48
Detroit, Michigan	15	.09	-19.50
Baltimore, Md.	50	.62	-15.69
Cleveland, Ohio	9	.04	-13.25
Boston, Mass.	24	.27	-2.49
St. Louis, Mo.	12	.06	-4.73
New Orleans, La.	15	.07	-6.75
San Francisco, Ca.	26	.29	+71.58

Sources: U.S. Department of Commerce, Bureau of the Census, City Government Finances in 1975-76; and U.S. Advisory Commission on Intergovernmental Relations, Significant Features of Fiscal Federalism, Vol. I, 1973-74, Table 58. Data for New York were taken from the State Charter Revision Commission for New York City, Preliminary Recommendations of the State Charter Revision Commission for New York City, Table I, p. 32, and from census data.

partial explanation since New York City encompasses five counties and San Francisco is coterminous with a county, yet neither of these two cities comes close to Baltimore's relative share. On the per capita difference between welfare and highways, Baltimore comes out on the plus side of dollar expenditures. Nonetheless, its figure of +15.69 is behind New York and California, the only other states that spend more dollars per capita on welfare than they do on highways.

After Maryland, New York, Massachusetts, and California surface as leading meliorist states. New York is highest in per capita welfare aid over highways with California second, but both require local governments to meet a significant part of the cost.

The states that offer the least direct assistance to their biggest cities were also cited earlier as having less favorable revenue policies, namely Ohio, Missouri, and Louisiana. Illinois is less generous with its major city than most other states, but does have a less damaging distribution of welfare/highway funds than either Ohio, Missouri, or Louisiana.

Once again, the states which fall into an ambiguous middle are Pennsylvania and Michigan. This middle group of states is the least defined with some (like Illinois) falling into or out of it, depending on the measure being used.

Despite the variations, it is feasible to make nominal categories for these states based on a meliorist/reinforcing dichotomy. Those states with indirect revenue policies, sympathetic toward exterior cities and awarding cities higher direct assistance payments, fit well as meliorist states. These states are "interventionist" because they seek to mitigate the effects of local fragmentation through a state dominated system of graduated taxes. Direct assistance to cities has a softening effect, and it should be noted that while welfare aid does little to change the core of urban poverty it does make that condition marginally easier. At the opposite end, those states with weaker tax policies increase competition between city and suburb (as well as with other states) and can be classified as reinforcing states. The limited amount of direct assistance they afford exterior cities does nothing to stem the flight of the middle class and the natural push of privatism.

These states are broken down into the three basic categories as follows. The listing is alphabetical and not by rank.

Meliorist	Mixed or Ambiguous	Reinforcing
California	Illinois	Louisiana
Maryland	Michigan	Missouri
Massachusetts	Pennsylvania	Ohio
New York		

With the mounting concern about the need to adopt a national urban policy, some policymakers have expressed an interest in strengthening the state role. In no small part, the concern has been spurred on by state lobbying organizations and by the prospect of federal bonuses for those states that take the lead. Some states have already promulgated an urban strategy which, though largely a product of the governor's staff, represents an effort to control the economic and political environment of their cities. It remains to be seen how far state legislatures will take an urban stretegy, but for some states there is a format which has been put to paper.

Massachusetts and California, both meliorist states, have attempted to establish themselves as pace setters in this effort. New York, Maryland, and Massachusetts have taken singular steps, particularly in housing and community development. These steps are even more noteworthy than paper efforts, because they are tangible and their achievements and failures could be felt in urban communities. How California undertook the Bay Area Rapid Transportation (BART) project also tells us something about meliorist states.

For obvious reasons, the "mixed" and reinforcing states have not been as active in urban policymaking. Michigan has been attempting to formulate urban related policies and has provided inducements for economic development. Illinois services Chicago with an old but reasonable rail system drawing on revenue from the surrounding region. Pennsylvania and Missouri have established neighborhood assistance programs in which local businesses receive tax credits for contributions they make toward community betterment. In Philadelphia, a group of clothing manufacturers used this tax credit to run training programs, rehabilitate housing, and stimulate commerce. Compared to the immensity of deterioration in Philadelphia, St. Louis, and Chicago, these are pallid efforts. Indeed, most of what states finally undertake is modest, and it is rare to see urban policies implemented that are commensurate with the size of the problem. Whether it is recognized or not, any discussion of state action to alleviate the crisis of exterior cities is bound to find itself on the shoals of public policy. States simply have not had the energy nor the will to attempt a massive social uplift, and it is only in the last ten years that some have even recognized the problem. Any classification of states as "meliorist" is relative. Given the choice of doing something rather than nothing at all, meliorist states have chosen to do something, but in most it has been a case of too little and too late.

THE MELIORIST MEA CULPA:
PICKING UP THE PIECES AFTERWARD

The environment that meliorist states have created for their localities
is the product of vigorous activity in certain areas and complete passivity in others. It was often easier for states to act with vigor in
areas that did not require continual supervision, such as the creation
of major universities and the construction of major highway systems.
(13) In the mundane concerns of establishing rules for the regulation
of daily life, states were generally "non-interventionist." By ideology
and by temperament, Americans are great practitioners of local
government, so as long as localities acted within prescribed limits
they could fix the rules of ordinary behavior. Local governments
were free to raise property or sales taxes, determine zoning practices,
and establish local ordinances. Over the long run, this blend of fragmented, local discretion and private enterprise was a very potent
combination in precipitating the decline of central cities. Whether by
ignorance, inadvertence, or calculation, state power was instrumental
in the exodus from the city. Washington may have provided the bulk
of the money for giant roadways, but state highway departments applied
for the grants and determined the routes.

In many instances, state governments were simply reacting to
the politics of localism and private interest that had already begun to
flourish. Many states conditioned their highway programs on local
approval, and when that approval was not quickly forthcoming construction was begun in more sparsely populated areas. Fewer residents
usually meant less displacement, less trouble, and a rise in the price
of real estate. This kind of highway building is akin to the land use
policy of "leap frog" zoning, where land too expensive to build on is
bypassed in favor of undeveloped land. The upshot is an ugly spread
of industrial parks and tract housing which soon surround the more
expensive land and ripen it for similar development. "Leap frog"
highway construction has occurred throughout suburbs in Boston,
Baltimore, and New York City.

In Massachusetts, the most rural parts of Interstate 90 were
completed in Hampden and Worcester Counties a number of years before highway segments in metropolitan Boston. The same development occurred with Massachusetts' Interstate 93 which was constructed
in less densely settled communities well to the north of Boston. Baltimore fell prey to six and eight lane highways which circumvented the
city and short-circuited its traditional transportation routes. The object was to bypass the city and speed traffic through the emerging
Bos-Wash complex. As a consequence of these routes, Maryland

suburbs sprung up – not for the city of Baltimore but for the burgeoning industries of law and lobbying in the nation's capital. In New York, the titan of highway builders, Robert Moses, ticker-taped the surrounding countryside with 416 miles of parkways. The parkways were not for use by buses, but were hidden away in exclusive suburbs as semi-private tracks for automobile owners. Moses exercised his right to build through an interlocking directorate of state positions and rose to his enormous prerogative with the blessings of some of New York's most popular governors. (14)

Both federal and state highway policy was enacted as a stimulant to economic development, and that often meant development which was land extensive. The stated objective of an earlier highway plan for Massachusetts was "to serve committed future development" – not past development or the rehabilitation of worn out communities, but "future development" which could open up new land. (15) As a land extensive technology, highway construction favors open spaces, and many state allocation formulas take account of this by funding for road mileage rather than density of use. Trolleys and rail transport were once the staples of urban development, and communities would flourish around their junctures and stations. Today, only four states in the Union (New York, New Jersey, Massachusetts, and Maryland) spend more than 15 percent of their transportation budget on mass transit. (16) The rest goes to highways.

The use of land extensive highways by the states has had its intended effects. Valuable coastline and green space have been consumed by private development in the Bay State. Former wetlands and acres of potato farms have been covered over by concrete and bridges in New York State. And in California, 15,000 to 20,000 acres of agricultural land are lost each year to a spreading urbanization. (17)

The loss of coastal land has become so serious in California that special state and regional commissions have been established to control the private expropriation of this natural resource. More than half of California's 1,072 miles of beach is in private hands, and many of the public beaches are ringed by privately owned parcels, making them impossible to reach without committing an act of trespass. (18) Despite previous state legislation to regulate coastal zone development, local governments have now wrestled away much of that authority and conservationists are fearful that the abuses will return.

States have also taken direct methods to promote economic development with little regard for their major cities. Most states in the union offer incentives to attract new industry. The list of potential benefits to corporations is huge and consists of: (19)

Services & Giveaways	Direct Financial Ass't.	Tax Benefits
Free land.	Loan guarantees for equipment and	Accelerated depreciation for industrial
Sites for industrial parks.	machinery.	equipment.
	Loan guarantees for	Corporate income tax
University facilities for research and	building and construction.	exemption.
development.		Sales use tax exemption on new goods.
	Industrial development bonds.	
Employee recruitment and screening.		Tax exemption on raw
	Aid for plant expansion	material used in manu-
Employee training.	and construction.	facture.

The meliorist states of California, Maryland, Massachusetts, and New York offer some or all of these incentives. In services and giveaways, these states provide concessions on land for industrial parks and employee services for newly located firms. California offers the least direct financial assistance. Perhaps because California is already saturated with corporate investments, or perhaps because it has begun to feel the liabilities of smog and sprawl, the state has been reluctant to do more for corporations and is rated by one consulting firm as the 47th worst state for business advantages. Maryland, Massachusetts, and especially New York have no such inhibitions and provide a full panoply of advantages to privatism. Loan guarantees, development bonds, and plant expansion are available to interested firms, in addition to the construction and leasing of first rate facilities. Also, while individual income taxes are relatively high in these three states, averaging more than 40 percent, corporate income taxes are remarkably moderate, averaging less than 10 percent.

Hardly any of these incentives are consciously applied to benefit central cities. (20) Most tax incentives are indiscriminately given across the state and, since many of the benefits are loaded in the direction of new facilities, rural and suburban areas are the leading beneficiaires. Plant construction and land concessions most easily take place in open spaces, and states are happy enough to stimulate this business. Expecting the states to steer privatism toward distressed cities is contrary to the habit of their politics.

Moreover, it is questionable whether providing incentives truly creates new industry or just shifts the existing ones around. Understandably, most states are not enthusiastic about examining this issue. Local competition and arguments about state aid are severe enough without giving them an official format. As an exception to the rule, Massachusetts has taken a peek at the consequences and the results are not encouraging. In an extraordinary admission of mea culpa, the state made a study of how its policies were affecting older communities. One of these policies provides for establishing Industrial Development Finance Authorities (IDFAs) in the localities. Local IDFAs can, with the permission of the state, issue tax exempt bonds, and, with the proceeds, turn them into loans for expanding manufacturers. While it was hoped that IDFAs might be of some use to the cities, it was never anticipated that they would be deleterious to them. The Massachusetts study found that:

> ...these bonds have been used extensively to support the re-
> location of industry from existing centers to suburban industrial
> parks. Of the approximately $100 million industrial revenue
> bonds...nearly $90 million has been approved for suburban and
> rural IDFAs.... (21)

Out of the total number of projects funded, 20 involved relocation and 8 of those were by industries moving from urban to suburban sites. According to the Massachusetts' findings, these locations: "...had the effect of diminishing the tax base of older urban areas and forcing urban workers to commute by private automobile if they wanted to retain their jobs." (22)

A more disturbing result of the study was the realization that extensive subsidies through IDFAs may not have been necessary. Many of the recipient firms, such as the Radio Corporation of America (which is at the top of the "Fortune 500"), could have financed themselves or gone to private banks. And every firm receiving IDFA money had previously been located within the state. (23)

The Massachusetts study is too confined to draw definitive conclusions for programs in other states, but it does point in a direction. The study also pinpoints inadequacies in Massachusetts' own investment policies: school construction that is turned away from perfectly good urban space in favor of more costly suburban space; sewer and wastewater policies that favor new lines rather than the rehabilitation of old ones; housing policies that place black welfare families in old congested cities and reserve the best spending for a handful of elderly whites in suburban towns.

Remaining silent about the effects of industrial sprawl and mis-directed state investments does not lessen their visibility. In other meliorist states, less quick than Massachusetts at self criticism, anti-urban policies are in full swing with very little being said about where or why the investments are being made. Bidding for manufacturing plants occurs at an unprecedented rate by state departments of commerce and business. New York state makes its upstream waters available for the dumping of chemical wastes for fear that stronger environmental laws will discourage business. Pennsylvania goes all out to attract a Volkswagen plant to be located in the countryside.

Often the more meliorist a state has been in the past, the more it is willing to bend over backwards to recoup its losses. Meliorism creates hazards when a state extends itself too far. These hazards take the form of high budgets, corporate raiding by other states, and crises of performance. The only perceived way to rebound from these hazards is to become "fiscally responsible" again, win back corporate confidence, and, as one state advertisement suggests, "Stop Giving Business The Business." (24) In other words, adopt a strategy of sharp reinforcement and encourage private money into the state wherever it may flow.

The precedents which led to this turnaround by meliorist states are significant for how they worked. The mechanics of those failures in housing or mass transit tell us why they failed.

CASES IN HOUSING AND MASS TRANSIT:
UDC AND BART

Housing Policy

The bulk of state housing policy is carried out by state units called housing finance authorities, or HFAs. More than half the states in the Union including all four meliorist states have HFAs. These units do not build housing, nor do they generally manage it. They do serve as lenders and insurers for private housing developers who want to take advantage of government subsidy programs.

HFAs accomplish this by raising capital through the issuance of tax exempt bonds. With the proceeds from these bonds, low interest mortgages can be made available to builders who meet the state's specifications. In other instances, these authorities loosen up the money market by buying outstanding mortgages, so that banks will have a larger amount of capital to disperse. Less frequently, HFAs acquire land for private developers and help them assemble housing projects.

The conception behind HFAs is that of a miniature government conduit, modified by cautions that are attendant to most state governments. Certainly, it was Washington's involvement in urban policy that spawned HFAs as a model of public intervention. Under Section 236 of the 1968 Housing and Development Act, the federal government made money available on rental housing which could be used to shave down interest rates on mortgages. States could either leave it up to the initiative of separate builders to get the subsidies, or intercede by organizing the applications. Typically, HFAs would invite development proposals and agree to finance a number of them. Subsidies allowed under Section 236 were "piggybacked" onto the agreed upon proposals and the conduit functioned under an expanded federal-state-private partnership.

In theory, everyone involved derives an advantage from this approach. Bond investors get safe paper that is often backed by the "full faith and credit" of the state plus a tax exemption on the interest they earn. HFAs obtain cheap money because the interest rates can be kept low. Developers enjoy low interest loans on housing that is built for low and moderate income tenants. And tenants who inhabit the sponsored buildings theoretically have the savings passed on to them through inexpensive rents.

In actuality, there is another side to HFAs that plays havoc with all these neat pieces of the conduit. At the onset, there was a nagging doubt as to whether the states were really getting their money's worth by allowing tax exempt bonds for this purpose. Politicians could boast about HFAs not cutting into their budgets, but there was bound to be a diminution on the tax receivable accounts. Regardless of which coffer the money was taken from, the state and federal treasuries would be emptier and deficits would have to be made up by those whose incomes were not tax exempt.

Despite the preparations and supports, most HFAs were ineffectual and a good many were completely dormant. Nearly half of all HFAs in 1973 had not financed a single housing unit, and most of those remaining had a paltry few thousand units to their credit. New York and Massachusetts alone accounted for almost 75 percent of all state financed housing. (25) HFAs in other states seemed like empty administrative shells.

It was not a shortage of money which wrought such disappointing results, but a lack of enthusiasm about low and moderate income housing - especially when black families were to occupy that housing. California's HFA rental units are subject to Article 34 of the state constitution, which provides that local elections must be held for projects developed by a public authority. The few places where referenda have passed are in big cities like San Francisco, Oakland, and Los Angeles.

HFAs not only incurred the stigma of publicly supported housing, but also the fiscal restraint of privately built housing. Because bonds would come due and construction loans would have to be paid off, the average HFA administrator was as cautious as the downtown banker.

Housing that could not meet investment obligations was avoided and risky tenants were shunned. After the patina of "public support" was washed away, HFAs were businesses motivated by the imperatives of the bond and housing markets.

New York State's Urban Development Corporation: I've Got the 20, If You've Got the 80.

It was this vacuum in housing policy that New York's Urban Development Corporation (UDC) sought to fill. UDC had diverse origins, but its richest vein of support came from the unmatchable supply of the Rockefellers. David Rockefeller made a speech in Washington saying that low and middle income housing ought to be built on the basis of four dollars of private capital for every one dollar of public money. Not one to miss a chance on government innovation, Governor Nelson Rockefeller called his brother the next morning saying, "David, I've got the 20 cents, if you've got the 80 cents." (26) The suggestion stuck, and a leading housing official used this ratio of four to one in promoting the UDC to a group of bankers.

The Rockefellers had a reputation as political liberals, and led the moderate, eastern wing of the Republican party. At the nucleus of that philosophy was the partnership approach between government and the private sector, and this portended some operational changes in the tax laws. Hitting at the crux of meliorism, David Rockefeller told a Senate subcommittee:

... To attract such substantial funds we must take steps to make investment in urban redevelopment more appealing in comparison with other opportunities. For instance, a closer examination of our existing tax structure is in order to stimulate private investment in our cities and to avoid driving out private investment. (27)

Three years later, the Tax Reform Act of 1969 made housing a preferred investment for people in high income brackets by providing for tax shelters of up to 50 percent on earned income and putting accelerated depreciation clauses into the law. Though not an unmixed blessing, these changes broadened the appeal of enterprises like UDC. (28)

New York was the first state to begin an HFA and the first to initiate a new type of organization for housing and urban development. UDC began where New York's HFA left off. Where HFA was slow and orthodox, UDC was rapid-fire and imaginative. Where HFA functioned like a business for the sake of the market, UDC functioned like a social catalyst for the sake of public policy.

The man Nelson Rockefeller chose to head this special unit was
Ed Logue, an urban renewal entrepreneur who earned a high reputation for his work in New Haven and Boston. Logue had previously
turned down a job as top housing administrator for New York City because it did not give him enough challenge, and he was determined to
make sure that UDC had sufficient powers to complete its mission.

Logue had a suitable counterpart in Governor Rockefeller who
collaborated with him in creating a public corporation with unusual
latitude. For UDC's revenue raising authority, Rockefeller brought
in a cagey bond attorney named John Mitchell, who was better known
as Nixon's Attorney General. Mitchell was employed by Rockefeller
to find a way around the state's requirement that revenue raising bonds
be approved by a public referendum. The legal circumvention used by
Mitchell to replace the "full faith and credit" guarantee of the state
was the "moral obligation" bond. "Moral obligation" bonds are a legal
figment which accomplish two seemingly contradictory purposes. On
the one hand, they oblige the state to consider the apportionment and
payment of funds to restore a public corporation's capital reserve
fund, should that fund be insufficient to cover one year's debt service.
On the other hand, the bonds are expressly stated not to be a debt of
the state. Since the state was obliged only to consider the appropriation of money, not necessarily approve it, the requirement for a public
refendum did not hold. Backing all of this up was the power of Nelson
Rockefeller, who was regarded as a Governor with great control over
the state legislature.

Rockefeller and Logue had other stipulations for UDC. Among
them was an initial bond raising authority of $1 billion, a substantial
amount of seed money which was to rise even higher in later years.
Another power given to UDC was the prerogative of overriding local
zoning laws. This was a point of high priority with Logue, who knew
that if localities could veto UDC projects his sphere of action would be
very limited. In the final frame of UDC, a concession was meted out
to local legislators which rested the override power in a two-thirds
vote of UDC's Board of Directors. That was still a big victory for a
man of Logue's experience, who had dealt with part-time overseers in
the past.

Getting the UDC through the state legislature was Rockefeller's
chore. The Governor believed the bill was on its way to passage when
the State Senate approved it by a strong vote of 40 to 12 in April 1968.
Rockefeller left Albany to attend the funeral of Martin Luther King.
In his absence the State Assembly defeated the bill and the surprised
Governor reacted sharply. First he plied the King episode through
public opinion and publicized a Message of Necessity urging that UDC
be passed immediately. Next he worked on the private perquisites of

individual legislators, and directed a long distance lobbying campaign
from Atlanta to Albany. Rockefeller's efforts brought the Assembly
around and UDC was passed. When asked at the bill signing ceremony
whether he promised favors in exchange for votes, the Governor responded with that insouciant tone of a veteran politician, "No, I put it
the other way around...that I would be unable to do personal favors."
He also denied that a handsome pension bill for the lawmakers that was
awaiting his signature had anything to do with the Assembly's vote. (29)

    With UDC inscribed as law, Rockefeller and Logue began to put
the corporation into action. (30) The first step was to make the national
money markets available to UDC and, for this, Rockefeller approached
Mr. George Woods, director and former chairman of the First Boston
Corporation. Though Woods disclaimed having any knowledge about
housing or urban development, he was offered the chairmanship of
UDC's Board of Directors. Woods accepted on the condition that First
Boston be the senior managing underwriters for UDC's bond issue. (31)

    Mr. Woods was an obvious success with the bonds, and they sold
at an interest rate just a notch above the state's "full faith and credit"
securities. Seven firms participated in the underwriting syndicate,
among them Chase Manhattan, Citibank, Morgan Guarantee, Saloman
Brothers and, of course, First Boston. Between them the profit was
$3.9 million on an initial offering of $250 million. (32)

    With some initial capital available, it was now Logue's task to
operate what was going to be the second biggest housing and development agency in the nation. UDC did not eliminate the governmental
conduit - its entire financial backbone was a product of bank investment firms - but it could venture into areas prohibited to most HFAs.
It could raise start up capital, acquire land, plan a project, and put
a housing "package" together.

    In some ways, UDC shortened the governmental conduit by serv-
ing as a developer and a public interest speculator. Obviously, it needed to do this if it wanted to develop where private firms saw no profit.
In other ways, the conduit was strengthened by UDC's fiscal lifeline
through the banks and the almost frenetic building pace that Logue pursued. Logue's strategy was to build and develop just as fast as he
could - and, often, faster than he could. Sites were acquired and planning investments poured in from prospective projects across the state.
Conventional rental housing was begun in the midst of Harlem's slums;
voguish "new communities" were started in the suburbs of upstate New
York; and the foundation was laid for a modern complex on a near
abandoned island in the middle of the East River. The latter project,
on Roosevelt Island, was one of Logue's visions for the future. Roosevelt Island was to be a self contained community, mixed along racial and
income lines, with no cars, and within a short tramway ride to Manhattan.

UDC even undertook projects for economic development, most of
which were outside center cities. Facilities were made available for
a leading optical company, a department store, and a brewery. The
brewery was to be established in the still unbuilt "new community" of
Radisson which prompted the jest, "Schlitz - the beer that made
Radisson feasible."

Within 18 months after UDC was signed into law, it had begun 50
projects in 23 cities. In this short time, it had over 45,000 housing
units under consideration, which was well above the combined total of
the other 49 states. Every surge for UDC meant an increasing debt,
and the state was willing to increase the corporation's bond authorization so long as Nelson Rockefeller gave assurances and bankers were
willing to buy the paper. In the first six years of operation, UDC's
cumulative financial and construction costs zoomed from $290 million
in 1969 to $1.4 billion in 1971 and to $2 billion by 1974. (32) Logue
was very conscious of this and wanted to go higher. Testifying before
an investigating commission years later, he told its members that he
would not have taken the job in the first place, "...if all I was going
to do was be involved in a billion dollar operation..." Rockefeller endorsed Logue's approach and told the same commission that he was
"not running a bank" nor was he "running a corporation for profit"
but "a social institution trying to help people." The former Governor
continued to tell the commission that he was "always ready to err on
the side of achieving social objectives" even if that meant taking
risks. (33)

Yet the risks that both men were willing to take weakened their
command over the process and showed just how vulnerable they were
to banking underwriters. The more UDC built, the greater it needed
to sell bonds, and the greater that need became, the more bankers
could exert power over what UDC was doing.

UDC's vulnerability was exacerbated too by its reliance on Section 236 subsidies. Like conventional HFAs, the corporation used
federal subsidies to reduce the cost of the mortgage interest on buildings, thereby "piggybacking" federal dollars onto its own financial
supports. UDC was so aggressive in pursuing 236 money that it estimated receiving over 50 percent of the total distributed by Washington
to all the HFAs in the country.

UDC's entire operation was like a house of cards, and the most
precarious card of all was Logue's own method for "fast track" building. "Fast tracking" meant cutting the paper work and engaging in
site selection, planning, and start up costs before the subsidies were
formally assured. On Section 236 funds, Logue frequently went ahead
with projects on the basis of an informal understanding with HUD officials. Most of UDC's projects had little more than their foundations

laid and were not drawing revenues to pay off outstanding debts. In
the meantime, the strategy for UDC was to build, build, build, without
ever being legally certain that all of its commitments had enough financing to carry them to completion.

By 1973, the house of cards was poised against the wind and
ready to fall. The Nixon White House started the first gust when it
announced a moratorium on all housing subsidies, including those
from Section 236. Some 58 UDC projects under construction lacked
firm subsidy contracts and their condition threatened the entire UDC
operation. Governor Rockefeller flew down to Washington and intervened through John Ehrlichman. After a nervous pause of a few months,
the promised subsidies were made available. But that was all that
could be expected, and the discomfitting signals from the White House
worried the financial community.

Next came a burst of wind emanating from Albany itself. UDC
had been embroiled in Westchester County over low and moderate income housing it was hoping to place in some of the richest and whitest
townships in the United States. Lurking as the ultimate weapon against
these townships was the corporation's power to override zoning laws.
The townships resisted, complained of an infringement on home rule,
and the state legislature responded by clipping UDC's power to override local zoning laws. The incident was enough to shake UDC's confidence and cause others to wonder about its real strength.

The next news from Albany was far more serious. In December
1973, Nelson Rockefeller resigned as the Governor of New York State,
ending a reign that had lasted for 15 years. With Rockefeller's personal obligation to the state gone, the moral obligation of the state to
outstanding bonds could be in question. Members of the underwriting
syndicate had been clamoring about UDC's bonding authority and demanded that the corporation slow down. Now one major bank, Morgan
Guaranty Trust, had withdrawn as an underwriter bringing an additional chill to the air.

The last bit of news was enough to precipitate the actual collapse
of UDC and bring its entire house of cards down. It came within months
of Rockefeller's resignation when, in April 1974, the Port Authority
Bond Covenant between New York and New Jersey was repealed. The
Bond Covenant guaranteed that the Port Authority would not make investments in an unprofitable mass transit system, aside from the minimal commitments it had already agreed to support. Though the Port
Authority was an issue apart from UDC, it did involve the commitment
of another public authority to the financial well-being of its bondholders.
The repeal of that commitment by two states was enough to conjure up
doubts about the worth of UDC's moral obligation bonds.

Within a month after the repeal, the interest rate on UDC bonds
was so high that offerings had to be withdrawn. UDC was virtually

locked out of the bond market and it knew it. Logue later claimed that
the bankers had decided to test New York's willingness to stand behind
UDC, and teach it a "lesson that you'd better not repeal bond covenents."
The bankers conceded that after the Port Authority episode they had
grave misgivings about "moral obligation" bonds, but also pointed to
irresponsible accounting practices by UDC and a "disastrous market"
that was beyond their control. (34)

Whatever weight is assigned to each of these complex causes, the
UDC strategy had failed. It was paying astronomical interest rates, it
was unable to meet its daily expenses, and debts were coming due which
it could not meet. By the winter of 1974, UDC was spending $1 million
a day just to keep up with its 500 staff employees and 8,000 construction workers. With only a trickle of revenue coming in from fees and
a few completed projects, UDC was broke and unable to go further. On
February 25, 1974, UDC's treasurer notified the managing bank of a
lending syndicate that it was unable to pay outstanding notes. New York
State's Urban Development Corporation had formally defaulted.

The crisis of UDC was now brought to a head. After months of
negotiations and task force reports, the apparent decisions were made.
Logue was fired as soon as Hugh Carey became Governor. A large
section of UDC's technical staff (particularly those in design, construction, and legal departments) were also let go.

In a foray of negotiations with top investment bankers the state
worked out an agreement whereby it agreed to give UDC additional
funds and the banks agreed to lend the corporation additional money.
In exchange, the reconstituted UDC promised not to undertake any new
projects. Notwithstanding John Mitchell's legal refinements, the banks
insisted that UDC's obligations constituted a de facto state debt. Eventually, the state paid over $200 million to restore UDC's credit. Though
there were threats and compromises over the details of finance, the
"social objectives" approach was a patently ridiculous issue for discussion. The state was in bad financial condition, New York City had
to borrow huge chunks of money to keep abreast of its spending, and
everyone knew who controlled the bond market.

Mass Transit Policy

The major source of decay for exterior cities in the northeast and
north central states lies in their stagnant economies and wasted housing
stock. This is what prompted New York and Massachusetts to support
a UDC or an aggressive HFA. California is in a newer period of development and its major cities suffer not so much from the corrosive
aspects of age as they do from the consequences of wildcat growth.

More so than other Americans, Californians are addicted to the automobile and to the building of freeways. California has more automobiles per capita than any other state, and at last count exceeded other states in total number of registered motor vehicles by 75 percent. More than 4,000 miles of freeway have been built since the Pasadena freeway was constructed in 1940, and the state has a long-term plan to build over 12,000 more miles at a cost of over $10 billion. (35) To pay for this, the state has its own highway trust fund and has embedded an amendment into its constitution which effectively prohibits the diversion of these funds for anything but highway use.

Auto addiction is more acute in the southern half of the state than it is in the San Francisco Bay Area. Modern Los Angeles was made for the automobile. It is carved out by freeways which twist through every part of it. Most of that city has been swallowed up by the debris of the auto culture. Gas stations, feeder streets, and parking lots as big as football fields cover Los Angeles. In its land use pattern, Los Angeles lacks a coherent "downtown" commensurate with its size, and two-thirds of its remnant business district is given over to the automobile. Residents of Los Angeles County spend over $5 billion each year to feed their habit, and this does not include the financial cost of keeping up the highways nor the social cost of smog and pollution. And yet, voters in the Los Angeles area have turned down more than one referendum for mass transit. (36) Despite the urging of some political and business leaders, Los Angeles has not been able to develop a workable mass transit system. The city and its surrounding suburbs are not built for it, and citizens are not willing to pay for public transportation when it is easier to travel by car.

The San Francisco Bay Area is another story. That area has an extensive public service through buses and trolleys and a strong tradition of mass transit support. Land use patterns in San Francisco are more akin to traditional cities like Philadelphia or Boston. Business and cultural enterprises are closely knit and designed for pedestrians rather than cars. Residences are tied into the commercial fiber of the city instead of segregated from it by distant shopping malls. San Francisco is an exterior city where mass transit can thrive because it is easy and cheaper for urban dwellers to use than the automobile.

Outside of San Francisco the land use patterns change into low density suburbs which, like Los Angeles, were built around the automobile. Nonetheless, planners contended that these suburbs were suited for mass transit (particularly fixed rail systems) because of their confinement along either side of the Bay. San Francisco's suburbs are molded into narrow strips that run parallel to each other on the east or west parts of the Bay. These strips converge in San Francisco (West Bay) or in Oakland (East Bay) and are linked by bridges at various points.

BART: Mass Transit for the Few/Highways for the Many

As highways and cars from the suburbs began to crowd the passageways
into San Francisco, pressure for a mass transit solution intensified.
Much of the stimulus came from the business community in San Francisco, and this was quickly joined to official or quasi official designation by the state. As early as 1944, the state of California established
the Bay Area Council (BAC), whose roster held the most prestigious
business names in the Bay Area. Bechtel, Kaiser, Standard Oil of
California, Hewlett Packard, and the Bank of America all had executive representation on BAC's board of trustees. For the first years,
BAC was state supported, but by 1945, it became a non-profit group
with funds pledged by its corporate progenitors.

    With economic recovery a prime objective after World War II,
BAC set out to promote San Francisco's business climate, and transportation was a top priority. Staff workers bandied about the possibilities for mass transit, and BAC lobbied at the state legislatures for a
public instrument which could move plans beyond the stage of speculation.

    Besides BAC, there were other sources of support for mass
transit. (37) Under the leadership of Marvin Lewis, a San Francisco
supervisor, an ad hoc group of local officials, businessmen and civic
activists was formed called the Bay Area Rapid Transit Committee.
The Committee recognized the regional nature of the problem and was
composed of representatives from six counties - San Francisco,
Alameda, Contra Costa, Marin, San Mateo, and Santa Clara. Within
a short time, the affiliation with the Committee had spread to 9 surrounding counties and 36 cities.

    With BAC and the Committee serving as a nucleus, the Califor-
nia legislature was prodded into creating an alphabetocracy of Bay
Area abbreviations which could put the force of officialdom behind
mass transit. Through the decade of the 1950s the precursors for
BART were activated by the state. By 1951 the Committee had been
superseded by a state created Commission called the Bay Area Rapid
Transit Commission (BARTC). Interestingly, 13 of the 26 BARTC
commissioners had been members of BAC, and these close ties with
the business sector continued through BART's formative period. (38)

    BARTC was charged with conducting a systematic investigation
of rapid transit problems and delivering recommendations on what
might be done about them. By the early 1950s those recommendations
were in order and submitted to the state legislature. BARTC's major
suggestion was for the creation of a coordinated rapid transit plan for
nine counties within and around San Francisco. In addition to San
Francisco, four of those counties were located near the heart of the

central city (Alameda, Contra Costa, Marin and San Mateo). The
sixth county, Santa Clara, was at the south end of the West Bay and
San Francisco's pull on it was less strong. The seventh, eighth, and
ninth counties (Sonoma, Napa, and Solano) were lightly populated and
not as dependent on the daily traffic which poured into the central city.
Still, what BARTC was seeking was a comprehensive regional system
which would ultimately include rural or semi-rural areas.

In 1957, the California state legislature responded. Though
BART enthusiasts did not get all of what they wanted, a substantial
chunk of their ideas remained when Sacramento established the Bay
Area Rapid Transid District (BARTD). BARTC had successfully ex-
pired, and BARTD took its place with five counties as members instead of nine. San Francisco, Alameda, Contra Costa, Marin, and
San Mateo were the most populated counties within the Bay Area and
their inclusion into BARTD signaled a promise of things to come. For
the first time in fifty years, a mass transit system stood ready to be
built. All that the state of California required was the concurrence of
each of the counties in arranging the financial and political details.

For its part, the state had given BART the power to levy taxes
within the district, to issue bonds as a source of capital, and to compose a board of directors with representatives from the member counties. There were constraints put on these powers such as limitations
that taxes could not exceed a certain amount of the assessed property
value within the district and limitations on the bond debt which the district could incur. The most telling limitation was that, before BART
could begin to act as a public entity, the five counties would have to
approve its most fundamental steps. The first of these steps required
each county to agree to its incorporation into the district. The second
required that bond authorization be approved by a two-thirds popular
vote of the entire district. In short, though the state had given BART
the breath of life, its continuance was placed back into the respiratory
system of the localities.

BART was soon put to some disappointing tests. In December
1961, the San Mateo Board of Supervisors unanimously rejected the
plan for BART and voted to withdraw from the district. There were
many reasons for San Mateo's decision, but, quite clearly, realtors
in the county feared that better transit to San Francisco would threaten
the growth of shopping centers in their county. Two realtors in particular were very influential with San Mateo's supervisors and made it
clear that a vote for BART would jeopardize their political futures. (39)
Also, the Southern Pacific Railroad exerted a strong influence against
BART. The railroad opposed the introduction of another transit system into the county because it would be forced to maintain the unprofitable remnants of an expanded commuter service. A retired vice-

president of Southern Pacific held office as a San Mateo supervisor, and he was a conspicuous influence in the county's withdrawal. (40)

Once the choices were placed back into spheres of local politics, BART suffered from a lack of confidence which spread to other counties. San Mateo's decision was affected by the earlier exclusion of Santa Clara and by Marin County's anticipated withdrawal from BART. No doubt the psychological impact of a shrinking membership prompted supervisors to question the efficacyof mass transit, and this was aggravated by the realities of land use politics. On the West Bay, electronic and aircraft industries were sprawling just to the south of San Mateo in neighboring Santa Clara. This spurred a belief that San Francisco would not hold the key to the Bay Area's economy, and that it would be foolish to make such a heavy investment in a fixed rail system. San Mateo also looked northward and saw that BART was having enormous trouble in building a track on the Golden Gate Bridge so that it could reach into Marin County. The bridge authority resisted the idea of allowing BART to run on an additional deck and exercised its autonomy by denying BART access. By force of circumstances, Marin County and BART were compelled to cancel their plans.

By 1962, BART had been whittled down to three participating counties (Alameda, Contra Costa, and San Francisco) and was about to undergo its second test in obtaining district approval for its bond issue. Sensing more trouble ahead, BART leaders lobbied the legislature for a revision of its enabling legislation concerning bond approval. Normally, special districts need only gain a majority of voter approval for a bond issue. The legislation for BART hoisted that requirement to a two-thirds approval until BART officials managed to reduce it to 60 percent. This resuscitated BART's chances for survival, since an analysis of past bond votes in the Bay Area showed that half of all bond turndowns could have been avoided by lowering the margin a mere 6 percent.

Various accounts of the BART story attempt to paint it as the product of a big business conspiracy against the rest of the Bay Area. (41) The interpretation is not so much overdrawn as it is misleading. Business interests were split depending upon where they were located in the Bay Area and whether they stood to lose or gain from BART's passage. Certainly, the greatest BART boosters came out of BAC's leadership which consisted of established firms with considerable investment in the central city. But newer corporations that were situated in the suburbs and rural land speculators were dead against BART.

Whatever the nuances of the interpretation, certain parts of privatism were anxious to see BART built and gave their time and money to that end. Carl Wente, a former top executive with the Bank

of America, was contacted and asked to spearhead a campaign for the
passage of the bond issue. His efforts bore financial fruit when some
of the largest enterprises in San Francisco backed the campaign. These
included the Bank of America, Wells Fargo, Bethlehem Steel, West-
inghouse Electric, the Kaiser Corporation and many others. As Wente
relates his fund raising encounters:

> I solicited (Edgar) Kaiser and I told him at the time, "You are
> interested in this for several reasons. First place you are
> interested from a civic standpoint; it is a good thing for the city.
> You have your office here. You are in the cement business, you
> are in the aluminum business, you are in the engineering busi-
> ness, you are in all kinds of... Your outfit ought to be interested
> in this from every conceivable angle. " (42)

With the help of corporate money the bond vote passed. The reduction in the approval margin turned out to be the difference between
success and failure. San Francisco gave BART its biggest victory
with almost 67 percent of its voters approving, in Alameda the vote
was slightly over 60 percent, and in Contra Costa only 54 percent of
the voters approved of the bond. Had the vote been by county instead
of district, BART would have failed.

BART could have gone either way at any time in its history, and
this is reflected in the constituency it served, its design, and its basic
objectives. BART had to appeal to interests which could win political
acceptance and it had to offer a dramatic vision of the future to make
the financial stakes worthwhile. Only 7.5 miles of BART's 75 mile
route are located within San Francisco. It is not a system for the
entire city of San Francisco, but for its central business district and
financial community. Aside from parts of the Mission District, few
of San Francisco's neighborhoods have direct access to BART, and
rather than knitting the city together BART opens it up to the surrounding suburbs. Of the system's 34 stations, only 8 are located within
San Francisco, and most of these are at business junctures. BART
serves suburban commuters who come to the city to carry out their
business. Individuals in upper income brackets constitute a disproportionate amount of its riders. (43) More than a few of BART's
boosters stood to gain from increased property values on buildings
located near transit stations.

BART is sleek in its design and built to impress viewers. The
engineering was done by companies that earned their income through
defense contracts and by aerospace firms. Train speeds reach 80
miles an hour and are controlled by electronic sensing devices, trans-
mitters, and receivers. Coordination and scheduling is done by com-

puter and everything is automated, including devices which detect
trains that are running too close to one another.

The virtues of Pentagon technology also have their vices, fos-
tering the claim that BART was over-engineered and stacked with unnecessary gadgetry. Often the gadgetry went wrong. "Phantom"
trains which were never really there were spotted by unreliable machinery bringing passenger-filled trains to an abrupt halt. Doors
would open while trains were en route, or failed to open when trains
reached their stations. The opening of BART was marred by a major
accident when a faulty speed code caused a train to go off its track.

These technical failures were compounded by more serious financial and political failures. Cost overruns by companies which
were used to an absorbent Defense Department threw BART into a financial crisis. Millions of dollars in underestimated expenses and
cost overruns piled up and threatened to bring construction to a halt
in 1968. BART and supervisors within the three-county district appealed to Sacramento for help. A number of taxing proposals went
before the state legislature and some passed one house. There were
bills to increase the taxes on auto use, suggestions were made to divert highway funds, a sales tax on gasoline was proposed, and the
state senate passed a measure to increase bridge tolls to subsidize
mass transit.

None of these found their way into the statute book, although
some bridge tolls were already diverted to BART under the rationale
that mass transit would reduce auto congestion on bridges. The California highway lobby (partly composed of the Automobile Club, the
Motor Car Dealers, and the Highway Users Conference) snuffed out
whatever chances there were of getting auto users to subsidize mass
transit. Then Governor of California, Ronald Reagan, commented that
he would not approve any general statewide tax for the purpose of aiding mass transit. Reagan's statement narrowed the options and the
legislature was unable to come up with a state solution. The only
choice left was to throw the burden of mass transit back on a regressive tax within the district. Hence, a .5 percent regional sales tax
was enacted and signed into law.

By the time BART became operational in the early 1970s, it was
perceived as a white elephant on wheels. Critics attacked it from all
corners. Academics derided it for being impractical and cost inefficient. Studies were done showing that it would have been less costly
and more effective to maintain a bus service instead of a fixed rail
mass transit. Surveys attempted to prove that BART had little or no
impact on reducing auto congestion, and that half of its ridership was
drawn from other types of mass transit. Because BART is mainly
supported by property and sales taxes, lower income households were
said to be paying for mass transit for the rich. (44)

In Sacramento, officials chafed at the shortfalls in BART fares. Less than half of the expected patronage was riding BART so instead of promised surpluses the system was running into large operating deficits. In Washington, officials in both the Ford and Carter administrations were looking askance at fixed rail, mass transit systems that were planned for other cities. A memorandum was passed along from President Carter to his Secretary of Transportation questioning the advisability of fixed rail systems and pointing to the BART experience. Despite the energy crisis and the carcinogens from automobile fumes, people began to wonder whether mass transit was worth it. They were also wondering about a problem which was fundamental to the exterior city - there can be no mass transit where there is no mass.

Lessons from UDC and BART

UDC and BART were two of the most substantial attempts by the states to deal with the crises of exterior cities. In the case of UDC, New York attempted to inject its power into the fabric of local government. California was non-interventionist and allowed the initiative to well up from the localities. All the state did for BART was give it enabling legislation and allow the localities to tax themselves.

What went wrong? At the outset there were problems of basic strategy. Though it purported to help distressed cities, UDC built everywhere, and quite often in open spaces and "new communities." The UDC commitment to the crisis of the city was only surface deep; it failed to target its efforts toward the most blighted areas. In much the same way that private developers seek new land, UDC built on a near vacant Roosevelt Island and sought fresh suburbs to relocate urban dwellers.

The same difficulty might be attributed to BART which was built more for the area around San Francisco than for the city itself. It was not Hunter's Point that BART sought to salvage but Montgomery Street. Perhaps bringing suburban commuters into the central city is an important step toward urban recuperation. More business creates more jobs and opportunities within the city. But to build mass transit almost exclusively for upper income suburbanites and to avoid ghetto communities is hardly an urban program.

Moreover, the influence of privatism in UDC and BART was paramount. UDC was entirely reliant on banking underwriters for its finances. Once the banks decided to put a halt to the dollar flow, UDC was helpless. The line between policy decisions and financial support is very thin, and this eventually brought down the entire effort.

BART was also very much a product of the business community. Thus, its entire design and function had to satisfy those interests.

Like most public policies, it was run through a conduit with the state, and when it failed another government enterprise was discredited. This is not necessarily to contend that privatism ought to be barred from public enterprises, but only to point up that government needs to guard its prerogatives jealously. Once the state assumes the ultimate responsibility, it ought to take care that public purposes are served.

Neither UDC nor BART possessed any real capacity to produce wealth on their own. Both enterprises acted as stimuli for the production of private wealth. Public policy carried the burden of investment and private enterprise took the profit from its overspill. Under the best of circumstances, this might yield an increase in tax revenues, but, under less favorable outcomes, governments must absorb the deficits. For both UDC and BART, the most optimistic possibilities followed the tactics of a "trickle down" strategy. If public investment works, private entrepreneurs profit and pass the rewards down to ordinary citizens.

Though UDC and BART were state initiatives, the power of individual localities was significant. Neither New York nor California overcame the power of their suburbs. Technically, the states could impose their will. Politically, they could be resisted by suburban legislators who sat at the state capital or by local supervisors who deliberated in the counties. In the case of UDC, a powerful governor managed to ram it through the Assembly, but even he was reversed once UDC threatened the suburbs with its zoning override. For BART, the state never presumed to supersede the discretion of local government to join the district. Counties were given the right to withdraw from BART and acted according to their perceived interests.

This raises some disturbing questions about the de facto efficacy of state sovereignty. Historically, the states have displaced local jurisdictions when they saw fit. This has been done with individual localities and especially to exterior cities. Most recently, the New York State legislature enacted an extension for New York City's Emergency Financial Control Board, without even consulting the City Council. But can a state act against a coalition of suburban localities? The evidence from UDC and BART indicates that it apparently cannot, or at least does not choose to encourage such a confrontation.

Finally, the federal presence on all policy is pervasive. Much like state government, Washington cannot escape its influence on the cities or the suburbs. For UDC this was quite apparent. The impetus for state housing policy came from Section 236 subsidies, and when those were frozen UDC went into a tailspin. Washington not only gave birth to agencies like UDC, but it shaped the method for building low cost housing. For BART the federal role was more subtle. Most of California's highways were built with federal money, yet Washington's

contribution to BART was miniscule. Out of the $1. 6 billion to con-
struct and equip BART, only $315 million, or about 19 percent, came
from Washington. Yet it was the federal infusion of highway money
which created the need for BART by making automobile congestion
possible. Californians complained about chronic deficits in mass
transit because they had to pay the bill through higher sales and property taxes. In the meantime, federal assistance was going into a
highway program ten times as costly as BART and little was heard
about deficits. What made mass transit imperative for the Bay Area
was what made it unfeasible. Federally funded highways at once
brought on the urban congestion and scattered the population to the
suburbs.

8 Cities, Suburbs, and the Colonial Syndrome

Law is the clothes men wear
Anytime, anywhere,
Law is Good-morning and Good-night.

Others say, Law is our Fate;
Others say, Law is our State;
Others say, others say
Law is no more
Law is gone away.

And always the loud angry crowd
Very angry and very loud
Law is We,
And always the soft idiot softly Me.

Auden, 1945

Urban scholars have gone to considerable lengths to disprove what seems apparent to the public eye. If it appeared to ordinary people that big cities were rotting at their core and that most suburbs were clean and prosperous, urbanists did not ask why this need occur but questioned whether it was occurring at all. A leading text in the field claimed that disparities between cities and suburbs were "over emphasized," and that suburbia was "not the exclusive domain of the country club set," but was increasingly typified by "blue collar workers, clerks and salesmen." (1) Another book, written by Thomas Murphy and John Rehfuss, begins by debunking "popular assumptions" about stereotypes of "Beverly Hills" or "Scarsdale," and goes on to

shade in the variations that differentiate suburbs from one another.
Typifying much of the thinking among specialists, these authors point
out that there are suburbs which are poorer than central cities, and
that along with white migration many blacks have also moved to the
suburbs. (2) For Murphy and Rehfuss, these events are sufficient
reason to discuss problems which lie just outside of the central city
as part of a "suburban crisis." So close has the suburban race toward
critical status become, that its problems are explained as a mere
"subset of the urban crisis" and it is argued that there is "no typical
suburb." (3)

No doubt, there are suburbs which have come to their full share
of the urban crisis. The contention here is that these are relatively
few in number and largely relegated to suburbs in close vicinity to the
central city. Stereotypes can be as misleading as they are helpful and,
if one tries hard enough, differences can be found within any phenomenon. For those who choose to concentrate at this level of microanaly-
sis, a lifetime can be spent in making fine distinctions between the
normally inconspicuous. After all, there are differences between the
common varities of the apple. McIntosh apples have a different shape
than Red Delicious; Red Delicious have a different color than Golden
Delicious; and so on. But apples are not coconuts - central cities are
not suburbs - and this kind of approach runs the risk of magnifying
nuances to the detriment of the larger picture. Most big cities are
radically different from most outlying suburbs and, as the old Bob
Dylan lyric suggested, "You don't need a weatherman to tell you which
way the wind is blowing." Seeing is also knowing and the overall evidence on central city/suburban disparities is overwhelming. Some
statistical evidence on differences between the exterior city and its
outlying suburbs was presented in Chapter 1, and an additional dimension is shown in Table 8.1. This table lists ten critical exterior cities
compared to their suburbs in per capita income, manufacturing employment, and retail sales.

Note that the per capita income of every listed city is lower than
that of its suburbs. Expressed as a ratio of city to suburban earnings,
for every dollar made by a suburbanite in the New York metropolitan
area, the inhabitant of the city earned only 84 cents. The Chicago resident earned 80 cents to the suburban dollar, the Baltimore resident
only 79 cents, while Cleveland had the most severe disparity with only
66 cents to the suburban dollar.

These differences are also widely repeated in manufacturing and
retail activity. Of those cities listed, only three of them (New York,
Baltimore, and New Orleans) held 50 percent or more of the manufacturing jobs in their metropolitan areas. The remaining cities fell
below the 50 percent mark, with Boston barely able to hold a fifth of

Table 8.1. Disparities Between Ten Exterior Cities and Their Suburbs on Per Capita Income, Manufacturing Employment, and Retail Sales

Metropolitan Area	Per Capita Income, 1973			Mfg. employment, 1972 (in thousands)			Retail Sales, 1972 (in millions of dollars)		
	city	suburb	ratio of city to suburb	city	suburb	city share in metro area %	city	suburb	city share in metro area %
New York	$4309	$5088	.84	757	233	76%	$14,691	$9,457	61%
Chicago	3984	4975	.80	430	479	47	6,619	9,461	41
Philadelphia	3678	4394	.83	203	295	41	3,378	6,770	33
Detroit	3817	4736	.80	180	359	33	2,673	7,160	27
Baltimore	3595	4517	.79	91	89	51	1,740	2,777	39
Cleveland	3160	4773	.66	131	138	49	1,361	3,016	31
Boston	3678	4617	.79	59	214	22	1,625	5,204	24
St. Louis	3292	4179	.78	98	158	38	1,163	3,833	23
New Orleans	3319	3544	.93	29	26	53	1,170	1,137	51
San Francisco	4762	4964	.95	69	112	38	2,796	4,833	37

Source: Data compiled from U.S. Advisory Commission on Intergovernmental Relations, "Trends in Metropolitan America," 1977, Tables 10, 13, and 14.

the manufacturing employment, and Detroit fast losing its place as an industrial center. Retail sales, long the symbol of "downtown hubs," held a relatively minor proportion of business for the city. In all but two instances (New York and New Orleans), the suburbs swallowed up most of the merchandising traffic.

The important clues to the problem, however, are not to be found in the absolute fact that cities have a smaller share of the metropolitan economy, but in relative trends which portend still further shrinkage for the city. Table 8.2 shows how cities have slipped in these same activities over the last decade or more.

Table 8.2 reveals a trend for the city which is uniformly ominous. In every single instance, cities lost their share of the metropolitan economy, while their suburbs made commensurate gains. During this period, the gap between city and suburban income widened by six cents on the dollar for the Chicago dweller, by eight cents for people in Detroit, and ten cents for the resident of New Orleans. Only New Yorkers and Philadelphians seemed to be fending off further disparity. The ratio of central city to suburban income widened over a 13 year period and continues to do so. The ten cities declined an average of 8.4 percent in manufacturing employment, and by a whopping 14 percent in retail sales. What is more, this attrition has continued through the late 1970s and, by the time the toll is taken after the 1980 census, these cities will have lost nearly a fifth of their manufacturing base and more than a quarter of their sales volume. (4) Commercial life is easily drained by vicious cycles (just as it feeds on upward spirals) and this downward drift is not likely to half without some significant change in the nation.

The trends seem plain enough, and the essential question is not to quibble over the size of city/suburban differences, but to understand why these have come about and what the relationship between city and suburb really means. Only if we appreciate the underlying connection behind the fall of the city and the rise of the suburb can we formulate alternatives; otherwise all that we do is pour the best of our resources down an open sieve.

CITIES, SUBURBS, AND THE IDEA OF
DOMESTIC COLONIALISM

In Chapter 1 it was suggested that the relationship between exterior cities and their outlying suburbs was not unlike a colonial exchange, where a dominant power exacted value from a subordinate area without giving much in return. The application of this colonial analogy

Table 8.2. Decline and Prosperity in Ten Exterior Cities and Their Suburbs

Metropolitan Area	Change in Income Ratio: City/Suburb 1960 to 1973	% Change in Mfg. Employment 1963 to 1972		% Change in Retail Sales 1963 to 1972	
		city	suburb	city	suburb
New York	00	-5%	+5%	-6%	+6%
Chicago	-.06	-12	+12	-13	+13
Philadelphia	+.01	-8	+8	-10	+10
Detroit	-.08	-8	+8	-16	+16
Baltimore	-.11	-3	+3	-16	+16
Cleveland	-.02	-11	+11	-16	+16
Boston	-.02	-6	+6	-7	+7
St. Louis	-.04	-12	+12	-14	+14
New Orleans	-.10	-10	+10	-19	+19
San Francisco	-.08	-9	+9	-11	+11

Source: U.S. Advisory Commission on Intergovernmental Relations, "Trends in Metropolitan America" 1977, Tables 10, 13, and 14.

to domestic life has been used by scholars to describe race relations and to point up how white society exploited blacks. Such an exploitation has focused on groups of people; little attention has been given to the role of territorial units in the exercise of domestic colonialism. (5) Yet classic colonialism almost invariably involved crossing over from one area into another, and a territorial distinction between the colonizer and the colonized was a central component of its makeup. So it is with the domestic variant of colonialism as it takes place between the territory of the central city and that of the suburb. Race, ethnicity, and and class all interact with territory to create a syndrome which is very much like classic colonialism.

The syndrome of domestic colonialism draws its qualities from city/suburban relationships and the fact that the prosperity of one area feeds on the misfortune of another. More precisely, this syndrome is characterized by 1) a social distinction based on the racial/ethnic and class characteristics of the people who respectively inhabit cities or suburbs, 2) an exploitative pecuniary relationship between territories in which the resources of central cities (as colonies) are depleted and put to the use of suburbs (as colonizers) and, 3) a set of political/legal devices which are used to sort out groups in order to perpetuate unequal relationships.

Taken singularly, these features constitute a random imbalance within the social system that meliorists have attempted to redress. Taken collectively, however, they constitute a systematic way in which central cities are used as well as used up by the suburbs, and for which there is little redress within the meliorist context.

Race, Ethnic, and Class Segregation
Between Cities and Suburbs

Classic or international colonialism usually transpired between members of different nationalities or races. The British takeover of the dark Indian subcontinent, the French rule over the Indochinese peninsula, and Belgium's colonization of black Africa are examples which readily come to mind. These examples of colonialism were compounded by class differences writ on a national scale, where a territory of poor peasants was exploited by a wealthy industrial power.

Admittedly, the domestic variant of colonialism is not as clear cut, but the tendencies are apparent and, in some cases, racial apartheid between inner city and outer suburb is almost complete. Why it is that particular racial or ethnic groups (Puerto Ricans, Chicanos) are segregated within central cities relates to the role in which cities have been cast as reservations for the despised minorities of our

society. As other territories have grown in worth, blacks have either
been displaced from the countryside (as in the South) or have been prevented from migrating to newly developed suburbs (as in the North).
As automation threw blacks off the tobacco and cotton fields during the
1950s, they flocked to nearby cities in search of employment. Jackson-
ville, New Orleans, and Atlanta became the immediate stop-offs for
those without subsistence. In the North, cities like New York, Detroit,
and Cleveland became reservations for migrating blacks when whites
barred them from the growing suburbs. Race became a recognizable
badge, congruent with lower class life styles, and this set the stage
for the subject population to be quarantined within the oldest urban
neighborhoods.

The movement of racial groups between 1960 and 1970 is truly
dramatic and could take place only as a result of powerful factors
which could simultaneously infuse the cities with unwanted minorities
and block them from the suburbs. In America's largest cities, one
out of every four residents is black, compared with only one out of
twenty in the suburbs. Over three million blacks were added to the
cities during the 1960s (almost three times the black increase in outlying areas), despite the fact that suburbs were growing twenty times
faster than cities. (6) In national terms, nearly 60 percent of all
blacks compared to 30 percent of the whites lived in the central cities
in 1970. Only 15 percent of the nation's blacks lived in the suburbs
compared to about 40 percent of the nation's whites. Since 1970 white
population in central cities has dropped more rapidly than ever, nearly
3 percent each year, while black population remained stable or increased. (7)

Still a different view on the same demographic phenomenan is
offered in Table 8.3 which reflects the results of this population shift
at the end of the last decade. Here the congruence between territory
and race (or for Hispanics, ethnic features) is equally striking. The
figures indicate absolute numbers and percentages of Blacks and Hispanics residing in ten exterior cities as well as their suburban rings.

With only one exception (San Francisco), blacks are clustered
into the exterior cities and left out of the suburbs. As noted in Chapters
1 and 7, San Francisco is one exterior city which excuses itself from
most prevailing norms and there are several reasons for this. One
explanation is purely technical and has to do with the fact that the city
Oakland is counted within the San Francisco SMSA along with the suburbs of the area (see table 8.3). All the remaining exterior cities contain a preponderance of blacks, with most of them absorbing more
than 75 percent of the nonwhite population. New York, Chicago,
Philadelphia, Detroit, Cleveland, and Baltimore hold more than 85
percent of black families in their respective SMSAs.

Table 8.3.   Racial/Ethnic Segregation in Exterior Cities
and Their Suburbs: 1970*

Metropolitan Area	Black Families		Hispanic Families	
	Number	%	Number	%
New York				
Central City	394,904	90	200,676	96
Suburbs	45,328	10	7,192	4
Chicago				
Central City	244,626	90	53,473	76
Suburbs	36,671	10	16,775	24
Philadelphia				
Central City	147,664	88	5,637	85
Suburbs	20,239	12	1,021	15
Detroit				
Central City	150,769	88	5,697	46
Suburbs	20,599	12	6,581	54
Baltimore				
Central City	89,920	87	1,753	43
Suburbs	13,613	13	2,290	57
Cleveland				
Central City	67,181	86	3,054	65
Suburbs	10,627	14	1,610	35
Boston				
Central City	23,438	83	3,896	49
Suburbs	4,722	17	4,054	51
St. Louis				
Central City	55,067	67	1,377	39
Suburbs	27,149	23	3,490	61
New Orleans				
Central City	59,099	84	6,259	60
Suburbs	11,457	16	4,166	40
San Francisco				
Central City	22,307	29	23,596	27
Suburbs	53,383	71	63,147	73

* The term "central city" includes only those cities listed and
excludes other "central cities" which are within the same SMSA.
These other "central cities" have been coupled with nearly suburbs, giving the data a conservative bias. Thus, Yonkers is
counted as a "suburb" of New York City, Oakland as a "suburb" of
San Francisco, and so forth. This accounts for the low level of
ethnic/racial segregation in San Francisco, but even with such
a conservative tilt in the data the racial/ethnic dicotomy for
all the other metropolitan areas is astounding. In the case of
San Francisco Central City, if we exclude Oakland as a "suburb"
the statistics on blacks and Hispanics change substantially. If
we include Oakland as part of San Francisco central city, 47 per
cent of all black families and 30 percent of all Hispanic families in the Bay Area SMSA are clustered within San Francisco.

Source: Data gathered from U.S. Department of Commerce, Bureau
of the Census, 1970 Census of Population, "Characteristics of the
Population," Tables 89, 94, and 100.

The rule of territorial segregation is not as strong among Hispanic populations, although it should be borne in mind that there are few Hispanics outside of New York, Chicago, and San Francisco. In four areas where Hispanics predominate in the suburbs (Detroit, Baltimore, Boston, and St. Louis) the total number of Spanish surnamed families does not exceed 17,000. At the other end of the spectrum, New York with its large Puerto Rican population has an Hispanic concentration which exceeds that of blacks. Only 4 percent of this minority can be found in its suburbs. The city of Chicago also has a sizable Hispanic concentration (mostly Chicano and Puerto Rican) with only a small portion of it in its suburbs.

To be sure, most exterior cities still have a majority of whites living within them, though projections are that many will "tip" toward nonwhites within the next few decades. Chicago, for example, is projected to become 60 percent black and Hispanic by 1990 and 80 percent black and Hispanic by the year 2000. Today even those whites left in the city are predominantly working class and have poorer paying jobs than those who have gone to the suburbs. By and large they are older, and one can see white ethnic neighborhoods fast losing their younger generations because the sons and daughters of Italian and Polish Americans can afford to buy homes elsewhere.

Class membership is an important determinant of residence in the colonized areas; less well off whites or the elderly are also victims of the process. When class segregation is compounded by racial or ethnic segregation, domestic colonialism is more visible. As a rule, urban blacks and Hispanics are far worse off than any group living in the suburbs. Among blacks themselves suburban migration is led by families of higher status, proving that domestic colonialism is not simply a matter of racial oppression but contains the necessary condition of lower class status. In one study of 24 suburbs, selected because of their high black in-migration, family income was above the earnings of inner city blacks in all but three instances. (8) By criteria as varied as counting those below the "poverty line" to the number of female headed households, escape to the suburbs symbolized a badge of middle class status.

For blacks in particular, city life is the life of the lower class. Subordinate status as a racial group coincides with the subordinate position of blacks as an economic class, and this combines with territorial segregation to make blacks first among the colonized people of the central cities. A useful question to test this proposition is: Does having been born into a minority group dramatically increase a member's life chances of being poor, intermittently employed, or dependent upon welfare payments? If the answer is "yes," the chances are also greater that members of these minorities will be counted among the

newly arrived of the central cities. Obversely, should the response to
this question be negative, the chances are greater that an individual
would be counted among the upwardly mobile residents of suburbia or
as part of the regional migration toward the open spaces of the sunbelt.

Racial stigma coupled with lower class status makes urban minorities especially vulnerable to domestic colonialism because of their
dependency on white suburbia. Dependency is the logical consequence
of weakened populations living in cities whose wealth is controlled from
the outside. What made inner city ghettoes a fortress for previous
ethnic groups was that they were able to work and own small businesses
(grocery stores, tailor shops, small construction firms) at a time when
commerce was not overwhelmed by giant corporate chains. For blacks
and many Hispanics, there is no way out of the ghetto - they own very
little within the inner city and are extremely dependent on an outer world
for job opportunities or welfare subsistence. Dependency has always
been a major feature of the colonial syndrome. It renders the subject
population helpless, and ultimately grateful for the meager benefits
they are allowed to enjoy from time to time. Dependency also functions
to bewilder and confuse the colonized populations with doubts about
their self worth and their ability to control things for themselves.

When conservative politicians talk about the demoralizing and
debilitating effects of welfare, they are quite correct. Liberals and
some radical ideologues show a naive tendency to justify the existence
of welfare for able-bodied people on grounds that it is necessary for
young mothers to stay at home, or that jobs that do exist do not pay
enough and lack dignity. Yet this rationale fails to appreciate that
nonproductivity and the denial of an earned stake in society does, in
fact, rob people of confidence in themselves as controlling individuals.
To deny a whole population gainful employment is to set the psychological and economic conditions for controlling them.

The paradox of the dependency syndrome is that it contains the
visible aspects of a free, uncaring life style, but beneath it is an abiding
social control which teaches submission. To be jobless is a reminder
of how tentative an individual's judgments really are, and to be habitu-
ated to temporary escapes from these shackles is itself a way of learn-
ing how to return to them. Ask an Afrikaaner from Capetown and a
businessman from Newark why it is that blacks are held in an inferior
position, and they will probably offer the same response. In both instances, they are likely to explain that their subject populations are
content enough as they are, and are not equipped to aspire toward anything else. In both cases, too, the answers will be a self-serving
rationalization for the acceptance of the status quo and the continuance
of social control.

Two useful measures for analyzing the class status of urban
minorities and its relationship to dependency can be found in their

rates of unemployment and welfare. We are all familiar with the general trends. Black and Hispanic unemployment have been about double the rate of whites and welfare is substantially higher. What is interesting about these measures is their confinement to the central cities and their territorial circumscription. Table 8.4 provides a statistical profile of this observation for ten exterior cities.

As expected, the rates of black unemployment and welfare are concentrated within the exterior cities, while the suburban rings contain only a fragment of these populations. Thus, as our earlier observation pointed out, black segregation in the cities is strikingly coupled with their dependent status. New York, Chicago, Philadelphia, Baltimore, Cleveland, and Boston are near or above the 90 percent mark on both unemployment and welfare for blacks. St. Louis and New Orleans are not very far behind, while San Francisco is the only exterior city which reverses the pattern. However, if the city of Oakland is not counted as a "suburb" within the Bay Area SMSA, the figures for blacks are substantially changed. Thus, without Oakland 49 percent of all black welfare and 50 percent of all black unemployment are found within San Francisco. For Hispanics the statistical change is not as dramatic, with only 38 percent of welfare families and 38 percent of unemployed individuals clustered within San Francisco. Note, too, that welfare and unemployment rates have a greater concentration than segregation which is solely based on demographics.

For Hispanics, much the same pattern prevails, although it lacks the same uniformity. For either unemployment or welfare, the only cities to reverse the pattern are Philadelphia (unemployment only) and San Francisco. Interestingly, those cities which were pointed out as containing fewer Hispanics than their suburbs (Detroit, Cleveland, Boston, and St. Louis) now exceed their suburbs in Hispanic unemployment and welfare or in one case (St. Louis) equals them. Again (with the exception of New York, Chicago, and San Francisco) the absolute number of Hispanics is small.

What is particularly disturbing about these figures, is the high absolute number of dependent minorities who are confined to the cities. A high percentage of dependent people within a single racial/ethnic category is subject to prejudice carried out throughout the society. When these particular groups also constitute a substantial mass of the populace within well-defined territories, the colonial analogy looms even larger, and one must suspect how exterior cities are being used by other people. During each workday, white bureaucrats (social workers, unemployment office supervisors) administer the flow of subsistence payments to black families; public and private enforcement officers (policemen, judges, bill collectors) regulate human conduct; and middle class businessmen (doctors, insurance agents, retailers)

Table 8.4. Race Ethnicity and Dependency Between Exterior Cities and Their Suburbs

Metropolitan Area	Black Unemployed Number	%	Black Families/Welfare Number	%	Hispanic Unemployed Number	%	Hispanic Families/Welfare Number	%
New York								
Central City	32,162	91	81,902	93	15,502	97	59,586	99
Suburbs	3,169	9	6,440	7	423	3	837	1
Chicago								
Central City	26,997	90	43,234	95	5,549	81	4,682	91
Suburbs	2,936	10	2,068	5	1,287	19	470	9
Philadelphia								
Central City	16,270	90	29,178	92	580	25	1,573	94
Suburbs	1,788	10	2,531	8	1,777	75	103	6
Detroit								
Central City	25,738	88	22,956	89	810	54	483	70
Suburbs	3,548	12	2,845	11	681	46	211	30
Baltimore								
Central City	9,909	92	16,764	95	150	63	104	69
Suburbs	916	8	899	5	87	47	43	31
Cleveland								
Central City	7,890	89	10,931	93	284	74	292	87
Suburbs	1,010	11	758	7	98	26	44	13
Boston								
Central City	2,397	88	7,433	93	555	64	1,201	81
Suburbs	328	12	568	7	311	36	276	19
St. Louis								
Central City	8,460	87	11,099	90	100	50	103	76
Suburbs	1,218	13	1,198	10	100	50	33	24
New Orleans								
Central City	7,186	82	11,929	86	534	60	494	73
Suburbs	1,533	18	1,897	14	352	40	182	27
San Francisco								
Central City	21,764	28	4,988	29	3,249	37	2,791	32
Suburbs	56,754	72	12,452	71	5,513	63	5,922	68

Source: Data compiled and calculated from U.S. Department of Commerce, Bureau of the Census, 1970 Census of the Population, "Characteristics of the Population," Tables 85, 89, 92, 94, 98, and 100.

derive profits from ghetto consumers. Where these administrators and entrepreneurs come from and how they spend or invest their earnings is an important piece of the city/suburban dynamic.

The Pecuniary Relationship Between
Cities and Suburbs

The capacity to selectively penetrate a colonized territory is another feature of classic colonialism. Penetration need not be widespread but rather pinpointed to the objectives at hand, that is, to extract resources efficiently and with the least political controversy. One advantageous system for doing this is "indirect rule" in which visible authority is given to a native class of civil servants or tribal chieftains, while commercial enterprises manage productivity and carry out financial transactions. Great Britain used this method with considerable success in Africa and India. At the same time, large business firms, like the East India Company, siphoned off the colony's wealth and provided lucrative earnings for a new class of colonial administrators. Much of this wealth was exported back home, either to support a luxurious living style or build industry in the mother country.

Again, the analogy of domestic to classic colonialism has its imperfections, but a common syndrome resonates through these seemingly distant occurrences as similar roars may come from oceans that are far apart. Analyzed from a domestic perspective, selective penetration can be translated as suburbanites commuting to the central city in order to obtain values from it. Pecuniary advantage can be looked at from the vantage of income earned by those who commute to the city and live in the suburbs. And the exportation of local resources can be understood as a question of how suburbs derive their affluence and how the vested resources of the city are used by them.

Specific data concerning these questions is scanty, but the accumulation of available evidence is suggestive. Beginning with the broadest gauged statistics on commuter traffic and income within metropolitan areas, we see that in 1970 over 40 million people traveled to work, and close to half of all those living within Standard Metropolitan Statistical Areas (i.e. central cities and their outlying suburbs) earned their living within the core city. Table 8.5 provides data on the "Commuting Workforce Within Central Cities and Suburbs" for all metropolitan areas of 250,000 or more within the United States.

Within low and moderate income brackets (people earning less than $14,999 per year), the percentages of those working within the central city and outside of it remain fairly constant. Slightly more than half of these wage earners (unskilled or semiskilled laborers and

Table 8.5. Commuting Workforce Within Central Cities and Suburbs Living and Working Within Same SMSA (250,000 or more): 1970

Earnings in 1969	Total 16 years old and older	Working in Central City	Working outside Central City
	40,815,970	23,044,693	17,771,277
$1 – 4,999	14,836,459	55%	45%
5,000 – 9,999	15,602,427	58%	42%
10,000 – 14,999	6,241,538	55%	45%
15,000 – 24,999	2,293,613	56%	44%
25,000 or more	862,510	62%	38%

Source: Data compiled from U.S. Bureau of the Census, Department of Commerce, 1970, Journey to Work, p.233.

low status clerks) work within central cities. Those in the next income category (better paid craftsmen, middle managers, and some
professionals) hover at about the same or slightly higher proportions
in identifying their place of work. The real jump occurs in the category at or above $25,000 per year; 62 percent of these individuals work
in central cities. For the most part, these people are found in executive, professional, or entrepreneurial positions. They manage, and in
many cases, own the financial houses, manufacturing concerns, and
retail outlets which are located in the central cities. A broad, though
fair, statement is that those in the highest income brackets are most
likely to gain their living from central city locations.

While this may tell us something about income and workplace it
does not separate suburban commuters from central city residents,
so that we can get some notion of where income is spent. Moreover,
the inclusion of metropolitan areas with populations as low as 250,000
obfuscates the role played by the handful of our older, deteriorating
cities (Detroit, Philadelphia, Cleveland) as the territory through which
colonial extraction actually takes place. To get at this issue, I have
singled out the greater New York metropolitan area and its patterns
of income and occupation between central city and suburb. The data
presented in figures 8.1 and 8.2 represents a ten year average between
1960 and 1970 in relative earnings and occupations held.

The most salient point to be gleaned from these figures is the
concordance between class structure (as reflected in earnings or occupation) and territorial residence. Both figures show that more highly
paid individuals and those in managerial (i.e. controlling) occupations
are far more likely to be suburbanites who commute to the city. In
contrast, residents of the city predominate in the lowest paid jobs,
earning about half the income of suburban commuters. They are far
more likely to be working in unskilled jobs as dishwashers, janitors,
or press operators. Though 18.3 percent of the city's work force is
made up of commuters, they held 42 percent of the professional and
managerial positions. A third of Nassau County's labor force commuted
to New York City and that third produced 43 percent of the income
earned by Nassau residents. (9)

Given the nature of the data and the predominant trends which
they point up, a logical inference is that much of the wealth and resources of the urban core are controlled by commuters who come into
Manhattan on a daily basis and leave for their suburban households
after work. Another inference is that a disproportionate amount of
the income which the central city generates, flows out to the suburbs
through a managerial (and owning) class and is spent in the outlying
suburbs. Houses are bought and constructed in the suburbs, property
taxes are paid to local townships, and goods are purchased at local

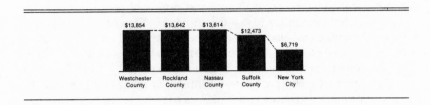

Fig. 8.1. Earnings of Manhattan workers by place of residence: 1960-70.

Source: U.S. Department of Labor Bureau of Labor Statistics, New York, May 20, 1976.

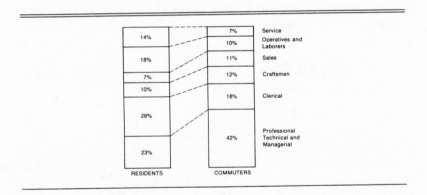

Fig. 8.2. Occupational profile of residents and commuters at work in New York City: 1960-70.

Source: U.S. Department of Labor, Bureau of Labor Statistics, New York, New York, May 20, 1976.

shopping malls. The suburbs not only sustain themselves by absorbing
disproportionate income from the central city, but derive their value
from a protected proximity to the urban core. Expensive housing,
spacious surroundings, and even cheap domestic help are all made
possible by invisible costs which are borne by the central city. Meanwhile, the central city must pack huge members of less affluent residents into tenements or apartment buildings; it must build on open
spaces and cut down greenery to make way for bustling businesses;
and it often uses its rivers and harbors as cesspools for factory waste.
Every day, thousands upon thousands of suburban commuters descend
upon the central cities to use their transit facilities, their streets,
their theatres - all without directly paying for costs of cleaning or po-
licing these facilities. In Manhattan alone, over 1. 6 million people
throng into the central business district each workday, taxing its facilities to the breaking point. (10) Where would the suburbs be without
these facilities? Scarsdale, New York would be a different village if
it were not within penetrating distance of Manhattan. Grosse Point,
Michigan would not have premium real estate if it did not have ready
access to Detroit. Suburbs derive their value from the very city
whose problems they seek to close off. Posh, suburban Bronxville,
located in Westchester County, does in reality possess slums - they
can be found in the Bronx.

The Politics and Legality of Sorting Out Groups
Between Cities and Suburbs

Any colonial relationship must maintain a territorial separation between
dominant and subject populations. Too great a violation between boundaries, much as too great an intermixture of living styles, would make
it difficult to perpetuate a one-sided advantage. In the absence of some
kind of separation, the colonizer's territory would be vulnerable to
economic incursions by an alien population, and it would lose some of
its qualities (commodious living arrangements) as a land of privilege.
This is the reason for national quotas against immigration. For a time,
Great Britain allowed some former subjects into the country and so,
too, did France and the Netherlands. Most of that immigration has
now been curtailed or has stopped.
     Suburbs also maintain quotas against immigration from the cen-
tral city, and are able to regulate both the kind and the number of individuals who wish to reside in them. This may sound like a harsh interpretation, but racial/ethnic/class imbalances between cities and
suburbs did not come about through happenstance. Sorting out populations is complex and is based on a multiplicity of practices. It is

accomplished through formal as well as informal rules of governance - through conscious attitudes of what kinds of people should be permitted entry to the suburbs as well as tacit understandings - and it occurs through acts of personal intervention as well as through the perfunctory operations of the housing market.

At a visible level, the practices are formal and legalistic. They consist of seemingly reasonable ordinances like setting acreage requirements per housing unit, or specifying housing designs so they conform to community ambience. The law, however, is often what local magistrates say it is, and law can be made to work with the "marketplace" to regulate population. Thus, larger acreage requirements and elaborate construction standards drive up the cost of housing. The higher the costs, the fewer who can afford it, and the more exclusive the resulting class composition.

Two examples from suburbs that have different class features serve to point up how the sorting out process works. One suburb, Edgmont Township, is a solidly middle class community located outside of Philadelphia in Delaware County. The second suburb, New Castle Township, is an upper-middle to upper class community situated in Westchester County, and within commuting distance of New York. In 1970, Edgmont had a median income of $14,229, well above that of Philadelphia, and the median value of a house was about $30,000. For New Castle the median income during the mid-1970s was $34,600, and most houses in the area sold for between $80,000 and $100,000. Both of these townships are almost entirely white - better than 99 percent of Edgmont is white and New Castle has less than 110 blacks and Hispanics among its population of 16,000. (11)

What is more, these suburbs are growing whiter and richer with the passage of time. At one time, Edgmont had 17 blacks in its population, but census takers could find only 7 at last count. New Castle's substantial growth in population makes its small number of blacks appear as a few dark sprinkles in what one demographer has called a "vanilla suburb." In Edgmont, the proportion of low income residents declined dramatically in the last decade. Looking at Edgmont's population in terms of income quintiles, the lowest three-fifths of families dropped by 77 percent. Those in the upper two-fifths of the income notch increased by 32 percent, with most of the growth occurring at the very top. (12)

New Castle tells something of the same story, with an accent on its upper class disposition. There, the only quintile to experience a proportionate increase in the last two decades was made up of the highest income families. The bottom four-fifths of the town's population declined by 25 percent, while the highest fifth increased by 25 percent. (13)

Aside from their exclusivty, both of these suburbs have another attribute in common; a vast amount of their land remains unoccupied. Nearly 40 percent of Edgmont land is vacant, while New Castle prefers to spread most of its population onto parcels of two acres or more. Since building lots cannot be bought in either of these townships for less than $8,000 per acre, and since the cheapest house cannot be constructed today for less than $35,000, the class composition of these suburbs is assured. In the 1970s a relatively low cost house of $43,000 precluded any family with an annual income of less than $21,500, since as a rule of thumb a house should cost no more than twice the annual income of a family. Almost 90 percent of the nation's 23 million blacks cannot purchase a home in the suburbs.

The arithmetic of the sorting out process is simple when it applies to a conventional single family dwelling. But what of less conventional housing which can be clustered together to save acreage or multifamily housing? As we have seen in earlier chapters, the federal government provides subsidies for modestly designed single family houses, as well as for renters who can find apartment units. Here, the arithmetic of the marketplace needs to be bolstered by the fine hand of administration.

On the face of it, exclusionary zoning is the practice of applying housing or lot requirements in excess of what is needed to maintain health, safety, or environmental quality, but it often results in restricting a particular class or race from a community. (14) Its most common manifestation is zoning building lots above one-quarter of an acre for a single housing unit, and this has been used effectively to exclude the poor. In New York City's suburbs (which include parts of New Jersey and Connecticut) two-thirds of the vacant land is zoned for lot sizes of more than one-half an acre. (15)

Behind these zoning legalities some suburbs have manipulated their official profile to create the impression that land remains open for multiple unit development. Land which is already built upon is zoned for high densities, while vacant land is zoned for much lower densities. Other suburbs simply cast the onus of responsibility on those seeking cheaper housing by refusing to map the permitted uses for land. Thus, all vacant land is zoned at the lowest possible density within their ordinances, and any other residential construction requires a zoning change. Since zoning changes must go through a board made up of local citizens, there is ample opportunity for discouragement.

There are also suburbs which use their discretion over building codes to sort out residents. Bogus architectural standards are regulations which serve questionable aesthetic or safety purposes, but can be used to maintain the homogeneity of the population. Some communities have "look-alike" or "nonlook-alike" ordinances which either demand conformity with other housing designs or preclude common

features from appearing too frequently. Other ordinances require that
buildings have a minimum size, that floor space be of certain dimensions, and that landscaping amenities (fences, walls, screening) be
installed. All this gives leverage to town people anxious to determine
the demographic complexion of the area.

Even greater leeway is given to suburban officials through the
power of their clerkships. Dilatory administrative procedures can
force prospective builders or buyers through a maze of architects and
lawyers. Elaborate checking, filing, or inspection procedures can be
imposed. There are instances where builders have been forced to
abandon projects because of the unforeseen costs for professional fees
which were needed to obtain clearance. Many more builders refuse to
even consider construction in certain areas because of the legal fees
necessary to override local statutes. The argument against opening
the suburbs to the urban poor is especially convincing because it is
quicker and more profitable to build for the upper-middle class that
it is to fight against prevailing trends. Time is money for the builder
and very few are willing to beat a new path in the interests of social
justice.

The Courts and the Legality of
Sorting Out Populations

For those who have taken a less trodden path, their ventures have been
none too rewarding. In the last ten years, housing sponsors (mostly
nonprofit organizations) have attempted to break through suburban
barriers by appealing to the federal courts. Their legal arguments
seemed persuasive and were drawn from earlier struggles for black
civil rights. Exclusionary zoning, they argued, was a denial of the
"equal protection clause" of the Fourteenth Amendment, it was a denial
of the right to travel, a denial of due process, and an unlawful restric-
tion against interstate commerce.

After a few slivers of victory were grasped against the most
blatant forms of housing discrimination, (16) the full weight of local
home rule came down against the challengers. The courts have always
presumed that zoning laws were permissible so long as they bore some
rational relationship to a legitimate public objective. Judges reasoned
that by its nature zoning entailed exclusion - certain uses could properly be excluded from a community if they violated its health, safety,
or morals. The proverbial glue factory being built amidst a row of
neat family houses is a case in point of a community's right to protect
itself against industrial intrusion. Later, that right to exclude others
was extended to protect "family values," "quiet seclusion, " and the
retention of a "small town('s) character. " (17)

What had not been clearly decided was how far zoning could be taken if it resulted in the exclusion of economic classes or racial/ethnic minorities. The issue of economic discrimination was a weighty one, since all America was constructed on the basis of some class discrimination. Whole neighborhoods within cities can be identified by their class composition, and suburbs are a political convenience for extending the geographic distance between income groups. Clearly, it would take a revolution to overturn this arrangement, and the federal courts were not inclined to make so disruptive a decision.

Though the courts had ruled against economic discrimination on issues involving the vote and access to the appellate courts in criminal matters, the judges felt no compulsion to extend similar rights to low income housing. The distinction was made between a fundamental right which ensured other rights, and rights which were simply a matter of social policy. Thus, voting and access to the courts could be judged fundamental because they guarded against arbitrary government and its abuse. Presumably, housing was a service which could be undertaken at state or local discretion, and the federal courts had no power to impose their views of what constituted a wise social policy. (18) This reasoning was a bit ingenious since good housing also connects to better education, jobs, and a host of economic rights. But the courts were on the horns of a dilemma of whether to support class upheaval or rule against the expansion of constitutional rights, and who is to argue with a presiding judge once his decision is made.

Despite the hopes of egalitarians, the cause of class equality never had much of a chance when it came to housing. Racial discrimination, however, was another issue. Americans have always been uneasy about racism because it belied their belief about this nation as a land or opportunity where all men are created equal. To rationalize a person's low economic status because of inability was one thing, but to attempt to explain away poverty on the basis of "bloodline" became increasingly unacceptable.

As a legal position, racial discrimination could not be used to constrict equal opportunity, regardless of whether or not the right in question was fundamental. In one case, the federal courts ruled that a history of blatant racial discrimination was sufficient reason to intercede in the traditional prerogatives of local government. Zoning and housing were no longer sacrosanct where a clear pattern of racial exclusion existed. The court found that in such circumstances a locality "must show a compelling governmental interest in order to overcome a finding of unconstitutionality." (19)

Though this seemed like a beginning, the realities of land use politics do not easily fit into juridical notions of what constitutes racial discrimination. Just how far the federal courts would be willing to interpret the facts of a case in order to find racial discrimination was unknown until January, 1977. In that month Arlington Heights v. Metropolitan Housing Development Authority had wended its way through the legal labyrinth and reached the Supreme Court. The background of the case was akin to the suburban experience of Edgmont and New Castle - a wealthy white suburb on the outskirts of a big city which, through its right of self government, had excluded blacks and other minorities. The Village of Arlington Heights had once been a small farming community located 25 miles from Chicago. During the years after World War II its population exploded, and by the mid-1970s it had close to 70,000 residents who enjoyed one of the highest median family incomes in the vicinity. Less than 500 of Arlington's residents are black or members of a minority. (20)

At issue was the refusal of Arlington to change its zoning restrictions to accommodate integrated multiple family housing. The Metropolitan Housing Development Corporation (MHDC) had purchased land and drawn up plans for 190 low and middle income housing units, to be assisted with federal subsidies. When MHDC found itself unable to carry out its plans, it brought suit together with three black residents against the Village. Unlike other test cases of housing discrimination, there was little here that smacked of an overt conspiracy against blacks. Arlington was a typical suburb which had zoned its land in a typical manner, making it improbable that blacks or law income families could live there.

Cognizant of the import of the challenge, a lower federal court had ruled that such zoning had an adverse impact on blacks and decided against the Village. This court reasoned that blacks constituted a far greater percentage of the Chicago region than Arlington was willing to admit as residents, and there was no compelling government interest for the Village to continue its exclusionary practices. The issue now before the Supreme Court was whether a discriminatory result could be used to overturn Arlington's zoning restrictions.

In short order, the nation's highest court issued its declaration. Discriminatory results were no grounds on which to mount a challenge to suburban zoning. To be unconstitutional, the Court declared, there must be an "intent" or "purpose" to discriminate. Nay, too, should there even be evidence of "intent," a suburb could justify its actions so long as there were other reasons for the zoning. (21) Thus, exclusionary zoning based on race could be legally sustained if it also entailed preserving the configuration of a community or maintaining low densities for its citizens.

The single crack left in the exclusionary wall rested on unmitigated "intent," "purpose," or "motive." And to establish one of these the Court suggested that a challenging party should obtain the minutes of official meetings, produce reports from planning or zoning boards, or examine witnesses. The suggestion was hardly consoling to the most stubborn optimist who thought it unlikely that local boards would ever write into their records "for the purpose of excluding blacks," much less admit to it in a courtroom. Like most decent people, those who live in exclusionary suburbs are not happy to acknowledge they may be motivated by race. After the Supreme Court had spoken, the lawyer for Arlington Heights expressed relief that this would "clear up the completely unfair labeling of the village as being racially discriminatory." Later he added, "It is economics, not zoning, which has impaired the right of blacks to live in Arlington Heights." (22)

Though the Supreme Court had disposed of the Arlington case so far as the U.S. Constitution was concerned, matters were still left open for the state courts. Localities are given the power to enact zoning laws by their respective state constitutions in exercise of the police power to promote the general welfare of all the people. Logic would have it that, since local government is "a creature of the state," any abuse of that police power could be overriden in the state courts or legislatures. Technically, the suburban wall was not inviolable and could be breached if it were shown that local prerogatives needed to be outweighed by the welfare of the larger region. In actuality, the suburban wall is buttressed by political complexities, and the handful of states which have attempted the hurdle (including California, Michigan, New Jersey, New York, and Massachusetts) found themselves tripped by one obstacle or another.

One of the best known cases to come before the state courts was the Mt. Laurel controversy, which exemplifies the durability of exclusionary suburbs. Mt. Laurel Township is a fast growing "sprawl" suburb on the outskirts of the small city of Camden, New Jersey and within a daily commute to Philadelphia. By the undisputed facts of the case, Mt. Laurel had zoned its land so that poorer citizens could be kept out, and better educated, middle class residents could contribute to its boon. In 1975, the Supreme Court of New Jersey ruled that this township had misused its police power and violated substantive due process and equal protection of the laws under that state's constitution. The Court concluded that land use regulations must take into account the "regional need" of the area, and that "developing communities" like Mt. Laurel must provide a "fair share" of low and moderate income housing for prospective residents. As the Court pointed out:

> . . . Mount Laurel must, by its land use regulations, make realistically possible the opportunity for an appropriate variety and choice of housing for all categories of people who may desire to live there, of course including those of low and moderate

income. It must permit multifamily housing, without bedroom or similar restrictions, as well as small dwellings on very small lots, low cost housing or other types and in general, high density zoning without artificial and unjustifiable . . . requirements as to lot size, building size and the like . . . . (23)

The court pinned its "remedy" to these strong words nullifying the town's zoning ordinance and giving it 90 days to "correct the deficiencies." Afterward, it commented that Mt. Laurel should have the "full opportunity" to encourage development in order to fulfill its regional obligations to the surrounding cities. (24)

More than three years after the court's action results have been negligible. In Mt. Laurel itself, no construction has begun for low and moderate income housing. Seven communities in New Jersey have been the subjects of Mount Laurel-type decisions, but few shovels of earth have been turned to fulfill the intent of the decision. (25) Why suburbs have been able to resist judicial directives bears upon the ineffectuality of the courts as suitable institutions for carrying out policy; discretion remains rooted in the localities.

Neither the courts nor the suburbs build housing. Private construction companies build housing, so long as it is profitable and local governments make it easy for them to do so. Rarely can court decisions of the Mt. Laurel variety be self executing. They must, instead, rely on a measure of cooperation from suburban governments and builders alike. For private builders, cooperation may be induced by profits (government subsidies, ability of renters and moderate house buyers to pay). But for suburbs there is much to be lost (low income residents drive up taxes) and they are apt to employ all their means of resistance.

Suburbs have managed to thwart judicial efforts by playing on the weaknesses of the law, and have exempted themselves by claiming they are not "developing communities" and, therefore, not subject to the obligation to meet "regional needs." More than a half dozen localities in New Jersey have suddenly dropped their once-proud appellation of "growing suburbs" and now claim to be fundamentally rural. Other suburban governments have made use of their considerable discretion on land use and have decided to replan their communities. For every such replanning, builders must wait, and their expenses climb. Twenty acres of land to support 200 housing units may be valued at $600,000. We should add to this a carrying cost for mortgage charges, taxes, insurance, cost of litigation, rising construction costs, and what a builder could "earn" on his money if it were invested in a safer venture. On top of this, some suburbs have kept their zoning and building ordinances "fluid" by changing them frequently or making them indeterminate, throwing the builder off balance. Still other suburbs have "co-operated" by rezoning available land, but the access routes may take five years to build. (25) The list of technical obstacles that suburbs have put up is enormous, and one could go on ad nauseum discussing their refinements. The most effective tactic has been to play on the notion that time is on the side of the locality, and hope that unwanted builders either leave them alone or drop dead. The tactic seems to be working not only in New Jersey but in New York and California where similar suits have been undertaken.

The foundations on which the sorting out process rest are strong and the most sustained legal efforts have failed to weaken them. The pecuniary, demographic, and locational advantages that suburbs enjoy are constructed on the blocks of fragmented, self governing suburbs. There should be little wonder about the consequences of this arrangement. As long as immediate gains accrue to a locality, its body politic will act in response to those gains, regardless of the moral issues raised by critics, or the legal abstractions voiced by the courts. The irony of the colonial syndrome is that in the longer term it also does damage to the very suburbs which indulged in its benefits.

THE SYNDROME REFRACTED AS
SUBURBAN BLIGHT OR SPRAWL

Black and Blue Suburbs

At the beginning of this chapter it was mentioned that not all suburbs are ridden with luxury, and indeed some have come to experience an "urban crisis." Darby is a worn down industrial suburn located just outside Philadelphia; East Cleveland is heavily black and known as "The Annex" to the larger city it adjoins; while the Village of Port Chester, New York is as dilapidated and drug infested as the streets of Harlem. These are working class suburbs which look every bit like central city neighborhoods and suffer as much from commercial evacuation.

Usually suburbs in crisis are found within the immediate rings outside of the central city. Suburbs like Darby are scattered around Philadelphia on both the Pennsylvania and New Jersey sides of the Delaware River. Cleveland's black suburbs are an extension of its oldest ghetto neighborhoods, and like East Cleveland are on the eastern side of the city. Port Chester is one of several suburban slums in a tier which border on the northern part of New York City. All of these suburbs are nearly as old as the major city each adjoins and has developed in a common cycle with it, absorbing factories and cheap housing to accommodate immigrant laborers. Today they parallel the central city and large numbers of blacks have moved in to make them black and blue (collar) suburbs. Actually, "suburbs" like Darby, East Cleveland, and Port Chester are urban backyards, and they can be called "suburbs" only because they function in the shadow of the exterior city. These suburbs grew up as resources for smaller industries which could not afford to locate in the larger city. Often they were incubators for businesses which were just beginning and needed low tax districts. They also provided cheap land for the construction of wood frame houses or small tenements. The rich occupied other sections of these suburbs, and built stately mansions along tree lined streets. With the onset of decline, these mansions have been converted into rooming houses or partitioned into smaller apartments.

The legal status of black and blue suburbs varies a good deal. Darby is incorporated as a borough, East Cleveland as a municipality, and Port Chester as a village. The designations remain despite the fact that their relative densities, buildings, and streets make them appear as "cities" to any passerby. Socially and politically they are also treated like cities. They have been zoned for use by factories, garages, and junkyards. Moreover, as land values began to plummet, black and blue suburbs have become receiving stations for welfare recipients.

Intrinsically, there is nothing in a "suburban" status which affords these communities any special privilege or allows them to exploit the exterior city. Along with Philadelphia, Cleveland, and New York, sections of black and blue suburbs have become blighted and riddled with dependent populations. In many instances, they may even be worse off than big cities because they lack a large "downtown" commercial base to give them any redeeming value. When initial investments are thin and there is little left for profit, whole areas can be quickly discarded.

What shaped the configuration of black and blue suburbs was largely the same as what shaped the exterior city. Industrial and commercial development by privatism took place at the turn of the century and brought about a similar type of urban form. To be sure, these suburbs bear a closer resemblance to smaller neighborhoods of the exterior city than to its downtown business districts. But it is an urban form, nonetheless, with concentrated populations interspersed between retail stores, movie houses, and industry.

What causes the contemporary depression of black and blue suburbs is also largely the same as what causes the plight of the exterior city. It is their obsolescence to new industry and, like the exterior city, these suburbs are being "used up" by that sector of privatism which still remains. The colonial syndrome is not precipitated by

suburbs themselves, nor by the people who live in them. Localities
are merely the agents of a larger economic push and they make themselves available for that role because the incentives are great enough
for them to do so. But just as the colonial syndrome takes its toll on
Philadelphia and Darby, so, too, does it affect the sprawl suburbs
around Edgmont.

Sprawl Suburbs

The majority of American suburbs are not black and blue, but over-
whelmingly white and middle class. Their populations spread outward,
connected only by belts of roadway and shopping centers which are used
in common. For the suburban family, a trip to "town" often means a
visit to a massive parking lot outside the local K Mart or Piggly Wiggly
chain store. These suburbs not only deconcentrate their housing and
commerce, but assimilate only those assets which meet their perceived
objectives.

Like all local governments, sprawl suburbs are driven by the
need for growth, and compete with each other to manage their tax burdens. Shopping centers and "clean" industry (corporate headquarters,
electronics firms) contribute handsomely to that tax base. Real estate
speculators, developers, bankers, and professionals need growth in
order to continue with their businesses. More business means more
employment, more employment means more development, and the
spiral escalates. For many, the choice is perceived as one between
growth or death; for should growth cease, residents would be out of
work, mortgages would be foreclosed, and the spiral would be set in
reverse. Put simply, the more a local economy pumps itself up through
selective development, the more it must do to keep up the motion of
that development.

In order to maintain that economic momentum, whole counties
have given themselves away to private developers. Santa Clara is one
suburban county in California which allowed its agricultural land to be
torn up. Twenty years ago, this county was one of the richest agricultural areas in the nation, filled with acres of vineyards and fruit or-
chards that were nestled below the mountains of the Coast Range. Its
major city is San Jose which served as "town" for farmers in the
county. Today the vineyards are almost all gone and replaced by private tract houses and commercial strips. One cannot tell when he has
moved from one "municipality" into another because the houses and
shopping centers are built without recognition of community character
or purpose. Signs get larger and larger, colors get wilder, and lights
get brighter to attract the motorist's attention. At night the signs are

illuminated, twirling and flashing in a combination of different colors.
Even the buildings are designed to win the attention of passing motorists. A hamburger stand may be housed in a structure shaped like a
giant pink shoe with a figure of a little old lady outside of it. Aside
from the aesthetic liabilities, there are consequences for traffic and
safety. Each business demands its own entrance, exits, and parking
lots, creating a string of openings for vehicles which dart in and out
of the roadway. Traffic control is at times impossible because it is
difficult to determine a fixed point of activity. During peak hours an
entire roadway will become one big snarl. (26)

Planning for Sprawl.

This description of Santa Clara County is an example of what strip zoning can do to an area. It is called strip zoning because elongated
stretches of land, crisscrossing the county, have been reserved for
commercial exploitation. Strip zoning is also joined by rezoning, spot
zoning, and leap frog zoning, which are made available to privatism as
land use conveniences. These conveniences may represent the worst
of sprawl suburbs, but they also point up how developers can run wild
in communities which need them. The mechanics of sprawl are easily
manipulated, if the new inhabitants bring the likelihood of profits.
Just as low income housing can be kept out of suburbs by a locality's
control over land use, so can profitable establishments be let in. The
process usually occurs in successive waves. First, real estate speculators come in and buy up land from farmers. Some farmers may
hold out not wishing to give up their livelihoods, so the speculators
buy up land in huge checkerboards. This first wave of buyers holds
the land for a number of years until it is ready to be resold to a second
wave of mass scale developers or builders. Large concerns of this
type (Boise Cascade, Levitt Brothers) are in a position to get the land
rezoned and provide sewerage, utility lines, streets, and lighting for
prospective buyers. These concerns have resources in cash and legal
talent to win over reluctant town or planning boards. On the eastern
seaboard and suburbs of Long Island, large scale developers are heavy
contributors to the Republican Party. One study of a Long Island township found large builders to be politically well connected and able to use
businessmen and town officials to smooth the way for development.
Instances of money changing hands through legal fees, commissions,
and surreptitious payments were plentiful. (27) On the West Coast,
and especially the suburbs of Santa Clara, campaign contributions are
freely given to officials in exchange for friendly appointments to planning commissions. Most of these commissions are known to be stacked
with developers and realtors who have taken an interest in civic affairs.
(28)

After mass scale developers have done their work, a third wave of spot builders comes in to take up land which is left over. Spot builders take advantage of the utilities already provided and may only need to obtain a variance to the local zoning ordinance in order to construct on a smaller lot. Houses built on spot zoned lots are sold as custom-built single family structures at a higher price.

Not all these waves occur in a continuous swell. Those farmers who have held out may find themselves in the midst of heavy suburbanization, and their land climbs further in value. If the farmers do not sell directly to builders, long-term speculators buy out the land, anticipating that the market will rise even higher. This causes developers in search of cheap land to leap frog over rural land and build in large suburban swatches. Leap frog zoning encourages sprawl to grow in many directions at once, and the suburbs take the shape of twisted amoebas scattered aimlessly along highway routes.

Speculators and builders are not the only sector of privatism which bring about sprawl suburbs. Industrial corporations which no longer find the exterior city useful also feed the spiral. With a few twitches from a giant corporation, sprawl suburbs have risen amongst scenic wonders and mountain ranges. Consider the following newspaper account of how one company changed the landscape and the lives of thousands.

[The Johns-Manville Corporation] had formerly been based in New York and New Jersey. Its executives, like those of so many corporations, grew tired of problems of the Northeast and chose to flee, not just out of the city, but also out of the region. And the company, once it had chosen to move to Colorado, made it clear that it did not want to try city life again, either - Johns-Manville not only didn't want to be in New York, it didn't think much more of Denver.

So the company bought the former Ken-Caryl cattle ranch, a safe hour's drive from downtown Denver, and its officials talked excitedly about the problem-free land to which they were moving.

All well and good in theory. But the reality is a bit harder to accept. Much of the land between Johns-Manville's sprawling site and the city of Denver had been farmland until recently, but the coming of the corporation, with almost 2,000 workers - which means 2,000 households - has changed all that. Real-estate developers bought up the farmland in anticipation of Johns-Manville's arrival, and now much of the land has been built up with suburban subdivisions, just like those one would see anywhere else.

So Johns-Manville, which wanted to trade the crowded Northeast for the land where the buffalos roam, has ended up causing
a lot of that land to be turned into something not so very different
from the place it left. The company itself is apart from this
suburban sprawl, of course - its enormous site affords it protection from the changed landscape. The views from the executives' windows are of a pure, perfect, virgin landscape. But
over the ridge, it is something else. (29)

If this episode tells us anything, it reveals that sprawl is not unplanned. Contrary to common impressions, sprawl is very much prepared by a constellation of private entrepreneurs who find it to be lucrative and convenient. A retinue of private interests followed Johns-
Manville's lead and are reaping substantial profits by changing the face
of the Rocky Mountains. Likewise, in typical sprawl suburbs, the
planning is led by speculators who gamble on the price of land, by
large developers who build private houses en masse, by spot builders
who need the utilities to put houses up on a single shot basis, and by
bankers, lawyers, and others who need the business. Without sprawl
there would be less fluctuation in the price of land and less waste in
the home building industry. But sprawl is the bedrock of the suburban
economy, and the private interests which spring from it have created
an entire life style for one-third of America's people.
    Planning for sprawl is largely in the hands of privatism, though
cooperation with suburban governments is necessary for it to be carried out. There are suburbs like Santa Clara County and on Long
Island where passive cooperation is sought out. Here, the initiative
is with the developers in obtaining special permits, rezonings, and
variances. Land use politics is big business in many suburbs, and
local people make an occupation of guiding acceptable projects to completion. On Long Island, scandals erupt periodically around illegal
dealing in land. The incidents abound with such regularity that they
have become institutionalized methods for district attorneys to win re-
putations as "crime busters" and for reporters to do "investigative
stories." (30)
    There are also suburbs where active cooperation is provided by
the local government. Here, the suburbs actually invite and provide
incentives for select private interests to establish themselves on vacant land. In the Mount Laurel controversy discussed earlier, the
township zoned nearly 30 percent of its land for light industry, while
the remainder was zoned for single-family, detached dwellings, one
house per lot. The scheme was specifically designed to accommodate
large-scale developers who wanted to sell their product to upper middle
income families. Under the town's general ordinance, no attached

townhouses, apartments, or mobile homes (except on farms for workers) were permitted. (31) According to the findings of the courts, land
use in Mt. Laurel was exclusively geared to "attract a highly educated
and trained population ... to support nearby industrial parks ... as
well as businesses and commercial facilities." (32) Even the township's
own poor were ignored and faced "hostility" when they sought relief
from "substandard accommodations" in the older parts of town. (33)

Mt. Laurel follows another characteristic of the colonial syndrome.
The township is laced with highways built with federal, state, and local
support that allow it to sap the strength of nearby Camden and the
Philadelphia region. In the past 30 years, manufacturing and jobs have
faded from these cities and their tax base is being severly eroded.
During that same 30 years, Mt. Laurel has grown by over 500 percent
and laid aside a hefty 4,000 acres for industry with almost all of that
land located on either side of a state turnpike and interstate routes. (34)

Reinforcing Policies and Sprawl

Within the conceptual theme of this book, suburbs have acted as reinforcers for privatism, encouraging it to expand its push through land
use policies. Not surprisingly, the lower the level of policymaking,
the greater will be the propensity to pursue reinforcing approaches
simply because localities have been placed in a financial race with one
another. Also, given the narrow base and scanty resources available
to localities, they are more dependent on privatism to foster their
economies. Reinforcement through land allocations, low taxes, and
the assimilation of "useful" populations are the best ways for suburbs
to attract corporations.

By the same token, sprawl suburbs could not act as reinforcers
if there were not strong policy support from federal and state sources.
Highway construction is a necessary service to privatism if it is to
make use of suburban opportunities. At the moment, two of the famed
"Fortune 500" corporations are planning such moves which are dependent on federal largess for highways. Union Carbide plans to move its
headquarters, along with 4,000 jobs from New York City to a 500 acre
site near Danbury, Connecticut; and Mobil Oil is anticipating a similar
transfer to a 130 acre tract in Falls Church, Virginia. Both of these
relocations out of the central city depend upon funding of multi-million
dollar highway interchanges. Union Carbide has already aroused opposition in some lonely corners because $14 million of public money is
being used to construct a highway link to a site which is likely to reduce
the company's black and Hispanic workers. The site, the interchange,
and the access roads were designed for Union Carbide with the help of
state and local officials. (35)

Other reinforcing policies which abet sprawl can be found in the elaborate tax codes of all three levels of government. Federal and state tax laws permit fast depreciations on old buildings and large credits for new investments, thus giving owners a double dip into the public treasury. On the first dip, a person can purchase a tenement and write off the paper value of that building each year against his income tax, without ever putting a cent into rehabilitation. (After the tenement is exploited as a tax loss, it can be sold to a new landlord who can repeat the process.) On the second dip, this same person can take a credit against any taxes owed to the government by simply investing in new real estate. If that person uses the land for speculation and turns it over quickly, he is entitled to a reduced tax rate under the capital gains provision of the income tax laws. The faster one buys and sells, the less one pays in taxes. The whole mentality is to buy-sell, sell-buy as quickly as possible and to keep money working in new ventures. The income tax is perhaps the most potent domestic policy devised. To return to Santa Clara County for the sake of illustration, the amount gained by speculators from capital gains provisions in just one year exceeded the total expenditures in that county by HUD. (36)

These calculations do not even touch the tax benefits homeowners enjoy by being able to deduct mortgage interest payments from taxes they owe (no such benefits accrue to apartment renters). Nor do they take into account how state and local property taxes work against the rehabilitation of old structures by taxing improvements and additions. Even the time-worn method of assessing property for only part of its real value operates as a reinforcer, because large corporations are typically under-assessed for what they truly own. Local officials are often reluctant to assess large companies too heavily for fear that they will relocate or that word of an "adverse financial climate" will spread within the business community. In one study of a large suburban county in California, the owners of the most under-assessed and the most over-assessed parcels were identified. The results showed that there were five times more corporations (mostly insurance, banking, and large development firms) in the under-taxed category than in the over-taxed group. (37)

Reinforcing Policies and the Colonial Syndrome

What can we make of this? Do suburbs really gain by shielding themselves from the crises of the exterior city and attracting corporate investment through reinforcing policies? There is evidence to suggest that immediate "booms" may be followed by intermittent "busts" in the future. Like colonial powers which reaped immediate benefits only to

pay the cost in aid and racial strife later on, suburbs, too, may be
"mortgaging their future. " (38)

The benefits of quick, mass scale development are immediate
and tangible, but the costs of sprawl are gradual and amorphous. Concessions given to corporations such as roads, sewers, and tax abatements require long-term financial absorption. Many of these are capital investments. That means not only must they be paid for over a
lengthy period of time, but they must be maintained at local expense.
Taxes which are already on the rise and a bane to homeowners will
continue to increase. More significantly, for every development there
is likely to be an increase in the school burden, particularly as families mature and children reach school age. These, too, are long-term
costs which must eventually be met. And as communities are spread
a further distance from one another, duplicate services must be provided, whether that is in the form of maintaining under-utilized schools
or in ordering new buses to transport children longer distances.

The colonial syndrome refracts on suburbs in ways which are
not only a drain on the public purse, but damaging to community ecology.
If it is true that the real costs of sprawl are deferred, we can also
assume that each spurt of growth will generate still more demand for
expansion in order to keep up with impending expenses. (39) Of necessity, all land must be filled and relatively little green space will be
left. Anything less than this frenetic pace will burst the speculative
bubble and set off a recession. Sprawl is a highly addictive pattern of
development, and it is an irony of the suburbs that most of its residents
originally moved there to enjoy green spaces which are now disappear-
ing at an uncontrolled rate.

Another facet to this irony is that the very development which is
planned to preserve green space - i.e., multiple dwellings clustered
on limited amounts of land - is barred from suburbia because of the
colonial need to sort out populations. In the end, there are few villians
and many victims. Central cities lose their role as concentrated areas
for commerce and culture, while the countryside becomes transformed
into a motorized city and transfixed on the necessity of growth.

To be sure, there may be a "suburban crisis" ahead, but it is of
a different order than that which confronts exterior cities. Where
these cities are faced with the threat of decay and commercial shrinkage, sprawl suburbs must confront the consequences of their own expansion.

Epilogue

After Jimmy Carter and his team occupied the White House in 1977 there was a great stir about the creation of a national urban policy. Messages came from the President's closest advisers and HUD that urban problems were slated for a fresh review, and cities could expect some sympathy after eight years of Republican indifference. Carter had assigned the task of formulating an urban policy to an interdepartmental group of Cabinet members and their assistants. Within a year of the President's inauguration, urban proposals were being tested in the press and assistant secretaries were flying around the country speaking about the administration's new initiatives.

It is the tenor of national politics that major portents can be discerned from routine events. In the midst of this buzz, two incidents occurred which showed something about the assumptions and content of White House planning. The first of these was a statement made by an important HUD policymaker at a meeting in San Francisco that, "The urban problem was not created by the federal government and it will not be solved by the federal government." (1) The second incident was a rendering of Carter's urban policy given by people in Washington who were in the process of making up its details. Assistant secretaries and officials from the Treasury and Commerce Departments described the President's economic program for the cities as one which would be "a radical shift in emphasis" from previous policies. Asked what that "radical shift" might be, the policy planners responded that it would place its primary "reliance on the private sector" and instead of public service jobs, the government would provide subsidies to companies which were willing to locate in "distressed areas." (2)

Was it historical myopia that the Carter White House was experiencing in approaching urban policy as if the past 25 years had never taken place? No matter what the reality, perceptions are difficult to change once stereotypes are ensconced in the public psyche. The ruin of the exterior city may not be wholly a product of the federal government - problems of that magnitude rarely have singular causes - but as much as any institution can be singled out for its mistakes, Washington surely did its damage. The HUD official was saying more than, "We'll try to help but don't hold us responsible." In his own way he was reducing the expectations about what the federal government would or could do. He was also inferring that Washington could neither prevent huge swatches of industry from moving south nor jawbone northern suburbs into rendering any support for their central cities.

If the denial of responsibility is one way to curb assumptions about the federal promise, confirmation of limited alternatives is another way to shape the content of policies. The Commerce and Treasury officials who presented urban economic policies as a "radical shift" from previous programs were pretending that public employment had been a major weapon against unemployment, that it had failed, and that something new was at hand.

The two incidents did more than provide a glimpse at a limp attempt to deal with the cities. They also revealed the extraordinary sticking power of old ways and the effort to adjust public expectations to those ways. Limiting policy expectations by drawing a circle around federal responsibility would keep the cities from demanding a full loaf. At the same time, pronouncements about fresh policies and innovative approaches would keep the liberal embers burning. Though few liberals asked when Washington had intervened without the hand of private enterprise, it made no matter because the statement was made and reported in the press as a fact. Public perceptions about the culpability of cities and the congenital ineptitude of government were solidified.

CARTER AS A POLICY TEST

The Carter White House fits within the broadest traditions of past Democratic administrations. It has a meliorist orientation to urban policy, though it is far closer to John Kennedy's caution than to Lyndon Johnson's bold and rapid strokes. Like his predecessors, Carter must respond to an urban constituency within the Democratic Party - mayors, blacks, trade unions and the Urban League. Should he fail to do this, he runs the risk of a challenge from the left side of the party. Assuaging that wing of the party with reworked meliorist responses rather than antagonizing it is the President's wisest course of action. Nonetheless, should antispending and antitax fever run high, Carter would

have to hold most meliorist policies at a steady state. This appears
to be his probable course of action into 1980 - few dramatic initiatives,
hold down further rises in the urban budget, but keep existing commitments flowing so that allies are not completely alienated.

It is the meliorist aspect of Carter's presidency which is most
intriguing because it puts the theory of this book to the test. Whether
or not a policymaker can be categorized as one type or another is not
nearly as important as whether meliorism and reinforcement accurately explain how policy works. Explanation, not categorization, is the
key to understanding. At any rate meliorism and reinforcement are
"ideal types" with no individual being a perfect exemplar of either
type. Presidents fall on a continuum between the two poles, so that
Johnson would come closest to the meliorist ideal while Kennedy and
Carter veer further away from it.

Meliorism has been described as "intervening policies" which
seek to divert the natural push of privatism toward sore spots in American society. The mechanisms for this diversion are direct subsidies,
loans, and compensatory opportunities for private enterprise to earn
a profit should it choose risky ventures. These mechanisms are linked
through a government conduit which ties national and middle governments into a financial relationship with privatism so that benefits can
trickle down to people or places in which they live.

There are other features to meliorism which highlight its evolution. Meliorist presidents have a penchant for urban populism, and a
belief in the efficacy of voluntary, extra-governmental action. This
led the Johnson White House to attach layers of citizen groups (CAPs,
Model Cities) onto urban efforts during the 1960s. Apprehension about
the possible conflicts with city halls led meliorist policymakers to hold
these organizations on a political and financial leash. Whether it was
a CAP or a Model Cities agency, urban populism showed itself to be
vacuous; to offer more bluster than substance; and to be searching for
a nebulous, imprescribable end. Though there are exceptions, federally sponsored voluntarism is not known for its successes. Meliorism
also attempts to skew federal aid toward depressed cities, but invariably trips on its own initiatives by spreading those dollars so thinly
that the impact is lost. This typified Model Cities and a host of other
Great Society programs which fell prey to the congressional pork-
barrel. As much as congressional pressures bring about this spreading effect, the dynamics of White House politics also contributes to it.
The very position of a meliorist president as someone who must deliver
something in a short time to an impatient constituency, makes his
leadership vulnerable to political pressures. For the president who
seeks to alter market forces by taking a political hand to them, life
on Capitol Hill can be very frustrating.

Incrementalism: Piecing an Urban Policy Together

There was no fell swoop which brought anything resembling a coherent
urban policy to the Carter White House. Policies are rarely made that
way and, while the media talked about a fresh, comprehensive look at
the cities, Jimmy Carter is a man skeptical about the federal government's ability to alter social problems. The new president's posture
could be characterized by what policy analysts call "incrementalism,"
which is the gradual accretion of one policy upon another with only
scant view of an overarching scheme. As the term suggests, incrementalism is policymaking by a series of small steps which build up
slowly, often with unintended consequences.

The first step in Carter's incrementalism was to deal with the
leftovers from the Nixon/Ford years. The Housing and Community
Development Act of 1974 (HCDA) wrought some disastrous aid formulas for exterior cities. Had the "hold harmless" safeguards of
HCDA been phased out without changing its aid formula, seven out of
ten exterior cities would have faced reductions in community development funds. By the spring of 1977, the White House and key congressional committees had worked out a compromise which would provide
an escape. The compromise involved the creation of a dual formula
under which federal money could be dispensed. Since the old formula
favored many cities in the "sunbelt," an alternate choice was developed
for the "frostbelt." The new formula accented the distress which
northern cities incurred by weighting averages for age of housing
stock, loss of population, and poverty. Cities could elect to choose
any one of the two formula choices. As the Housing and Community
Development Act of 1977 was signed into law, the immediate conflict
between "frost" and "sun" belts had abated. The unmentioned burden
was to the national budget, which contained more community development aid to more communities than had ever existed before.

The next step in the incremental process was to tinker with the
existing machinery so that central cities could obtain some additional
relief. This was accomplished through an administrative tightening in
the executive departments and additional granting authority which was
given to Cabinet secretaries. (4) HUD secretary Patricia Harris, who
had established herself with the old civil rights coalition and pro-urban
groups in Washington, successfully lobbied the Congress and her own
president for discretionary money which could be applied to the most
severely pressed communities. Harris' own objective was to extend
Washington's hand directly to these communities through Urban Development Action Grants (UDAGs) and a special fund made available to the
secretary. The idea was to "leverage" the possibility of private investments in particular areas by using the lure of federal loans and

subsidies. Like many of the categorical programs a decade earlier, the new HUD provisions were competitive and would be given to those areas showing the greatest need and presenting the strongest proposals.

The single action by the Carter White House which comes closest to a statement of policy intent for the cities is something entitled "The New Partnership," implying that programs would have to be worked through a combination of dollars from Washington, administration by the localities, and the operation of private manufacturers and developers. Presumably leveraging could be accomplished by getting the states and localities to complement federal dollars with their own contributions, and then using these public resources to win over private investments. The theory is to apply some money to bring in more money, and then pyramid the entire pot onto private investments in order to begin capital formation in distressed areas.

Targeting, or the effort to shift money into urban areas, is another priority of the "New Partnership," though this has run into difficulties since Congress and governors are worried that some states would be given short shrift. Nonetheless, targeting provides the Carter White House with the opportunity to turn away from the revenue sharing mentality of Nixon/Ford by discouraging the tendency to diffuse federal aid. For other reasons of parsimony and efficiency, the Carter staff would also like to see federal aid flow to where it is needed.

As a last component of the "New Partnership," the Carter White House included its own version of voluntary group action to cope with urban problems. Voluntarism has been tacked onto this urban package with a measure of caution and some doubt, but it is present in some form to meet the populist impulses of some policymakers.

Leveraging, targeting, and voluntary group action are familiar components of the meliorist tradition. Leveraging must lead to trickle down benefits if it is going to be successful; targeting attempts to channel some of the federal flow to cities in order to divert a much larger "push from privatism"; and voluntary group action is a kind of supplementary government to city hall which draws its energy from citizen participation. When all of its sundry pieces are cast into one great scheme "The New Partnership" sounds expansive, even imaginative. Seen in historical perspective and analyzed item by item it is old medicine being sold with new labels. In figure E.1, major items are broken down in terms of their objectives.

The reception accorded the "New Partnership" can at best be called restrained disastisfaction. Senator Daniel Moynihan, a longtime scholar and critic of urban policy refused to see any virtue in the Carter proposals. In an essay on how government has gotten so clumsy, Moynihan underscored Carter's proposal as "contain(ing) no

I. Leveraging Private Investments

A. Differential Tax Investment Credit,
designed to bring industry back into depressed urban areas. An additional five percent tax credit would be applied to existing
credits for firms which made capital investments in "distressed communities." Firms
located in these designated urban areas
would apply to the Commerce Department for
a "Certificate of Necessity" which would be
decided upon within 30 days. Once certi-
fied, a firm would be able to write off a
percentage of its investments against
federal taxes it would normally pay.

B. Employment Tax Credit, designed to
deal with the problem of hard core urban
unemployed. Private employers of young,
disadvantaged, or handicapped workers
would be entitled to an additional $2,000
tax credit for every eligible worker hired
during the first year of employment and
$1,500 during the second year.

C. National Development Bank, designed
to stimulate an influx of capital in depressed urban areas. This bank could
provide outright grants, subsidized loans,
and furnish a secondary mortgage market
for private banks which lent monty to
entrepreneurs. The actual grants could
cover as much as 15 percent of a firm's
capital costs (up to a celing of $3
million) while loans could be provided
for 75 percent of a firm's capital costs
(up to a celing of $15 million). As an
example of how the program would work, a
businessman who wanted to establish a
$1 million toy factory on the south side
of Chicago could receive $150,000 in a
grant, and $640,000 in a subsidized loan
leaving him to raise $210,000 on his own.
Meanwhile, private banks would be alerted
to the fact that the federal government
was buying "mortgage paper" for loans on
eligible projects. This would give private banks an incentive to lend additional
money so that the Chicago toy entrepreneur
could raise his remaining $210,000 in
capital costs.

D. Institute for Community Investment,
designed to improve lending practices in
needy urban communities. The Institute
would bring together appraisers, realtors,
lenders, builders, and insurance companies
to develop a consistent approach toward
urban lending and to train urban lending
specialists. Another instrument to encourage
lending is a proposal for Neighborhood Commercial Investment Centers which are supposed
to bring together merchants, commercial
banks, and local organizations in order to
stimulate business lending.

Fig. E.1. Carter's "New Partnership."

II. Targeting Federal Urban Assistance

A. Supplemental Fiscal Assistance, designed to
put the federal aid funnel directly into localities with high rates of unemployment. Under
earlier legislation to combat economic recession,
states and localities received "counter-cyclical"
funds when national unemployment rose above six
percent. Carter's new program would bypass the
states and do away with the national unemployment
"trigger," and instead give funds directly to
localities whenever local unemployment reached
above 4.5 percent. In addition, the Carter
administration made it possible for localities
to qualify for aid if their growth rates lagged
below the national average.

B. Grants to the States, designed to sensitize
states to respond to the needs of hard pressed
localities through better planning and increased
assistance. Originally this plan contained a
carrot and stick provision which would penalize
unresponsive states by cutting back on their
revenue sharing allocations and reward activist
states by awarding them additional allotments.
The penalty aspects were politically volatile
(despite some enthusiasm for it in the House)
and Carter dropped the opportunity to use the
stick. Under the final proposal, Carter offered
the states incentive grants for those which
submitted the most promising proposals. The
grants would be awarded on a competitive basis
and would total $400 million over a two-year
period.

III. Voluntary Group Action

A. Neighborhood Self Help, designed to activate
community groups and allow them to play a role in
housing and neighborhood revitalization. This
program functions like a categorical grant to
neighborhood groups which submit plans to Washington. Individual projects would be funded according to community need and the worth of the project.
Each funded project would require the concurrence
of the mayor.

B. Urban Volunteer Corps, designed to recruit
individuals with professional talent and skills
to serve neighborhood groups and work on community
projects. The program would be initiated by a
federal agency (ACTION), which, in turn, would
select the details of the program. Planners,
architects, and lawyers would provide technical
skills to community projects. Concurrence of
the local government is required.

new initiatives of any consequence" and described it as a "complex agreement" that allocated new resources to "already established programs." (3)

The "New Partnership" is not only warmed over stuff from the "New Frontier" and the "Great Society," it is condensed and made for instant disappointment. Despite the great confidence in leveraging, there is no evidence that tax, loan, and grant incentives can actually bring significant capital into deteriorated sections of the central city. Similar tactics were attempted in President Kennedy's Area Redevelopment Act and in Johnson's sequel to it, the Economic Development Act. Appalachia and the rural regions for which these acts were designed are as depressed as ever, and their most popular source of relief is migration. The precedent is not encouraging for the cities.

Subsidies have been tried in manpower programs at both the federal and state levels. The results are disappointing. Subsidies were used in Johnson's housing programs for the urban poor - Sections 235 and 236 of the 1968 Housing Act. The results were disappointing and Congress virtually cancelled the programs. (4)

Beyond this negative history, leveraging has its costs. The Differential Tax Investment Credit would cost $200 million, the Employment Tax Credit is pegged at $1.5 billion, and the National Development Bank is authorized to guarantee investments of $11 billion in the space of a few short years. For leveraging alone, the total is nearly $13 billion more than the combined yearly revenues for nine exterior cities (excluding New York City, whose expense budget is over $13 billion). As far as can be determined, Carter's proposals were made without a shred of data on the efficacy of leveraging in distressed communities.

Neither is it difficult to envision how leveraging programs can run amuck with abuse and corruption. Entrepreneurs have found innumerable ways to use federal grants, loans, and tax credits. They have set up bogus corporations, paid themselves inordinate salaries with the investments, misappropriated funds, and even used nonexistent workers to reap trainee benefits. The experience of Section 235 shows how leveraging can turn big profits. The history of abuse in the Small Business Administration is full of it; and graft between giant corporations and governments does occur. The irony is that blame is attributed to government programs. Success is a new idea carried out by private industry; failure is the residue of those ideas that never made it and belong to Washington.

The targeting aspects of the "New Partnership" are weak and do not change the structures of relationships between Washington and the states or the cities. Under Supplemental Fiscal Assistance, about 26,000 cities and towns across the nation would receive aid as "dis-

tressed communities. " Some of these are prosperous suburbs which
have been included to assuage influential congressmen. While some
big cities would benefit, the program amounts to an urban revenue
sharing scheme which is neither specified to change long term ills nor
pinpointed to achieve tangible results. The only "targets" of Supplemental Fiscal Assistance are some of the all purpose governments
which would receive it. Otherwise, it operates on the forlorn hope
that simply pumping more federal dollars into bottomless urban budgets will change fundamental conditions.

Carter's plan for discretionary grants to the states is little better. With the penalty aspects of the plan deleted, the White House
shied away from the mildest of efforts to snap the states out of their
indifference. Putting up $200 million each year for which 50 states
are supposed to compete is not realistic. There are innumerable
federal grants a state can tap, and the amount from any one source
constitutes a fraction of a state's budget. Under the circumstances,
Carter's plan is hardly an incentive, but rather another opportunity for
states which already have "urban plans" to send them off to Washington
for funding. The real questions for the states are whether they will
continue to permit suburbs to zone out urban burdens and zone in urban
assets, and whether they will continue to raid each other for industry
and permit corporations to spread over their unused land. Unless
something is done about these problems corporate flight will continue,
and discretionary grants from Washington are not likely to resolve
anything.

The "New Partnership's" plans for voluntary group action are
well intended but not designed to change the urban picture. Little has
been proposed that has not been tried before, but Carter's suggestions
are more cautious. Care has been taken to avoid the pitfalls of the
1960s by requiring the concurrence of city hall. This may be a plus
in strengthening coordination between citizen groups and the localities,
and it settles the question over who is the boss. The plan, however,
is much too open ended, and its ambiguous objective of "neighborhood
revitalization" smacks of the same liabilities which stymied CAPs and
Model Cities. At this stage, "neighborhood revitalization" sounds as
definitive as "curing poverty" or "improving local planning. " If experience is any teacher, the Carter White House had better take care
that its voluntary groups have substance and precision to them.

Moynihan's assessment of the New Partnership was correct. It
does little but pile an addenda onto a set of dubious precedents - a kind
of incrementalism which has lost its beginning and its end. Nothing
points this up more sharply than Carter's preamble to the urban policy.
"Total assistance to state and local governments has increased, " the
President said, "by 25 percent from $68 billion in... 1977 to $85 billion

in... 1979. These increases are the direct result of actions we have taken... They are as much a part of my Administration's urban policy as the initiatives I am announcing today. " One can only sit in astonishment and ask what an increase from $68 billion to $85 billion has accomplished in two years besides to discredit the very notion of an urban policy. (6)

THE POLITICS OF URBAN POLICY

As the 95th Congress moved to adjournment in 1978, very little had been enacted into law. Some of the ideas for voluntary group action had been tagged onto amendments to the Housing and Community Development Act. These were innocuous enough and involved marginal amounts of money. Supplemental Fiscal Assistance had been altered, partly dropped, and failed to pass the House on its first try. Discretionary grants were set aside and failed to evoke enthusiasm. The National Development Bank met with a storm of criticism and was dropped for the time being. Policy had run into political obstacles and Congress was in no mood to fool with old ideas that cost new money.

What happened to "The New Partnership" was that it met the exertion of power - qua politics - over the execution of decisions which were supposed to resolve public problems - qua policy. Trying to separate policy from politics is a tough job. One must live with the political implications of a policy choice, and all presidents have done this in one way or another. There are, however, different ways in which this can be done. One is to shape policy so that it is politically palatable and make whatever accommodations are necessary in order to win its passage. Kennedy did a little of this and fumbled with the Congress. Johnson did a lot of it and triumphed over the Congress. Nixon manipulated the self seeking impluses of Congress with partial success. Ford was a short timer and carried the Nixon impetus a bit further. Carter tried to carry on in the Kennedy/Johnson tradition but has not won much from Congress.

An alternative way to cope with the restrictions of politics is to accept them as reducing the chances for policy passage. Having done this, the next step would be to proceed with policies which are not an outgrowth of precedent or existing habits. "Totally unrealistic" is the proffered retort to such a suggestion. Policy without political strength is simply a theory which can be of benefit to no one.

Before rejecting the alternative, policymakers should ask themselves, what is "realistic" about decades of incrementalism which continues to ply old methods for stubborn problems which only grow worse. In sticking with these methods, Carter lost on both counts. As policy, "The New Partnership" was stale. As politics, "The New Partnership" has not been a success. Carter was further subject to the charge of throwing good money after bad at a time when politicians are beginning to recoil from rising budgets. This is a serious charge and one which promotes a cynical belief that nothing can be done to reverse urban deterioration. As one sympathetic official confided, "We can't change St. Louis an awful lot. Maybe all we can do is make it a little bit better. It'll be great to do even that."

Carter's policy staff came to Washington hoping to find a new way to do things. Within a few months they were under siege by the very groups which helped put them in the White House. Campaign promises to do something about the cities came back to haunt the administration and it grabbed hold of what was familiar.

Politicians and policymakers do not respond to social problems; they respond to their own problems by putting them in a social context. This is how the Carter White House responded, and it was unrealistic to believe they would respond differently. The only check on such behavior is through self-recognition that each policymaker is a speck in a long chain of events which repeats variations of itself. Otherwise each policymaker becomes wedded to his own scheme, defensive about his choices, and obsessed with prolonging his tenure of office. The implusion toward self-protection is political. The cost is to policy and to the problem itself.

Notes

INTRODUCTION

(1)   Figures are taken from Fortune, May 1976, and are applicable for the year 1975. A notable exception to the shortcoming of dividing public and private power is Grant McConnel, Private Power and American Democracy (New York: Knopf, 1966).

(2)   Sam Bass Warner, The Private City (Philadelphia: University of Pennsylvania Press, 1968), p. 4.

(3)   Santayana, Obiter Scripta.

(4)   For a discussion of spatial factors as a method of analysis, see Frederick Cleaveland, Congress and Urban Problems, (Washington; The Brookings Institute, 1969), p. 5.

CHAPTER 1

(1)   Sam Bass Warner, The Urban Wilderness (New York: Harper & Row, 1972), pp. 101-04. For a fuller exposition of how swirls of commerce and manufacture feed into one another to create cities see Jane Jacobs, The Economy of Cities (New York: Random House, 1969).

(2)   Milton Kotler, Neighborhood Government (Indianapolis: Bobbs
       Merrill, 1969), Chapters 1 and 2. For a history of New York's
       annexation and development, see Wallace Sayre and Herbert
       Kaufman, Governing New York City (New York: W.W. Norton,
       1960), Chapter I; and Roger Starr, "Power and Powerlessness
       in a Regional City," The Public Interest, No. 16, (Summer,
       1969) pp. 3-24. It is interesting to note that the center city used
       a variety of inducements, such as tax advantages, bridges, and
       more commerce, as well as intimidation, in order to draw sur-
       rounding territories into it.

(3)   Warner, The Private City, pp. 58-59.

(4)   The so-called "Chicago School" of sociology took its roots in
       this kind of urban setting. See Robert E. Park and Ernest
       Burgess, The City (Chicago: University of Chicago Press, 1967),
       pp. 50-77.

(5)   Max Weber, The City (New York: Free Press, 1958). For a
       modern day elaboration of this, see Norton Long, The Unwalled
       City (New York; Basic Books, 1972), especially Chapter 1.

(6)   Oswald Spengler, "The Soul of the City," in Classic Essays On
       The Culture of Cities, edited by Richard Sennett (New York:
       Appelton-Century-Crofts, 1969), pp. 66-76.

(7)   Robert Caro, The Power Broker (New York: Knopf, 1973),
       pp. 147-48.

(8)   See for instance, Edward Banfield, Political Influence (New York:
       Free Press, 1961), Chapters 8 and 9; and Edward Banfield and
       James Q. Wilson, City Politics (New York: Random House, 1963),
       Chapters 9-11.

(9)   An excellent analysis of reformist attitudes and style can be
       found in James Q. Wilson, The Amateur Democrat (Chicago,
       University of Chicago Press, 1962), especially note Chapter 1.

(10)   The best known of these is Robert Merton's "The Latent Func-
       tions of the Machine," in Urban Government, edited by Edward
       Banfield (New York: Free Press, 1969). See also Banfield and
       Wilson, City Politics; and Urban Bosses, Machines and Pro-
       gressives, edited by Bruce Stave (Lexington, Mass.: D.C.
       Heath, 1972), Part II.

(11)   An excellent analysis of the anti-labor activities of the machine
       can be found in Allen Rosenbaum "Machine Politics, Class
       Interest and the Urban Poor. " Paper presented at the Annual
       Meeting of the American Political Science Association, New
       Orleans, September, 1973, p. 26.

(12)   The best known of these is Lincoln Steffens, The Autobiography
       of Lincoln Steffens (New York: Harcourt Brace & World, 1931);
       and Lincoln Steffens, The Shame of the Cities (New York: Hill &
       Wang, 1957).

(13)   Theodore Lowi, At the Pleasure of the Mayor (New York: Free
       Press, 1964), pp. 194-99.

(14)   See Steffens, The Shame of the Cities, p. 20.

(15)   See James Bryce, The American Commonwealth, Volumes 1 and
       2, particularly Volume 1, pp. 642-3, and Chapters 48-52. (New
       York: Macmillan, 1909)

(16)   Monte A. Calvert, "The Manifest Functions of the Machine, " in
       Stave, Urban Bosses Machines and Progressive Reformers
       (Lexington, Mass.: D. C. Heath & Co., 1972), pp. 45-54.

(17)   For details see, Harold Zink, City Bosses in the United States
       (Durham, N. C.: Duke University Press, 1970), especially p. 37.

(18)   Sayre and Kaufman, Governing New York City, pp. 497-502.

(19)   Lincoln Steffens, The Shame of the Cities, pp. 162-94.

(20)   Samuel P. Hays, "The Politics of Reform in Municipal Govern-
       ment in the Progressive Era, " Pacific Northwest Quarterly 55
       (October 1964): 157-69.

(21)   Apparently, the old interior politics of graft and patronage have
       not been wiped clean. Much of this is still a part of contempor-
       ary urban politics, though its forms have changed. For instance,
       much of the graft occurs through private business connections,
       which allot high fees from business clients to politically active
       lawyers, architects, and insurance brokers. The popular Amer-
       ican phenomenon of the lawyer legislator is as much due to the
       advantages of drawing clients as any other reason. Also, while
       working class patronage has decreased and been replaced by a

civil service, middle class patronage is at its apogee, especially
at the judicial level where judges are known in cities to have
"mortgages" on their judgeships and the price of a seat on the
bench is determined by party leaders. The bench is a very popular means for setting politicians "out to pasture" for a comfortable retirement. We might conclude, then, that many aspects
of interior politics are with us, but are overlaid with other relationships and have taken different forms. For details on corrupt modern politics see, Martin and Susan Tolchin, To the
Victor...(New York: Random House, 1971).

(22)   For journalistic accounts of Mayors Lee and Daley, consult
        Allan R. Talbot, The Mayor's Game (New York: Praeger, 1967);
        Bill Gleason, Daley of Chicago (New York: Simon & Schuster,
        1970); and Mike Royko, Boss (New York: E.P. Dutton, 1971).

(23)   "Politics" is defined in this sense as the struggle for power,
        while "policy" is conceived as decisions or programs that are
        intended to resolve social problems. Admittedly, politics is
        often linked with policy, but each stresses a centrally different
        objective.

(24)   Most of the data relating to measures of urbanism are based on
        the Standard Metropolitan Statistical Area (SMSA). According
        to SMSAs, an area is considered urban if it is made up of one
        city with a population of at least 50,000, or two cities with con-
        tiguous borders which have a combined population of at least
        50,000. Two or more adjacent counties each having a city or
        cities which meet one of the above criteria may be considered
        an urban area if the cities lie within 20 miles of each other and
        are economically integrated. Social and economic interrelation-
        ships are an important factor in determining SMSAs, and these
        may be included across boundaries. I have used different
        measures of urbanism, such as the "great metropolitan area,"
        the megalopolis, and the "metropolitan region," all of which
        are explained in the text, or in accompanying footnotes.

(25)   See for example David Elazar, "Are We a Nation of Cities?"
        Studies in Urban Politics, Reprint #16, Temple University, 1966;
        and James Wilson, "The Urban Unease," The Public Interest,
        Summer 1968, pp. 25-39.

(26)   Elazar, "Are We a Nation of Cities?" p. 43.

(27)   Jerome Pickard, "U.S. Metropolitan Growth and Expansion,
       1970-2000, With Population Projections, The Commission of
       Population Growth and the American Future," Population Dis-
       tribution and Policy, Vol. V., ed. Sara Mills Mazie (Washing-
       ton, D.C.: U.S. Government Printing Office, 1972), p. 146.

(28)   Ibid. For a full account of the development of the megalopolis
       on the Atlantic seaborad see Jean Gottman, Megalopolis (Cam-
       bridge, Mass.: MIT Press, 1961).

(29)   Herman Kahn and Anthony Weiner, "The Next Thirty Years: A
       Framework on Speculation," Daedalus, 96 (1967), 705-32.

(30)   Robert Redfield, "The Folk Society," in Sennett, Classic Essays
       on the Culture of Cities, p. 148.

(31)   Edward Higbee, Farms and Farmer in An Urban Age (New York:
       Twentieth Century Fund, 1963), pp. 60-61. Quoted in Amos
       Hawley, Urban Society (New York: Ronald Press, 1971), p. 233.

(32)   Report of the Commission on the Cities, The State of the Cities
       (New York; Praeger, 1972).

(33)   The mayoralty has never been a particularly good stepping stone
       to higher office, and this is still by and large true. However,
       national exposure and mobility are not one and the same thing,
       and the big city mayoralty has become a very visible office.
       For an interesting view on the political immobility of the office,
       see Marily Gittell, "Metropolitan Mayor: Dead End," (Public
       Administration Review, XXIII March, 1963), 20-24.

(34)   Donald Haider, When Governments Come to Washington (New
       York: Free Press, 1974), p. 98.

(35)   The so-called Pittsburgh Renaissance is the upshot of an earlier
       effort to get business to reinvest in that city and was quite suc-
       cessful under Mayor David Lawrence. Many of that city's larg-
       est companies joined this effort including the Mellon interests,
       Westinghouse and Jones and Laughlin Steel. Pittsburgh, at the
       time, was in an advanced state of decay, and pollution from the
       mills was threatening life within the city. See Jeanne Lowe,
       Cities In A Race With Time (New York: Random House, 1968),
       Chapter 3.

(36)   Long, The Unwalled City, p. 90; see also Peter Tropp, "Governors' and Mayors' Offices: The Role of the Staff," National Civic Review 63 (May 1974): 246.

(37)   The USCM/NLC have had on and off again mergers. Currently they share staff and work closely together, publishing many joint periodicals. They do, however, hold separate meetings and represent different constituencies with the USCM reflecting the viewpoint of large cities and their mayors; the NLC is more inclined to favor small to medium sized cities. See Donald Haider, When Governments Come to Washington, Chapter 1 and particularly pp. 7 and 20, for data on membership and staff. Also see Suzanne Farkas, Urban Lobbying (New York: New York University Press, 1971).

(38)   The New York Times, June 19, 1978, p. 1.

(39)   Michael Reagan, The New Federalism (New York: Oxford University Press, 1972) pp. 34 and 55.

(40)   The New York Times, June 19, 1978, p. B4.

(41)   For a history and account of urban fiscal crises see Advisory Commission on Intergovernmental Actions, City Financial Emergencies, (Washington, D.C., July 1973), p. 49.

CHAPTER 2

(1)   David Truman, The Governmental Process (New York: Knopf, 1960); Robert Dahl, Who Governs (New Haven: Yale University Press, 1963); Banfield, Political Influence; and Sayre and Kaufman, Governing New York City; and William Mitchell, The American Polity (New York: Free Press, 1970). A more critical interpretation of this process can be found in Theodore Lowi, The End of Liberalism (New York: W.W. Norton, 1969).

(2)   John Locke, "The Second Treatise of Civil Government" in Two Treatises of Government, edited by Thomas Cook (New York: Hafner, 1947), p. 132.

(3)   For a philosophical and theoretical exposition of this theme see Leo Strauss, Natural Right and History (Chicago: University of

Chicago Press, 1953); Harold J. Laski, The Rise of European Liberalism (London: George Allen & Unwin, 1962) and H. Mark Roelofs, The Language of Modern Politics (Homewood, Ill.: Dorsey Press, 1967).

(4) Charles Beard and Mary Beard, New Basic History of the United States (Garden City: Doubleday, 1960), p. 292.

(5) Ralph Nader, "The Case for Federal Chartering," in Corporate Power in America, edited by Ralph Nader and Mark Green (New York: Grossman, 1973), pp. 69-71.

(6) Congress and the Nation: 1945-64 (Washington, D.C.: Congressional Quarterly, 1964), p. 553.

(7) John Hicks, The American Nation (Cambridge, Mass.: Riverside Press, 1955), p. 133.

(8) Garbiel Kolko, The Triumph of Conservatism (New York: Free Press, 1963), p. 135 and chapters 5 and 6, passim.

(9) Ibid., Chapter 6.

(10) See for example, Jack Plano, Milton Greenberg, Roy Olton and Robert Riggs, Political Science Dictionary (Hinsdale, Ill.: Dryden, 1973).

(11) John Galbraith, The New Industrial State (Boston: Houghton Mifflin, 1971), pp. 74-75.

(12) Edward Greenberg, Serving the Few (New York: Wiley, 1974), p. 39.

(13) Ibid., p. 39.

(14) Greenberg, Serving the Few, p. 39.

(15) Jacobs, The Economy of Cities, pp. 123-25.

(16) Kirkpatrick Sale, Power Shift (New York: Random House, 1970), pp. 51-53.

(17) See for example, George Sternlieb and James Jughes, "Post-Industrial America: Decline of the Metropolis," Nation's Cities

(September, 1975) pp. 14-18; and George Sternlieb and James Hughes, Post Industrial America (New Brunswick, N.J.: Rutgers University Press, 1975). Also see The Wall Street Journal, April 6, 1976, p. 1, and June 16, 1976, p. 1.

(18) U.S. News and World Report, April 5, 1976, p. 62.

(19) Lowi, p. 88; see also chapters 2 and 3, passim.

(20) Research and Policy Committee of the Committee for Economic Development, Modernizing Local Government (New York: Committee for Economic Development, 1966), p. 13 and 17.

(21) Allen Manvel, "Metropolitan Growth and Government Fragmentation," Commission on Population Growth and the American Future: Research Reports, vol. IV, Governance and Population, ed. A.E. Keir Nash (Washington D.C.; U.S. Government Printing Office, 1972), p. 181. By the term metropolitan areas we are referring to Standard Metropolitan Statistical Areas.

(22) Ibid., p. 187.

(23) For a sympathetic, neoclassical economic treatment of this issue, see Robert Bish, The Public Economy of Metropolitan Areas (Chicago: Markham, 1971), Chapter 5.

(24) Michael Danielson, "Differentiation, Fragmentation, Segregation and Political Fragmentation in the American Metropolis," Governance and Population, p. 162.

(25) Henry Etzkowitz and Roger Mack, "Imperialism In The First World," paper presented to the Pacific Sociological Association, San Jose, California, March, 1975.

(26) The point is made by Frederick Wirt in his Power In the City (Berkeley, University of California Press, 1974), p. 352. Wirt quotes a phrase from Machiavelli, "a wise man will see to it that his acts always seem voluntary and not done by compulsion, however much he may be compelled by necessity."

(27) New York Times, February 29, 1976.

(28) New York Times, July 25, 1976.

(29) See for example, Dahl, Who Governs; Banfield, Political Influences and Sayre and Kaufman Governing New York City. See most especially Nelson Polsby, Community Power and Political Theory (New Haven: Yale University Press, 1963); and Richard Merelman, "On the Neo-Elitist Critique of Community Power," American Political Science Review, LXII, No. 2 (June, 1968), 451-60.

(30) There are two landmark studies which do account for the definition of alternatives and have set a framework to explore undersurface questions: E. E. Schattschneider, The Semisovereign People (New York: Holt, Rinehart, & Winston, 1960); and Peter Bachrach and Morton Baratz, Power and Poverty (New York: Oxford University Press, 1970). Also see H. V. Savitch, "Powerlessness In An Urban Ghetto," Polity V, no. 1 (Fall 1972): 19-56.

(31) The figures were compiled from a report issued by Drexel Burnham & Company, August 13, 1975 (New York, 600 Broad Street).

(32) A distinction should be made between wealth and income. Private wealth is the value of an individual's property and possessions, such as real estate, home, stocks, trust, retirement, boats, etc. Income is the regular monetary yield from a job, ownership, or investment. Yet much of the financial return from wealth is not counted as income. The most notable are unrealized capital gains and increases in the value of possessions that have not been sold for cash. While the top fifth of American families have over 40 percent of the income, these families hold an astounding 80 percent of the wealth. Also, the distinction is important for practical considerations. In 1974, a family with an income of $20,400 was in the top fifth of earners, and a husband and wife earning $10,200 each could belong in this category - but were they rich? See Lester Thurow, "Tax Wealth, Not Income," New York Times Magazine, April 11, 1976, pp. 32-108.

(33) Figures are garnered from charts presented in Greenberg, Serving the Few, pp. 131-36; and Thomas Dye, Understanding Public Policy (Englewood Cliffs, N.J.: Prentice-Hall, 1975), pp. 98-100.

(34) Greenberg, Serving the Few, pp. 146-47.

(35) Donald Haider, When Governments Come to Washington, pp. 144-52.

(36)   Arthur Miller, "Political Issues and Trust in Government: 1964-
       1970, " American Political Science Review, LXVIII, No. 3
       (September, 1974), 951-72.

(37)   "1976 Study of American Opinion: Concerning Public Attitudes
       Toward Business and Government" sponsored by the Marketing
       Department of U.S. News and World Report. In an earlier
       study, Greenberg reports that on a Harris national survey, 96%
       of the population believed that "free enterprise had made this
       country great. " Another 91% of the respondents believed that
       "business in America has changed for the better since depression
       days, " and 76% felt that "most businessmen are genuinely in-
       terested in the well being of the country. " See Greenberg,
       Serving the Few, p. 57.

(38)   For a broader interpretation see, Larry Sawyers, "Urban Form
       and the Mode of Production, " The Review of Radical Political
       Economics, 7, No. 1 (Spring 1975), 52-67.

(39)   Ibid. , p. 58.

       "Special Report: Government and the Auto, " National Journal,
(40)   VIII, No. 1 (January 3, 1976), 2.

(41)   Quoted in Sawyers, "Urban Form and the Mode of Production, "
       p. 55.

(42)   For particulars, see Bradford Snell, American Ground Trans-
       portation, 93rd Congress, U.S. Senate, Committee on the Judi-
       ciary, Subcommittee on Antitrust and Monopoly (Washington,
       D.C.: U.S. Government Printing Office, 1974). Historical
       anecdotes are also quoted in Sawyers, "Urban Form and the
       Mode of Production, " p. 55.

(43)   Congress and the Nation 1945-1964, p. 524.

(44)   New York Times, July 8, 1975, p. 31.

(45)   James O'Connor, The Fiscal Crisis of the State (New York: St.
       Martin's, 1973), p. 105.

(46)   Ibid. , pp. 105-06. It is difficult to estimate the absolute cost of
       a highway mile, but the Federal Highway Administration estimates
       that the cost of one lane of interstate highway for one mile is

$3,443,400. Multiplied by four, assuming a four lane highway, the total for one mile comes to $13,773,600 at rates prevailing in 1975.

CHAPTER 3

(1) The transcript for this conversation was prepared by the House Judiciary Committee. For the interested inquirer, an extended version of this conversation can also be obtained by consulting The New York Times, July 20, 1974, p. 14.

(2) James MacGregor Burns, Presidential Government (Boston: Houghton Mifflin, 1965), p. 148.

(3) These are treated in this book as ideal types. Obviously no president contains all the features of a meliorist or a reinforcing type, but has a predominance of one or the other. Of the presidents discussed in this chapter, none can be considered a "mixed" or "hybrid" type. See Max Weber, Basic Concepts in Sociology (New York: Citadel Press, 1963); and The Methodology of the Social Sciences (Glencoe: The Free Press, 1949).

(4) For a historical perspective on how the White House responded to cities during the years of the Great Depression, see Mark Gelfand, A Nation of Cities (New York: Oxford University Press, 1975), p. 31.

(5) Ibid., p. 34.

(6) Ibid., p. 33.

(7) Francis Piven and Richard Cloward, Regulating the Poor (New York: Random House, 1971), p. 53.

(8) Transcript of the U.S. Conference of Mayors, February 17, 1933, pp. 77-78 (Washington, D.C.).

(9) For this and other narratives by those who experienced the strife of the cities during the Great Depression, see Studs Terkel, Hard Times (New York: Random House, 1970), esp. p. 396.

(10)   Gelfand, A Nation of Cities, p. 41.

(11)   Arthur Schlesinger, Jr., The Coming of the New Deal (Boston:
       Houghton Mifflin, 1958), p. 193.

(12)   Ibid., Chs. 20-22.

(13)   "Work Relief" is more closely connected to direct government
       employment as an alternative to the dole. Both the Civil Works
       Administration (CWA) and the Works Progress Administration
       (WPA) conducted programs of this kind. Public works more
       often referred to contracts let out by government for the con-
       struction or rebuilding of public properties and did not necessarily
       involve unemployed workers. A good example of this is the Public
       Works Administration (PWA). For purposes of simplification
       we use work relief and public works interchangeably.

(14)   Schlesinger, The Coming of the New Deal, p. 270.

(15)   L. Laszlo-Ecker-Racz, "Financing Relief and Recovery," in
       The Municipal Yearbook: 1937 (Washington, D.C. International
       City Management Association), p. 372; and Emerson Ross "The
       Works Progress Administration," in Donald Howard, The WPA
       and Federal Relief Policy (New York: Da Capo Press, 1943),
       pp. 437-41.

(16)   Schlesinger, The Coming of the New Deal, p. 264.

(17)   Ibid., p. 274.

(18)   For useful bits and pieces of information on each of these parts
       of the government conduit as they function in housing policy,
       consult Michael Stone, "Federal Housing Policy: A Political
       Economic Analysis," in Jon Pynoos, Robert Schafer, and Chester
       Hartman, Housing Urban America (Chicago: Aldine, 1973),
       pp. 422-33; also Henry Aaron, Shelter and Subsidies (Washington,
       D.C.: Brookings Institute, 1972), especially chs. 5 and 6.

(19)   Robert Connery and Richard Leach, The Federal Government and
       Metropolitan Areas (Cambridge: Harvard University, 1960),
       p. 15.

(20)   Ibid., pp. 15-16.

(21) See Harold Wollman, Politics of Federal Housing (New York;
      Dodd Mead, 1971), p. 28.

(22) See Stone, "Federal Housing Policy," p. 432, on how "Fannie
      Mae" subsidizes private investors.

(23) Congress and the Nation: 1945-64, p. 481.

(24) Ibid., p. 478.

(25) For details on how one mayor and his staff in New Haven utilized
      urban renewal and applied the rules of the program, see Allan
      Talbott, The Mayor's Game, pp. 153-61. For how urban renew-
      al worked in Newark, see Harold Kaplan, Urban Renewal Politics
      (New York: Columbia University, 1963). Actually, New Haven
      was the most proficient city in using renewal funds and spent
      the highest per capita sum ($88.8) of any city in the country be-
      tween 1949 and 1960. Washington D.C. and Norfolk trailed far
      behind with per capita expenditures of $20.9 and $38.2 respect-
      ively. The very largest cities in the country, New York, Chicago,
      and Philadelphia spent the least dollars during these years,
      averaging a little over $8.4 per capita. For a conservative view
      on the deleterious consequences and operations of urban renewal,
      see Martin Anderson, The Federal Bulldozer (Cambridge: MIT
      Press, 1964).

(26) Housing Act of 1949 (63 stat. 413).

(27) See for example, the exchanges in Congress, Hearings on Hous-
      ing and Urban Redevelopment 81st Congress, first session 1949
      (Washington D.C.: U.S. Government Printing Office), pp. 1606-
      99, 1909.

(28) Harold Wollman, Politics of Federal Housing (New York: Dodd,
      Mead and Co., 1971), p. 37.

(29) See Anderson, The Federal Bulldozer, for a comprehensive
      account of the consequences of urban renewal. For statistics,
      see especially pp. 67 and 93. It should be noted that the Eisen-
      hower White House cooperated with city mayors in reducing the
      amount of land within urban renewal tracts which were to be re-
      served for residential use. Urban mayors, pinched by rising
      costs for municipal services, were anxious to have commercial
      structures erected, so that their tax base could be increased.

(30)   One of the more poignant accounts of how stable ethnic enclaves
       were disrupted is Herbert Gans, The Urban Villagers (New York:
       Macmillan, 1962), which describes an Italo-American community
       in the West End of Boston. What mistakenly appeared to be a
       slum to local planners and officials was a tightly knit neighbor-
       hood which nurtured elderly, lonely, and widowed residents.
       Jane Jacobs in The Death & Life of Great American Cities (New
       York: Random House, 1961), describes similar episodes,
       albeit happier ones, of communities fighting off their eradication.

(31)   Anderson, The Federal Bulldozer, p. 69.

(32)   Morton Grodzins, "Centralization and Decentralization in the
       American Federal System," in A Nation of States, edited by
       Daniel Elazar (Chicago: Rand McNally, 1963), p. 5.

(33)   Connery and Leach, The Federal Government and Metropolitan
       Areas, pp. 135-36.

(34)   Adams had the official and unassuming title of Assistant to the
       President and was, next to Eisenhower, the most powerful man
       in the White House. Some journalists in Washington believed that
       Adams was even more powerful than the passive President and,
       while Eisenhower lay ill with a heart attack, a mocking joke could
       be heard about what would have happened if Adams had been
       struck and Eisenhower forced to become President. See Louis
       Koenig, The Invisible Presidency, (New York: Rinehart, 1960),
       pp. 338-404.

(35)   Gelfand, A Nation of Cities, pp. 266-72. See also Sherman Adams,
       First Hand Report (New York: Harper Brothers, 1961); and Inter-
       view with Sherman Adams Tapes 1-5, Oral History Project,
       Columbia University.

(36)   Gelfand, A Nation of Cities, p. 273.

(37)   Dwight Eisenhower, Mandate for Change (Garden City, New York:
       Doubleday, 1963), pp. 548-49.

(38)   Ibid.

(39)   "The Crisis in Local Transit," Business Week, July 23, 1955,
       p. 120. Quoted in Gelfand, A Nation of Cities, pp. 231-33.

CHAPTER 4

(1)   See Gelfand, A Nation of Cities, pp. 294-306.

(2)   The figures were estimated by Arthur Schlesinger, A Thousand
       Days (Boston: Houghton Mifflin), pp. 708-09.

(3)   John F. Kennedy, Public Papers: 1961 (Washington, D. C.:
       Government Printing Office) p. 87. See also Bruce Miroff,
       Pragmatic Illusions (New York: David McKay, 1976), chapter 5.

(4)   Kennedy's aggressiveness during the "steel crisis," when he re-
       sorted to forceful government measures (threats of antitrust in-
       vestigations, harrassment of corporate executives, withdrawal
       of government contracts), represents the apogee of White House
       willingness to apply the federal jawbone to privatism. Never-
       theless, it is significant that these were limited measures and
       that some time later Kennedy permitted these same major steel
       companies to raise their prices with hardly a squawk from
       Washington. See Grant McConnell, Steel and the Presidency
       (New York: Norton, 1963); and Hobart Rowan, The Free Enter-
       prisers: Kennedy, Johnson and the Business Establishment
       (New York: G. P. Putnam, 1964).

(5)   Schlesinger, A Thousand Days, p. 660.

(6)   Confidential interview with a member of the Kennedy administra-
       tion.

(7)   Judith Parris, "Congress Rejects The President's Urban Depart-
       ment, 1961-62," in Congress and Urban Problems edited by
       Frederic Cleaveland (Washington, D. C.: Brookings, 1969),
       pp. 173-223.

(8)   Gelfand, A Nation of Cities, p. 326.

(9)   Parris, "Congress Rejects...", p. 210.

(10)   Quoted in James Sundquist, Politics & Poverty (Washington,
       D. C.: Brookings, 1968), p. 137.

(11)   Hugh Sidey, A Very Personal Presidency (New York: Athenium,
       1968), p. 103.

(12) See for example the description of HUD in <u>Congress and the</u>
<u>Nation: 1965-69</u>, (Washington, D. C.: Congressional Quarterly),
pp. 183-87.

(13) The accolade was given to HUD by one adviser to the poverty
program, Jack Conway; according to conversations and interviews I have held with other White House intimates, the view is
widely shared. Also see Bernard Frieden and Marshall Kaplan,
<u>The Politics of Neglect</u> (Cambridge: MIT Press, 1975), p. 40.

(14) Aaron, <u>Shelter and Subsidies</u>, p. 134.

(15) Ibid.

(16) For a technical critique of section 235 and how it failed to supply
benefits, see Robert Schafer and Charles Field "Section 235 of
the National Housing Act: Homeownership for Low-income
Families," in Jon Pynoos, et al., <u>Housing Urban America</u>,
pp. 460-71.

(17) Congress conducted extensive investigations and hearings on
the subject. See "Investigation of Abuses in the Low Income and
Moderate Income Housing Programs," <u>Hearing Before The Com-</u>
<u>mittee on Banking and Currency of the House of Representatives</u>,
Ninety First Congress, Sec. Sess., December 16, 1970 (Wash-
ington D. C.: U. S. Government Printing Office), as well as
<u>Staff Report and Recommendations</u>, Committee on Banking and
Currency, House of Representatives, Ninety First Congress,
Sec. Sess. (Washington, D. C.: U. S. Government Printing
Office).

(18) In addition to congressional hearings, energetic reporters turned
up a good deal of information not available to public officials.
See <u>The New York Times</u>, December 11, 1975, and December 12,
1975. Also Brian Boyer, <u>Cities Destroyed For Cash</u> (Chicago:
Follet, 1973).

(19) <u>Congress and The Nation 1965-69</u>, p. 188.

(20) A similar point is made and treated in an article dealing with
the particulars on the War on Poverty in James Anderson,
"Poverty, Unemployment and Economic Development: The
Search For a National Antipoverty Policy," <u>Journal of Politics</u>
(February, 1967), pp. 70-93.

(21)   Daniel Moynihan, Maximum Feasible Misunderstanding (New
       York: Free Press, 1969), p. 80.

(22)   Piven and Cloward, Regulating the Poor, p. 259.

(23)   One political scientist has developed an entire thesis around this
       idea of political ambiguity, claiming that it is a by-product of a
       political system which rests on the necessity to parcel out
       sovereignty and policymaking to interest groups. "Interest
       group liberalism" is the designation given to this system, which
       deliberately constructs vague objectives so that special groups
       can gain control over policy implementation. While this may be
       true, it is not as novel a phenomenon as one might think. I
       would contend that interest group liberalism is more closely
       related to the meliorist tradition of enlisting privatism because
       of a corporate monopoly over the marketplace which has a deep
       economic compulsion behind it. For the "interest liberalism"
       thesis, see Theodore Lowi, The End of Liberalism.

(24)   See Piven and Cloward, Regulating the Poor, chapter 9.

(25)   Joseph Califano, a top Johnson aide after 1965, explicated this
       thesis in a speech given before a liberal Jewish organization,
       "Remarks by Joseph A. Califano, Jr., Special Assistant to The
       President Before National Representatives of B'nai B'rith,
       June 27, 1968," The White House, June 27, 1968 (Mimeograph).

(26)   Lyndon Johnson, Vantage Point (New York: Holt, Rinehart &
       Winston, 1971), p. 72.

(27)   Piven & Cloward, Regulating the Poor, p. 335.

(28)   Pete Hamill, "The Revolt of the White Middle Class," New York
       Post, April 14, 1969, pp. 24-29. Also quoted in Daniel Moynihan,
       The Politics of A Guaranteed Income (New York: Random House,
       1973), p. 105.

(29)   Robert Fogelson, Violence as Protest (Garden City, New York:
       Doubleday, 1971), p. 26. The statistics on collective rioting
       between 1965 and 1968 are derived from Moynihan, The Politics
       of A Guaranteed Income op. cit. p. 102 and from The Statistical
       Abstract of the United States: 1971 (Washington: U.S. Govern-
       ment Printing Office), p. 144. For the year 1968 the term "col-
       lective rioting" includes only "major" and "serious" acts.

(30) Quoted in John Donovan, The Politics of Poverty (New York:
      Pegasus, 1967), p. 57.

(31) For the history and rationale behind model cities see Frieden
      and Kaplan, The Politics of Neglect, as well as Charles Haar,
      Between The Idea and The Reality (Boston: Little Brown, 1975).

(32) Message from the President to the Congress on "City Demonstra-
      tion Projects," H. R. Doc. No. 368, 89th Congress, Sec. Sess.,
      January 26, 1966.

(33) Confidential interview with a Johnson adviser.

(34) See U.S. Congress House Committee, Subcommittee on Housing,
      Banking, and Currency, Hearings: Demonstration Cities, Hous-
      ing and Urban Development and Urban Mass Transit, 89th Con-
      gress, Sec. Sess., 1966, p. 35.

(35) Frieden and Kaplan, The Politics of Neglect, p. 66.

(36) One consultant to HUD became distressed over whether partici-
      pation meant citizen control or their co-optation by local officials,
      and so resigned from her position. See an article written by
      her on the various ways in which "participation" can be inter-
      preted, Sherry Arnstein, "A Ladder of Citizen Participation,"
      Journal of The American Institute of Planners, XXXV, no. 4
      (July, 1969) 216-24.

(37) Moynihan, Maximum Feasible Misunderstanding, p. 137.

(38) Johnson, The Vantage Point, p. 323.

(39) Ibid., p. 323.

(40) 68 Stat. 617, see Title VIII of the Act (S 3497-PL 90448).

CHAPTER 5

(1)   Richard Nathan, The Plot That Failed (New York: Wiley, 1975),
      p. 101.

(2)   Quoted in Daniel Moynihan, <u>The Politics of a Guaranteed Income</u>
       (New York: Random House, 1973), pp. 76-77.

(3)   "Meliorist" and "reinforcing" seats are calculated on the basis
       of a Representative's or a Senator's willingness to use federal
       aid to solve urban problems. Actual differences between
       meliorists and reinforcers are more complex (see discussion
       in Chapter 2), but a willingness to spend money for cities is an
       adequate measure for assessing the voting disposition of Con-
       gress in this case.

(4)   See <u>Congressional Quarterly Guide,</u> Spring, 1977, p. 73.

(5)   The assertion here is that political circumstance shapes behavior.
       This is somewhat of a modification of the Lasswell-Barber argu-
       ment which views personality and individual character as con-
       stants, see James Barber (Englewood Cliffs, N.J.: Prentice
       Hall, 1972) and Harold Lasswell, <u>Power and Personality</u> (New
       York: W.W. Norton, 1948). In Nixon's case the political align-
       ment of forces probably accentuated certain personality traits
       and as his presidency matured grated against Nixon's aggressive
       instincts.

(6)   Revenue sharing type programs is a generic term used by the
       writer to describe general revenue sharing, special revenue
       sharing and block grants. Each of these programs has its own
       complex characteristics and functions.

(7)   The example is not entirely hypothetical since HUD, under Nixon
       and Ford, experimented with a housing "income strategy" and was
       hoping to move more closely to these kinds of policies to provide
       housing for the poor. The so-called "voucher system" in educa-
       tion, which quite conceivably could replace segments of the pub-
       lic school system by providing recipients with an "educational
       voucher" with which they could "purchase education" for a child
       is a good example of the "income strategy" approach. Thus,
       instead of remedial programs such as OEO's "Headstart,"
       which were funded by categorical grants, families might be able
       to seek out remedies for themselves by applying an "educational
       voucher" to whatever school they deemed best. The "voucher
       system" never did gain widespread use in primary and secondary
       schools, but something very similar to an "income strategy"
       was initiated by the Nixon-Ford White Houses in higher education

when grants were shifted from funding universities and colleges
to supplying students directly with stipends to be used wherever
the individual chose.

(8)   *National Journal Reports*, March 10, 1973, p. 329.

(9)   Ibid., p. 331.

(10)   States which stood to receive less of a dollar return than their
       size and populations warranted were Pennsylvania, Ohio, and
       Texas. As a rule, low tax and low density suburbs also received
       smaller revenue sharing totals. See note 13 for details.

(11)   As passed under the Nixon White House, general revenue sharing
       guaranteed a minimum per capita grant to every local govern-
       ment of at least 20 percent of the statewide average. Under this
       general revenue sharing act, the maximum per capita grant for
       localities was 145 percent of the statewide average.

(12)   For an idea of how other mayors from all sizes of cities began
       to favor Nixon, see an article by Pete Wilson, a Mayor of San
       Diego, entitled, "Nixon's Urban Record," in *City*, VI (No. 4,
       Fall 1972), 8.

(13)   "State of the Union Message to the Congress on Law Enforcement
       and Drug Abuse Prevention," March 14, 1973, in *Public Papers
       of the Presidents* no. 79 (Washington, D.C.: U.S. Government
       Printing Office) p. 193 (herein referred to as *Public Papers*).

(14)   For a detailed exposition of how Nixon handled categorical grants,
       see Michael Reagan, *The New Federalism* (New York: Oxford
       University Press, 1972), especially p. 136. Also see for sub-
       stantiating information, *National Journal Reports* April 13, 1974,
       pp. 556-57; and April 28, 1973, p. 622.

(15)   See for example, *National Journal Report*, February 9, 1974,
       which details the Nixon budget and spending patterns.

(16)   For the mayors' reaction to Nixon's housing policy see, *National
       Journal Reports*, July 28, 1973, pp. 1101-02.

(17)   *The New York Times*, March 1, 1970, p. 1.

(18) For details on Nixon impoundments and cutbacks see, Congres-
      sional Quarterly Alamanac: 1973, pp. 252-56; Congressional
      Quarterly Almanac: 1972, pp. 352, 419 and Congressional Quar-
      terly Weekly Report, February 10, 1973, p. 270.

(19) Congressional Quarterly Almanac: 1973, p. 980.

(20) New York and the Urban Dilemma (New York: Facts on File,
      1976) p. 82.

(21) Congressional Quarterly Weekly Report, January 1, 1973, p. 40.

(22) Ibid., January 27, 1973, p. 139.

(23) National Journal Reports, February 28, 1973, p. 1100.

(24) Congressional Quarterly Weekly Reports, January 20, 1973,
      pp. 73-74; and January 27, 1973, p. 139.

(25) A negative income tax is an idea popularized by Professor Milton
      Friedman, a laissez faire economist, who promotes the virtues
      of free enterprise and competition. Basically, Friedman argues
      that if a progressive income tax takes money from individuals as
      they earn more, a negative income tax should return money to
      individuals if they earn less or nothing at all. The idea has a
      particular applicability to marginal workers who may earn a
      decent income in one year and pay a goodly amount in income
      taxes, but in a subsequent year not earn anything at all. Under
      a "negative income tax," such individuals could be "reimbursed"
      for taxes paid in previous years. Gradually, Friedman came to
      believe that a "negative income" could be a permanent device
      for persons who never entered taxable income brackets and paid
      out routinely, in lieu of welfare.

(26) For an elaborate and full account of FAP see Daniel Moynihan,
      The Politics of Guaranteed Income (New York: Random House,
      1973).

(27) Congressional Quarterly Weekly Reports, March 3, 1973, p. 431.

(28) Ibid., p. 433.

(29) Ibid., p. 433.

(30)   Congressional Quarterly Alamanac 1970, p. 557.

(31)   The percent increase for violent crime (murder, rape, robbery,
       assault) and for property crimes (burglary, larceny, auto theft)
       for 1970-72 are as follows: murder (+14%); rape (+21%); robbery
       (+59%); assault (+14%); burglary (+5%); larceny (+2%) - only auto
       theft declined (-7%). Crime rates continued to rise through 1975
       with serious crime up 11% in the first nine months of 1975 - rob-
       bery during that year increased 11%, larceny 13%, burglary 10%,
       assault 7%, murder 3%, and rape 2%. Overall, cities with over
       100,000 population had a 9% crime rise and suburbs and other
       locales 12%. By contrast, civil disturbance showed an overall
       pattern of decrease with major disturbances showing a drop as
       follows:

| | | Disturbance | | |
Year	Total	Major	Other	Related Deaths
1969	57	8	49	19
1970	76	18	58	33
1971	39	10	29	10
1972	21	2	19	9

(32)   Nathan, The Plot That Failed, p. 40.

(33)   For a stinging and readable account of Nixon's difficulties with
       Romney and other cabinet appointees see, Dan Rather and Gary
       Gates, The Palace Guard (New York: Warner, 1975).

(34)   Confidential interview.

(35)   Radio Address, October 21, 1972, "The Philosophy of Govern-
       ment. "

(36)   Radio Address, "The New Budget: Charting A New Era of Pro-
       gress," January 28, 1973, Public Papers, #20, p. 30.

(37)   Ibid.

(38)   National Journal Reports, December 13, 1975, p. 1690.

(39)   The fact that Ash's conglomerate, Litton Industries, was also in-
       volved in a significant number of cost over-runs in contracts for
       the military caused quite a stir in Washington. One Defense De-
       partment official noted that "General Eisenhower must be twitch-

ing in his grave" over the "military-industrial-executive department complex" suggested by Ash's position as head of OMB.
Senator William Proxmire, an outspoken and unorthodox Democrat from Wisconsin, charged that "here we have one of the most
difficult and conspicuous conflicts that I have ever seen." Congress, in fact, sought to require confirmation of the OMB Director, but was successfully vetoed by Nixon. For his part, Ash
was candid about his business affiliation and likened running the
federal government to managing the "biggest conglomerate of
them all." James Lynn, who was Ash's successor at OMB, had
been the Nixon insider sent in to displace Romney at HUD in
early 1973. Lynn went on to an even tighter relationship with the
President after he earned his trust at HUD, and later became the
number one man at OMB under both Nixon and Ford. For a view
of OMB under Ash see John Herbers, "The Other Presidency,"
New York Times Magazine, March 3, 1974, pp. 16-41.

(40)   For an account of some of these personnel changes consult
        National Journal Reports, March 10, 1973, p. 335.

(41)   Ibid. , p. 335.

(42)   Radio address, "State of the Union Message on Community De-
        velopment," March 14, 1973, Public Papers #68, pp. 164-65.

(43)   President Ford: The Man and His Record (Washington: Con-
        gressional Quarterly, 1974), p. 27.

(44)   Discriminatory norms are subtle, but nonetheless recognizable,
        and can range from a lack of credence and speaking time made
        available to minorities to behavioral pressures which make min-
        orities ill at ease and unwilling to press their claims. More
        formal political/legal blockages are not uncommon, either in the
        North or the South and include gerrymandered electoral districts
        which preclude minority representation, rigged voting systems
        which make it difficult for minorities to field winning candidates,
        and prejudicial judges who eliminate minority candidates from
        getting their names on a ballot for frivolous and contrived reasons.

(45)   Bernard Frieden and Marshall Kaplan, "Community Development
        and the Model Cities Legacy," Working Paper, No. 42, Joint
        Center For Urban Studies of MIT and Harvard University, p. 41.

(46) Ibid. , p. 30.

(47) For an extensive study on HCDA and how model cities has been
      given short shrift in most cases, see a study done by the Brook-
      ings Institution for HUD, Block Grants For Community Develop-
      ment (Washington, D. C.: U. S. Department of Housing and Ur-
      ban Development, January 1977), especially, p. 167.

(48) The concept of "triage" was summarized by Anthony Downs as
      follows: "When combat surgeons are faced with far more cases
      of wounded personnel than they can handle in the time available,
      they supposedly divide those cases into three categories: people
      who will probably get well whether the surgeons operate or not,
      people who are so badly hurt they will probably die whether they
      are operated on or not, and people for whom what the surgeons
      do will probably make the difference between life and death. In
      theory, the surgeons then give pain-killing medicine to the first
      and second groups, and operate only upon the third group. This
      allocation technique maximizes the effectiveness of their scarce
      abilities and time in terms of final outputs, which in the case of
      medicine is the number of persons who are well. " (U. S. Depart-
      ment of Housing and Urban Development Block Grants for Com-
      munity Development [Washington D. C.; HUD, January 1977]
      pp. 331-32.)

(49) Frieden and Kaplan, "Community Development and the Model
      Cities Legacy," p. 40.

(50) Block Grants For Community Development, p. 180.

(51) Ibid. , pp. 156-161.

(52) See the transcript and accompanying stories on each of these
      presidential documents in the New York Times, January 20,
      1976, and January 22, 1976.

(53) For example see the New York Times, January 22, 1976, p. 25.

(54) Confidential interview.

(55) Confidential interview.

(56) New York Times, June 28, 1976, p. 1.

(57) New York and the Urban Dilemma, p. 120.

(58) Ibid., p. 164.

(59) Ibid., p. 134.

(60) The New York Times, October 19, 1975, p. 48.

(61) The headline won instant attention throughout New York and other
      parts of the country and probably was instrumental in losing
      New York State for Ford during the 1976 election. See The New
      York Daily News, October 30, 1975.

(62) New York Times, October 30, 1975, p. 46.

(63) Ibid., p. 46.

(64) Over the years Lockheed has been involved in over-charging the
      Defense Department for contracted work or in "cost over-runs."
      The company has also been involved with making bribes to offi-
      cials of foreign governments in order to obtain contracts from
      those governments.

(65) New York and the Urban Dilemma, p. 133.

(66) New York Times, November 7, 1975, p. 51.

(67) A subsequent study of New York's fiscal condition of 1977 by the
      Comptroller General of the United States concluded that the
      "fiscal and economic base of NYC continues to deteriorate..."
      and "barring major policy shifts at the State and Federal levels,
      1977-85 will be an extremely difficult period for the city." See
      Report to the Congress by the Comptroller General of the United
      States, Summary: The Long Term Fiscal Outlook For New York
      City (Washington, D. C.: U.S. Government Printing Office,
      1977), pp. 2-3; and the full report, The Long Term Fiscal Out-
      look for New York City (Washington D. C.: U.S. Government
      Printing Office, 1977).

CHAPTER 6

(1)   Hearing before the Committee on Banking, Housing, and Urban
        Affairs, U.S. Senate, 95th Congress, nomination of Patricia
        Roberts Harris to be Secretary of the Department of Housing and
        Urban Development, January 10, 1977.

(2)   Actually, Senator William Proxmire has been one of the more
        outspoken critics and skeptics within the Congress. As some-
        thing of a maverick Senator, he has built his career on incisive
        and relatively candid discourses on bureaucratic bungling and
        corporate irresponsibility. Despite this, his remarks still prove
        the rule that members of Congress are loathe to make the same
        kind of public lambastes about their own legislative practices.

(3)   See, for example, some landmark studies on the subject by Ran-
        dall Ripley, such as Power In the Senate (New York: St. Martins
        Press, 1969); Party Leaders In the House of Representatives
        (Washington: Brookings Institution, 1967); Majority Party Leader-
        ship In Congress (Boston: Little Brown, 1968). See also Richard
        Fenno, Congressmen in Committees (Boston: Little Brown, 1973);
        as well as some popular accounts such as Joseph Clark, The
        Senate Establishment (New York: Hill and Wang, 1963); and
        Richard Bolling, Power In The House (New York: Capricorn,
        1974).

(4)   The committee chairmen in the House who were moved were F.
        Edward Hebert (D/La.) from Armed Services, W.R. Poage
        (D/Texas) from Agriculture, and Wright Patman (D/Texas)
        from Banking, Currency, and Housing.
            The new Senate rules made it slightly easier to invoke
        a cloture against a filibuster and placed a check against chair-
        men by Senate Democrats. The procedure to carry out the
        chairmanship reforms provides that a list of nominees be dis-
        tributed to all Democrats. Democratic Senators have the
        right to place a check-mark next to the name of any nominee
        they wish to subject to a secret ballot, without having to sign
        their own name. If at least 20 percent of the Democrats in-
        dicate that they would prefer a secret vote on a nominee, this
        vote is held by the caucus two days later.

(5)   For the 95th Congress, on the House side Carl Albert (Ark.) was
        replaced by Thomas (Tip) O'Neill (Mass.) and James Wright
        (Texas) and John Brademas (Ind.) moved into leadership positions
        as Majority Leader and Whip respectively. At the time of their
        rise, O'Neill was in his mid-60s (not an old age for a speaker-
        ship, which places importance on the aspirant's ability to out-
        wait or outlive his colleagues), while Wright and Brademas were
        at the dawn of their 50s. Other influentials in the House were Al
        Ullman (Or.), Chairman of Ways and Means; Henry Reuss (Wis.)
        Banking, Finance, and Urban Affairs. Thomas Ashley (Ohio) is
        another influential member of the Banking, Finance, and Urban
        Affairs Committee and has been important on housing policy.
        The Senate has undergone less dramatic changes, though its
        Majority Leader Mike Mansfield was succeeded by Robert Byrd
        (W. Va.), and Howard Baker (Tenn.) appears to be taking things
        in hand for the Republicans as their Minority Leader.

(6)   See Donald Matthews, U.S. Senators and Their World (New York:
        Random House, 1960). For more up-to-date data see Fenno, C
        Congressmen in Committees, Ch. 5.

(7)   Quoted in Doris Kearn, Lyndon Johnson and the American Dream,
        (New York: Harper and Row, 1976), pp. 221-22.

(8)   Actually, the tide began to turn first with the large mass of pub-
        lic opinion and these changes were felt by Congress. For example,
        in mid-October only 42 percent of the American public expressed
        any support for making funds available to New York City, while
        49 percent of those surveyed opposed the idea. By early Novem-
        ber, a majority of Americans had changed their mind on the issue
        and a poll showed that 55 percent of the public favored the idea
        and 33 percent opposed it. See New York and the Urban Dilemma,
        pp. 150-51.

(9)   Richard Fenno, Congressman In Committees (Boston: Little
        Brown, 1973), p. 87.

(10)   For a legislative history on the initial stages of the "War on
        Poverty" bill see William Selover, "The View from Capitol Hill:
        Harassment and Survival, " in On Fighting Poverty edited by
        James Sundquist (New York: Basic Books, 1969), pp. 158-186.
        See also the discussion of this in Chapter 3.

(11) Donald Haider, When Governments Come to Washington (New
      York: Free Press, 1974), p. 70.

(12) Much of the following discussion on NAHB is drawn from William
      Lilley, "The Homebuilder's Lobby, " in Housing Urban American,
      pp. 30-48.

(13) Ibid. , p. 34.

(14) Ibid. , p. 33.

(15) Ibid.

(16) Congressional Quarterly, Weekly Report, April 6, 1974.

(17) These observations are not as apparent as may seem at first
      glance. For example, many political scientists have argued that
      party affiliation and not constituency is the determining variable
      for how a legislator votes. Demetrios Caraley purports to esta-
      blish that Democratic or Republican party affiliation determines
      "pro" or "anti" urban voting. The motivations behind urban
      voting, I believe, are more subtle than using party as an exclu-
      sive referent since there are significant cross pressures com-
      ing from a legislator's constituency. See Demetrios Caraley,
      "Congressional Politics and Urban Aid, " American Political
      Institutions In The 70's, ed. Demetrios Caraley (New York:
      Columbia University Press, 1973), pp. 312-38.

(18) Fenno, Congressmen in Committees, p. 104.

(19) In a study of congressional committees between 1955-65, Richard
      Fenno found that of six House committees, Education and Labor
      had the lowest median seniority for its members (. 78 years of
      prior service) while Ways and Means had the highest (6. 6 years
      of prior service). Of the six committees studied, Education and
      Labor also fell somewhere in the middle in terms of the fre-
      quency of committee turnover with an average rate of 27 percent.
      See ibid. chapters 2 and 4. In spite of this history of relatively
      low preference and low credibility, Education and Labor did quite
      well for itself during Johnson's initiatives with Great Society
      legislation. With a boost from the White House, the Committee's
      efficacy soared, and so, too, did its importance in the House.

(20)   The word "image" is used deliberately because stereotypes can
       be deceptive. While Education and Labor was stigmatized in the
       House because of its conspicuous rowdyism, at least one member
       of Ways and Means was acting quite bizarrely off the Congressional
       floor. More than a few staid members of Congress and committee
       chairmen were discovered to have some very ribald patterns of
       behavior, while the so called "crazies" turned out to be very con-
       ventional individuals.

(21)   Fenno, Congressmen in Committees, p. 55, and see John Manley,
       "Wilbur D. Mills: A Study In Congressional Influence, " American
       Political Science Review, LXIII (No. 2, June 1969), 448.

(22)   Using the Congressional Quarterly's composite index of "conser-
       vative coalition support" to indicate a propensity toward reinforc-
       ing policy choices and away from meliorism, the Committee on
       Eucation and Labor comes out with total scores of 43.21 (94th
       Congress) and 36.63 (93rd Congress). By contrast, Ways and
       Means had much higher "conservative coalition support" scores
       of 56.41 (94th Congress) and 54.35 (93rd Congress). The "con-
       servative coalition support" scores for these Congresses were
       based on a percentage of roll call votes in which committee mem-
       bers voted "for" issues supported by right of center interest
       groups. On this subject see also Fenno, Congressmen in Com-
       mittees, p. 52.

(23)   Fenno, Congressmen in Committees, p. 169.

(24)   Fenno illustrates this through data showing that Finance had a
       very preferential standing in terms of transfer rates. It also
       had a low percentage of freshman appointments (18 percent)
       among the six committees he studied. See ibid., Ch. 5. One
       freshman Senator who did make it into the Finance Committee
       during the 95th Congress, after publicly stating his preference
       for it, was Daniel Moynihan, Democrat from New York. Moyni-
       han, of course, had good reason for wanting Finance because it
       was the crucial committee in the upper chamber for managing
       welfare reform legislation; a subject Moynihan had intimate ex-
       perience with during the Nixon White House.

(25)   Congressional Quarterly, Weekly Report, December 6, 1975,
       p. 2624.

(26)   The New York Times, October 31, 1975, p. 1.

(27)   Congressional Quarterly, Weekly Report, June 11, 1977, p. 1194.

(28)   See "Special Report: Government and the Auto," National Jour-
       nal VIII, (No. 1, January 3, 1976), especially 2-3.

(29)   Congress and the Nation, III, 1969-72, 150.

(30)   There are numerous ways to estimate federal contributions to
       highways vis-a-vis roads, and one can come up with startlingly
       different figures depending on the time frame used, whether
       funds are actually spent or just earmarked, and which programs
       are included or excluded in defining "mass transit." According
       to House Committee figures, the federal contribution to roads
       actually spent since 1977 amounts to $88.2 billion. Money
       actually spent on mass transit, since legislation was enacted in
       1964, is $6.4 billion. Much more money is earmarked for both
       highways and mass transit. For a brief article on the subject
       see New York Times, May 30, 1976, Section IV.

(31)   For background and detail of how Anderson made the fight in the
       House see Congressional Quarterly Weekly Report, October 14,
       1972, pp. 2286-89.

(32)   Ibid., p. 2688.

(33)   Congressional Quarterly Almanac: 1975, p. 736.

(34)   Congressional Quarterly, Weekly Report, October 14, 1972,
       p. 2688.

(35)   For part of the story on Kluczynski see National Journal Reports,
       February 24, 1973 VIII, p. 286; and Haider, When Governments
       Come to Washington, p. 253.

(36)   The nine House conferees and their constituencies were as follows:
            James Wright (D/Tex.) 59% central city
            John Stanton (R/Ohio) 0% central city
            John Kluczynski (D/Ill.) 100% central city
            John Blatnik (D/Minn) 21% central city
            William Harsha (R/Ohio) 0% central city
            James Cleveland (R/N.H.) 15% central city
            M.G. Snyder (R/Ken.) 0% central city

Harold Johnson (R/Calif.) 0% central city
Donald Clawson (R/Calif.) 18% central city
The seven Senate conferees came from the following states:
Lloyd Bentsen (D/Tex.)
Jennings Randolph (D/W. Va)
Joseph Montoya (D/N. M.)
Howard Baker (R/Tenn.)
Robert Stafford (R/Vt.)
Edwin Muskie (D/Maine)
James Buckley (C-R/N. Y.)

(37) For an account which is thorough and quite favorable to the Bentsen and Wright roles see Michael Malbin, "Transportation Report One Long Deadlock Ends In Compromise Opening. Highway Trust for Mass Transit," in National Journal Reports, August 11, 1973 V (No. 32), pp. 1163-71.

(38) Ibid.

(39) For a criticism of the administrative and fiscal restrictions of this legislation see, Statement of the Honorable James Robinson, Mayor of Montgomery, Alabama, "On the Federal Highway Act of 1975," House, Public Works and Transportation, September 11, 1975, Made on Behalf of the National League of Cities/the United States Conference of Mayors, September 11, 1975 (Mimeograph; USCM/NLC; Washington, D. C.).

(40) For a detailed and statistical account of how this legislation has been implemented across the country and of how minimally cities have been able to use it, see Report of the Secretary of Transportation to the United States Congress, "Urban Systems Study," (Washington, D. C.: U. S. Government Printing Office, 1977), especially pp. 1-40.

CHAPTER 7

(1) The analogy is drawn from a well known piece by Morton Grodzins, "Centralization and Decentralization In The American Federal System," A Nation of States (Chicago: Rand McNally, 1961), pp. 1-24.

(2)   See John Grumm and Russell Murphy, "Dillon's Rule Reconsidered,"
        The Annals (November, 1974),p. 123.   This article offers a fuller
        exposition on the subject and treats the legal question as com-
        pounded by contemporary realities of state and bureaucratic
        politics.

(3)   For a revealing history of state prejudice toward cities see Mark
        Gelfand, A Nation of Cities, pp. 7-17.

(4)   J. F. Dillon, Commentaries on the Law of Municipal Corporations
        (5th ed. , 1911), pp. 449-50.

(5)   Frank Michelman and Terrance Sandalow, Materials on Govern-
        ment In Urban Areas (St. Paul, Minnesota: West Publishing,
        1970), pp. 252-53.

(6)   F. J. Macchiarola, "Local Government Home Rule and the
        Judiciary," The Journal of Urban Law 48 (1971): 335-59.

(7)   Reynold v. Simms, 377 U. S. 533 (1974) and Wesberry v. Sanders,
        376 U. S. 1 (1964).

(8)   Consult Macchiarola, "Local Government Home Rule."

(9)   For an interesting set of commentaries and critiques of state
        policies toward cities see Alan Campbell, ed. , The States and
        The Urban Crisis (Englewood Cliffs, N. J.: Prentice-Hall, 1970);
        for a defense of state policies see Ira Sharkansky, The Maligned
        States (New York: McGraw Hill, 1972).

(10)   Quoted in Rochelle Turner, "Carter's Urban Policy and the
        States," Publius VIII (Winter, 1978), p. 39.

(11)   Consult "Special Report: Where the Funds Flow," The National
        Journal, June 26, 1976, p. 881.

(12)   The figures are rounded and are for the total number of recipients
        on public assistance. The percentage of AFDC recipients is sig-
        nificantly higher. See U. S. Advisory Commission on Intergovern-
        mental Relations, Fiscal Balance in the American Federal System,
        Vol. II, p. 41.

(13)   For a different kind of treatment of this subject and one that
        measures a larger and indiscriminate universe of state actions,

consult Ira Sharkansky, "Government Expenditures and Public Services in the American States," American Political Science Review 61, no. 4 (December 1967): 1066-77; Ira Sharkansky and Richard Hofferbert, "Dimensions of State Politics, Economics and Public Policy," and Jack Walker, "The Diffusion of Innovation Among the American States," both of which can be found in The American Political Science Review 63, no. 3 (September 1969): 867-99. Also, see a series of articles on "Innovation in State Politics," by Douglas Rose, Virginia Gray, and Jack Walker in the American Political Science Review 67, no. 4 (December 1973): 1162-1193.

(14) For an account of Moses' activities, see Robert Caro, The Power Broker (New York: Random House, 1974).

(15) See Towards a Growth Policy For Massachusetts: A Preliminary Draft, Office of State Planning, Commonwealth of Massachusetts, October, 1975, especially p. 64 (herein referred to as Massachusetts Growth Policy).

(16) See Notes by Professor Troy Westmeyer in the National Civic Review (July 1976), p. 358.

(17) Urban Development Strategy for California: Review Draft, Office of Planning and Research, State of California, May, 1977, p. 25.

(18) Barbara Swain, "The New Coastal Commission, More Bad News for Developers," California Magazine (March, 1977), p. 87.

(19) For comprehensive listings of state programs consult any of the most recent editions of The Book of the States, published by the council of State Governments, Lexington, Kentucky.

(20) These are some state programs which are targeted to distressed communities. These include state supported training of the "hard core" unemployed (California, Maryland, Massachusetts, and New York); and state, city, or county incentives for establishing industrial plants in areas of high unemployment (California, Maryland, Massachusetts, and New York).

(21) Massachusetts Growth Policy, p. 65.

(22) Ibid., p. 72.

(23)   Ibid., p. 80, 81.

(24)   The New York Times, August 2, 1978, p. A21.

(25)   The figure includes units built by New York State's Urban Develop-
       ment Corporation. See Michael Stegman, "Housing Finance Agen-
       cies: Are They Crucial Instruments of State Government?" Jour-
       nal of the American Institute of Planners (September, 1974),
       p. 315.

(26)   Described in "Nelson A. Rockefeller," in Governing New York
       State, edited by Robert Connery and Gerald Benjamin (New York:
       The Academy of Political Science, 1974), p. 11.

(27)   Eleanor Brilliant, The Urban Development Corporation (Lexing-
       ton, Mass.: D.C. Heath, 1974), p. 24.

(28)   Ibid., p. 24. The act also placed more severe tax restrictions on
       industrial and commercial development, which UDC was interested
       in undertaking.

(29)   The incident is described in Richard Lehne's Reapportionment of
       the New York Legislature: Impact and Issues (New York: The
       National Municipal League, 1972), pp. 40-41.

(30)   The best and fullest account of UDC can be found in A Report to
       the Governor by the New York State Moreland Act Commission on
       the Urban Development Corporation and Other State Financing
       Agencies, March 31, 1976, "Restoring Credit and Confidence"
       (herein referred to as Moreland Act Report).

(31)   The role of underwriter is to buy a given issue of bonds en masse
       and then market them to other buyers. Usually several underwrit-
       ing firms get together to form a syndicate which manages the
       first issue of bonds collectively. The senior manager of a syndi-
       cate usually receives the largest share of the profits and plays
       the leading role in directing the transaction. Bond profits are de-
       rived from the difference between what underwriters pay for the
       bonds and what they receive from their subsequent sale. Usually
       an underwriting syndicate buys bonds at a discount and sells them
       at their face value or at a premium above their face value. Thus,
       if a $100 million bond issue were sold at a two percent discount
       for $98 million, the underwriters would realize a $2 million pro-
       fit on a subsequent face value sale. If the bond sold at a premium

of $102 million, the underwriters would earn a profit of $4 million.
Under these same procedures, it is not difficult to see how a syndicate might also lose money, but this is rare and underwriters
are known for retaining a portion of a discounted bond issue for
themselves. Considering the profits from just having bought a
discounted bond, plus the interest, plus the tax exempt status,
we can understand why the largest underwriting banks have held
a disproportionate share of bond issues.

(32)   Ibid. , p. 127; and Jack Newfield and Paul Dubrul, The Abuse of
       Power (New York: Viking Press, 1977), p. 25.

(33)   Moreland Act Report, p. 127.

(34)   The New York Times, October 15-18, 1975.

(35)   Neal R. Peirce, The Megastates of America (New York: W.W.
       Norton, 1972), p. 612.

(36)   For a telling article on the defeat of mass transit referenda in
       southern California and the costs of the automobile, see Peter
       Marcuse "Mass Transit for the Few, " Society XIII, (No. 6,
       September/October, 1976), 43-50.

(37)   The BART Case has generated a controversy around "who" and
       which groups were its movers. Those who believe in the "con-
       spiracy" theory of BART claim that it was the work of business
       classes. See for example, Stephen Zwerling, Mass Transit and
       the Politics of Technology (New York: Praeger, 1973); and Les
       Shipnuck and Dan Feshback, "Bay Area Council: Regional Power-
       house, " Pacific Research and World Empire Telegram IV (No. 1,
       November, December, 1971); and Greg De Freitas, "BART:
       Rapid Transit and Regional Control, " Pacific Research and World
       Telegram IV (No. 1, November, December 1971). On the other
       side, a more pluralist interpretation can be found in studies
       commissioned by the U. S. Department of Transportation under the
       BART Impact Program. See A History of the Key Decisions In
       the Development of Bay Area Rapid Transit, U. S. Department of
       Transportation, August 1975, Report No. 3-14-75. (Herein re-
       ferred to as A History of Key BART Decisions.) Most of the
       factual material in my account is drawn from the latter.

(38)   See De Freitas, "BART Rapid Transit, " p. 14, and Shipnuck and
       Feshback, "Bay Area Council, " p. 7.

(39) A History of Key BART Decisions, pp. 36-38.

(40) Ibid. , p. 38.

(41) See Zwerling op. cit. and Shipnuck and Feshback loc. cit. , De
      Freitas loc. cit.

(42) De Freitas, "BART Rapid Transit, " p. 15.

(43) See Melvin Webber, The BART Experience - What Have We
      Learned? Monograph No. 26, Institute of Urban and Regional
      Development, University of California, Berkeley (October 1976),
      p. 22.

(44) Ibid. ; and see Zwerling, Mass Transit and the Politics of Tech-
      nology.

CHAPTER 8

(1)   John C. Bollens and Henry Schmandt, The Metropolis (New York:
      Harper & Row, 1970), pp. 51-52.

(2)   Thomas Murphy and John Rehfuss, Urban Politics in the Suburban
      Era (Homewood, Illinois: Dorsey Press, 1976), p. 20.

(3)   Ibid. , pp. 2 and 73. For a similar point of view see, Louis
      Masotti "Prologue: Suburbia Reconsidered - Myth and Counter
      Myth, " in The Urbanization of the Suburbs, Urban Affairs Annual
      Reviews, VII (Beverly Hills, California: Sage, 1973), pp. 15-22.

(4)   These are conservative estimates. In recent years the annual
      rate of job loss in manufacture has been declining by 5. 3% in the
      east and by 3. 1% in midwestern cities. For a more complete
      picture of this decline see a document submitted by the President's
      Urban and Regional Policy Group entitled "Cities and People In
      Distress" (November, 1977), especially pp. 15-16.

(5)   See for example, Stokely Carmichael and Charles Hamilton,
      Black Power (New York: Knopf, 1967), p. 6; Robert Blauner,
      "Internal Colonialism and Ghetto Revolt, " Social Problems XVI
      (No. 4, Spring 1969) 393-4; and Mario Barrera, Carlos Munoz,
      and Charles Ornelas, "The Barrio as an Internal Colony, " Urban

Affairs Annual Reviews: People and Politics in Urban Society, VI (Los Angeles; Sage Publications, 1972) 484.

(6)   Statistics are derived from Michael Danielson, "Differentiation, Segregation and Political Fragmentation in the American Metropolis," Commission on Population Growth and the American Future; Research Reports IV, Governance and Population, ed. A. E. Keir Nash (Washington, D. C.: U. S. Government Printing Office, 1972), pp. 151-52.

(7)   Regional Plan Association, "The Region's Agenda," vol. I, no. 1 (New York: Regional Plan, 1975) pp. 1-2.

(8)   Harold X. Connolly, "Black Movement Into the Suburbs," Urban Affairs Quarterly IX, (No. 1 September 1973) 104.

(9)   New York Times, June 13, 1976, Section IV, p. 7.

(10)   For a scathing account of what suburbs have done to cities and how American cities have been transformed, see Murray Bookchin, The Limits of the City (New York: Harper & Row, 1973), p. 74.

(11)   Data for Edgmont is derived from research done by the Suburban Action Institute for the Commonwealth of Pennsylvania, Department of Community Affairs, A Study of Exclusion, I & II, (December 1973), especially pp. 4-10 in Volume I. For New Castle Township see, Mitchell Berenson & Appellants v. The Town of New Castle, State Of New York, Court of Appeals (December, 1975, Mimeograph), as well as Mitchell Berenson, Morris Black and Leo Kagan v. The Town of New Castle, Supreme Court of the State of New York, County of Westchester (December, 1977, mimeograph).

(12)   A Study of Exclusion, II, p. 6.

(13)   Paul Davidoff and Virginia Gordon, A Study of Growth and Segregation (New York: Suburban Action Institute, 1975), p. 33.

(14)   Some of the best work on the problem of exclusionary zoning has been done by Paul Davidoff, Linda Davidoff, and Virginia Gordon of the Suburban Action Institute, New York City. Much of the foregoing discussion on the use of architectural and building design to exclude low and moderate income groups has been based

on the excellent two volume research entitled A Study of Exclusion, see especially Volume I, Part I.

(15) Spread City, Regional Plan Association (1962) quoted in A Study of Exclusion I, p. 26.

(16) Among the most notable of these cases is Kennedy Park Homes Association, Inc. v. City of Lackawana, U.S. Court of Appeals, Second Circuit, 1970 436 F 2d 103 (herein referred to as Kennedy Park Homes).

(17) For landmark cases on this subject see Village of Euclid v. Ambler Realty Co., 272 U.S. 365 (1926) and Village of Belle Terre v. Bruce Boraas, 416 U.S. 1. 39 L. Ed. 2d. 797 (1974).

(18) For an historical recapitulation and analysis of this subject, see "Segregation and the Suburbs: Low Income Housing, Zoning and the Fourteenth Amendment," Iowa Law Review 56, (1971) 1298-1322; also see Harper v. Virginia Bd. of Elections, 383 U.S. 663, 667 (1966); Reynolds v. Sims 377 U.S. 533, 561-62 (1964); Yick Wo. v. Hopkins, 118 U.S. 356, 370 (1886).

(19) See Kennedy Park Homes.

(20) See Arlington Heights v. Metropolitan Housing Development Corporation, __ U.S. __ 97 S. Ct. 555, 50L. Ed. 450 (1977).

(21) Ibid., the Court pointed this out in an important footnote to the decision.

(22) The New York Times, January 12, 1977, p. B6.

(23) Southern Burlington County NAACP, Camden County, CORE, Camden County NAACP, Gladys Clark, Bell Weal and Angel Perez, et al. v. Township of Mount Laurel, Supreme Court of New Jersey All (September 1973) pp. 45-46 (herein described as the Mount Laurel Case.)

(24) Ibid., pp. 51-54.

(25) See William C. Brack, "There's A Long, Long Trail Awinding," in After Mount Laurel, ed. Jerome Rose and William Rothman, (New Brunswick; Center for Urban Policy Research, 1977) pp. 279-288.

(26) For a critical account of sprawl in Santa Clara County, see the
      Nader Report on Land Use in California, published as The Poli-
      tics of Land, directed by Robert Fellmeth, (New York: Gross-
      man Publishers, 1973), especially pp. 393-95. (Herein referred
      to as Nader Report on Land Use).

(27) See Mark Gottdiener, Planned Sprawl (Beverly Hills, Calif.:
      Sage, 1977), chapters 4 and 5.

(28) Nader Report on Land Use, p. 382. See also "National Growth
      Policy" Hearings Before the Subcommittee on Housing of the
      Committee on Banking and Currency, House of Representatives,
      Second Session, June 6 and 7, 1972 (Washington, D.C.: U.S.
      Government Printing Office, 1972), pp. 227 and 246-48. (Herein
      referred to as House Hearings on National Growth).

(29) The New York Times, April 27, 1978, p. B1.

(30) Gottdiener, Planned Sprawl, chapters 4 and 5.

(31) The Mount Laurel Case, pp. 7-10.

(32) Ibid., p. 17.

(33) Ibid., p. 19.

(34) Ibid., p. 8.

(35) Complaint to the Director of Civil Rights, United States Depart-
      ment of Transportation, Regarding Federal Funding Proposal
      for the Improvement of Interstate 84 From the Vicinity of the
      New York State Line to the Vicinity of Route 7 in Danbury. Sub-
      mitted by: Suburban Action Institute, 257 Park Avenue South,
      New York, N.Y., 10010, Of Counsel: Eisner, Levy, Steel, and
      Bellmen, 351 Broadway, New York, N.Y., 10013.

(36) Estimates of HUD expenditures in Santa Clara during 1969 were
      $5.4 million. By contrast capital gains estimates in the County
      for the same year vary from a low of $13 million to as much as
      $42 million. See House Hearings on National Growth, p. 238.

(37) Nader Report on Land Use, p. 362.

(38)   The phrase was coined in a Rand Corporation, report on Santa
        Clara County. See House Hearings on National Growth, p. 167.

(39)   This assumption was put into a scientific design and mathematical-
        ly tested by the Rand Corporation. The results confirmed the
        hypothesis and revealed that employment was highly dependent
        on the need for high growth. See "Alternative Growth Strategies
        for San Jose: Initial Report of the Rand Corporation, " in Hear-
        ings on National Growth, especially pp. 164-92.

                              EPILOGUE

(1)   The New York Times, December 6, 1977, p. 5.

(2)   The New York Times, April 4, 1978, III, p. 1.

(3)   See "Imperial Government, " Commentary XIV (June 6, 1978): 30.

(4)   Administrative changes were to take place through the executive
        departments and involved modification of federal procurement and
        construction policies to favor central cities, better coordination
        between federal agencies, the submission of urban impact state-
        ments by agencies in order to assure that executive goals were
        not contradictory or damaging to cities, and changes in the man-
        agement of water and sewer programs. In addition to more money
        given to HUD, there were bonus funds for the Economic Develop-
        ment Administration (Commerce Department) as well as for youth
        training (Labor Department) and for education (HEW).

(5)   Modifications of the program were contained in the Housing and
        Community Development Act of 1974, but they were not operable
        and continued only on a pilot basis.

(6)   Office of The White House Press Secretary "To the Congress of
        the United States" (March 27, 1978, mimeograph), p. 3.

Index

About the Author

H. V. SAVITCH is Associate Professor of Urban Affairs and Public Policy at the State University of New York, Purchase. Dr. Savitch has taught courses in public policy and served as director of projects dealing with the operation of federal and local governments. In addition he has authored articles which have appeared in Polity, New York Affairs, The Annals, and other publications.

Pergamon Policy Studies